APL

AN INTERACTIVE APPROACH

APL

AN INTERACTIVE APPROACH
Second Edition Revised Reprinting

Leonard Gilman
*International Business
Machines Corporation*

Allen J. Rose
*Scientific Time-Sharing
Corporation*

John Wiley & Sons, Inc.,
New York, Santa Barbara, London, Sydney, Toronto

Library of Congress Cataloging in Publication Data:
Gilman, Leonard, 1930
    APL: An Interactive Approach

    Published in 1970 under title: *APL360*: An
Interactive Approach.
      Includes index.
      1. APL (Computer program language) I. Rose, Allen J.,
joint author. II. Title.

QA76.73.A27G54 1976   001.6'424   76-22478   Card No.
ISBN 0-471-30022-5

Printed in the United States of America

10 9 8 7 6 5 4 3 2 1

APL★PLUS® is a registered service mark of
Scientific Time Sharing Corporation.

To Laurie Gilman

Foreword

APL is a language for describing procedures in the processing of information. It can be used to describe mathematical procedures having nothing to do with computers, or to describe (to a human being) how a computer works. Most commonly, however, at least at this time, it is used for programming in the ordinary sense of directing a computer how to process numeric or alphabetic data.

The language was invented by Kenneth E. Iverson while at Harvard, and was described in a 1962 Wiley book appropriately titled *A Programming Language*. In 1966 an experimental time-sharing system for the IBM System/360 became available within IBM, and is now an IBM program product. A number of universities and at least one public school system (Atlanta) are using *APL* on a wide scale for student instruction, and several universities and computer manufacturers are currently producing implementations for various computers. *APL* is clearly gaining acceptance at this time as a computer programming language.

This acceptance is not hard to understand. *APL* is one of the most concise, consistent, and powerful programming languages ever devised. Operations on single items (scalars) extend in a simple and natural way to arrays of any size and shape. Thus, for instance, a matrix addition that in other languages might require two loops and a half dozen statements, becomes simply $A + B$ in *APL*. Since computer programming typically involves a great deal of work with various kinds of data structures, the simplification offered by *APL*'s rich and powerful handling of arrays is central to its strength.

Again, since so many computer operations are describable by single *APL* operators, since data declarations are seldom required, and since procedure definitions are always independent of other definitions, *APL* is ideal for on-line interactive use of computers. Programs can readily be checked out in easy-to-manage segments.

From a pedagogical standpoint *APL* has a number of advantages. The material can be taught and used in small pieces. A student can be trying his hand on simple operations after five minutes of instruction. What he doesn't know won't hurt him (a statement that cannot be made about most other languages). If he tries something illegal, such a division by zero or adding a number and a letter, he gets an understandable error message and is free to try something else. Nothing the user can do will cause the system to crash.

As a new user becomes familiar with simple *APL* features, he moves on to more advanced concepts. Perhaps he tries operations on vectors, or samples the *APL* operator called reduction, which with two character strokes replaces complete loops in other languages. Some users will never have any occasion to become intimately familiar with all *APL* operators; their work will just not require them. Those who do need the advanced features will find the effort needed to master them rewarded with the availability of some extremely powerful operators, the equivalent of which are not to be found in other programming languages.

It is indubitably true that a "clever" programmer can use these advanced operators in such a way as to produce an "opaque" program, that is, one so compact and concise as to be nearly impossible for anyone else to understand. Whatever else may be said about such programs, which are questionable in many contexts anyway, they should not be used in demonstrations of *APL*. Experienced programmers who have seen *APL* demonstrated in terms of the fantastic cleverness angle sometimes criticize the language as being hard to understand, when their criticism more properly should have been directed at the demonstrator. Such misplaced cleverness is not to be found in this book. All operators are thoroughly covered, but there is no attempt to show off the ingenuity of the authors in writing ingeniously condensed programs.

APL is being taught successfully to high school students, in courses where the intent is more to teach mathematics than to teach programming. It is being used by engineers and statisticians to assist in their work, employing *APL* program packages designed to make such work easier. And it is also used for various kinds of text processing, such as checking out compiling schemes and writing *APL* interpreters of other languages. Many other application areas could be cited. *APL* may not be all things to all men, but, to a greater degree than is true of most programming languages, it is many things to many.

This book concentrates on no special class of users. The features of the language are explained thoroughly, in a sequence chosen to facilitate learning. The authors have very extensive experience teaching *APL* to a wide variety of users. As the subtitle indicates (*An Interactive Approach*), the presentation is built around the assumption that the reader has access to an *APL* terminal. This, of course, is unquestionably the best way to learn *APL*, and such a reader will find the book well suited to his needs.

Nonetheless, the reader who wants to find out what *APL* is all about, not yet having access to a terminal, will discover that the presentation is easily readable. The text displays the terminal printouts just as they would appear to a user executing the commands under discussion. Being on a terminal oneself is surely the best way to learn an interactive language, but if that is not possible this may be the next best thing.

Daniel D. McCracken
Ossining, New York
June, 1970

Preface

Since the publication of the first edition of *APL \360 - An Interactive Approach* in 1970, both the number of *APL* users and available new features and extensions to the language have grown significantly.

This revised second edition of *APL - An Interactive Approach* has been renamed to reflect the fact that several versions of *APL* are currently being offered (in particular, Scientific Time Sharing Corporation's *APL ★PLUS* ® Time Sharing Service and IBM's *APLSV* Program Product and 5100 Portable Computer). In recognition of *APL*'s growing use in business applications, more examples and problems in this area have been included, and the body of the text itself has undergone a modest shift in orientation toward commercial uses of *APL*.

Readers will also note that the separation of functions and examples according to the ranks of the arrays on which they were operating, which characterized the sequence of topics in the first edition, has been mostly eliminated. Based on comments from many users of the text, as well as on personal experience of the authors in presenting *APL* to hundreds of students, primitive functions are illustrated in this edition with examples and exercises involving scalars and one- and two-dimensional arrays presented in the same chapter. Higher dimensional arrays are found toward the latter part of the text. This change allows the introduction of more meaningful and useful examples at an earlier point in the text than was feasible before.

Additional functions and features now available in both the IBM and Scientific Time Sharing implementations have been included in this edition, and the chapters on workspace management and function definition have been substantially rewritten and provide additional graphic aids to the student. Where appropriate, sections have been included on distinctive features of the IBM 5100 Computer. The conversational style characteristic of the first edition has been retained so that users will continue to find the text usable for self-study as well as in a classroom environment.

We are indebted to Daniel Dyer for the many services generously provided by Scientific Time Sharing Corporation in the production of this edition; to Robert A. Smith, Lawrence M. Breed, Harold A. Driscoll, Robert J. Beilstein, Alan W. Holmes and Thomas J. Pritchard for their explanations of *APL ★PLUS* ® features; to Eugene McDonnell and Paul C. Berry for their help in describing Shared Variables; to Calvin Rice, William Kleis and Donald Link for their contributions to the material about the IBM 5100; to Carol Thompson for her assistance in photocomposition; to William D. Hauptman and Bruce P. Nemlich for their careful proofreading and suggestions on the drafts; and to the many readers of the first edition whose suggestions have been incorporated in this edition.

We are especially grateful to Philip S. Abrams, whose responsiveness and impartial good judgment have been helpful to us in matters of style and insights into the development of the language; and to Alan G. Konheim, who gave many hours of his personal time to organizing the typography of this book.

Leonard Gilman and Allen J. Rose
June, 1976

Preface to the first edition

As a result of increasing interest in *APL*, a formal educational program was begun in 1967 at the Thomas J. Watson Research Center in Yorktown Heights, New York. Within a year an *APL* "curriculum" had evolved which has been put on videotape. This text follows the same instructional sequence and uses essentially the same examples given on the videotapes.

With but a few exceptions not necessary to the understanding of the topics following, the level of mathematical sophistication required does not exceed that associated with most current high school mathematics programs. In addition, no previous programming experience on the part of the reader is assumed. The authors believe, therefore, that the text is suitable for use by both secondary school and college-level classes, as well as by those in business and industry who are interested in the data processing capabilities of *APL*. Preliminary versions of the text have been used extensively in classroom situations and independent study by many individuals.

At the end of each chapter except the first are problem sets with drill exercises and practice in the writing of *APL* expressions and programs (function definition). These have in general been chosen to emphasize and reinforce the concepts presented in the chapters which they follow. Past experience has indicated that students readily develop their own applications of *APL* once having learned the language.

Finally, nearly all of the example functions that the student will encounter in the text have been placed in a block of storage (called a *workspace* in *APL*) which has the name 1 *CLASS*. If not in your system, this workspace is obtainable from Scientific Time Sharing Corp. The work of the student will be facilitated if he has access to this workspace.

We wish to acknowledge our debt to the many individuals who gave us their helpful comments and suggestions with regard to the layout and contents of the text. In particular we want to give credit to the following persons: Robert Hurley, for invaluable technical assistance in the early development of the course; Miss Colleen Conroy, for proofreading the text at several stages in its preparation; Eugene McDonnell, for suggesting solutions to a number of problems; Horst Feistel, for his ideas and exercises in the section on cryptography (Chapter 19); Miss Linda Alvord, for her work in graphing (on which the latter part of Chapter 25 is based); Raymond Polivka, for his kind permission to use a number of problems which he had developed earlier in his own *APL* teaching. And last, but by no means least, in gratitude for a task that at times appeared endless, thanks are due to Mrs. Frances Verzeni and Mrs. Ann Tiller for preparing the copy for publication.

Leonard Gilman and Allen J. Rose
Yorktown Heights, New York
June, 1970

Contents

Chapter 1:
Getting started

Communication with the computer

Language is the means whereby we, as users, can tell the computer what to do, and it, in turn, can tell us what it has done with the information we have furnished it. It would be highly desirable to have a language that is as near as possible to what people ordinarily use. At the same time, the computer has to be able to interpret the given commands and execute them.

As a result of the development of time-sharing, in which regular telephone lines are used to connect remote inexpensive typewriters equipped for teleprocessing ("terminals") to a single central computer, a number of specialized languages have appeared with features adapted to this environment. Among them is *APL*, the name being an acronym for *A Programming Language*, which is the title of a book by Dr. K. E. Iverson[†] (New York, John Wiley, 1962) defining the language in detail.

Since it is similar in many respects to algebraic notation and, in addition, contains many useful functions not expressible concisely with conventional symbols, it has proved to be very efficient for describing algorithms (problem-solving procedures). The text, therefore, will concentrate on the use of the *APL* language for problem-solving on the terminal, following a brief introduction to the operation of the terminal and the establishment of the telephone connection. Little consideration will be given to the characteristics and operation of any of the other elements of the *APL* system since the user of a time-sharing system is removed from the immediate vicinity of the computer, and need not, in general, be concerned with anything other than his terminal.

What the *APL* system does

The following is a typical session in which a user interacts with the central computer via an *APL* terminal. The student is cautioned that the display of terminal copy below was obtained from a terminal with access to programs in storage not necessarily available to him, such as $STATISTICS$, which will result in a $VALUE\ ERROR$ message if execution is attempted.

```
        2 + 2
4
        3 ÷ 4
0.75
```

[†]Presently an IBM Fellow, APL Design Group, General Products Division, IBM

```
      3.1×5
15.5
```

As the illustration shows we can use the terminal as a desk calculator, with instructions and data entered by the user via the keyboard (beginning six spaces to the right of the margin). Following the entry the RETURN key is depressed to signal the computer that the user is finished. The response of the computer begins at the left margin.

Or we can assign a string of numbers to a variable called X, and ask the computer to execute the instruction shown, $+/X$, with response 17.1:

```
      X←3   4   1.1   3   6
      +/X
17.1
```

This is the sum of all the numbers assigned to X.

The variable X can be further operated on, as, for example,

```
      2+X
5 6 3.1 5 8
```

And we have the ability to call upon programs previously stored in the system. Here is one that enables us to carry out statistical calculations on data:

```
      STATISTICS
ENTER DATA
□:
      4 3 4.4 5 1 6 2
6 OBSERVATIONS ENTERED
AVERAGE IS 3.933333333
RANGE IS 5.2
STANDARD DEVIATION IS 1.787363048
TO TERMINATE TYPE  STOP
□:
```

The program is expecting yet another set of data, which will now be entered:

```
      8  9  7.8  6.4
4 OBSERVATIONS ENTERED
AVERAGE IS 7.8
RANGE IS 2.6
STANDARD DEVIATION IS 1.070825227
TO TERMINATE TYPE STOP
□:
      STOP
```

As the instructions indicated, we terminated execution by typing $STOP$.

The hardware

Let's take a brief look at the physical equipment. It will be assumed in the remainder of this book that the communications terminal you will be using is equipped with the **APL** character set, and capable of corresponding with an **APL** computer system via a dataset or acoustic coupler.

PROBLEMS

Define the functions as required in problems 1 to 6:

1. Dyadic, explicit result: to calculate the FICA (social security tax) at the rate of P percent on gross yearly income IN up to a maximum of \$15300.

2. Dyadic, no explicit result: to store under the name T the square of the difference of two arguments.

3. Monadic, explicit result: to generate prime numbers, using Fermat's formula,

    $$2^{2^n} + 1 \text{ (conventional notation.)}$$

4. Monadic, no explicit result: to calculate the ceiling of X, using the residue function.

5. Niladic, explicit result: to produce four random numbers from 1 to 100.

6. Niladic, no explicit result: to see if either one of two previously defined variables divides the other evenly.

7. What is wrong with the following function headers (A, B are arguments)?

    ```
    A SQA B
    ∇ Z←B HYP
    ∇ A 1FIB B
    ∇ A HYP B C
    ```

8. Enter the function HYP (see page 84) and use it to evaluate each of the following:

    ```
    ( 3 HYP 4 ) HYP 3 HYP 1
    4+3 HYP 4-3
    (4+3) HYP 4-3
    ```

9. After executing the command $)LOAD$ 1 $CLASS$, define a dyadic function called D which returns an explicit result and gives the larger of the two arguments. Explain the system's response.

10. Assume that you have a monadic function AVG that returns an explicit result (there is one in 1 $CLASS$. Write a one-line **APL** expression which uses AVG to obtain the average of a vector of numbers X, stores the result under the name A, and calculates and stores in F the 10-log of A.

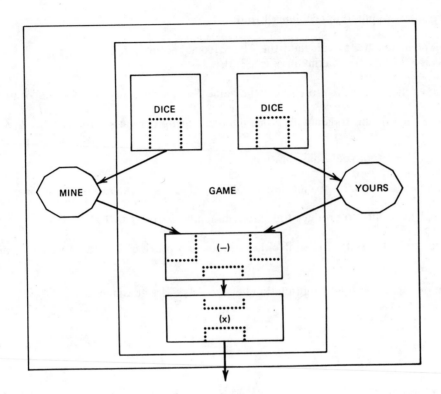

Another function like *GAME* that you have already encountered is *EASYDRILL* in the workspace 1 *APLCOURSE*. This also required no arguments and returned no explicit results. It typed out the answers and accepted inputs, but you couldn't do any computations with them. Functions of this type are commonly called *main programs*.

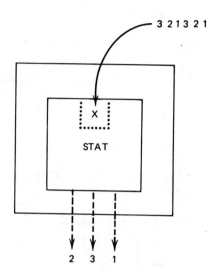

Since no explicit results are returned, it doesn't make any sense to work further with them. If we try it, we get an error message as before:

```
      2×STAT 8 1 4 10
11.5
10
1
VALUE ERROR
      2×STAT 8 1 4 10
      ∧
```

To complete the table on page 84, display the function *GAME*:

```
      ∇GAME[□]∇
   ∇ GAME
[1]   MINE←DICE
[2]   YOURS←DICE
[3]   ×MINE-YOURS
   ∇
```

After executing this function a few times

```
      GAME
⁻1
      GAME
⁻1
      GAME
0
```

you should be able to see that this function simply generates one of the three random integers ⁻1, 0, 1, using the niladic function *DICE*.

The interface diagram of *GAME* shows the results of *DICE* being ultimately deposited in permanent (as opposed to temporary) storage boxes in the **APL** system:

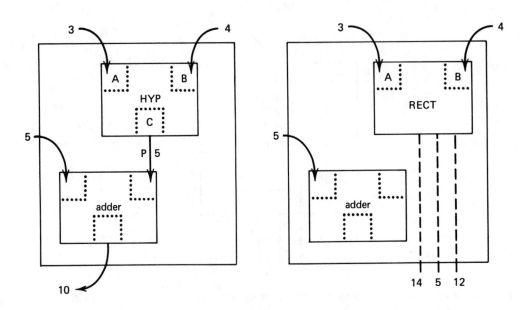

In the diagram of $RECT$ on the right, one of the input paths has no values to feed into the adder, since the output from $RECT$ was "deposited" on the paper and not retained anywhere. By contrast, the output from HYP was stored temporarily in C to permit its moving along path P to the adder.

The two headers differ in that a specification is made in HYP and not in $RECT$, and in the body of $RECT$ again there were no assignments of results to any variables. We will have more to say about the significance of the variables used in the header and in the function itself in Chapter 13.

Now consider the monadic function $STAT$:

```
        ∇STAT[□]∇
    ∇  STAT X
[1]     N←ρX
[2]     (+/X)÷N
[3]     ⌈/X
[4]     ⌊/X
    ∇
```

Again there is no explicit result expressed in the header, and the output will be three lines. The first two give us the average of the elements of X, and could easily be combined into one line. N is just a convenient handle for transferring the result of line 1 (which is the number of elements) to line 2. Lines 3 and 4 print the largest and smallest elements of X. Executing $STAT$, we get

```
    STAT 3 2 1 3 2 1
2
3
1
```

Here is the interface diagram of $STAT$:

Functions without explicit results

So far, we have seen three types of function headers, requiring none, one or two arguments. They all returned explicit results, that is, a result that could be used for subsequent computation. Now let's look at one that doesn't give explicit results, but merely prints them on the paper.

Display the function $RECT$:

```
      ∇RECT[□]∇
   ∇  L RECT H
[1]    2×L+H
[2]    L HYP H
[3]    L×H
   ∇
```

The first thing that should hit your eye is that there is no arrow in the header. Line 1 gives the perimeter of a rectangle of length L and height H; line 2 is the length of the diagonal, using the previously defined HYP; line 3 is the area of the rectangle.

Notice also that there is no specification arrow on any line. This means that the results of that line aren't stored anywhere and will, as mentioned above, be printed on the paper, as for example:

```
      3 RECT 4
14
5
12
```

The purpose of this function, as defined, is to give information, not for further work. Watch what happens when we try to use its "result" for further computation:

```
      5+3 RECT 4
14
5
12
VALUE ERROR
      5+3 RECT 4
          ∧
```

Here the results of the three lines of the function again are printed, but we can't add 5 to these results because the numbers weren't stored anywhere, as contrasted to

```
      5+3 HYP 4
10
```

Interface diagrams point up immediately what the key differences are:

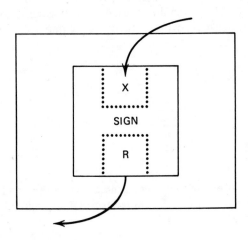

Now type $DICE$ several times and display it.

```
      DICE
6
      DICE
7
      DICE
3
      ∇DICE[□]∇
   ∇ R←DICE
[1]    R←+/? 6 6
   ∇
```

This is simply the sum of a random roll of two dice. Notice in the header that $DICE$ has no arguments. It is a *niladic* function, to coin a word. The function really doesn't need any arguments. It is designed to select the numbers for the roll itself, using the random number generator as shown by the following interface diagram. Note that since no external input path is shown, the data required must come from within the **APL** system itself (dotted arrow):

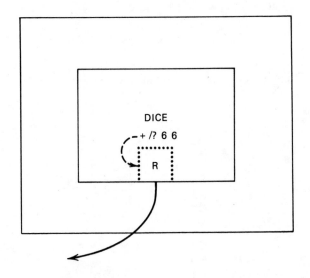

Examine the keyboard, reproduced below:

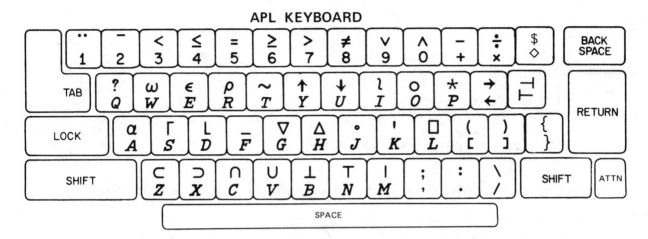

The alphabetic and numeric characters are in the standard positions, but you will find most of the remaining symbols are unfamiliar, and the conventional symbols are not all located where you might expect them to be.   There may, however, be minor differences in the number and arrangement of the keys, depending on the terminal manufacturer.

The SHIFT key is used in the usual manner for upper shift characters, and the RETURN key on the right tells the system that you, the user, are finished with whatever you are entering, and are now ready for the terminal to respond.

To the right of the return key is the ON-OFF switch, which is the main power control for the terminal. The space bar is at the bottom of the keyboard. Also located on the terminal may be a switch marked COM-LCL.   When the switch is in the LCL position ("local") the terminal can be used as an ordinary electric typewriter.   The COM ("communicate") position is the correct one for *APL*.

Sign-on

At this point, turn the terminal on and set the COM-LCL switch to LCL.   Practice entering the following with the terminal in the local mode:

>)*USER NUMBER*:*LOCK*

with

>)*1421*:*JAY*

as an example.

The use of the lock is optional, but strongly recommended for security reasons. If a lock is not used, the sign-on command is simply

>)*USER NUMBER*

If you forget to hold down the shift key, you will get] instead of). This is an incorrect entry and you will not be able to sign on. Repeat the above exercise. When you are finished practicing, put the COM-LCL switch back on COM and leave the power switch on.

Now examine the dataset. You will be concerned only with the two rightmost buttons, TALK and DATA. When the TALK button is depressed, the dataset is a conventional telephone (more or less depending on the model). Use it to dial the computer.

If you have made a proper connection, you will hear a high-pitched tone. At this point, press the DATA button, replace the handset, and you are ready to sign on as above.

Here is a summary of the sign-on procedure:

1. turn ON-OFF switch on
2. put COM-LCL switch to COM
3. depress TALK button
4. dial telephone number
5. on tone, press DATA button
6. replace handset
7. enter) your user number : lock (if any)
8. press RETURN key

Alternatively, if you are using an acoustic coupler, the sign-on procedure is somewhat different:

1. turn ON-OFF switch on
2. put COM-LCL switch to COM
3. dial telephone number
4. on tone, place handset in acoustic coupler receptacle
5. turn coupler ON-OFF switch on
6. enter) your user number : lock (if any)
7. press RETURN key

The complete sign-on with the terminal response looks like this

```
     )1500:DG
OPR:  SYSTEM AVAILABLE TO 8 PM TONIGHT
057)  9.44.03 10/25/73 LGILMAN

     APL*PLUS SERVICE
```

057) tells on which port (telephone line) you are coming into the computer, and is followed by the time in hours, minutes and seconds, the date and the user's name. The next line identifies the system. At times there may also be a message from the operator with **APL** news for all users.

Having signed on, we can now do simple calculations:

```
     3+5
8
     2+2
4
```

There may well be variations in the above sign-on procedure in different **APL** systems and with different terminals, some of which may be wired directly to the computer. For example, if you are using an ASCII terminal at 30 characters per second, you must enter ○ (upper shift O) before the right parenthesis. You should consult your computer center for specific sign-on information.

Sign-off

At this point you are ready to work. In the scheme of things, it is foreordained that somebody is bound to come in and interrupt you. If the interruption is a lengthy one and you are unable to continue at the terminal for some time, you will need to know how to sign off. Do *not* sign off at this point unless you have to leave the terminal.

Here is the sign-off procedure:

1. enter)*OFF*
2. press RETURN key
3. after terminal response, turn ON-OFF switch off and
    if using an acoustic coupler, hang up the telephone.

The terminal's response will show how long you were connected and the actual time the central processing unit (CPU) of the computer was working for you both since sign-on and cumulatively since the last billing:

```
    )OFF
057   10.04.15 10/25/73 LGI
CONNECTED 0.20.12 TO DATE   4.19.26
CPU TIME  0.00.01 TO DATE   0.01.03
```

All times shown are hours, minutes and seconds. The cumulative connect time for this user in this billing period is 4 hours, 19 minutes and 26 seconds. The cumulative computer usage time is 1 minute and 3 seconds.

Different *APL* systems may use accounting displays other than the one shown here, and in any case it is wise to make sure you understand how you're being charged or budgeted. Contact your Marketing Representative if you are using a commercial system, or the Computing Center management otherwise.

Additional sign-off commands which will keep the line open for a short period after sign-off, allow users to change or remove locks on their user numbers, or automatically save material on which work was done during the current session will be treated in Chapters 14 and 15. Also to be taken up later will be a series of commands that on some systems will permit users to send messages to the computer operator or others signed on at the time.

IBM 5100 portable computer

This desk-top computer, a diagram of whose console and keyboard appears below, may be used as a stand-alone *APL* system, with most of the language features and facilities of *APLSV*; or as a remote terminal when equipped with a communications adapter. It uses a 16-line display screen 64 characters wide instead of a printer. Tape cartridges provide external storage.

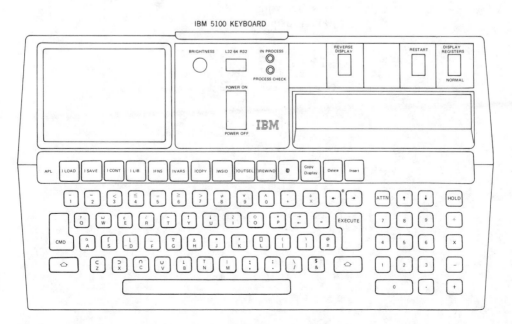

On some keyboards you will find that several extra characters, such as @, & , #, $ are available.

Since only one person at a time can use the 5100, no user number is needed. To start, turn the power on and wait until the 5100 finishes its internal checks. If no error has been detected, the message *CLEAR WS* will appear in the lower left corner of the screen. The 5100 is now ready for use as a stand-alone *APL* system. Should the message not appear, press RESTART again. No sign-off is necessary; simply turn the power off.

To use the 5100 as a terminal on a time-sharing system, repeat the instructions in the last paragraph. Then insert the special communications cartridge, enter the command *)MODE COM* and press the EXECUTE key.

The next steps require you to know something about the *APL* system you want to use and its data transmission rate. Specifically, enter &SYSTEM followed by APL.SV. The underscored ampersand character is obtained by pressing the alphanumeric 1 key while holding down the CMD key. All communications commands on the 5100 begin with this character. The 5100 is now functionally equivalent to a Selectric® terminal.

Now enter &RATE followed by either 134.5 or 300. These values are the number of bits per second transmitted (see Chapter 32 for a discussion of *bits*) supported by the computer you plan to connect to. If this command is not entered, the 5100 assumes that you intended 134.5. Don't confuse the 300 bits per second rate on the 5100 with ASCII conventions. This means that you can't use the 5100 on a port configured for 300 bits per second ASCII.

There are other variations and restrictions with these commands when the optional printer or tape unit is attached, or when nonswitched lines are used. Consult the IBM 5100 Communications Reference Manual SA 21-9215 for further information.

After these commands are entered, establish the line connection with the computer as on pages 3 and 4. Remember that the EXECUTE key on the 5100 keyboard is equivalent to the RETURN key on most other keyboards.

An extra line on the bottom of the display screen is used to report the status of the 5100. In particular, for communication, it indicates one of the following in display positions 58 and 60:

    ☐ ↓   no line connection
    ☐ ↑   line connection established
    ☐ ←   5100 is receiving
    ☐ →   5100 is transmitting

Chapter 2:
Some elementary operations

From this point on, we assume that you are seated at an active terminal, or have ready access to one. Many of the chapters will have instructions to get you into a special workspace, which is a block of internal storage (called "memory"), and in which there are a number of programs and exercises that you will use. More about this later.

In the early chapters, try to get as much finger practice as you can. Remember that the slowest link in the *APL* system is you, the user. You are limited by the speed with which you can enter information via the keyboard.

Elementary arithmetic operations

We'll begin with the simple arithmetic operations, + × - ÷, the symbols for which are in the upper right portion of the keyboard. The decimal point, which will be introduced here, is in the lower right part of the keyboard. All these symbols are used in the conventional manner.

Addition:

```
      3+4
7
      .5+.6
1.1
      1.45+5.99
7.44
```

You've just barely started, but already there is one error that you are free to make. Suppose we type

```
      3+
```

You ask: 3+ what? Clearly this isn't a meaningful statement because you haven't indicated a second value for the plus symbol to operate on. The response of the computer is to type out the following error message:

```
SYNTAX ERROR
      3+
        ^
```

The caret marks where the error was detected. In plain English, the error message means that the statement has been improperly formulated in *APL*, i.e., is "ungrammatical" in the sense that we are using perfectly good symbols, but using them incorrectly.

Multiplication

```
      5.1×7.9
40.29
      3×6
18
```

Subtraction

```
      5-2
3
      2-5
¯3
```

Notice the overbar in the last response. This symbol means "negative." In a way it is a description (like the decimal point) attached to the number that follows it. It is *not* an indication of an operation to be performed. For this, the subtraction sign is used.

Let's try some additional examples using the negative sign (upper shift 2):

```
      3+¯2
1
      ¯2+3
1
      -2+3
¯5
```

If you think that there's something peculiar about the last example, where a subtraction sign was used in place of the negative, relax - the distinction will be made in Chapter 9.

Division

```
      3÷5
0.6
      5÷3
1.666666667
```

By now you have probably noticed in your own practice with the arithmetic operations that at most ten significant figures will be printed in the response. *APL* carries out all calculations to approximately sixteen figures and rounds off to ten figures in the output (5 on the IBM 5100). Zeros on the right are not printed. In Chapter 21 a command will be introduced that will allow the number of places printed to vary from 1 to 16.

So far so good. Now how about

```
     5÷0
DOMAIN ERROR
     5÷0
     ^
```

Here we see a second type of error occurring. The explanation is that the operation ÷ is a valid one, but we tried to divide by 0, which is not in the "domain" of possible divisors in our number system.

This seems reasonable enough, until you try 0÷0; you get a 1. The version of *APL* used here follows the rule that any real number divided by itself is 1.

Corrections and comments

Now suppose we have to enter one or more numbers that are a little harder to type than what we have been using thus far, and (heaven forbid!) we make a mistake. Specifically, suppose, as in the following example, we typed 2×3.14169 and really meant 2×3.14159, but haven't yet pressed the RETURN key.

There is a simple way to make corrections. We strike the BACKSPACE key gently (it may be a "repeating" key on some terminals) to move the typeball over to where the error begins. If we then press the ATTN (attention) key, an inverted caret will appear under the character at that point. This signifies that everything above and to the right of the caret has been wiped out from the memory of the system and the corrections may be typed. Note: The examples following were done on a Selectric® terminal. On ASCII terminals, use the LINEFEED key instead of ATTN. The behavior is the same, except that the inverted caret is not printed.

Here are some illustrations:

```
     2×3.14169
              v
              59
6.28318
     2×1.1058
           v
2.2
```

In the following example we want 23×506 but actually type 3×506. All we need do is to backspace just before the 3 and type 2 as shown, provided, of course that RETURN hasn't yet been pressed:

```
     23×506
11638
     3×506
1518
     3×506
    2
11638
```

The fact that the 2 is shown on another line is immaterial, since the system doesn't "know" that we moved the roller and paper manually for illustrative purposes here. We can also glean from this example that the order in which characters are entered at the keyboard is immaterial. What you see on the paper is what you get in *APL*.

You have undoubtedly guessed by this time that the way to get rid of a whole line is to backspace all the way to the beginning and make the correction:

```
     1234567×12345678
 v
```

The correction mechanism may also be used to enter comments:

```
THIS IS A COMMENT
∨
```

Otherwise the system doesn't recognize the entry and an error message is printed.

While we're on the subject, the combination upper shift *C* ("cap") and the small circle (upper shift *J*), nicknamed "jot," overstruck is interpreted as indication that a comment follows. It may contain any **APL** symbols and calls for no response from the system.

```
Ɐ THIS IS A BETTER WAY TO MAKE A COMMENT
```

This doesn't mean that all combinations of overstruck characters are possible in **APL**. The times and divide signs have been overstruck in the example below, with a resulting *CHARACTER ERROR*. (Those combinations which are legal will be taken up in succeeding chapters.)

```
      34✳73
CHARACTER ERROR
      34@                      (the paper was manually moved forward one line here)
        ×73
2482
```

Note that the original input is reproduced only up to the first illegal character (here indicated by the @ symbol, which from this point on in the text will be used only as an indicator of where the typeball comes to rest. It is *not* a character printed on the terminal.) At the same time the keyboard is unlocked and ready to accept the correct characters for processing and output, following the usual carriage return.

Occasionally the computer will report an error even when you haven't made one. At other times there may be misprints not traceable to mechanical or electrical problems in the terminal itself. This happens when there is a faulty telephone connection. If errors are reported frequently, hang up the phone and dial in again. At times transmission difficulties may result in a *RESEND* message. When this occurs, the input line is lost and must be reentered.

An introduction to vectors

Imagine a store which, following a disastrous fire, is left with just three items for sale, A, B, C. Here is the sales record of the number of items sold over a two-week period:

	A	B	C
WEEK 1	9	7	8
WEEK 2	3	4	5

Before they go out of business, what are the total sales for each item? The obvious answer is to add the weekly totals for each item separately as

```
      9+3
12
      7+4
11
      8+5
13
```

But there ought to be a more compact way and, in **APL**, there is:

```
      9 7 8+3 4 5
12 11 13
```

This leads us into a unique and time-saving feature of *APL* - its ability to process arrays of numbers. In the previous example the array was one-dimensional, with the elements all arranged in a single chain, called a *vector*. We shall see later that *APL* can handle multidimensional arrays as well.

Let's now change the problem:

	A	B	C
WEEK 1	9	7	8
WEEK 2	5	5	5

Treating this as a problem involving vectors, we enter

```
      9  7  8+5  5  5
14  12  13
```

To save still more typing time, where all the elements of one of the vectors are identical, it suffices to type just one of the numbers in that vector, leaving it to the system to extend it automatically to match the other vector in length:

```
      9  7  8+5
14  12  13
```

Now for some do's and don'ts. First, suppose we run all the numbers together:

```
      978+555
1533
```

The absence of space between the digits causes the system to interpret the series as a single number. Again, what you see is what you get. Does this mean that the numbers (or the operation symbol, for that matter) must be separated by any fixed number of blanks? The following example makes clear that one blank is sufficient as a separator, but extra blanks don't hurt:

```
      9     7  8+     5
14  12  13
```

What if the two vectors don't have the same number of elements?

```
      9  7  8 + 5  3
LENGTH ERROR
      9  7  8 + 5  3
              ^
```

Here we get an obvious error message because the computer doesn't know which number goes with which. The only exception to this is where all the elements are identical (as in the previous example) and only one element needs to be typed.

You might argue that if we had

```
      9  7  8+5  3  0
14  10  8
```

we ought to be able to leave off the zero since it doesn't contribute anything to the sum. But zero is not the same as a blank. The former means that the element in that position where it occurs has the value of zero, while the latter occurs in the place of some unknown element, possibly, but not necessarily, zero, and impossible for the computer to determine.

This *parallel processing* of vectors, to give it a name, works equally well with other arithmetic operations:

```
    1  2  3  4×2
 2  4  6  8
```

If, for example, a cookie recipe required 6, 4 and 1 cups respectively of three ingredients, and we wished to make only one-third of a batch, then the required amounts are

```
    6  4  1÷3
 2  1.333333333  0.3333333333
```

Again, suppose that the above three ingredients cost respectively 1, 5 and 7 cents per cup. What is the total cost for each ingredient?

```
    6  4  1×.01  .05  .07
 0.06  0.2  0.07
```

As we shall see in subsequent chapters, not only are there a large number of operations that can be used with vectors, but we will also be able to invent functions that behave just like our ordinary arithmetic operations, in that they also can be used with vectors.

Data display on the IBM 5100

The display screen on the 5100 has room for 16 lines of maximum width 64 positions. There are actually 128 input positions available on the bottom two lines of the screen, which are normally used for input when the 5100 is a stand-alone. When used as a terminal the bottom line is the status line (page 6). Your cue as to where your next character of input will be displayed is called the *cursor*, a flashing under-score.

You can control the cosmetic appearance of the display by the three-position L32 64 R32 switch (which gives the normal display or enlarges the leftmost or rightmost 32 characters), the brightness switch and the reverse display switch (black on white or vice versa).

Each additional line of information is displayed at the bottom of the screen, rolling the previous lines up. The scroll keys (above the numeric 8 and 9) with the arrows ↑ and ↓ move the display up or down. When the 5100 is used as a stand-alone, lines moved off the screen are lost. When used as a terminal, there is an extended display capability which stores the transmitted and received data. Its size (1000 to 49000 characters) varies with the model used. The display will show only the first 64 characters of the 14 most recent lines. With the scroll keys, however, you can access any part of the extended display.

The bottom line shows the status of the display. Positions 1 through 5 indicate the character position in the extended display that appears in position 1 on the display screen. Position 64 is the line indicator. If the symbol → appears, it is an indication that at least one line on the screen is longer than is shown. A ↑ tells you that the longest line displayed just fits, and no arrow in position 64 means that there is some room remaining to the right of the longest line displayed.

Besides using the scroll keys, you can move the image by holding down the CMD key and pressing any of the following numeric keys (right side of keyboard). These shift the display as shown:

Key	Shift
2	20 positions to left
3	20 positions to right
5	14 lines up
6	14 lines down
8	1 position to left
9	1 position to right

The normal (*home*) position of the display can be restored by pressing CMD and the 8 key on the typewriter keyboard.

Sometimes it happens that an output display is created which is large in size (such as a big table) and which you want to examine before it goes off the screen. Pressing the HOLD key once stops all processing in local mode. Pressing it again will cause processing to resume.

Error correction on the 5100

When the 5100 is used as a stand-alone *APL* system, error correction is more versatile on the display screen than described for the printer terminals earlier in the chapter. The ability to scroll data on the screen allows you to do a number of things not possible on other kinds of terminals. For instance, here is a display of data with the cursor shown awaiting input:

```
      3 × 7
2 1
      _    (cursor)
```

If the scroll-down key is used to move the display one line down (don't hold the key down or it will continue to scroll), we have

```
      3 × 7
2 1   _
```

The value 2 1, since it is on the input line, can now be captured as input:

```
      3 × 7
2 1   + 8
2 9
      _
```

To correct typing errors use the backspace (←) or forward space (→), both located just above the EXECUTE key, to position the cursor at the character to be corrected. Like the scroll keys, these will continue to move if held down. Once the cursor is positioned, type in the correct character. It will replace what was previously in that position. When the cursor is used in this way, it is no longer an underscore but a flashing character.

If a character is to be deleted, move the cursor, hold down the CMD key and press the backspace key once. The characters to the right will then be moved one position to the left. To insert a character, move the cursor to the desired position, hold down CMD and press the forward space key once. Now type the character to be inserted.

The cursor can also be used with ATTN to correct a section of a line in the same way as on other terminals. However, even if the line has been executed (as long as it remains on the screen) you may scroll it down to the input line and correct it. This luxury is denied you on print-oriented terminals.

Finally, when the 5100 is used as a terminal, the correcting capabilities described above must be initiated by first moving the line to be edited to the input line, holding down CMD and pressing the alphanumeric 2 key. This starts the edit operation. Not only do you have at your disposal all the previous editing techniques, but you may also delete all characters on the input line above and to the right of the cursor (CMD and alphanumeric 3 key), and shift the line to the right when the cursor is at the left edge of the screen (backspace key) or the left when it is at the right edge (forward space key).

Lines which have been edited can be transmitted by pressing EXECUTE. There is a price to be paid for this, however: all characters in the extended display after the edited line are deleted. Pressing CMD and the alphanumeric 8 key restores the display but does *not* transmit the edited line or delete the characters following it in the extended display.

PROBLEMS

1.   DRILL. (Some of the drill problems may result in error messages.)

```
6 8 2 4+3 9 1 1          5 4 3×6              1 2 8÷1 2 0

1 0 9 8-4 2 2 3          10÷10 5 2 1          ¯2 0 .81+15 6 ¯5

3-¯1 ¯56.7 0 ¯.19        3 4×1 2 3            2¯¯3
```

2.   Additional finger exercises (use BACKSPACE and ATTN to delete each statement in turn):

   NOW IS THE TIME FOR ALL GOOD MEN TO COME TO THE AID OF
   IF AT FIRST YOU DON'T SUCCEED, TRY AGAIN
   HOW NOW BROWN COW
   PRACTICE MAKES PERFECT
   THE SLOWEST PART OF THE APL SYSTEM IS GENERALLY THE USER

3.   At a basketball game a ticket seller sold 155 adult tickets at 1.25 each, 89 student tickets at .50 each, and accepted 45 courtesy passes at .25 each. Write an *APL* expression which gives the income from each class of tickets.

4.   A taxi fleet owner recorded mileages of 1263, 2016, 1997 and 3028 for each of his four cars. Operating expenses for each car during the same period were 59.50, 72.50, 79.50 and 83.00, respectively. What was his cost per mile for each car?

5.   Type 3 - 2. Backspace and overstrike the subtract sign with + before pressing the RETURN key. Account for the result.

Chapter 3:
Useful tools

Up to this point, all of our work has been done in desk calculator or *execution* mode. This has the disadvantage that once we type in the numbers and the operation symbol to be used and then press RETURN, execution proceeds and we get an answer (unless we tried something illegal). But the work is lost. No longer is it available to us for any future calculation, except as noted previously for the IBM 5100.

To handle problems such as described above, you will now be introduced to a data storage feature of **APL**. Then, as an extension of the concept of a vector, two-dimensional arrays will be examined in the latter part of the chapter.

Assignment

Any good calculator has the ability to store constant factors so that they can be used over and over again without having to be reentered each time. For instance, suppose we are given a series of problems all involving the constant 0.75:

```
      2×.75
1.5
      4+.75
4.75
      .75×.75
0.5625
```

As it stands, .75 has to be typed each time. What we'd like is some way to save this number and have it available for reuse. It may seem trivial at this point because our repeated factor, .75, doesn't take many keystrokes, but what if the expression you had to repeat had a large number of characters in it?

In **APL**, the terms *specification* or *assignment* are used to describe the placing of the results of an expression in storage. It works this way:

```
      A←.75
```

The expression above is read as "A is assigned the value .75", or "A is specified as .75". The name A is given by means of the arrow ← to the quantity .75 and from this point on, unless the contents of our workspace are destroyed or a different value is assigned to A, typing A will be the same as typing .75.

Since A is a name to which we are free to assign any value we want (even though we have chosen a specific one here), it and other names used in a similar manner are called *variables*.

Here are some calculations we can do with A:

```
      2×A
1.5
      4+A
4.75
      A×A
0.5625
      A
0.75
```

Flushed with success, you ought to be ready to try your hand at another assignment:

```
      B←1  2  3  4  5
      2×B
2  4  6  8  10
```

A, like death and taxes, is still with us. So try

```
      A+B
1.75  2.75  3.75  4.75  5.75
      B×B
1  4  9  16  25
```

If we keep this up, sooner or later we are going to run out of letters of the alphabet. What then? The next logical step is to use multiple letter names:

```
      PI←3.14159
      PI×PI
9.869587728
```

The name in the example above was not chosen haphazardly. Subject to restrictions on length and usable characters (to be discussed later in this chapter), you have a wide choice of possible names for objects in **APL**. We suggest as a general rule that names be chosen for their mnemonic utility. This simplifies identification and enhances consistency, making it easier for you (and others) to follow what has been done.

You should have noticed by now that when an assignment is made, the terminal does not print its result on the paper. This is reasonable enough, since all we are asking when we make an assignment is for something to be placed in storage.

A is still in storage. Here it is again:

```
      A
0.75
```

What happens if we mistakenly (or otherwise) use A for a second assignment? For instance,

```
      A←2+B
```

If we call for A now, we get

```
      A
3  4  5  6  7
      2+B
3  4  5  6  7
```

The new values of A replace the old, which are lost. Moral of the story: If you want to save the values stored under a variable name, don't override the assignment. Use a different name.

There are several ways to extend the number of possibilities for variable names. Underlining (upper shift F) is one way:

```
      A←3.2
      A+5
8.2
      A
3  4  5  6  7
```

$\underline{A}$ is clearly different from A, which still has its last assigned value. In effect, this gives us 52 letters to choose from, alone or in multiple character names like

```
      DATA←5  2  7  8
```

APL recognizes up to 77 characters in a variable name, but it doesn't pay to make it too long. Remember, *you* are the one who will have to type it. Numbers can also be included in any position except the first, as shown by

```
      X3Y2←20
      3XY2←20
SYNTAX ERROR
      3  XY2←20
         ∧
```

but special symbols for operations, spaces and punctuation marks may not be used in a name. Exception: The symbol Δ (upper shift H) is treated exactly as though it is an alphabetic character.

As an aside, *APL* actually put the value 20 (see above) in storage under the name $XY2$:

```
      XY2
20
```

APL lets you make multiple specifications on the same line. In certain cases this turns out to be a handy timesaver. Here is an example:

```
      A←2+B←3  1  5
      B
3  1  5
      A
5  3  7
```

Now let's try asking for

```
      A+W
VALUE ERROR
      A+W
         ∧
```

It should be obvious what's wrong. The computer didn't recognize the variable name W because there hasn't been any value assigned to that name. Hence the error message. A is still a valid variable, but not W:

```
      A
5  3  7
```

```
        W
VALUE ERROR
        W
        ∧
```

This raises another question: How can you find out what variable names you already have in storage? The command)$VARS$ (abbreviation for "variables") produces an alphabetized listing of the variables in storage:

```
        )VARS
A       B       DATA    PI      XY2     X3Y2            A̲
```

A partial listing of the variable names beginning with a given letter, say P, to the end of the alphabet, can be obtained with

```
        )VARS P
PI      XY2     X3Y2            A̲
```

In the case of a long listing, if you don't want to continue the output, pressing ATTN (or BREAK on an ASCII terminal) effectively interrupts the printout. Note that the underlined A̲ comes after the nonunderlined letters of the alphabet. ATTN can be used to interrupt execution of any expression at the end of the statement currently being processed. On the IBM 5100, pressing ATTN twice immediately stops execution.

Expressions which begin with a right parenthesis followed by a word or abbreviation are known as *system commands*. You have already used two of them, sign-on and sign-off, and $VARS$ is another. More will be introduced in succeeding chapters as the need arises.

Getting back to our $VALUE\ ERROR$, if we give W a value and then call for $A+W$, we no longer get an error message,

```
        W←0.1
        A+W
5.1 3.1 7.1
```

and not only is execution successful, but W is added to the list of variables in storage:

```
        )VARS
A       B       DATA    PI      W       XY2     X3Y2            A̲
```

Now W behaves just like the other variables and can be respecified:

```
        W←2×W
        W
0.2
```

Suppose that you want to get rid of one or more variables while still actively working in **APL**. Typing

```
        A←
```

buys you nothing since the response of the system is

```
SYNTAX ERROR
        A←
          ∧
```

and entering $A←0$ also gets you nowhere, since the only thing that happens is that the value 0 is assigned to A.

Another system command, *ERASE*, is useful here. This command is followed by the name(s) of the variables to be erased. Its execution elicits no response from the system other than the typeball moving over 6 spaces:

```
)ERASE A B DATA
@                  (typeball comes to rest at the position marked @)
)VARS
PI      W        XY2          X3Y2            A
```

An introduction to matrices

While useful in and of itself, the notion of a vector, as introduced at the end of the last chapter, is far too limited in the real world. We would certainly stand accused of myopic vision if, like the strange inhabitants of Flatland, we didn't recognize the need for arrays which are multidimensional.

The sales record table on page 10

```
          9    7    8
          3    4    5
```

is an obvious case in point. For tabulating data and correlating information which purports to relate two quantities, an array of two dimensions, called a *matrix*, is clearly a necessity.

We could, of course, continue this discussion and come up into a general n-dimensional array, but our finite minds are likely to boggle at the conception of any array beyond three dimensions. Even the latter can't be spatially portrayed on two-dimensional paper, given the constraints for printing imposed by the terminal.

Since the great majority of users of arrays don't normally require more than two dimensions, we will stick with two dimensions until much later in the text, after a firm foundation has been laid.

Now for the meat. Before using matrices, we have to know how to create them. Unlike vectors, which can be created in **APL** by simply typing the elements in a single line, matrices require two additional pieces of information: how many rows and how many columns; or to put it another way, how big - along each dimension - is the array. Incidentally, the word *coordinate* is frequently used to refer to a direction along which an array extends in space. Loosely speaking, it is somewhat interchangeable with the word *dimension* as we used it previously.

More specifically, the example matrix

```
          3    7    2      8
          4    7   1.06   14
```

has 2 rows and 4 columns, i.e., its *shape* is 2 4. The first coordinate, which gives the number of *rows*, is of length 2, which corresponds to the size of one column, while the second coordinate gives the number of *columns*, and corresponds to the size of one row.

If you're still with us, let's now take a look at how we can build these matrices. The operation ρ (upper shift *R*) is employed for array construction. In use, the numbers on the left specify the shape of the resulting matrix, and consist of two integers detailing the number of rows and columns, in that order. The numbers on the right are the elements to be included in the array, with these elements ordered by rows. Here are some examples:

```
      2 3ρ4 7 8 2 4 6
  4   7   8
  2   4   6
```

```
      A←4  2ρ7  8  4
      A
7  8
4  7
8  4
7  8
      B←3  4ρ1  2  3  4  5  6  7  8  9  10  11  12  13  14
      B
1   2   3   4
5   6   7   8
9  10  11  12
```

Two pertinent comments need to be made at this point. First, if there are not enough elements to make up the array, **APL** goes back to the beginning of the "storage pile" on the right and starts over, as in A above. Second, if there are too many elements, only those needed are used and the rest ignored, as in B.

The symbol ρ used in this manner is called *reshape*. Its effect is to take what is on the right, which could be a single number, vector, matrix, three-dimensional array or bigger, and reshape it according to the specifications of the numbers on the left. The following example is illustrative:

```
      2  3ρB
1  2  3
4  5  6
```

The shape of the result is dependent on the number and magnitude of the elements on the left:

```
      8ρ3  0  1
3  0  1  3  0  1  3  0
      2  3  4ρ7  8  2  2  3  6  8
7  8  2  2
3  6  8  7
8  2  2  3

6  8  7  8
2  2  3  6
8  7  8  2
```

One element on the left results in a vector, two in a matrix, three in a three-dimensional array, etc. Don't get alarmed by the last example, which is three-dimensional, consisting of 2 planes, or pages, each of which contains 3 rows and 4 columns. It is included at this point only for illustrative purposes.

Operations with matrices

Now that you know how to build and store matrices, there are a number of things we can do to manipulate their elements. We begin by defining two matrices M and N:

```
      M←4  3ρ1  2  0  1  3  2  3  4  2  3  3  0
and
      N←4  3ρ2  3  7  8  1  4  2  5  0  0  7  6
      M
1  2  0
1  3  2
3  4  2
3  3  0
```

```
        N
2   3   7
8   1   4
2   5   0
0   7   6
```

As an extension of our earlier work with vectors in the last chapter, we can add 2 to each element of M,

```
      2+M
3   4   2
3   5   4
5   6   4
5   5   2
```

or divide it by 3:

```
     M÷3
0.3333333333      0.6666666667      0
0.3333333333      1                 0.6666666667
1                 1.333333333       0.6666666667
1                 1                 0
```

We can multiply the two together,

```
      M×N
2    6    0
8    3    8
6   20    0
0   21    0
```

and subtract one from the other:

```
       M-N
⁻1   ⁻1   ⁻7
⁻7    2   ⁻2
 1   ⁻1    2
 3   ⁻4   ⁻6
```

From this point on, examples used in the text will include both vectors and matrices as appropriate.

PROBLEMS

1. On one line, assign the vector 3 4 5 6 7 to the name A and make B equal to two times A.

2. Which of the following are valid variable names in **APL**?

   A) $SPACEMAN$ D) $\Delta 3X$

   B) $X\ SQUARED$ E) $SIXTY\text{-}FOUR$

   C) $B+ALPHA$ F) $4BY5$

3. Construct a matrix M with 5 rows and 3 columns, consisting entirely of the number 7. Ditto for a matrix Q of the same size as M, each of whose rows contains 4 9 11.

4. Convert the matrix M from problem 3 into a matrix N of all 1's in at least two different ways.

5. A store sells 3 items, A, B, C. Over a one week period, the amounts sold are respectively 8, 15, 7. The following week's sales record is 12, 4, 0. Put this data in a matrix S, each of whose rows represents a week's sales. The prices of A, B, C the first week are respectively 3.10, 2.00, 4.17, and because of rapid inflation, these prices increase to 3.50, 2.75, 4.35 the second week. Put this data in a matrix P and use it to construct a table of total sales revenue by item over the two-week period.

6. Assign arbitrary values to the vector variables A and B and execute $A\ B$. Note the error message which results. Now try $A\ \textbf{,}\ B$.

Chapter 4:
Additional operations and tools

In the previous chapters we dealt with individual numbers, which we will now call *scalars*; chains of numbers, for which the term *vectors* was used; and two-dimensional arrays, which we called *matrices*. Left partially unanswered at that time was the question of what combinations of these are allowed in *APL*, as well as what the shape of the result might be. Let's now address ourselves to the question by formulating a few simple rules and giving appropriate names for the concepts to be considered.

Primitive scalar dyadic functions

There are seven rules that govern the ways in which vectors, scalars and matrices can be combined. In what follows, the symbol f stands for any of the arithmetic operations that we have already introduced. Later in this section we will further classify and categorize these operations to make more evident their connection with other operations yet to be defined.

Rule	Result	Arguments
1	scalar ←	scalar f scalar
2	vector ←	scalar f vector
3	vector ←	vector f scalar
4	vector ←	vector f vector
5	matrix ←	scalar f matrix
6	matrix ←	matrix f scalar
7	matrix ←	matrix f matrix

The terms under "result" tell us the shape of the result when various operations are performed on quantities having the shapes on the right.

This is as good a place as any to introduce a little additional terminology. Why? you ask. Naming something doesn't tell us any more about it and, in fact, can mislead us by enabling us to talk more glibly of things we may not know much about. But mathematicians especially, being the perverse creatures that they are, insist on more formal names for the tools and concepts they work with. And having a name for something does have the advantage of letting the namer identify without ambiguity (we hope!) that which is under discussion.

First, if f stands for an operation to be performed, the things it is to operate on will be called *arguments*. Thus, in 5×6, 5 is the left argument and 6 is the right argument. Both arguments can be scalars (rule 1),

```
      3 + 5
8
```

or one can be a vector, either on the right or left (rules 2, 3),

```
      2 + 3  5  7
5  7  9
      5  6  8 × 3
15  18  24
```

or both arguments can be vectors (rule 4),

```
      3  6  8 ÷ 2  1  4
1.5  6  2
```

the only stipulation being that both arguments must be of the same length. As an obvious corollary, the lengths of the resulting vectors in the two examples given above are the same as those of the vector arguments.

By substituting the word *size* for *length* in the last two sentences, the same reasoning can be shown to hold for various combinations of matrices and scalars (rules 5, 6, 7). In fact, an inspection of the seven rules and the examples should serve to convince you that they can all be boiled down into a single rule for operations on n-dimensional arrays (n=0,1,2, with 0 being associated with scalars), provided that appropriate size restrictions in the arguments are observed. Can you state this rule?

The operators that we have been working with are more properly called *functions*, because a result is obtained as a consequence of the function operating on its argument(s). (One of the dictionary meanings of "function" is "performance" or "execution.")

Furthermore, the word *dyadic* is associated with these functions, since they require *two* arguments (at least as we have been using them thus far). They are also called *primitive* because they are immediately available on the **APL** keyboard. And finally (at long last!), they are sometimes referred to as *scalar* because functions of this type are defined first for scalars and then extended element by element to vectors, matrices and other arrays. In summary, the operations + - × ÷ are called *primitive scalar dyadic functions*.

Operation tables for the arithmetic functions

For each of the functions thus far introduced, we can construct an operation table, with the left arguments down the vertical column on the left and the right arguments across the top. To save space, only the integers 1 2 3 4 will be used as arguments:

```
+| 1 2 3 4        -| 1   2   3   4        ×| 1  2   3   4        ÷| 1   2    3    4
-+--------        -+------------          -+----------          -+---------------
1| 2 3 4 5        1| 0  ‾1  ‾2  ‾3        1| 1  2   3   4        1| 1  1÷2  1÷3  1÷4
2| 3 4 5 6        2| 1   0  ‾1  ‾2        2| 2  4   6   8        2| 2   1   2÷3  2÷4
3| 4 5 6 7        3| 2   1   0  ‾1        3| 3  6   9  12        3| 3  3÷2   1   3÷4
4| 5 6 7 8        4| 3   2   1   0        4| 4  8  12  16        4| 4   2   4÷3   1
```

Since it is a downright nuisance to construct these operation tables by hand, let's use this opportunity to introduce a new **APL** function which behaves somewhat differently from the simple arithmetic functions used so far, but which, nevertheless, will be a great timesaver for us in the future.

We will begin by introducing a problem that involves a large number of multiplications. It asks that we compute the taxes to be paid for items costing varying amounts and taxed at three different rates:

TAX		TAX RATES		
TABLE		.01	.02	.05
COST	1	.01	.02	.05
	2	.02	.04	.10
OF	3	.03	.06	.15
	4	.04	.08	.20
ITEM	5	.05	.10	.25

The result desired is the matrix which is obtained by getting all possible products of costs and rates. You can see that if the cost and tax rate vectors had large numbers of noninteger elements, this procedure could involve a lot of work.

Outer product

APL has a function which operates on arrays in precisely the way needed to fill in the table above. It is called the *outer product* or *outer result*. To illustrate it, let the left argument be the vector of costs A and the right argument the tax rates B:

```
      A←1  2  3  4  5
      B←.01×1  2  5
      B
0.01  0.02  0.05
```

The outer product is

```
      A∘.×B
0.01           0.02           0.05
0.02           0.04           0.1
0.03           0.06           0.15
0.04           0.08           0.2
0.05           0.1            0.25
```

which is read "A jot dot times B." The little circle, called *jot*, is the upper shift J. Clearly, the outer product gives all possible multiplications of the left and right arguments.

Any primitive scalar dyadic function can be used after the period in place of ×, as for instance,

```
      A∘.+B
1.01           1.02           1.05
2.01           2.02           2.05
3.01           3.02           3.05
4.01           4.02           4.05
5.01           5.02           5.05
```

Notice that the shape or dimension of the result is the catenation (chaining together) of the shapes of the two arguments. In this case it is a matrix with five rows and three columns.

The outer product lets us to do a variety of things. For example, an addition table can be generated by

```
        A ∘ . + A
  2   3   4   5   6
  3   4   5   6   7
  4   5   6   7   8
  5   6   7   8   9
  6   7   8   9  10
```

and the subtraction table by

```
          A ∘ . - A
  0  ¯1  ¯2  ¯3  ¯4
  1   0  ¯1  ¯2  ¯3
  2   1   0  ¯1  ¯2
  3   2   1   0  ¯1
  4   3   2   1   0
```

The other operation tables can be obtained in the same way. More about this interesting and useful function in Chapter 25.

In the meantime, to continue our story, here is one in which no function is specified. Can you guess what it is?

```
  |  1   2   3    4
- + - - - - - - - - -
1 |  1   1   1    1
2 |  2   4   8   16
3 |  3   9  27   81
4 |  4  16  64  256
```

Note: In this and subsequent operation tables displayed in the text, only the results are generated and printed by the **APL** system. The rest has been added manually for identification.

Power function

You should be able to see that the previous table represents raising to powers. The left argument values are raised to the powers indicated by the right arguments. This power function exhibits the characteristics we would expect from a primitive scalar dyadic function. All we need is a symbol for it. This brings up an interesting aspect (or failing, if you prefer) of conventional mathematical notation, and one which will become even more apparent as we go along.

Notice how we write the four arithmetic functions:

$$2 + 3$$
$$2 - 3$$
$$2 \times 3$$
$$2 \div 3$$

And then we come along and write for the power function

$$2^3$$

The operation to be performed is specified not by a symbol but by position, which is not only inconsistent but potentially dangerous, since it is very easy sometimes to miss the elevated position of the power in writing or reading.

In **APL**, the symbol $\star$ (uppershift P) is used to represent raising to a power, as in

```
      2*3
8
```

*, being a primitive scalar dyadic function, extends to vectors and matrices as well:

```
      2  4  3*2
4  16  9
      A←2 3ρ1 2 3 4 5 6
      A
 1  2  3
 4  5  6
      A*3
   1    8   27
  64  125  216
```

In mathematics courses roots are shown to be equivalent to fractional powers, e.g., the square root is the same as raising to the one-half power. So, instead of writing $\sqrt{2}$ to mean the square root of 2, in **APL** this is

```
      2*.5
1.414213562
```

Here is another example:

```
      9  64*.5
3  8
```

Negative powers, which are the equivalent of the reciprocal of the number raised to the corresponding positive power, are also available to the **APL** user, as in the following:

```
      2*¯2
0.25
```

Our power function can now be used to generate quite large numbers, as, for instance

```
      100*8
1E16
```

Scaled (exponential) notation

In the last example you saw a new notation, which some of you may recognize as being similar to what is used in other higher level programming languages and evidently intended to avoid writing a monster like 10,000,000,000,000,000. The E may be interpreted as "times 10 to the ... power."

This notation is equally convenient for very small numbers,

```
      .01*9
1E¯18
```

and can be employed in many different ways to express the same number, say, 530:

```
      530        which is    53×10
      5.3E2                   5.3×100
      .0053E5                 .0053×10000
      530E0                   530×1
      5300E¯1                 5300×.1
```

APL not only produces results in scaled notation, but it is possible to enter data this way:

```
      1+33
34
    · 1+3.3E1
34
      1+.33E2
34
      1+330E¯1
34
```

Users have considerable freedom in formatting their inputs (although the common practice of using commas to separate groups of digits is not allowed, the comma itself being an *APL* function to be discussed later). The results generated by the *APL* system are somewhat more restricted. Problems 1 and 2 should give you some clues as to these limitations.

PROBLEMS

1.   DRILL

```
   ¯2*.5                 2*.5 .333 .25 .2        ¯8*.3333333333333

   3*4 2 1 0 ¯5          1*0 1 10 100 1000       ¯7.11E4÷9.45E¯3

   21.268E1+4.56E¯2      8.3E0×7.9E¯3 56            346×2E3.7
```

2.   Key in $1E0$, $1E1$, ,... $1E11$. Do likewise with $1E¯1$,..., $1E¯6$. Note where the break point is in *APL* for the display on large and small numbers in E-notation.

3.   Given a cube each of whose edges have length L. Write in *APL* the steps needed to find its surface area. Execute for $L \leftarrow 3\ 7\ 15\ 2.7$.

4.   Specify $A \leftarrow 1\ 2\ 3\ 4$ and $D \leftarrow 3 \times A$. Execute $A \circ . \times D$ and $D \circ . * A$.

5.   Use the outer product to generate a table of squares and square roots of the integers 1 through 5.

6.   Express the number of seconds in the year (365 days) in scaled notation.

7.   A journeyman snail finishing his apprenticeship is now allowed by the union to travel at a snail's pace (12 ft. per day). Express this in miles per hour.

Chapter 5:
Five more primitive dyadic functions

This chapter will introduce a number of additional primitive dyadic functions available in *APL*. Some of these will be employed frequently by most *APL* users; others, like combinations and logarithms, will be of value to a more specialized fraternity, nonmembers of which should feel free to study them with no more than passing interest, or for that matter, ignore them completely.

Logarithms

There is another function which is closely related to the power function of Chapter 4: the logarithm function (the logarithm of a number N to the base B is that power to which B must be raised to equal N). In *APL*, this is written $B \circledast N$, the symbol being that for power ($*$) overstruck with the large circle (upper shift *O*).

Thus, since it is true that

```
      10*3
1000
```

the base-10 log (to use the usual abbreviation) of 1000 is

```
      10⊛1000
3
```

and

```
      10⊛100 1000 10
2 3 1
```

Similarly, since we know that $2 * 3$ is 8, then the log of 8 to the base 2 is 3:

```
      2⊛8
3
```

Notice that the base is the left argument and the number whose log is to be found, the right argument.

Maximum and minimum

Now try the following exercise, exploring the working of the symbol $\lceil$ (upper shift S):

```
      3⌈5
5
      5⌈3
5
      5⌈5
5
```

Lest you be tempted to think that $\lceil$ always generates a 5, look at

```
      3⌈3
3
```

If you experiment with this function for a while, you will see that it selects the larger of the left and right arguments and is appropriately named the *maximum* function. Its operation table looks like this:

```
      A←1  2  3  4  5
      A∘.⌈A
1  2  3  4  5
2  2  3  4  5
3  3  3  4  5
4  4  4  4  5
5  5  5  5  5
```

If there's a maximum function, analogously there ought to be a *minimum* function. This is found on the upper shift D key, and selects the lesser of the two arguments:

```
      3⌊5
3
      ¯5⌊2
¯5
      B←2  3ρ3  4  0  1  7  9
      C←2  3ρ1  2  3  4  5  6
      B
3  4  0
1  7  9
      C
1  2  3
4  5  6
      B⌊C
1  2  0
1  5  6
      A∘.⌊A
1  1  1  1  1
1  2  2  2  2
1  2  3  3  3
1  2  3  4  4
1  2  3  4  5
```

The symbols $\lceil$ and $\lfloor$ have the technical names "upstile" and "downstile" respectively. You can hardly go wrong, however, in referring to them as "maximum" and "minimum" as they are used here.

"Lesser" and "greater" are relative terms, and indeed the mathematician defines them according to position on the real number line:

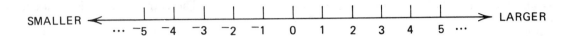

Thus, the lesser of two numbers is that one which is farther to the left, and the greater one, farther to the right.

Let's consider a couple of simple problems. There are three students who got grades of 90, 80 and 55 in a certain exam, and on a retest received 70, 80 and 75, respectively. The instructor wishes to record for each student only the greater of the two grades received. How can he do it?

The right answers are 90 for the first student, 80 for the second, and 75 for the third. In **APL** this is obtained by

```
      90 80 55⌈70 80 75
90 80 75
```

A second problem: We have purchased an odd lot of lumber consisting of 4 boards of lengths 5, 8.1, 10 and 7.9 feet. Unfortunately, our truck can carry boards no longer than 8 feet without running afoul of the law. Boards longer than 8 feet have to be trimmed to 8 ft. The "trimming" is done in **APL** by

```
      8⌊5 8.1 10 7.9
5 8 8 7.9
```

and the second and third boards are the ones to be cut down. These are two trivial examples, but as our store of new functions increases, we will be able to solve much more involved problems later.

Combinations

A relatively simple combinatorial problem in mathematics is to find the number of ways one can group 2 things out of a population of 4. Let's solve the problem by brute force, with 4 objects, A, B, C, D. Listing the possible combinations, we have

AB AC AD BC BD CD

We'll assume the order is not significant, so that CA and AC, for example, will be considered to be the same. Thus, there are 6 ways of grouping 2 things out of a population of 4.

In combinatorial theory it is shown that the formula

$$\frac{m!}{n!(m-n)!}$$

gives the number of ways of making m objects n at a time. For the case above, this would be

$$\frac{4!}{2!(4-2)!}$$

or 6. As a reminder to those of you whose math is rusty, m! means $m \times (m-1) \times (m-2) \times ... \times 1$, so that 4! is the same as $4 \times 3 \times 2 \times 1$.

As you might suspect, the process is somewhat easier in **APL**. It is done with the same symbol !
(whimsically nicknamed "shriek"). On the keyboard it is formed by striking the period, BACKSPACE and
the quote symbol (upper shift K) so that the two characters line up. The correct format is n!m and is, for
our example above

```
      2!4
6
```

This is the place to emphasize that ! like ⊛ is *not* a keyboard character, but is formed by overstriking as
described above. The symbols ' and . must be lined up. Otherwise a second quote is typed by the system,
followed in this case by a $SYNTAX\ ERROR$ message as shown,

```
      2.'4  (RETURN)
'
SYNTAX ERROR
      '
      ^
```

and we are back in execution mode once again. More about the use of quotes in Chapter 17.

! is a primitive scalar dyadic function and can take both vector and matrix arguments:

```
      0 1 2 3 4!4
1 4 6 4 1
      X←2 3ρ0 1 2 3 4 5
      2!X
   0  0  1
   3  6 10
```

Its operation table looks like this:

```
      E←0 1 2 3 4
      E∘.!E
1 1 1 1 1
0 1 2 3 4
0 0 1 3 6
0 0 0 1 4
0 0 0 0 1
```

What we generated above corresponds to the last column. That portion of the table consisting of the
nonzero integers can be removed to form what in mathematics is called Pascal's triangle,

```
            1
          1   1
        1   2   1
      1   3   3   1
    1   4   6   4   1
```

which, if you're interested, is a device for calculating and displaying the coefficients generated in the
expansion of an expression of the form $(a+b)^n$ by the Binomial Theorem.

Finally, to complete the picture, our arguments don't have to be integers:

```
      2.1!5.6
13.48487115
```

For the benefit of the more mathematically sophisticated, this is related to the complete beta-function of
probability theory. (Don't panic. It won't be mentioned again !)

Residue

The next primitive scalar dyadic function we will consider is one called *residue*. We can illustrate it with a trivial example. Assume that we are at the zoo with only 8 peanuts and 3 children who are to share the wealth evenly. We aren't able to cut up a single peanut. How many do we have left?

Clearly, the simple-minded way to do this would be to start with 8 and take away 3, leaving 5. Then take 3 more away, with 2 remaining, too few to distribute to the children. In formal language, the 3-residue of 8 is 2. This isn't, of course, the only way to do the problem. We could also divide 8 by 3, see that it goes in twice, and get a remainder of 2.

The symbol for residue is $|$, which is the upper shift M ("stile"). In **APL**, the 3-residue of 8 is entered as 3 | 8 and the result is 2.

Our peanut problem can be enlarged by considering the distribution of varying amounts of peanuts to the 3 children:

```
      3|0  1  2  3  4  5  6  7  8
0  1  2  0  1  2  0  1  2
```

Here is another problem in which 5 peanuts are distributed among 1, 2 and 3 children:

```
      1  2  3|5
0  1  2
```

The residue function is a handy one for generating all kinds of useful information. For instance, asking for the 1-residue of a number is a convenient way to get the fractional part of the number:

```
      1|2.5  31.23
0.5  0.23
```

Now what about the residues of negative numbers, say 3 | ⁻4? Previously we saw that a recurring pattern was generated by

```
      3|0  1  2  3  4  5  6  7  8
0  1  2  0  1  2  0  1  2
```

So when we try

```
      3|⁻4  ⁻3  ⁻2  ⁻1  0  1  2  3  4  5  6  7  8
2  0  1  2  0  1  2  0  1  2  0  1  2
```

we expect, and get a continuation of the recurring pattern. If you think about it a bit, you will see another way to obtain the residue of a negative number. For our example above, add 3 to ⁻4 to get ⁻1. Then add 3 again to get 2. In general, the rule is to keep adding until the result is 0 or positive.

Suppose the left argument is negative. Then the result is also negative, or 0 if the right argument is a multiple of the left argument:

```
      ⁻3 ⁻3|⁻4
2 ⁻1
```

Applications requiring negative left arguments are few and far between; however, if you insist on pursuing this, try a few examples and see if you can develop the general rule.

There is one residue class of particular interest in the computing industry, the 2-residues of the integers:

```
      2|0  1  2  3  4  5
0  1  0  1  0  1
```

Here we have a continuing pattern of 0 and 1 as the only elements of the pattern. If we so choose, we can let 0 represent the state of a circuit with the switch open (no current) and 1 with the switch closed. We'll have more to say about this later.

While all the new functions introduced, ⊛ ⌈ ⌊ ! | , are primitive scalar dyadic functions, the maximum and minimum functions mathematically are different from all others in one significant respect: no knowledge of an operation table is needed to use them, only the ability to distinguish greater and lesser. They are inherently simpler than even addition and subtraction. In fact, very young children can conceptualize ⌈ and ⌊ before they can + and -.

PROBLEMS

1. DRILL

    5 0 ¯22 15 3⌈3 7 ¯10.8 2 0   1|3.4 ¯2.2 .019

    2 3 4 5 6 10⊛2   0|1 2 3

    1 10⊛1   1 9 ¯5 ¯2⌊0 6 4 3

    10⊛0   1 9 8|3 4 6

    ¯2 4 ¯5|8 13 3.78   0 1 2 3 4!3 4 5 6 7

    ¯2⊛25   3|¯3 ¯2 0 1 2 3

2. Store A sells 5 vegetable items for 15, 20, 18, 32 and 29 cents a pound. At store B the prices are 18, 20, 15, 10 and 49 cents a pound, respectively. The policy of a third store C is to meet the competition's prices. Write an *APL* expression to determine store C's selling prices for the 5 items.

3. The pH of a solution is a measure of its acidity or basicity, and is defined as the logarithm (base-10) of the reciprocal of the hydrogen ion concentration in moles/liter of solution. Use *APL* to express the pH of a solution whose concentration is C.

4. Given that A and B are integers modulo 5 (i.e., A and B belong to the set S of integers generated by taking 5 | N for any integer $N \geq 4$), show that 5 | A + B, 5 | A × B and 5 | A * B are in S.

5. How can the residue function be used to tell whether one number A is divisible by another number B?

6. Write an *APL* expression to tell what clock time it is, given the number of elapsed hours H since 12:00.

7. For the equation   X + Y + Z + W = 50   find the number of possible solutions in all different positive integers. (Hint: Think of 50 units partitioned into 4 blocks by separators.)

8. How many quadrilaterals can be formed by joining groups of 4 points in a collection of 30 points in a plane, no 3 of which lie on a straight line?

9. If 1 | N produces the fractional part of N, how can the residue function be used to get the integral part of the number?

10. Write an expression to get the fractional part of a negative number.

11. You are given two matrices of prices, A and B. Define a new matrix C such that each element of C is the smaller of the corresponding elements of A and B.

Chapter 6:
Relational and logical functions

In this chapter we will introduce ten new functions falling into two classes, the relationals and logicals. If you think that this is far too many for a single presentation and will leave you hopelessly confused, you may breathe easier. All of these functions have one thing in common - they produce results of 0 or 1 only, which at this stage shouldn't be too taxing to keep in mind.

Relational functions

There are in *APL* six *relational* functions, $< \leq = \geq > \neq$, which are found on the keyboard as the upper shift 3 through 8. They have the usual mathematical meanings, *less than*, *less than or equal*, *equal*, *greater than or equal*, *greater than* and *not equal*, respectively. The reason they are called *relational* is that they inquire about the truth or falsity of the relationship between two quantities, say A<B.

This statement is really a question asked of the computer: Is A less than B? It calls for a response, yes or no, because either A is less than B or it is not. Let's try this on the terminal:

```
      3 < 5
1
      5 < 3
0
```

Clearly, a 1 response means the statement is true, and 0 false.

Vectors and matrices can be used with this function too:

```
      3 < 1  2  3  4  5
0 0 0 1 1
      A ← 2  3ρ1  2  3  4  5  6
      A
 1  2  3
 4  5  6
      2 < A
0 0 1
1 1 1
```

We can now use this function to help us in a selection problem. Suppose as a store owner we have a number of accounts, with \$3, \$ ‾2, \$0, \$2 and \$‾3 as balances, and we want to flag or mark those accounts which are overdrawn (represented by negative values). The "less than" function will solve our problem, although it is by no means the only way to do it:

```
      3 ‾2  0  2 ‾3 < 0
0  1  0  0  1
```

Does < have all the qualities of a primitive scalar dyadic function? Here is its operation table:

```
      B←1  2  3  4
      B∘.<B
  0  1  1  1
  0  0  1  1
  0  0  0  1
  0  0  0  0
```

By this time you ought to be able to convince yourself that "less than" meets our criteria for a primitive scalar dyadic function, as indeed do the rest of the relationals. We won't go through them all, but let's explore just one more, =. Typing

```
      3 ‾2  0  2 ‾3 = 0
0  0  1  0  0
```

generates a listing of those accounts from the previous example whose balance is 0, to complement the list of those overdrawn. You should be able to see many other possibilities. For instance, to get vectors of all 1's or all 0's, try

```
      0  1  2  3 = 0  1  2  3
1  1  1  1
      0  1  2  3 = 3  2  1  0
0  0  0  0
```

Logical functions

Not all the juice has yet been squeezed out of the subset 0 1 of the real numbers. Here is a function, ∧ (upper shift 0), called AND, whose operation table is

```
      C←0  1
      C∘.∧C
0  0
0  1
```

The result is 1 if and only if both arguments are 1.

You have probably noticed that only 0 and 1 were used as arguments in the table. Notice what happens when we try

```
      2∧0
DOMAIN ERROR
      2∧0
       ∧
```

The last time we got a *DOMAIN ERROR* was when we typed

```
      5÷0
DOMAIN ERROR
      5÷0
      ∧
```

It seems clear, then, that the arguments are restricted to 0 and 1.

For those who have some background in mathematical logic, the analogy between 0 and 1 and the true-false entries in the truth table for AND will be apparent. In any event, this function provides yet another means of generating 0's and 1's, and will be useful in writing programs later on. The AND function is an example of a class of functions called *logical* or *Boolean*.

Another logical function is ∨ (upper shift 9), called OR:

```
      C
0 1
      C∘.∨C
  0 1
  1 1
```

The result is 1 if either or both arguments are 1.

There are yet two more functions in this class, ⍲, NAND and ⍱, NOR. You may have guessed already that NAND stands for "NOT AND," and NOR for "NOT OR." The overstruck character ~ (upper shift *T*, "tilde") is used for negation. Below are their operation tables:

```
      C
0 1
      C∘.⍲C
  1 1
  1 0
      C∘.⍱C
  1 0
  0 0
```

Here are two examples:

```
      1⍱0
0
      D←2 2ρ1 0 0 1
      D
  1 0
  0 1
      1⍲D
  0 1
  1 0
```

You can see that everywhere 0 appears in the table for ∧, a 1 appears for ⍲, and vice versa. The same holds for ∨ and ⍱.

Although it was suggested earlier that the logical functions had a use in programming, for generating 0's or 1's at the appropriate point, there is another physical situation which could be represented by them, namely piping networks:

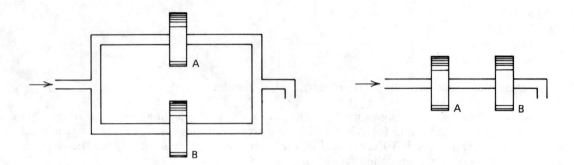

In the left figure, fluid flows if either valve A or valve B is open, while in the right figure flow occurs only if both A and B are open. Read "0" for closed and "1" for open, and the figures correspond to the OR and AND tables respectively. Keep in mind that it is a short step to go from pipes to electrical circuits (and onward to computer design).

Actually there are 16 possible logical connectives, of which we have taken up only 4. To illustrate how others can be generated, let's assume we want a function that gives us an EXCLUSIVE OR, with operation table

```
  |  0  1
 -+- - - -
 0|  0  1
 1|  1  0
```

the result being 0 if and only if both arguments are 0 or both are 1. Can we get this in **APL**?

The answer is yes. It is that part of the operation table for ≠ where both arguments are 0 or 1. A similar approach yields many of the others.

```
 _ _ _     0  1  2  3  ∘.≠0  1  2  3
|0 1|1  1
|1 0|1  1
 1  1  0  1
 1  1  1  0
```

Summary

Thus far, we have introduced and illustrated a large number of primitive scalar dyadic functions. Before going on, here is a brief recapitulation up to this point:

$A + B$	sum of A and B	$A < B$	
$A - B$	B subtracted from A	$A \le B$	
$A \times B$	product of A and B	$A = B$	1 if true
$A \div B$	A divided by B	$A \ge B$	0 if false
$A * B$	A raised to the power B	$A > B$	
$A \circledast B$	base-A logarithm of B	$A \ne B$	
$A \lceil B$	larger of A and B		
$A \lfloor B$	smaller of A and B	$A \vee B$	logical OR of A and B
$A \mid B$	A-residue of B	$A \wedge B$	logical AND of A and B
$A \,!\, B$	combinations of B items	$A \barvee B$	logical NOR of A and B
	taken A at a time	$A \barwedge B$	logical NAND of A and B

Keep in mind that any of these functions can be used to replace the symbol f in the rules (page 23) for combining scalars, vectors and matrices.

PROBLEMS

1. DRILL

   0 0 1 1∨0 1 0 1   2 3 0<5 ¯1 4

   1 0 1 0∧1 0 0 1   3 1 2≠1 2 3

   2 4 7 ¯2>6 ¯1 0 4   0 1 2 3=0 1 3 2

   4 ¯5 ¯1 ¯6.8≥4 1 ¯1 2   0 0 1 1⍱0 1 0 1

   8 7 6 5 4 3 2 1≤1 2 3 4 5 6 7 8   1 0 1 0⍲1 0 0 1

2. How can the functions = and | be used in *APL* to identify the factors of an integer N?

3. *A* is a vector of accounts, with the negative values representing those overdrawn. Use one or more of the relational functions to flag those accounts *not* overdrawn.

4. Write an *APL* expression to return a 1 if either condition A is true or condition B is false.

5. Execute 1 0 1 0 = 0 1 1 0. Compare this with the operation table on page 38. What name would be appropriate to assign to this logical connective?

6. You happen to have in storage a vector *S* of four positive elements. Use *S* to generate in at least five different ways: A) A vector *Z* of four zeros, and B) A vector *W* of four ones.

7. Write an algorithm which will produce a logical vector *C* with 1's corresponding to the even numbers in a vector *A*←¯6 7 2 4 ¯21.

8. Obtain as many of the remaining logical connectives as you can from the functions introduced so far.

9. Execute the following outer products for *A*←0 1:

$$A \circ . \times A$$
$$A \circ . \lfloor A$$
$$A \circ . \lfloor A$$
$$A \circ . \ast A$$
$$A \circ . | A$$
$$A \circ . ! A$$

What logical or relational functions is each equivalent to?

Chapter 7:
Algorithms, reduction and scanning

At this point it is appropriate to introduce the concept of an *algorithm*, which is nothing but a series of steps that together comprise a prescription for defining a function or solving a problem. Two main examples will be given. The first, taken from plane geometry, will involve no new **APL** functions and will be used to illustrate the concept of an algorithm. The second example, although very useful in its own right, quite frankly is an excuse to introduce one of the most widely used **APL** functions, *reduction*, which allows us to carry out operations among the elements of a single vector or matrix. It will be seen that the final function to be introduced in this chapter, *scan*, can be thought of as a "rich uncle" to reduction.

Algorithms

Here is the example referred to above, which everyone should recognize as the butt of numerous jokes and misspellings of its name. The problem is to calculate the hypotenuse of a right triangle, given the sides as shown:

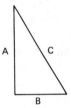

A convenient and time-honored rule for finding C is the Pythagorean Theorem. It states that to get C we have to square A and add it to the square of B, then find the square root of this sum.

Here is how this sequence of steps can be executed in **APL**:

```
A←3
B←4
A2←A*2
A2
```

```
        B2←B*2
        S←A2+B2
        S
25
        C←S*.5
        C
5
```

There is one point worth commenting on. We had to specify A and B initially in this sequence; otherwise, when we called for the values of $A2$, $B2$ and S along the way as checks on our work, we would have gotten *VALUE ERROR*s, or perhaps some previously assigned value. We'll see later, when we learn how to write and store programs, that this specification of values for the variables need not be done beforehand.

Meanwhile let's go through the same steps again, this time solving for a family of triangles:

```
        A←1  3
        B←1  4
        A
1   3
        A2←A*2
        A2
1   9
        B2←B*2
        B2
1  16
        S←A2+B2
        C←S*.5
```

As before, the result for C doesn't appear on the paper because our last step, which was an assignment of a value to C, merely put it in storage. So to get the result, we have to type C:

```
        C
1.414213562  5
```

If we didn't want to save the result by storing it in C, we could eliminate the assignment and have the results printed directly by typing

```
        S*.5
1.414213562  5
```

Finally, we can check on the variables in storage in the usual manner,

```
        )VARS
A       A2      B       B2      C       S
```

and the new variables specified in our right triangle algorithm are now included. Of course, your listing may differ from this if you happen to have defined additional variables in the current terminal session. However, it should contain at least these names.

Reduction

Previously you saw how the introduction of vectors and matrices enabled *parallel processing* of data to take place, with a resulting saving in time and number of typestrokes required. In the remainder of this chapter, this concept will be extended to show how meaningful operations can be effectively performed on the elements of a single vector or matrix. Continuing the analogy with electrical circuits, we may call such operations *series processing*.

Let's begin with a problem in invoice extension. Assume that several different items, each with its own cost, have been purchased. We'll use Q and C to represent the quantities and the costs, respectively.

```
Q←6  2  3  1  0
C←2  4  3  5  10
```

To get the vector of total costs, we execute

```
X←Q×C
X
12  8  9  5  0
```

But now, to obtain the grand total, we have to add up all the elements of this vector. In conventional notation, the mathematician indicates the sum of the elements of a vector by writing

$$\sum_{i=1}^{n} x_i$$

"Σ" means "sum" while "i" is a running variable from 1 to n, identifying the individual elements of the vector. n is the total number of elements, 5 in the invoice extension problem we are working on. If this seems potentially like a lot of work, don't be too concerned. In what follows we will show how to carry out the summation in **APL** with minimal effort.

Getting back to the problem at hand, our objective is to sum across the elements of a vector. We do this in **APL** by the use of $+/X$. This is read as "plus reducing X," or "the plus reduction of X." The symbol / (lower right corner of the keyboard) is called *reduction*, because it reduces the vector to a single element:

```
+/X
34
```

How this operation works is worth discussing in more detail. What the system does is to insert the function symbol which appears to the left of the / between each pair of elements of the vector, and group them (internally) so that the order of execution is 12+(8+(9+(5+0))).

The reason for the grouping is that in the **APL** system each function symbol operates on everything to the right of it. If you think about what this means, you will see that this is equivalent to operating on the rightmost pair of elements first, taking that answer together with the next element to the left, and so on. Following this through step by step, we obtain

```
12+(8+(9+(5+0)))
12+(8+(9+5))
12+(8+14)
12+22
34
```

You may be inclined to argue that we are making a big to-do about nothing, since with addition it doesn't really make any difference whether we work from right to left or left to right. We'll see later, however, that this property of independence of order of execution (called *commutativity*) is not general. For the time being, just remember that in **APL** execution is from right to left.

Times reduction

Now consider still another problem. A rectangular box has the dimensions 2"×3"×4". What is its volume? To answer the question we obviously want

```
2×3×4
24
```

If we assign the vector of the dimensions to Z, then $\times / Z$ should give us our answer:

```
    Z←2  3  4
    ×/Z
24
```

In this case, $\times$ is planted between each neighboring pair of elements, and the internal calculation is carried out in this sequence:

```
        2×( 3×4 )
        2×12
        24
```

Reduction on matrices

Since a matrix has two dimensions to be concerned about, reduction is somewhat more complicated. As an example, suppose we have sales information by weeks showing the numbers sold of each of five items, as shown in the table below:

```
        SALES |    I T E M S
              |   1   2   3   4   5
        - - - - - - + - - - - - - - - - - - - -
        WEEK  1 |  15  18   9   2   7
        WEEK  2 |   4  15   1   8   6
        WEEK  3 |   0   4   0   8   3
        WEEK  4 |  12  10  13   7   9
```

It is reasonable to ask what the sales record is by item for the month (i.e., over the 4-week period). This involves a summation along the columns, or, put another way, across the first coordinate of the matrix.

To show how this operation may be performed in **APL**, we first put the matrix in storage:

```
        S←4  5ρ15  18  9  2  7  4  15  1  8  6  0  4  0  8  3  12  10  13  7  9
        S
 15  18   9   2   7
  4  15   1   8   6
  0   4   0   8   3
 12  10  13   7   9
```

The desired summation is obtained by

```
    +⌿S
31  47  23  25  25
```

⌿ is the symbol for reduction overstruck with the subtract sign. It is used for summing the elements in each *column* of a matrix. The result is a vector with as many elements as there are *columns* in the matrix.

If in the above example we wanted gross sales records by weeks, we would obtain it by typing

```
    +/S
51  34  15  51
```

This sums the elements in each *row* of the matrix, that is, across the second coordinate. The result is a vector with as many elements as there are *rows* in the matrix.

In summary, $+⌿$ causes reduction across the *first coordinate* of any array, and $+/$ causes reduction across the *last coordinate* of any array. A vector has only one coordinate, so that $+⌿$ and $+/$ will have the same effect.

An algorithm for averaging

At this point we can profitably talk about an algorithm to get the average of the elements of a vector such as

$$X \leftarrow 2 \quad 4 \quad 3 \quad 3 \quad 2.5 \quad 2$$

To get an average we need two things: the sum of all the elements in the vector we are averaging, and the number of elements. The first is easy:

$$+/X$$
16.5

We can get the average by dividing this sum by the number of elements (obtained by manually counting them), but on the terminal there is a simpler, if somewhat sneaky, way to accomplish this. On your terminal type

$$X = X$$

Now it is obvious that each element of X is equal to itself, so the result is

1 1 1 1 1 1

As you can see, this generates a vector consisting of as many 1's as there are elements in X. Summarizing and storing the intermediate results,

$$M \leftarrow X = X$$
$$N \leftarrow +/M$$
$$N$$
6
$$T \leftarrow +/X$$
$$T$$
16.5
$$T \div N$$
2.75

we get 2.75 as the average of the elements 2 4 3 3 3 2.5 2.

A final comment on averaging: Plus reduction over $X = X$ does seem, and is rather awkward, to say the least. As a reward for your patience, we'll now introduce the monadic ρ, called the *shape* function. The term *monadic*, applied to an **APL** function, means that only a single (right) argument is required. Used monadically with any array, ρ returns the size of the array:

$$\rho X$$
6
$$A \leftarrow 2 \quad 3 \rho 1 \quad 4 \quad 5 \quad 6 \quad 8 \quad 9$$
$$A$$
1 4 5
6 8 9
$$\rho A$$
2 3

Our algorithm for averaging can now be more succinctly expressed as

$$T \leftarrow +/X$$
$$N \leftarrow \rho X$$
$$T \div N$$
2.75

Maximum, minimum and logical reduction

If + and × were the only functions that could be used with reduction, the operation wouldn't be particularly useful. But it turns out that all primitive scalar dyadic functions can be employed in this manner.

Here is an illustration using the maximum function. Remember Z, the vector of dimensions of the rectangular box we introduced earlier?

```
      Z
2  3  4
```

Suppose we wanted to get the longest dimension in Z, i.e., pick out the maximum value. Then by analogy, just as we had

$$2 + (3 + 4) \text{ is } 2 + 7 \text{ or } 9$$
$$2 \times (3 \times 4) \text{ is } 2 \times 12 \text{ or } 24$$

for $+/Z$ and $\times/Z$, respectively,

$$2 \lceil (3 \lceil 4) \text{ is } 2 \lceil 4 \text{ or } 4$$

and represents $\lceil/Z$.

On the terminal, try

```
      ⌈/Z
4
      ⌊/Z
2
```

The last example, the minimum function, is carried out like this:

$$2 \lfloor (3 \lfloor 4) \text{ is } 2 \lfloor 3 \text{ or } 2$$

Note that the symbol before the reduction sign is again placed between each pair of neighboring elements, and the groupings are the same as before.

Yet another simple application involves the logical functions in an accounts identification problem. Let X be a vector of balances:

```
      X←3  4  2  ¯2  1
```

Our job is to see if any of the balances are overdrawn (negative). The first step is to specify a vector of the same length as X, containing a 1 in each place where X is less than 0:

```
      LZ←X<0
      LZ
0  0  0  1  0
```

To complete the algorithm, enter

```
      ∨/LZ
1
```

(Remember that the logical OR returns a 1 if either or both arguments are 1.) Our answer can be interpreted as follows:

> if 1, then at least one account is negative
> if 0, then no accounts are negative.

Let's reset X and repeat the problem to illustrate the second possibility:

```
X←3  6  1  0  3
LZ←X<0
∨/LZ
```
0

Can you tell what the significance of the answers might be if we had used $∧/LZ$ in the algorithm instead of $∨/LZ$?

Minus reduction

We're not through with reduction yet. How about minus-reducing a vector?

```
-/3  2  1  4
```
⁻2

If you are puzzled by this result, the following step by step breakdown should help:

$$3-(2-(1-4))$$
$$3-(2-⁻3)$$
$$3-5$$
$$⁻2$$

Since $-⁻$ in succession is equivalent to a $+$, you should be able to see that the above is the same as $3-2+1-4$, done by hand from left to right. In other words, $-/$ is a way to get an *alternating sum*, to give this sequence its proper name.

Here is a somewhat messy example[†] that gives a value for π using $-/$:

$$\pi = 4 \times \frac{1}{1} - \frac{1}{3} + \frac{1}{5} - \frac{1}{7} + \frac{1}{9} \cdots$$

Let us construct an algorithm to obtain π. Our first requirement is to get the vector 1 3 5 7 9 11 13 15 17 19, stopping after 10 terms. Next, we take their reciprocals, find the alternating sum and multiply by 4, in that order.

Practically speaking, this isn't a very good way to get π because the series converges so slowly that a very large number of terms is needed to obtain an accurate value. However, it's dandy for illustrative purposes. First, we develop the vector 1 3 5 ... 19 from the vector 1 2 3 ... 10:

```
N←1  2  3  4  4  6  7  8  9  10
N←2×N
N
2  4  6  8  10  12  14  16  18  20
N←N-1
N
1  3  5  7  9  11  13  15  17  19
```

The respecification of N and $2×N$ and $N-1$ destroys the previously assigned values of N, as discussed on page 16.

The reciprocals can be obtained by specifying

---

† This comes from integrating $1 ÷ (1+x^2)$ termwise after dividing. The result is a series for arctan(x). If we let x equal 1, arctan(1) is $\pi÷4$, and substitution of 1 for x on the right hand side gives the expression in parentheses above.

```
      R←1÷N
      R
1 0.3333333333 0.2 0.1428571429 0.1111111111 0.09090909091
      0.07692307692 0.06666666667 0.5882352941 0.05263157895
```

and the alternating sum by

```
      T←-/R
```

Our answer for π (at last !) is

```
      PI←4×T
      PI
3.041839619
```

which is about 0.1 off because we used too few terms for such a slowly converging series. However, after all this work, you will be pleased to hear that **APL** provides a primitive function for π, that it is alive and well, and is discussed in Chapter 9 of the text.

If $-/$ is the alternating sum, then $\div/$ is the alternating product, which you can verify for yourself on the terminal. Note also that the result of reducing a vector is a scalar, while reduction of a matrix yields a vector. Hence, generalizing the operation, reduction can be thought of as a reduction in the *number of dimensions* (sometimes called *rank*) of an array. Thus, a matrix (rank 2) is reducible to a vector (rank 1), and a vector is reducible to a scalar (rank 0). More about this in Chapter 16.

Scanning

There are many instances when you may want to operate on the elements of an array one at a time and cumulatively with some primitive dyadic function, i.e., do a series of "partial reductions" as you "scan" the array. The simple example which follows illustrates the use of the *scan* function provided in **APL** for this purpose.

Suppose you opened a bank account. You deposit $100 the first week, and in weeks two, three and four you write checks for $25, $50 and $33 respectively. In the fifth week you deposit $80, and then withdraw $40 and $10 during the following two weeks. If you store the data in a vector M, using negative values to represent outgoing funds,

```
      M←100 ¯25 ¯50 ¯33 80 ¯40 ¯10
```

then the balance at the close of the seventh week is $+/M$ or $22. More interesting yet is keeping track of the balance on hand each week. Using reduction, you could find this by executing

```
      +/100
100
      +/100 ¯25
75
      +/100 ¯25 ¯50
25
      +/100 ¯25 ¯50 ¯33
¯8 (What is the significance of the negative sign?)
      +/100 ¯25 ¯50 ¯33 80
72
      +/100 ¯25 ¯50 ¯33 80 ¯40
32
      +/100 ¯25 ¯50 ¯33 80 ¯40 ¯10
22
```

The plus-scan, which uses the symbol \ ("slope"), found on the same key as /, does all this for you in a compact manner:

```
      +\100 ¯25 ¯50 ¯33 80 ¯40 ¯10
100 75 25 ¯8 72 32 22
```

Note that the shape of the result is the same as the shape of the argument, and that the last element is what would have been gotten had you performed a reduction instead of a scan.

Using the matrix S entered earlier in this chapter,

```
        S
 15 18  9  2  7
  4 15  1  8  6
  0  4  0  8  3
 12 10 13  7  9
```

you can scan across the second coordinate with

```
        +\S
 15 33 42 44 51
  4 19 20 28 34
  0  4  4 12 15
 12 22 35 42 51
```

or across the first coordinate:

```
        +⍀S
 15 18  9  2  7
 19 33 10 10 13
 19 37 10 18 16
 31 47 23 25 25
```

As you might expect, in the two examples above, the last column or row is the same as what would have been obtained by reduction along the same coordinate.

Any of the primitive dyadic functions can be used with scan, just as with reduction. Here is our π-finding algorithm using scan instead of reduction:

```
      R←1÷1 3 5 7 9 11 13 15 17 19
      T←-\R
      4×T
4 2.666666667 3.466666667 2.895238095 3.33968254 2.976046176
   3.283738484 3.017071817 3.252365935 3.041839619
```

With minus-scan you can see how the accuracy of the result improves as the number of terms in the sequence is increased.

PROBLEMS

1. DRILL

    +/3 7 ¯10 15 22   -/2 4 6 8 10   ×/2 4 6 8 10

    ÷/3 5 2   */3 2 1   ∧/1 0 1 1

    ∧/1 1 1   ∨/0 1 0 1   ∨/0 0 0

    =/3 2 2   >/1 ¯2 ¯4   ⌊/¯2 4 0 ¯8

    ⌈/1 ¯14.7 22 6   ×\3 2 7 9   ⌈\4 12 7 14

2. State in words what tests are represented by ∧/, ∨/ and =/.

3. For $AV \leftarrow 3\ 6\ 8\ 2\ 4$, evaluate $+/3 \times AV$.

4. Write a one-line *APL* expression to specify Q as the vector 1 7 ¯2 ¯3 and find the largest element in Q.

5. Set up an algorithm in *APL* to calculate the area of a triangle by Hero's formula, given below in conventional notation:

$$\text{Area} = \sqrt{S(S-A)(S-B)(S-C)}$$

    A, B and C are the sides of the triangle, while S is the semiperimeter. In your algorithm use S as the vector of sides of the triangle.

6. Write an *APL* expression to give the slope of the line passing through the points with coordinates $P(x_1, y_1)$ and $Q(x_2, y_2)$. By definition, the slope of a straight line is the difference in the values of the vertical coordinates of two points on the line divided by the difference in the values of the corresponding horizontal coordinates.

7. Each row of a matrix S represents sales of some item over a two-month period (by weeks). Create a new matrix SR which gives a running tally of cumulative sales over this time period.

8. A store maintains a matrix of accounts M, each column of which is associated with transactions by a single customer. The final row contains code numbers A or B placed there by the bookkeeper to flag overdue accounts (A) or current accounts (B). As a first step toward automating the store's accounting functions, write an *APL* expression to tell at a glance how many delinquent customers the store has.

9. Explain the action of each of the following on a logical vector LV: $\wedge \backslash LV$, $< \backslash LV$, $\vee \backslash LV$.

Chapter 8:
Order of execution

Further applications

In the last chapter we saw that in reduction the effective order of execution was from right to left, since each functional symbol operated on everything to the right of it. It was as a result of the operation of this rule that $-/$ gave us the alternating sum.

Does this order of execution concept apply to all functions in *APL*? You should make up a number of examples to convince yourself at this point that it does.

One good illustration is our previous problem (page 46) to calculate a value for π. There we used a large number of steps to get the result, but a much more elegant and neater way to write the algorithm is

```
PI←4×-/1÷¯1+2×1 2 3 4 5 6 7 8 9 10
PI
3.041839619
```

Here, working from right to left, the first thing the computer does is to multiply 1 2 3...10 by 2. Then ¯1 is added, which gives us the odd numbers 1 3 5.... These are divided into 1, yielding the reciprocals, and after $-/$ makes an alternating sum out of the reciprocals, the terms are multiplied by 4 to give π.

The same approach can be taken with our old friend the invoice extension problem (page 42). In this case the total cost of the products Q with individual costs C can be written as $+/X$, where X is the vector $Q \times C$. Numerically it can be expressed as

```
    +/6 2 3 1 0×2 4 3 5 10
34
```

Changing the order of execution

Don't be tempted by these examples into thinking that all problems can be solved this neatly. A case in point is our previous calculation of the hypotenuse of a right triangle. Without putting it on the terminal, let's figure out what would happen if we were so foolish as to write

$$C←A*2+B*2*.5$$

Going from right to left, 2 is raised to the .5 power, B is then raised to the power representing that result, and - we might as well stop here, because it is obvious we goofed.

Really what is needed is

$$C \leftarrow ((A * 2) + (B * 2)) * . 5$$

This is a good place to make three observations: (l) pairs of parentheses are used in **APL** in exactly the same way as in conventional mathematical notation, i.e., the normal order of execution is interrupted and expressions within parentheses are evaluated separately; (2) aside from the above use of parentheses, there is no hierarchy of functions specifying the order of execution in **APL**; and (3) a single right parenthesis is used in **APL** for system commands as contrasted to grouping, where a pair is required.

Getting back to the hypotenuse example, A and B are squared, then added, and finally this sum is raised to the .5 power. Let's execute this for specific values of A and B:

```
        A←3
        B←4
        C←((A*2)+(B*2)).5
SYNTAX  ERROR
        C←((A*2)+(B*2)).5
                         ∧
```

The error message is clearly due to the fact that a * was omitted before the .5, so that the line isn't a valid **APL** expression. Contrast this with the omission of × in conventional notation, where multiplication is implied by its absence.

Reentering the line correctly produces the answer for C:

```
        C←((A*2)+(B*2))*.5
        C
5
```

The parentheses around $B*2$ aren't necessary. Why?

```
        ((A*2)+B*2)*.5
5
```

Now, one more rehash of an old problem - the calculation of averages. We saw that it was necessary to get the sum of the elements of the vector X and divide this by the number of elements in X. In one line this is

```
        X←1  2  3
        (+/X)÷ρX
2
```

From right to left, ρX yields the number of elements of X, which in turn is divided into the sum of the three elements of X.

Parentheses aren't needed around the expression $+/X$ on the extreme left, but for a reason different from what you might expect. This can be shown by looking at $+/1\ 2\ 3$, which is arithmetically equivalent to $(1 \div 3) + (2 \div 3) + (3 \div 3)$, or 2. This exactly the same as $(1 + 2 + 3) \div 3$. It doesn't make one bit of difference if we divide the elements of the vector by 3 before summing or after, since, of course, the divisor (here 3) is the same for all the elements. However, it does make a difference computationally because it is a matter of three divisions and three additions in one case as compared to one division and three additions in the other. (The effects on computation time as a consequence of using different **APL** functions or groupings of variables are discussed in a 1973 paper, "Use and Misuse of **APL** - Efficient Coding Techniques," by Roy A. Sykes, Jr., obtainable from Scientific Time Sharing Corporation. Since the paper presupposes a reasonable acquaintance with **APL**, its reading should be deferred to the end of the book.)

A natural extension of this algorithm can be used to get row and column averages for a matrix. For example, specify

```
    M←3 4ρ6 7 9 10 4 0 4 8 3 1 9 7
    M
 6   7   9  10
 4   0   4   8
 3   1   9   7
```

The row averages can be obtained with

```
    ( +/M )÷4
8 4 5
```

and the column averages with

```
    ( +⌿M )÷3
4.333333333  2.666666667  7.333333333  8.333333333
```

Can you write a one-line expression to get the grand average of all the elements in the array? And while we're at it, can you think of a way to get the **APL** system to generate the number of elements in the rows and columns?

Every simple-looking procedure has its fly-in-the-ointment. The following is a case where omission of the parentheses is significant.

```
    3×2+4
18
```

In **APL**, 2 is added to the 4 to give 6, which is multiplied by 3. But in conventional notation, because of the accepted hierarchy of operations in which × takes precedence over +, 3×2 is 6, which, adding 4, gives 10. So if this is what you really want, you should write

```
    ( 3×2 )+4
10
```

or better still

```
    4+3×2
10
```

which requires fewer keystrokes.

The conventional rules in arithmetic aren't too bad to work with when only a relatively few functions are involved. Things tend to get a bit sticky, however, when you deal with the multitude of functions, primitive and defined, to which you have already been introduced or will soon encounter. It is here that the simplicity of the **APL** rule, that execution is from right to left subject only to the occurrence of parentheses, proves its worth.

At this stage of the game, as you start to build up expressions with many functions, don't hesitate to overparenthesize. When you are more at home in your understanding of the **APL** language, you will find yourself beginning to leave out the nonessential parentheses.

A polynomial illustration

An elegant demonstration of the order of execution rule and the power and versatility of *APL* can be seen in the following example showing how a polynomial can be written and evaluated.

Consider a typical algebraic polynomial expression

$$3 - 2X + 9X^2 + 4X^3 \text{ (conventional notation)}$$

which we want to evaluate for X, say 10. How can this be represented in *APL*?

We'll start with the most obvious, a direct transliteration from the conventional notation:

```
X←10
3+( ̄2×X)+(9×X*2)+4×X*3
4883
```

A little better version, which eliminates the parentheses, is

```
3+X× ̄2+X×9+X×4
4883
```

Working from right to left, to 4X we add 9, giving

$$9 + 4X \text{ (conventional notation)}$$

This is then multiplied by X (remember that without parentheses the X multiplies *everything* to the right of it),

$$9X + 4X^2 \text{ (conventional notation)}$$

 ̄2 is added,

$$- 2 + 9X + 4X^2 \text{ (conventional notation)}$$

X is again used as a multiplier,

$$- 2X + 9X^2 + 4X^3 \text{ (conventional notation)}$$

and finally 3 is added:

$$3 - 2X + 9X^2 + 4X^3 \text{ (conventional notation)}$$

But you can't really appreciate the economy of the *APL* notation until you have taken advantage of its ability to handle arrays. Here is the *pièce de résistance* of our problem:

```
+/3  ̄2 9 4×X*0 1 2 3
4883
```

In this version, X is raised to the powers 0 1 2 3 to give

$$1, X, X^2, X^3 \text{ (conventional notation)}$$

These are multiplied by 3 ̄2 9 4, yielding

$$3, - 2X, 9X^2, 4X^3 \text{ (conventional notation)}$$

and then + / results in

$$3 - 2X + 9X^2 + 4X^3 \text{ (conventional notation)}$$

Lines and statements

Now that you can express complete formulas on one line, you may be tempted to pack as much on a single line as possible. An exercise of this sort has its good and bad points. On the plus side, it has the effect of forcing you to review all the *APL* you know while looking for the proper combination of symbols and order that solves the problem. However, a word of warning. Lines of *APL* so written are frequently difficult for others to read and understand. To show that you have sympathy for others, as well as to enhance the concepts involved, you should arrange your lines so that each one represents a distinct part of the total algorithm and can stand more or less on its own feet.

Every *APL* author has his (or her) own stable of favorite horror stories in this connection. One of ours is the following, which happens to be a one-liner representing the calculation of the correlation coefficient from statistics. If you're not mathematically inclined, don't worry. This is not designed to scare you out of several days' growth, but rather to cause you to forswear such activity in the future. Here it is:

```
R←(+/X×Y)÷((+/(X←X-(+/X)÷ρX)*2)×+/(Y←Y-(+/Y)÷ρY)*2)*.5
```

In the above line, aside from the fact that it's almost impossible to read, there is the latent risk that in some future *APL* implementation it might not work at all A better arrangement for this algorithm would be

```
X←X-(+/X)÷ρX
Y←Y-(+/Y)÷ρY
R←(+/X*2)×+/Y*2
R←(+/X×Y)÷R*.5
```

If you are using *APL*★*PLUS*⍝ service, some of the economy of the one-liner can be achieved by employing the diamond ◊, formed by overstriking the < and > symbols on terminals which don't have the symbol as a separate key. The purpose of the diamond is to enable you to put statements that bear some meaningful relation to each other on the same line, while sacrificing neither brevity nor clarity. Each statement is separated by diamonds, and the *APL*★*PLUS*⍝ system calls for the first statement on the left to be executed, then the next, and so on until the last (rightmost) statement on the line is executed. The usual order of execution rules apply within each statement. Here is one way to write the above algorithm with the diamond:

```
X←X-(+/X)÷ρX ◊ Y←Y-(+/Y)÷ρY
R←(+/X*2)×+/Y*2 ◊ R←(+/X×Y)÷R*.5
```

The two lines above could have been pushed into one long one with another diamond, but that might look too formidable. In the final analysis, how much you put on one line is a matter of personal taste, but you should avoid constructing long lines (without the diamond) which could be interpreted in more than one way.

Another feature of the *APL*★*PLUS*⍝ system is that a comment can be placed on any line. The rule is that all characters to the right of the ⍝ symbol are ignored by the computer:

```
X←X-(+/X)÷ρX ◊ Y←Y-(+/Y)÷ρY ⍝ CENTER X AND Y
R←(+/X*2)×+/Y*2 ⍝ CALC DIVISOR--SQUARED
R←(+/X×Y)÷R*.5 ⍝ FINAL RESULT R IS CORRELATION
```

PROBLEMS

1.   DRILL

    4＊3⌈3＊4   1÷2+X←¯5 6 0 4 8 ¯6

    (4＊3)⌈3＊4   76÷+/2+3×1 2 3 4

    5＊3×5   6÷2-4＊3

2.   Of the following five expressions which have the same value?

    (B＊2)-4×A×C

    ((B＊2)-4×(A×C))

    B＊2-4×A×C

    (B×B)-(4×A)×C

    B×B-(4×A)×C

3.   Construct **APL** expressions for each of the following:

    A) Three-fourths plus five-sixths minus seven-eighths

    B) The quotient of the two differences: nine-sevenths
        minus eight-tenths, and one-third minus two-fifths.

4.   The geometric mean of a set of N positive numbers X is the nth root of their product. Write an **APL** expression to calculate this for $X←$ 1 7 4 2.5 51 19

5.   What is wrong with the expression $A+B=B+A$ to show that the operation of addition is commutative, i.e., the order of the arguments is immaterial?

6.   The Gregorian calendar provides that all years from 1582 to about 20,000 that are divisible by 4 are leap years, with the provisos that of the centesimal years (1600, 1700, etc.) only those divisible by 400 are leap years, and of the millenial years those divisible by 4000 are not. Write a one-line **APL** expression to determine whether a given year Y is a leap year.

7.   Why isn't the following a valid **APL** expression for $X^2 - 2XY + Y^2$ (conventional notation)? Correct it.
$$(X＊2)-(2×X×Y)+Y＊2$$

8.   Rewrite the following polynomial expression without parentheses. Do *not* use reduction:
$$(¯3×X＊4.)+(2×X＊2)-8$$

9.   Write an **APL** expression to compute the root-mean-square of the elements of a vector. (This is the square root of the average of the squares.)

10.   What is a possible interpretation of the following?
$$PROPOSE←RING∧WEATHER∧(JILL<JACK)∧JACK<AGELIMIT$$

11.   Write an **APL** expression to calculate the interest on P dollars at R percent compounded annually for T years. How would you change your answer to provide for compounding quarterly?

12.　You are required to make C equal to 5 if $A > B$, otherwise C is assigned the value 4. Similarly, if $A > B$ and $D < E$, then C is 10. Otherwise C is 8.

13.　Without executing it on the terminal, what is $2 + 2 \quad 2 + 2$?

14.　You are an industrial spy working for a bank, and have managed to "steal a vector" from a rival bank. The **APL** vector V contains all their accounts. Find

　　A)　How many accounts they have.

　　B)　The average value of the accounts.

　　C)　How many accounts are in the red.

　　D)　How many are exactly zero.

　　E)　The value of the largest (and smallest) account.

　　F)　The percentage of accounts above $100.

　　G)　The number of accounts between $100 and $200 inclusive.

　　H)　How many accounts in good standing are exact multiples of $100.

15.　Construct an **APL** expression that will yield a value A if A is greater than B, otherwise zero.

16.　The Sharp-as-a-Tack Company offers to sell one square inch of Klondike land for $0.25. Compute the gross income per acre (an acre is 160 square rods and one rod is 16.5 feet).

17.　A resort hotel charges $235 per person double occupancy for seven days, six nights (Modified American Plan). Extra nights are $39 per person. Children under 12 are half-price. With a service charge of $3.20 per person per day and $4 daily tax on the M.A.P. rate, what is the cost for a family of 5 (2 under 12) staying 10 days, 9 nights?

Chapter 9:
Monadic and circular functions

Primitive scalar monadic functions

Just as on page 24 we introduced the term *dyadic* to describe functions which require two arguments, so we will use *monadic* where only a single argument is needed. Let's take a look at how some monadic functions are represented in conventional mathematical notation:

$$-X \qquad \text{arithmetic negation}$$

$$X! \qquad \text{factorial}$$

$$|X| \qquad \text{absolute value}$$

$$1/X \text{ or } X^{-1} \qquad \text{reciprocal}$$

$$e^X \qquad \text{exponential}$$

$$\ln X \qquad \text{natural logarithm}$$

$$\sqrt{X} \qquad \text{square root}$$

$$\overline{X} \qquad \text{logical negative}$$

Whatever other merits this mishmash has, consistency certainly isn't one of them, for the symbol which is the functional indicator may appear on the left, the right, both sides, on top, or be in a special position, or be represented by an alphabetical label!

These same functions are effectively treated in *APL* as follows:

$-X$	arithmetic negation
$!X$	factorial
$|X$	absolute value
$\div X$	reciprocal
$*X$	exponential
$\circledast X$	natural logarithm
$X*.5$	square root (dyadic)
$\sim X$	logical negation

Notice that for all the monadics in this list, the symbol precedes the argument. Many of the symbols are also used for dyadic functions, but the interpretations may not always be closely related.

Let's run through some of them on the terminal. As you follow along, note that both scalars and vectors can be used as arguments. (The discussions on exponentials and natural logarithms may be omitted without loss of continuity if you have neither a demonstrated need nor a burning desire for them.)

Arithmetic negation

This function simply negates the argument that follows it:

```
      -3 4 ¯1 0 ¯8
¯3 ¯4 1 0 8
      -2 3ρ1 2 0 ¯3 ¯5 ¯8
¯1 ¯2  0
 3  5  8
```

Don't confuse the negative sign with arithmetic negation. As pointed out on page 8, the former should really be thought of as punctuation, *not* an operation to be performed; hence the error message in the following:

```
      A←3 ¯1 0
      -A
¯3 1 0
      ¯A
SYNTAX ERROR
      ¯A
      ^
```

Factorial

An expression like $!X$ (X is an integer) is to be interpreted as the product $(X)\times(X-1)\times(X-2)\times...(1)$. For example, we can execute

```
      !4
24
      1×2×3×4
24
      !1 2 3 4
1 2 6 24
```

```
      !2  2ρ1  3  2  4
  1    6
  2  24
```

If you got a *SYNTAX ERROR*, it was probably due to your failure to line up ' and . as discussed on page 32.

The domain of possible arguments of the factorial function is not confined to positive integers. Consider the following two examples:

```
      !2.5
3.32335097
      !0
1
```

For those with a considerable background in mathematics, the factorial can be defined by use of the gamma function, given by the following integral:

$$\Gamma(n+1) = \int_0^\infty x^n\, e^{-x}\, dx$$

which can be shown to be equivalent to !n with n not restricted to integer values. If n is 0, incidentally, the definite integral has the value 1, which justifies the terminal result for !0.

For those with minimal math background - forget it.

Absolute value

The absolute value function is defined as follows:

$$|X \text{ is } \begin{cases} X & \text{if } X \geq 0 \\ -X & \text{if } X < 0 \end{cases}$$

In plain English this means: take the magnitude of the number and ignore any negative sign that may be present. Here are some examples:

```
      |3  5  ¯2  7  ¯3
3  5  2  7  3
      |2  3ρ3  ¯1  0  1  ¯5  ¯6
  3  1  0
  1  5  6
```

Reciprocal

In *APL* the monadic ÷X is equivalent to the dyadic 1÷X.

```
      1÷1  2  3  4  5
1  0.5  0.3333333333  0.25  0.2
      ÷1  2  3  4  5
1  0.5  0.3333333333  0.25  0.2
      ÷2  2ρ1  ¯2.5  4  5
  1            ¯0.4
  0.25          0.2
```

Exponential

X is equivalent to raising e, the base of the system of natural logarithms, which has the value 2 . 7 1 8 2 8 ..., to the *X* power. This means that $*X$ is the same as 2 . 7 1 8 2 8 . . . $*X$. For example:

```
    *2.5 1
12.18249396 2.718281828
```

The second element gives the value of e itself.

Natural logarithm

⊛*X* yields the same result as the dyadic log, 2 . 7 1 8 2 8 . . . ⊛*X*, i.e., e⊛*X*. See page 29 for a discussion of the dyadic log.

Since the base e is very common, the practice is to use "ln" to stand for "$\log_e$". Base-2 would be represented as "$\log_2$," base-10 as "$\log_{10}$" or simply "log," etc. Logarithms were originally invented as an aid in doing calculations involving products, quotients, powers and roots. With the advent of modern calculators and computers they are rarely used nowadays for this purpose. More important, however, they do occur frequently in the solutions of equations representing a variety of physical problems, especially where the changes involved in the phenomena to be analyzed are exponential in nature.

Here is an illustration:

```
    ⊛10
2.302585093
```

In fact, from the definition of the logarithm, finding the logarithm and exponentiating are inverse processes, that is, each undoes the effect of the other, as the example below shows:

```
    ⊛*1 2 3
1 2 3
```

Furthermore, the general logarithm function *B*⊛*N* (page 29) can be defined as (⊛*N*) ÷ ⊛*B*.

Square root

Roots are fractional powers (see page 27) and the dyadic $*$ is used. For this reason, no special symbol is provided for square root in **APL**.

Logical negation

Like the other logical functions, ∧ ∨ ⍲ ⍱, logical negation can have only 0 or 1 as an argument. As you have undoubtedly guessed,

```
    ~1
0
    ~0
1
```

```
      ~1 0 1 1
0 1 0 0
      ~2 2ρ1 0 1 1
  0 1
  0 0
      ~~1 0 1
1 0 1
```

that is, logical negation is its own inverse. When we try to obtain

```
      ~3
DOMAIN ERROR
      ~3
      ∧
```

an error message results, since 3 is not an allowable argument for this function.

There are still more monadic functions in **APL** that for the most part have no corresponding symbol in conventional notation. These are given below and are taken up in sequence:

$\lceil X$ ceiling

$\lfloor X$ floor

$? X$ roll (random number generator)

$+ X$ additive identity

$\times X$ signum

$\circ X$ pi times

Ceiling

This is the monadic $\lceil$, and is defined as the smallest integer not smaller than the argument. Practically speaking, taking the ceiling of a number "rounds up" the number. Here are some examples:

```
      ⌈3.14
4
      ⌈4
4
      ⌈4.1
5
```

The U.S. Postal Service (at this writing) charges 13¢ for the first ounce of first class mail and 11¢ for each additional ounce. Any fractional ounces are counted as a full ounce. If X is the actual weight of a letter, then $.02+.11\times\lceil X$ is the cost in dollars.

Floor

Analogous to the ceiling function, this results in the largest integer not larger than the argument ("rounding down").

```
      ⌊3.14 3 2.999
3 3 2
      ⌊2 3ρ2.999 3.542 7.931 6 1.08 4
  2 3 7
  6 1 4
```

What about the ceiling and floor of a negative number? Let's try a few examples:

```
       ⌈ ¯4.1
 ¯4
       ⌊ ¯4.1
 ¯5
```

If this puzzles you, it can be cleared up by reference to the number line (page 31). Rounding up with ⌈ ¯4.1 gives the next largest integer, ¯4, while rounding down gives ¯5.

Finally, before going on to an illustrative problem, if we specify X as

```
    X←1.1 4.2 ¯3.9 3
```

then by executing

```
        ⌊X
1 4 ¯4 3
        -⌈-X
1 4 ¯4 3
```

and

```
        ⌈X
2 5 ¯3 3
        -⌊-X
2 5 ¯3 3
```

we can see that our **APL** system is richer by two identities, no simple equivalent of which exists in conventional notation. Additional identities will be introduced from time to time in the text.

Now back to earth. Here is a practical problem which uses the floor and ceiling functions. It involves rounding off bills with fractional pennies (so-called half-cent adjust). After studying the solution you should be able to come up with a number of other related applications.

For purposes of illustration let's specify a vector X as

```
    X←3 3.1 3.49 3.5 3.9 4
```

To make the half-cent adjust work properly, we round up if the fractional part is 0.5 or more, and round down if it is less than 0.5. So for the above values we look for the following result:

```
3 3 3 4 4 4
```

Looking at the floor of X, we get

```
      L X
3  3  3  3  3  4
```

This isn't exactly what we want. What about the ceiling?

```
      ⌈ X
3  4  4  4  4  4
```

which isn't right either.

Suppose we add 0.5 to each element of X and then try the floor again:

```
      X+.5
3.5  3.6  3.99  4  4.4  4.5
      L X+.5
3  3  3  4  4  4
```

Success ! And the result suggests that a half-cent adjustment that rounds down (i.e., makes 3.5 come out to 3 instead of 4) might be obtained by

```
      ⌈ X-.5
3  3  3  3  4  4
```

We can summarize these results in the following table:

X	3	4.1	3.49	3.5	3.9	4
$\lceil X$	3	4	4	4	4	4
$\lfloor X$	3	3	3	3	3	4
$X+.5$	3.5	3.6	3.99	4	4.4	4.5
$\lfloor X+.5$	3	3	3	4	4	4
$\lceil X-.5$	3	3	3	3	4	4
desired results	3	3	3	4	4	4

Roll

Let's execute the monadic function *roll* (upper shift Q, called "query"):

```
      ?6 6
1  5
      ?6 6
3  4
      ?6 6
2  1
      ?3 4ρ6
5  5  6  3
4  5  1  1
4  5  1  3
```

What kind of oddball function can this be that doesn't return the same result each time? We seem to be getting numbers at random from it. In fact, if you play around with it some more, you will see that $?X$ returns a random integer from 1 to X inclusive.

This means that $?6\ 6$ simulates the roll of a pair of dice, while $?2$

```
      ?2
2
```

could be a simulation of a coin toss, with 1 standing for heads, say, and 2 for tails.

```
      3 4ρ?6
2 2 2 2
2 2 2 2
2 2 2 2
```

In the last example we generated a single random value and then requested twelve repeats of that value, as contrasted to $?3\ 4ρ6$, which generated a matrix of 6's and then randomized the values.

When we try to execute the roll function with a noninteger, we get an error message:

```
      ?4.5
DOMAIN ERROR
      ?4.5
      ∧
```

The domain of this function consists of positive integers only.

In **APL** each time you sign on the terminal you will get the same sequence of random numbers if the same arguments are used. There is a practical reason for this. In checking out algorithms (debugging), it is often necessary for testing purposes to use the same set of numbers so that valid comparisons can be made each time through in the checking process.

Finally, the reason why the starting point is 1 and the way in which it can be altered will be shown in Chapter 32. Also in Chapter 32 is a way to change the "seed" from which grows the built-in **APL** algorithm for generating random numbers.

Additive identity

This function is included for completeness. $+X$ is equivalent to $0+X$, and should not be confused with $+/X$:

```
      +2 4 6
2 4 6
      +2 3ρ¯1 0 ¯3 4 5 6
 ¯1  0 ¯3
  4  5  6
      +/2 4 6
12
```

Signum

$×X$ results in 0, 1 or $¯1$ depending on whether the argument is zero, positive or negative:

```
      ×1 ¯3 0
1 ¯1 0
      ×2 2ρ¯1 4 0 ¯8
¯1  1
 0 ¯1
```

As before, it shouldn't be mixed up with $\times/X$:

```
      ×/1 ¯3  0
0
```

Pi times

$\circ X$ is equivalent to πX. This function uses the large circle $\circ$ (upper shift O):

```
      o2  3  ¯4
6.283185037  9.424777961  ¯12.56637061
      o2  2ρ¯2  0  2  3
  ¯6.283185307   0
   6.283185307   9.424777961
```

To get π itself, use

```
      o1
3.141592654
```

Calculation of the cosine

To show a useful application of some of these monadic functions, let's calculate the cosine of some angle X (in radians) in **APL**. The discussion which follows is for background only. Since the cosine example is used only for illustrative purposes, those not interested can skip the next three paragraphs.

The cosine is a trigonometric function which can be defined in a number of ways, including the following:

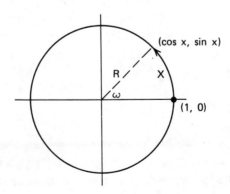

In a circle of unit radius, if we measure counterclockwise from the point (1,0) a distance X along the curve, the coordinates of the end point are defined to be cosine X (cos X) for the horizontal coordinate and sine X (sin X) for the vertical coordinate.

A radian is a unit of angular measure such that the angle omega (ω) shown in the figure, measured in radians, is the length of the curve intercepted, as indicated by the arrow, divided by the radius. Since the length of the whole circumference is $2\pi r$ and r is 1 in this circle, there are 2π radians in a unit circle. Arguments involving geometric similarity lead us to the same conclusions for all circles. Thus, π radians are equivalent to 180 degrees.

It can be shown in calculus, by application of a Maclaurin's series to the cosine function, that (in conventional notation)

$$\cos x = \frac{x^0}{0!} - \frac{x^2}{2!} + \frac{x^4}{4!} - \frac{x^6}{6!} + \frac{x^8}{8!} - \cdots$$

Notice the regularity of the terms, the numerators and denominators being all even and increasing regularly. This will help us in developing a compact **APL** expression for them.

Our first step is to set a value for X. Let's choose $\pi/4$ (45 degrees):

```
X←O÷4
```

Working with the numerators, we have

```
TOP←X*0 2 4 6 8 10 12
TOP
1 0.616849233 0.3805029763 0.2347129691 0.1447825149 0.0893089833
   0.05509017785
```

Similarly, the denominators can be assigned to a vector called BOT:

```
BOT←!0 2 4 6 8 10 12
BOT
1 2 24 720 40320 3628800 479001600
```

Our last step is to divide TOP by BOT and take the alternating sum,

```
-/TOP÷BOT
```

yielding as the cosine of $\pi/4$

```
0.7071072503
```

The steps taken above can be combined:

```
V←0 2 4 6 8 10 12
-/(X*V)÷!V
0.7071072503
```

We stored a vector of even numbers in the variable name V (since it is needed for both numerators and denominators). Next we got the factorials of V which were then divided into the vector $X*V$. Last, $-/$ gave us the alternating sum.

As a corollary to this problem, the Maclaurin's series for sin X is

$$\sin x = \frac{x^1}{1!} - \frac{x^3}{3!} + \frac{x^5}{5!} - \cdots$$

so that to calculate sin X all we have to do in our algorithm is to change V to $1+0\ 2\ 4\ 6\ \ldots$.

For those of you who have an interest, be it perverse or legitimate, in the circular, hyperbolic and pythagorean functions, they are available as primitive scalar dyadics. As with π, the function symbol is the large circle.

Circular functions

Strictly speaking, these functions, being dyadic, don't belong in this chapter, but are included to complement the examples used for those having a need to know at this time.

$0 \circ X$	$(1-X*2)*.5$		
$1 \circ X$	sine X	$^-1 \circ X$	arcsin X
$2 \circ X$	cosine X	$^-2 \circ X$	arccos X
$3 \circ X$	tangent X	$^-3 \circ X$	arctan X
$4 \circ X$	$(1+X*2)*.5$	$^-4 \circ X$	$(^-1+X*2)*.5$
$5 \circ X$	hyperbolic sine of X (sinh X)	$^-5 \circ X$	arcsinh X
$6 \circ X$	hyperbolic cosine of X (cosh X)	$^-6 \circ X$	arccosh X
$7 \circ X$	hyperbolic tangent of X (tanh X)	$^-7 \circ X$	arctanh X

In each case, the right argument is a scalar or vector (expressed in radians for the trigonometric functions). One precaution should be noted here: the inverse (arc) functions return only the principal value of the angle.

Finally, in addition to their uses in problems involving the trigonometric functions, to those who are familiar with the calculus, the value of having a complete set of circular functions readily available will be obvious. See any handbook containing tables of derivatives and indefinite integrals.

A drill exercise in *APL*

In the **APL** system (located in common library 1 of the system on which this text is based) there is a drill exercise in the various functions that have been described so far. This is a stored program, much like *STAT* was in the first chapter. The details of how such programs are written and stored will be covered in later chapters.

Follow this sequence carefully on your terminal. You should also check with your own system librarian to see what exercises (if any) may have been developed locally or duplicated for storage in the system you have access to. The more practice you get at this early stage, the better you will understand how they can be used in programming.

First execute the following command:

```
)LOAD 1 APLCOURSE
SAVED  11.07.53 09/01/69
```

A message comes back stating when the workspace named $APLCOURSE$ (a block of storage) was last saved. This command, about which more will be said later, in effect puts an exact image of the workspace $APLCOURSE$ into our own active workspace so that we can get access to it.

You will now go through an exercise in which you and the **APL** system will exchange roles. It will ask you to do problems and you will be required to type the answers in. To start off, type $EASYDRILL$ and put a Y under each function printed, as shown in the copy below. Be sure to type Y for the exercises in vectors because vectors are so important in **APL**. Ditto for reduction. None of the problems require answers which are not integers, and the problems are relatively easy computationally. We suggest, however, that the first time through, you stick with the easier functions in making your selection.

```
     EASYDRILL
TYPE Y UNDER EACH FUNCTION FOR WHICH YOU WANT EXERCISE
SCALAR DYADIC FUNCTIONS
+-×÷*⌈⌊<≤=≥>≠!|∧∨⊕⍟*⍱
YY          YY   YY
SCALAR MONADIC FUNCTIONS
+-×÷⌈⌊!|~
YY  YY
TYPE Y IF EXERCISE IN VECTORS IS DESIRED, N OTHERWISE
Y
TYPE Y IF EXERCISE IN REDUCTION IS DESIRED, N OTHERWISE
Y
```

Here are some sample problems generated by the program. These will be different each time you use it, and different for each user as well.

```
          ¯1 9 ¯9 5 > ¯8 ¯10 4 8
□:
     1 1 0 0
               -8 ¯6 ¯4 ¯3 0
□:
     ¯8 6 4 3 0
```

If the problem is correctly answered, you get another. Let's enter a wrong answer for the next one:

```
         ⊕/ 2 2
□:
       0 1
TRY AGAIN
□:
       1
```

You get three tries altogether, after which you are furnished with the answer and, to add insult to injury, you get another problem of the same kind.

```
         ∨/ 0 0 1 1
□:
      1
              ⌊ ¯2.333333333 ¯2 1.666666667 ¯2.666666667 ¯3
□:
       3 4 5 6
TRY AGAIN
□:
       4 2 10 4
TRY AGAIN
□:
       3 1 9 7
ANSWER IS  ¯3 ¯2 1 ¯3 ¯3
              ⌊ ¯1
□:
      ¯1
              + ¯7 ¯4
□:
      ¯7 ¯4
```

Typing *PLEASE* gives you the answer and another problem of the same kind, while typing *CHANGE* gives you the answer and moves you on to another problem generally involving a different function. However, since any valid *APL* expression equivalent to the answer is acceptable, the problem itself can be entered as its own answer - not particularly instructive from a pedagogical point of view, but it works. To get out of the drill, type *STOP*, after which you receive a record of your performance (only part of which is shown here). Typing *STOPSHORT* exits you from the program, but doesn't print your record.

```
            ∟ 1.333333333 ¯0.6666666667
☐:
      PLEASE
ANSWER IS   1 ¯1
            ∟ 0.5 1.75
☐:
      STOP
YOUR RECORD IS
```

FUNCTION	FIRST TRY	SECOND TRY	THIRD TRY	FAILED
+				
−				
>	1			
≠				
∨	1			
⊛			1	
+	1			
−				
⌈				
∟	2			1

PROBLEMS

1. DRILL

```
  L¯2.7|¯15            |3.1 0 ¯5.6 ¯8         ?10 10 10 10

  *3 4.7 ¯1.5          !3 5 7 4              ⊕14.1 86 .108

  Γ¯1.8 0 ¯21 5.6      L5.5 6.8 ¯9.1 ¯.12     ×¯5.6 0 42

  ?3 4 5               -¯1.2 ¯6.7 .52 19.5   +8.7 ¯19.1 23

  ÷3.5 ¯67 ¯.287       14×Γ5.8×¯31.046       1○○1 2

  ○1÷180               4○○1 2 3              ¯1 ¯2○1 1○.5
```

2. Using the residue function, write one-line definitions in **APL** of $\lfloor X$ and $\lceil X$.

3. If $A \leftarrow 3$, and $B \leftarrow 3\ 2\ 1\ ^-6$, evaluate

$$*2+A1 \leftarrow (\,^-1 + A*3\,) \div 2$$

$$\sim(2 \le A) \wedge \vee / 3 = B$$

$$C \ne \lfloor C \leftarrow ((A*2) + (A+1)*2) *.5$$

4. Write an algorithm to test an integer N for the following: if the final digit is deleted, the original number is divisible by the new one.

5. January 1 falls on Thursday (the fifth day of the week) in 1970. Determine the day of the week on which January 1 falls in any given year Y. For simplicity, assume any year divisible by 4 is a leap year.

6. Given a vector V which is made up of one- and two-digit integers,

   A) Write an expression that will yield a logical vector whose 1's correspond in position to the one-digit members of V.
   B) Do the same for the two-digit members of V.

7. After executing each of the following, write an expression to round a positive number N to D places to the right of the decimal point:

```
(10*¯1)×L.5+6.18×10*1              (10*¯2)×L.5+4.75×10*2
```

8. Let $M \leftarrow 84.6129999993$. Display M. Compare $1E5 \times M$ with $\lfloor 1E5 \times M$. (See *comparison tolerance* in Chapter 32 for an explanation.)

9. Construct an **APL** expression that will determine whether or not the first N significant figures of two whole numbers X and Y are identical.

10. A) You are given D dollars with which to make purchases of books at B dollars each. How many books can be purchased?
    B) How many books can be bought if it is required that the D dollars be used up and supplemented, if necessary?

11.   Carry out the following instructions and explain the answers:

$$A \leftarrow 15.8$$
$$B \leftarrow (A \leftarrow 4) \times A$$
$$B$$

16

$$A \leftarrow 15.8$$
$$B \leftarrow (A \leftarrow 4) \times \lceil A$$
$$B$$

64

12.   Write an *APL* expression that rounds numbers down if the decimal part is less than .5, and up if greater than .5. For numbers ending in .5, your expression should round to the nearest *even* integer.

13.   For $A \leftarrow 0\ 1\ 0\ 1$, $B \leftarrow 1\ 0\ 0\ 1$, and $C \leftarrow 1\ 1\ 0\ 0$ evaluate

$(\sim A) \vee \sim B$

$A \vee C \wedge B$

$(A \wedge \sim B) \wedge A \vee C$

$(\sim B) \vee A \vee \sim C$

14.   Show that the following identity holds: $\cos 2X = \cos^2 X - \sin^2 X$.

15.   Use reduction to express the identity $\sin^2 X + \cos^2 X = 1$.

16.   Write an *APL* expression to construct a 4 4 matrix made up of random integers in the range 1 to 100.

17.   A certain number N may be either positive or negative. Write a one-line *APL* expression to compute its square root if it is positive or its square if it is negative.

18.   Write *APL* expressions for each of the following. Use S for "Sam's a ham," J for "Joe is so-so" and T for "Teddy is ready."

A) Sam's a ham and Teddy is not ready.
B) Joe is not so-so or Teddy is ready.
C) Teddy is ready and Sam's a ham or Joe is so-so.

19.   For the arbitrary vectors $V1 \leftarrow 0\ 1\ 1\ 1\ 0\ 1$ and $V2 \leftarrow 1\ 1\ 0\ 1\ 0\ 1$ show that $\sim(V1 \wedge V2)$ is equivalent to $(\sim V1) \vee \sim V2$ and $\sim(V1 \vee V2)$ is equivalent to $(\sim V1) \wedge \sim V2$.

Chapter 10:
Function definition

Algorithms and functions

Earlier we introduced the idea of an algorithm for determining the hypotenuse of a right triangle. If you recall, at that time we stated the problem and went through a sequence of simple operations to solve it. Then we refined our treatment and reduced the number of steps needed by taking advantage of the simple order of execution rule in *APL*.

In a very real sense the operation of getting the hypotenuse exhibits the characteristics of a primitive scalar dyadic function. And it should be clear that what we did was by no means unique. Literally an infinite number of algorithms exist for solving all kinds of problems. And they behave much like our *hypotenuse function*, if indeed we may call it that.

This suggests that we need a way to name and record these algorithms so that they can be executed over and over again by using the appropriate name and arguments, just like the primitive *APL* functions studied so far.

More specifically, let's review what was done in the hypotenuse problem with our ultimate objective being to define it for repeated use:

(1)   *A* was specified
(2)   *B* was specified
(3)   *C* was specified as the sum of *A* squared and *B* squared, all raised to the one-half power.

This was our last revision, with the algorithm reduced to one line.

The defined function *HYP*

What is most desirable is to be able to give to the terminal values for *A* and *B* and a simple message to get the hypotenuse, much like asking for $2+2$ and getting 4 back. Here + is the simple message which tells the computer what to do.

By analogy, *A HYP B*, *HYP* being the message in this case, sounds like just the thing to do the dirty work of calculating the hypotenuse. Such a function has already been provided for you in the *APL* system.

Don't worry at this point how it got there. (Your attention is called to the note about the common library in the preface to the first edition. This common library will be heavily used from this point on.)

Now enter on your keyboard

      $)LOAD$ 1 $CLASS$

after which you should get a message back stating when this workspace was saved last:

$SAVED$ $15.02.39$ $04/15/74$

The workspace $CLASS$, incidentally, contains a large number of functions and illustrations which will be of considerable value to us in subsequent chapters.

Typing

      3 HYP 4

elicits the response

5

It works with vector arguments also, as the next example shows:

```
      1 3 12 HYP 1 4 5
1.414213562 5 13
```

Here we are finding the hypotenuses of three triangles simultaneously. In short, the function HYP acts just like + in the problem

```
      1 3 12 + 1 4 5
2 7 17
```

and apparently behaves and is used like a primitive scalar dyadic function.

Thus far we've looked at the external behavior of the function HYP. Before we can design our own functions we will have to be able to understand how HYP is constructed.

Function definition

There is a command which will display functions like HYP stored in the **APL** system. It is the following, which you should enter on your keyboard at this point. *Do not* press RETURN until your entry looks exactly like the one below. If you make a mistake, correct it before, not after, using the correction procedure introduced on page 9.

      $\nabla HYP[\Box]\nabla$

The symbol ∇ (pronounced "del") is the upper shift G and the box $\Box$ (called a *quad*) is the upper shift L. No attempt will be made at this point to explain the rationale behind the particular combination of symbols, but you will see in Chapter 12 how this command is related to a number of others that will be needed to define, display and edit functions.

Here is the system's response:

```
     ∇  C←A  HYP  B
[1]     C←((A*2)+B*2)*0.5
     ∇
```

The first line, beginning with ∇, is called the *header* of the function. HYP is the name of the function, and it has two arguments, A and B, with a *resultant* (i.e., the answer) which is stored under the variable name C. Notice that the arguments are separated by spaces from the function name. Can you imagine what would happen if the spaces were omitted?

Line 1 gives the rule for calculating C and is the same as before. If you are wondering what purpose the ∇'s serve, it should not be too difficult to see that since they open the function on the header line and close it after the one and only line needed (in this particular case) to complete the function, they must be a signal to the system that function definition is about to begin or is ending.

As we pointed out before, HYP can be used like a primitive scalar dyadic function, though an error results if we try to execute $HYP/3\ 4$, $HYP\backslash\iota10$ or $A\circ.HYP\ B$ in present **APL** implementations.

```
     1+3
4
     1 HYP 3
3.16227766
```

Interface diagrams

To help you understand the role of defined functions like HYP, here is a pictorial representation, which we will call an *interface diagram*, of the processes whereby the function gets entered and executed. The outer solid box stands for the **APL** system:

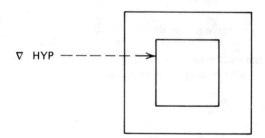

The first ∇ "opens the door" to an appropriate place in storage (inner box) for the instructions which follow, comprising the function HYP. Typing the final ∇ in effect "closes the door," and the system reverts to execution mode.

After entering, the paths leading to the dotted boxes A and B (diagram, top of page 75) and the path leading from the dotted box C are set up automatically as part of the instructions incorporated in HYP to allow for receipt of data (A and B) and for temporary storage of the answer C before release to the outside. It should be pointed out that the data paths shown exist only *potentially* because of the instructions. These latent paths are transformed into operational ones when the function is executed. Dotted boxes A, B and C have a similar ephemeral existence, coming into play only during function execution. In this example,

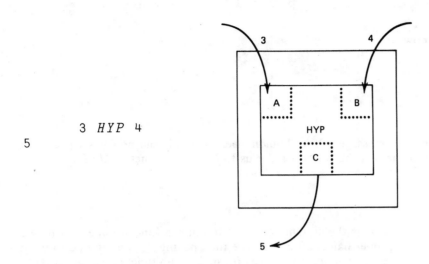

5   3 *HYP* 4

the process shown is really not much different from that involved in a simple addition problem involving the sum of 3 and 4 to give 7:

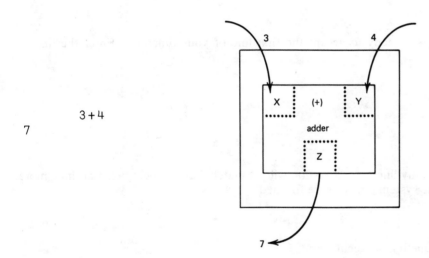

7   3 + 4

In the diagram, the temporary boxes have been given arbitrary names X, Y and Z. The two pictures are conceptually identical, except that in the second case the box representing the adder is a primitive part of **APL**, courtesy of the the designers and implementors of the **APL** system. You may wonder what purpose the dotted storage boxes serve. More about this a little later in the chapter.

Composing and entering functions

Let's now get some practice entering the function *HYP* ourselves. First type

)*CLEAR*

which is a system command that clears out your active workspace and replaces it with a fresh blank workspace, just like the one you received when you signed on. The response is

CLEAR WS

Suppose we try to execute *HYP* now:

```
      3 HYP 4
SYNTAX ERROR
      3 HYP 4
          ∧
```

Are you surprised that we got an error message? You shouldn't be. After all, our new workspace isn't supposed to have anything in it, and this leaves the way open for us to insert the function *HYP* ourselves. Start by typing

```
      ∇C←A HYP B
```

The initial ∇, as pointed out previously, tells the system you want to enter a function and "opens the door" to a place in storage. To give it its proper name, after you type the opening ∇, you are said to be in *function definition mode*, as opposed to execution mode. The rules for making up function names in **APL**, by the way, are the same as those for variable names (see page 17).

When you press **RETURN** you get the response

```
[1]
```

The system in effect tells you it is ready to accept the first line of your function. Enter the line as follows, then press **RETURN** again:

```
[1]    C←((A*2)+B*2)*.5
```

The response this time is

```
[2]
```

since the system doesn't know how many lines your function will ultimately have. There being nothing more to enter, type a second ∇ to signal the system that you are finished:

```
[2]    ∇
```

Having been duly entered, the function is executable:

```
      3 HYP 4
5
```

If at this point you don't get 5 type) *CLEAR* and enter the function again.

We haven't squeezed all the juice out of *HYP* yet. Just as we can type

```
      2+3×4
14
```

so we can ask the system for

```
      2+3 HYP 4
7
```

What makes this possible is the fact that the calculation involved in *HYP* produced a resultant which was stored away *temporarily* under the name *C* and hence was available for further calculations. Such a function is said to *return an explicit result*.

Using an interface diagram for this example, we can see that the existence of the temporary storage box C makes the result of 3 HYP 4 available to the adder, along with the argument 2, to yield the final result 7.

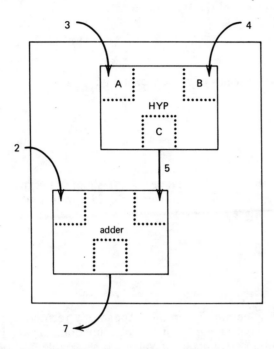

In the next chapter we will explore the uses and consequences of writing headers *without* resultants, equivalent in our diagram above to leaving out the box C.

A defined monadic function

For an example of a defined monadic function let's develop a square root function and complicate it a bit for purposes of illustration. If we had one called $SQRT$, then in HYP we could write for line 1

$$[1] \qquad C \leftarrow SQRT \ (A*2)+B*2$$

instead of what we actually have.

Now go ahead and define such a function with the header

$$\nabla R \leftarrow SQRT \ X$$

Again as a reminder, don't forget the space between $SQRT$ and X. Clearly, only the one argument X is needed here, namely the number we are calculating the square root of, and it is placed on the *right* of the function name. The system responds, as before, with

[1]

Incidentally, this suggests that a good way to tell whether you are in function definition or execution mode is to see if you get a number in brackets when RETURN is pressed. Just remember that if you do get it, anything you type from that point on until the closing ∇ becomes part of the function you are defining.

If you were to press RETURN again, you would get

[1]

and the system returns yet another indication to you that it is still waiting for line 1.

Now for the rule and the closing out of the function:

```
[1]     R←X*.5
[2]     ∇
```

A few examples show that $SQRT$ seems to work acceptably:

```
        SQRT 4
2
        SQRT 1 2 4
1 1.414213562 2
```

Since earlier we had indicated that $SQRT$ could be used to simplify the function HYP, and we have now defined $SQRT$, let's write another HYP function in which $SQRT$ can be embedded. Starting off as before, type the function header and wait for the response:

```
        ∇R←A HYP B
DEFN ERROR
        ∇R←A HYP B
                ∧
```

But this time it appears that something is wrong. Apparently reentering the function with the same name and in the same workspace doesn't wipe out the old function. There is no analogy between the behavior of a function header and an assignment of values to a variable, the old values of which are lost when a new assignment is made.

You may argue that this replacement feature could be a very handy thing to have around for function headers, but if you think about it you will see that it can have some grave consequences too. Suppose, for example, you had a big complicated function that was really valuable in your work, and you inadvertently used the same function name for something else. All your hard work, unless you kept a record of it somewhere else, would then be gone. So the **APL** system deliberately makes it hard for you to destroy defined functions accidentally.

This leaves you with two alternatives for redefining HYP: You can get rid of HYP by an appropriate system command (to be taken up later) or, better yet, use another name for your new function, say, HY. Here is the function HY:

```
        ∇C←A HY B
[1]     C←SQRT (A*2)+B*2
[2]     ∇
```

It appears to work just as well as HYP does:

```
        3 HY 4
5
        1 3 HY 1 4
1.414213562 5
```

An interface diagram for this shows $SQRT$ embedded within HY, along with, of course, the square and adder (not shown):

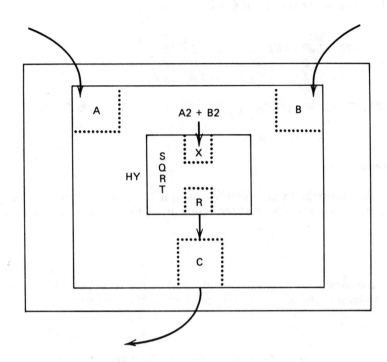

The arrow leading to the box X in $SQRT$ carries the result of the operations on A and B of the square and adder functions.

The cosine function (again)

For our final example in this section, let's define a monadic function which incorporates the cosine algorithm. In this problem, T is used for the resultant in the header and body of the function:

```
      ∇T←COS X
[1]   T←-/(X*0 2 4 6 8 10 12)÷!0 2 4 6 8 10 12
[2]   ∇
```

Here is the cosine of π divided by 4, along with the corresponding primitive expression:

```
      COS ○÷4
0.7071072503
      2○○÷4
0.7071067812
```

Documenting functions

The **APL** expressions and functions that we have seen so far are for the most part self-documenting to an experienced user. Suppose the function above had been called C instead of COS. How long might it have taken you to discover what it really does? You'd be wise to include comment statements in your functions to avoid the frustrating experience of not being able to figure out what you did a month or two later (and as a way of showing mercy to others who may be working with your functions).

With this in mind, here is a better version of COS:

```
      ∇T←COS X
[1]   ⍝WRITTEN BY GILMAN AND ROSE, 1975
[2]   T←0 2 4 6 8 10 12
[3]   ⍝T ABOVE IS USED AS A TEMPORARY VARIABLE
[4]   T←-/(X*T)÷!T
[5]   ⍝COSINE EXAMPLE. ACCURACY LIMITED.  USE 2○X FOR PRODUCTION.
      ∇
```

Some additional system commands

Our workspace, which was originally empty, now has four functions. As users we may at times want to find out what functions are in our workspace at the moment. This can be done quite easily by the system command

```
      )FNS
```

which works in exactly the same way as $)VARS$ did earlier; that is, it provides us with an alphabetized listing of the functions available in the active workspace. Here is the response:

```
COS      HY       HYP      SQRT
```

As was the case for the command $)VARS$, if the listing is long and we are interested only in whether a particular name, say, HYP is included we can ask for

```
      )FNS H
HY       HYP      SQRT
```

and we get that part of the listing from the letter H on. Printing of the list can be interrupted at any time by pressing ATTN.

We can observe the behavior of the system as we add and delete functions. For example, let's include the following simple monadic function designed to give the square of a number:

```
      ∇R←SQ U
[1]   R←U×U∇
```

Two observations should be made at this point. In the first place, the rule could have been stated in either of two ways: $U×U$ or $U*2$. Second, waiting until the next line number is returned by the system is really unnecessary. Since the function is finished at the end of line 1, it is perfectly proper to close it out there, as was done in this case.

SQ seems to be in working order,

```
      SQ 4
16
```

and in fact SQ and $SQRT$ are inverse functions, with one undoing the effects of the other:

```
      SQRT SQ 4
4
```

Displaying the list of functions now available, we see SQ has been added to the list:

```
      )FNS
COS      HY       HYP      SQ       SQRT
```

We haven't said yet how to delete a function from the workspace. This is done by the system command *ERASE* introduced earlier,

      `)ERASE HYP`

and a new display of functions shows that *HYP* is gone:

      `)FNS`
```
COS     HY     SQ     SQRT
```

As a side note here, the *ERASE* command can be used to delete more than one function at a time, as well as variables, so that the proper syntax for its use is `)ERASE FN1 FN2...VAR1...`, depending on what is to be deleted. Of course, to get rid of all the functions and variables at once, type

      `)CLEAR`
```
CLEAR WS
```

and then the command `)FNS` elicits an "empty" response from the system, the typeball merely moving over six spaces.

In the *APLSV* version of *APL*, if you are in function definition mode and enter the *ERASE* command, it will be accepted as a line of input. However, in execution it will result in an error message. The same is true for other system commands.

Some observations on function definition

Now that you have been introduced to function definition, some guidelines on the subject of programming are in order. Let's look first at what is involved: formulating the problem, developing the algorithm, translating the algorithm into *APL* instructions, testing and debugging the resulting functions and documenting.

The user's imagination and creativity are called on to a far greater extent in the first two of these activities than in the others, which are generally more mechanical. It is here that we separate the adults from the children. Half the battle is formulating the problem well. And victory can be almost guaranteed if, building on this foundation, intelligent algorithms can be developed. Many of the errors that must be identified and removed in debugging arise because the user rushed into an *APL* translation of a half-baked algorithm.

While it is true that *APL* instructions can be changed easily in defined functions (see Chapter 12), and error messages are usually a clue to what is wrong, nonetheless, in *APL* as in medicine, an ounce of prevention is worth a pound of cure. Our advice to you, therefore, is to spend more time thinking through the problem and how you plan to solve it. If you do this, you will spend considerably less time correcting mistakes after the fact.

PROBLEMS

1. Define a function EQ which evaluates the expression $(X-2) \times X - 3$ for various integer values of X and identifies the solutions to the equation $0 = (X-2) \times X - 3$.

2. Define a function BB which generates the batting averages of players by dividing the number of hits obtained by the number of times a bat for each player.

3. Define a function $HERO$ to calculate the area of a triangle by Hero's formula. (See problem 5, Chapter 7.)

4. The ABC Manufacturing Company reimburses its employees 100% of the first $200 spent per semester for college work in an approved program, and 50% of the next $300. No reimbursement is made for expenses above $500 per semester. Write a function called $REFUND$ that will calculate the refund due each employee in the program.

5. A well-known formula (Ohm's Law) in electrical work gives the combined resistance RT of several resistances R1, R2, etc., wired in parallel as follows (conventional notation):

$$\frac{1}{RT} = \frac{1}{R_1} + \frac{1}{R_2} + \cdots$$

   Define a function PR that will calculate RT for a vector M of resistances in parallel.

6. To find the standard deviation of a set of numbers, the following steps are necessary: (1) Compute the mean; (2) Find the difference of each number from the mean; (3) Square these differences; (4) Take the square root of the average of step 3. Write a function SD to compute the standard deviation of some data X. Assume you already have a monadic function AVG (which computes averages) in storage.

7. In relativity theory the mass of a body depends on its velocity V relative to the observer. Specifically, (in conventional notation)

$$m = m_0 \div \sqrt{1 - v^2/c^2}$$

   where m_0 is the mass of the object at rest and c is the velocity of light (3×10^8 meters/sec.). Write a defined function REL to compute the mass of a body moving at speed V and with a rest mass MR.

8. Define functions called $PLUS, MINUS, TIMES, DIVIDEDBY$ to give mathematical meaning to these words, e.g., 3 $PLUS$ 4 returns 7, etc.

9. As an extension of the "English" functions in problem 8, construct a series of functions to compute the sum of two values A and B by entering at the terminal $WHAT\ IS\ A\ PLUS\ B$

10. (For the more sophisticated): Rewrite HYP using one or more of the circular functions introduced in Chapter 9.

Chapter 11:
The syntax of functions

The last chapter discussed some of the ways in which functions can be designed and used. It should be apparent that they differ in a number of ways from the primitive functions, but the differences are of form and appearance rather than intent. As a matter of fact, if our keyboard had a hundred more keys on it, many of the more useful defined functions might then appear as symbols. If the function $SQRT$ happened to be one of these so favored, all that would be necessary to get a square root then would be to key in the appropriate symbol and argument. Practical considerations prevent the keyboard from being larger than it is, so only the most useful functions are incorporated.

The richness of the **APL** language is such that many other function types than have been introduced so far are possible. Already you have worked with two kinds, the dyadics HYP and HY and the monadics $SQRT$ and SQ.

A number of illustrative functions that will be helpful to us are stored in the workspace 1 $CLASS$, which was accessed in the last chapter. Let's reload this workspace and find out what is in it by executing the following sequence of commands. The system responses are included after each command:

```
        )LOAD 1 CLASS
SAVED   15.02.39 04/15/74
        )FNS
ADD       AGAIN     AREA      AUTO      AVG       AVG1      AVG2      AVG3
AVG4      AVG5      C         CHARMAT   CMP       CMPN      CMPX      CMPY
COMPINT   COS       CP        DEC       DENUMCODE           DESCRIBE
DICE      DUPLICATES          E         EVAL      FACT      FIND      FIX
GAME      GEO2      GEO3      GO        GRAPH     HEXA      HYP       IN
MEAN      NAMESONLY           NUMCODE   PEREL     PI        RECT      ROWNAMES
RUN       S         SD        SIGN      SLOPE     SORT      SPELL
SPLINECALC          SPLINEEVAL          SPRED     SQRT      STAT      STATEMENT
STATISTICS          SUB       SUBST     SUSPENDED           TRANSP    VIG
```

Your listing may not be identical with this one, since changes are made from time to time in the common library workspaces. Be that as it may, most of the functions in this list will be explained and used as we go through the remaining chapters. The ones we will be interested in at this time are HYP, $SIGN$, $DICE$, $RECT$, $STAT$ and $GAME$.

Remember that to display the contents of a function, type ∇name[☐]∇.

after which the system prints the function header followed by all the steps which comprise the function, including even the opening and closing dels. Our old friend HYP is an example:

```
      ∇  HYP[□]∇
      ∇  C←A HYP B
[1]      C←((A*2)+B*2)*0.5
      ∇
```

This display command will be useful as we examine in the rest of this chapter some additional ways of constructing defined functions.

Function headers

In **APL** there are six ways of writing function headers, and each has its own particular uses, as will be seen from the illustrative examples to be displayed. These six forms are summarized in the table below.

	Dyadic	Monadic	Niladic
Returns Explicit Result	∇E←A HYP B	∇R←SIGN X	∇R←DICE
No Explicit Result	∇L RECT H	∇STAT X	∇GAME

Don't worry for the moment about what all this means; all in good time.

Functions with explicit results

To start off, display the function $SIGN$:

```
      ∇SIGN[□]∇
      ∇ R←SIGN X
[1]     R←(X>0)-X<0
      ∇
```

It takes a single argument which, if negative, returns ‾1, if positive, 1 and if zero, it returns 0. In fact, it duplicates the monadic signum function introduced earlier. Executing this for various arguments, we get

```
      SIGN ‾5.2
‾1
      SIGN 0
0
      SIGN 569
1
      SIGN 3 ‾2 0
1 ‾1 0
```

If you look at the rule for $SIGN$, you should be able to see how it works by tracing it through. If X is negative, $X<0$ would be 1 and $X>0$ would be 0. So $0-1$ gives ‾1. Similarly, for X positive, $X<0$ is 0, $X>0$ is 1, with $1-0$ resulting in 1. And for $X=0$, $X<0$ is 0 and $X>0$ is also 0, so that $0-0$ gives 0.

Here is the interface diagram for $SIGN$:

Chapter 12:
Function editing

Up to now we have been examining the different ways to enter functions on the **APL** system, but have yet to consider how we might change a function which has already been entered. Since we can't do much without the capability for such change, this chapter will be concerned with ways of editing functions after they have been written and entered.

To speed things up, we'll use the prepared function $STAT$ in the workspace 1 $CLASS$.

```
      )LOAD 1 CLASS
SAVED  15.02.39 04/15/74
```

By way of review, let's look at what's in this workspace:

```
      )FNS
ADD       AGAIN    AREA       AUTO     AVG      AVG1      AVG2     AVG3
AVG4      AVG5     C          CHARMAT  CMP      CMPN      CMPX     CMPY
COMPINT   COS      CP         DEC      DENUMCODE          DESCRIBE
DICE      DUPLICATES          E        EVAL     FACT      FIND     FIX
GAME      GEO2     GEO3       GO       GRAPH    HEXA      HYP      IN
MEAN      NAMESONLY           NUMCODE  PEREL    PI        RECT     ROWNAMES
RUN       S        SD         SIGN     SLOPE    SORT      SPELL
SPLINECALC         SPLINEEVAL          SPRED    SQRT      STAT     STATEMENT
STATISTICS         SUB        SUBST    SUSPENDED          TRANSP   VIG
```

Our guinea pig function for this chapter is $STAT$. Remember how to display it?

```
      ∇STAT[□]∇
    ∇ STAT X
[1]    N←ρX
[2]    (+/X)÷N
[3]    ⌈/X
[4]    ⌊/X
    ∇
```

It isn't possible to enter it or redefine it because we already have a copy of it in our active workspace. Suppose we didn't know that it was already in and tried to reenter it:

```
      ∇STAT X
DEFN ERROR
      ∇STAT X
                ∧
```

An error message is obtained, showing, as was discussed earlier on page 78, that the system has built-in protection against accidental replacement of a function.

However, we can make changes in the function as already defined. This **APL** feature is a necessity, for otherwise finding errors and debugging and modifying functions would be considerably more tedious.

Adding a line

The four lines of the function as presently written give information on the average and largest and smallest elements of a vector X. Let's suppose we've decided to add a fifth line which will give the range (difference between the largest and smallest elements).

How is this done? The first step is to open up the function by typing a single ∇ and the function name, followed by RETURN as usual:

```
      ∇STAT
[5]
```

Notice that the system responds with [5]. In general the next available line number will be returned. It's as though we had just entered the first four lines and are ready to continue our writing on the fifth line. Incidentally, this is one way, if somewhat sneaky, to find out how many lines are in the function. Now enter

```
[5]    (⌈/X)-⌊/X
[6]    ∇
```

and the system has responded with a [6], waiting for the next line of input. Since we don't want to add anything further, a closing ∇ has been typed as a signal that we want to get back into execution mode.

Execution with a vector 2 9 1 gives us four lines of output, the fourth line being the range as we had intended:

```
      STAT 2 9 1
4
9
1
8
```

A display of the function now shows that line 5 has indeed been added:

```
      ∇STAT[□]∇
    ∇ STAT X
[1]    N←ρX
[2]    (+/X)÷N
[3]    ⌈/X
[4]    ⌊/X
[5]    (⌈/X)-⌊/X
    ∇
```

Replacing a line with another line

Also in the workspace 1 $CLASS$ is a function called AVG which computes the average of the elements of an argument X. Let's change line 2 of $STAT$ to AVG X. First we'll check out AVG to see if it works:

```
      AVG 1 2 3
2
```

To replace line 2, we need to open up the function as before by typing

```
      ∇STAT
```

The system's response is [6], which we override by typing [2]:

```
[6]    [2]
```

After pressing RETURN, the system replies with a [2] and we can now enter AVG X:

```
[2]    AVG X
```

Having accepted the change to line 2, the system prints [3], anticipating that's the next line you want to change. Since we don't plan at this point to make any further changes on line 3, ∇ is used to close out the function:

```
[3]    ∇
```

It should be emphasized that in making this change, lines 3, 4 and 5 are *not* affected.

Here is an execution of $STAT$ followed by a display of the revised function:

```
      STAT 2 9 1
4
9
1
8
      ∇STAT[☐]∇
    ∇ STAT X
[1]    N←ρX
[2]    AVG X
[3]    ⌈/X
[4]    ⌊/X
[5]    (⌈/X)-⌊/X
    ∇
```

The change has gone through, leaving the rest of the function unaltered.

Inserting a line between two other lines

Suppose we want to insert between lines 1 and 2 a statement whose purpose is to print the original values of X. This can be accomplished in the following way. First open up the function and type in some number in brackets between 1 and 2, say, [1 . 1], after the response [6]:

```
      ∇STAT
[6]    [1.1]
```

Any number will do as long as it is between the numbers of the two lines bracketing where the insertion is to be made.

The system returns $[1.1]$ and we can enter the single symbol X, which when encountered during execution will cause the values of X to be printed.

```
[1.1]  X
```

The next line number provided by the system is "one greater" in its last significant digit to provide for still other entries between lines 1 and 2. Since we don't want to close out the function just yet, let's ask first for a display of what we have so far while we're still in function definition mode, and then close it out:

```
[1.2]  [☐]∇
    ∇  STAT X
[1]    N←ρX
[1.1]  X
[2]    AVG X
[3]    ⌈/X
[4]    ⌊/X
[5]    (⌈/X)-⌊/X
    ∇
```

Your typeball should have moved over six spaces after this. If it does, you are in execution mode. However, if a number in [ ] was returned, then type ∇, followed by RETURN.

Of course, a line numbered 1.1 is somewhat awkward, to say the least. Fortunately, after the function is closed out, the steps are automatically renumbered, as seen in the following display:

```
       ∇STAT[☐]
    ∇  STAT X
[1]    N←ρX
[2]    X
[3]    AVG X
[4]    ⌈/X
[5]    ⌊/X
[6]    (⌈/X)-⌊/X
    ∇
[7]
```

The renumbering has actually taken place. But since [7] was returned, we are still in function definition mode. Pressing RETURN gives [7] again, and since there is to be no added entry at this time, we close out the function:

```
[7]    ∇
```

Now we are back in execution mode.

Doing several things at once

It is possible to put several of the editing instructions on a single line. For our example we'll take line 3, $AVG\ X$, change it back to what it was originally, and then return to execution mode. To do this, type the following:

```
       ∇STAT[3](+/X)÷N∇
```

Typing [3] gets control to line 3, what follows it is the new line 3, and the second ∇ closes it out after the change. We can now check this by displaying the function obtained in the usual manner:

```
        ∇STAT[▯]∇
     ∇ STAT X
[1]     N←ρX
[2]     X
[3]     (+/X)÷N
[4]     ⌈/X
[5]     ⌊/X
[6]     (⌈/X)-⌊/X
     ∇
```

Getting rid of a line

How do we remove a line completely? For example, suppose we want to get rid of line 4. As usual, we first open up the function and direct control to line 4:

```
     ∇STAT[4]
```

The computer responds with a [4] and in effect asks us what we intend to do with line 4. Pressing ATTN, followed by RETURN, is the *only* combination that will delete a line. Again, as you have already seen, **APL** makes it difficult to destroy things once entered.

```
[4]
        ∨ (RETURN)
```

Next, [5] is printed, and now we ask for a display of the function, but without closing it out:

```
[5]     [▯]
     ∇ STAT X
[1]     N←ρX
[2]     X
[3]     (+/X)÷N
[5]     ⌊/X
[6]     (⌈/X)-⌊/X
     ∇
```

Notice that line 4 has been deleted. The response continues with [7], but since we have nothing more to add, let's close it out:

```
[7]     ∇
```

The lines are now renumbered, as can be seen if the function is once more displayed:

```
        ∇STAT[▯]∇
     ∇ STAT X
[1]     N←ρX
[2]     X
[3]     (+/X)÷N
[4]     ⌊/X
[5]     (⌈/X)-⌊/X
     ∇
```

Just remember that if the number of ∇'s *you* (and not the system) have typed is even, you are in execution mode; if odd, you are in function definition mode.

Line n of a function can also be deleted by [∆n] on **APLSV**, and on the **APL★PLUS**® system line n can be deleted by [~n].

Displaying only part of a function

Thus far we have asked for the entire function to be displayed. What if the function is a long one and we are interested only in a single line, say, 4? The display command for this is very similar to what we have used previously:

```
      ∇STAT[4▯]∇
[4]    L/X
```

If there had been no second ∇, line 4 would have been displayed and then the system would "ask" us what, if anything, we wanted to do with it by returning a [4] again,

```
      ∇STAT[4▯]
[4]    L/X
[4]
```

and now we can close out the function by typing ∇

```
[4]    ∇
```

By now you should be getting the idea that the ▯ (quad) is used in **APL** to display things. Fancifully speaking, you might think of it here as a window to see what's going on inside the function. Just remember that

> [▯]   displays everything
> [4▯]   displays a particular line, here line 4.

Here is another useful variation which will display all lines beginning with the number specified:

```
      ∇STAT[▯3]
[3]    ⌈/X
[4]    L/X
[5]    (⌈/X)-L/X
      ∇
[6]
```

After listing lines 3, 4 and 5, the system offers the next available line number, 6, letting us continue adding lines. What's a user to do if the function has, say, fifty lines and he wants lines 3, 4 and 5 only? The way to display only these lines is to ask, as above, for lines 3 and on to be displayed and let the terminal print until you've seen what you need to see, and then press ATTN to stop the display. However, unless the original display command was closed with a ∇, you will still be in function definition mode after interrupting. Plan your next step accordingly.

Detailed editing of part of a line

Getting into more specific and limited changes, let's start over again from the beginning. Load a fresh copy of 1 *CLASS*.

```
      )LOAD 1 CLASS
SAVED   15.02.39 04/15/74
```

As has been discussed previously, this wipes out what was in the active workspace and replaces it with an exact image of the workspace loaded.

Now display *STAT*, but without closing out the function:

```
          ∇STAT[☐]
       ∇  STAT  X
[1]       N←ρX
[2]       (+/X)÷N
[3]       ⌈/X
[4]      ˙⌊/X
       ∇
[5]
```

It is again in its original form, and the system is waiting for us to add something on line 5.

Up to now we have made changes involving entire lines. But suppose a line is very long and complicated, and our change is to involve only a few characters without having to type the rest of the line over and quite possibly make a mistake. For example, say we'd like to change the letter N to $COUNT$ in lines 1 and 2 of $STAT$. Obviously, in this case we could type both lines over since they are quite short. However, it will be more instructive to use the detailed editing capabilities of **APL** to make the changes.

We're still in function definition mode, since pressing RETURN gets

```
[5]
```

To direct the typeball to specific characters that need revising, what we type in has the following format:

[line number ☐ estimate of what print position the first change occurs at]

In this case we'll deliberately make the typeball space over twenty positions (from the margin) and then backspace manually to the N to show that our estimate doesn't have to be accurate:

```
[5]     [1☐20]
```

The system will respond by displaying line 1 and then position the typeball twenty spaces over on the next line:

```
[1]     N←ρX
                    @
```

We wish to strike out the letter N. For this, the slash (same symbol as reduction) is used. $COUNT$ has five characters for which space needs to be provided. To be sure that we get enough space we type 8 after the slash as shown, once we have manually backspaced the typeball under the N. This inserts eight spaces just prior to the character (here ←) above the number typed:

```
[1]     N←ρX
        /8
```

After pressing RETURN, the system responds as follows:

```
[1]     @              ←ρX
```

and we can type $COUNT$ in the space provided.

```
[1]     COUNT    ←ρX
```

Having made this change we are asked if we want to do anything with line 2. Before doing anything else, display line 1:

```
[2]     [1☐]
[1]     COUNT←ρX
[1]
```

N is gone, $COUNT$ has been inserted, and the extra blanks deleted.

Now directing control to the eighth position on line 2, we use the same procedure to insert $COUNT$ at the end of the line. Eight positions are too few in this case, so we'll have to use the space bar to move the typeball over some more after it comes to rest in the eighth position:

```
[1]     [2□8]
[2]     (+/X)÷N
                 /
[2]     (+/X)÷COUNT
[3]     ∇
```

Since the insertion is to be made at the end of the line, no provision for extra space is necessary. Displaying the entire revised function, we see that the changes have been made:

```
      ∇STAT[□]∇
    ∇ STAT X
[1]    COUNT←ρX
[2]    (+/X)÷COUNT
[3]    ⌈/X
[4]    ⌊/X
      ∇
```

Here are more things you can do with detailed editing. First, the command [N□0] displays line N and moves the typeball to the end of the line to allow for additions on the right as shown,

```
      ∇STAT[2□0]
[2]     (+/X)÷COUNT@
```

and we can now add on to the line:

```
[2]     (+/X)÷COUNTESS∇
```

Second, if more than nine spaces have to be inserted at any one point in a line, the letters of the alphabet may be used, each letter being assigned a numerical value equal to five times its index position in the alphabet. Here is an example:

```
      ∇STAT[1□12]
[1]    COUNT←ρX
               B
[1]    COUNT@            ←ρX
```

The letter B causes 10 spaces to be inserted, and the typing element comes to rest at the position marked by the @ above. Now it's as though *you* had typed the line shown above, and you can make whatever additions you choose. In the example below, the letters ESS are entered in that space and then a ∇ typed at the end of the line:

```
[1]    COUNTESS          ←ρX∇
```

You can apply detailed editing to the line number itself. The effect is to generate a new line with the new number. The old line still remains. If you make other changes, those changes are carried to the new line, but the original line is not changed.

The ***APL ★PLUS*** ® system makes use of the comma and period to give added flexibility to detailed line editing. When a comma is typed, all characters following it are placed directly in the line to be changed, and then the line is redisplayed. The element comes to rest at the first created blank position, or at the end of the line if there were no blank positions created. For example:

```
       ∇STAT[1□7]
[1]    COUNTESS←ρX
       ////////,N
[1]    N←ρX@
```

Pressing **RETURN** now directs control to the next line, where the period is used to insert directly into the line the characters following it:

```
[2]    [2□10]
[2]    (+/X)÷COUNTESS
              ////////.N
[3]
```

It differs from the comma because it moves control directly to the next line.

The display screen of the IBM 5100 provides additional function editing capabilities. Say, for example, N on line 1 of $STAT$ is to be replaced by $COUNT$ as before. First enter [1□]. This displays line 1. The character N is deleted by moving the cursor to N and pressing the backspace key while holding down CMD. 5 spaces are then inserted by putting the cursor under the arrow and pressing the forward space key 5 times while again holding down CMD. Then press EXECUTE. Individual characters can be changed by positioning the cursor (flashing character) at the right place and entering the new character.

For the sake of completeness, we include again the system command which deletes an entire function from the active workspace:

```
       )ERASE STAT
       @
```

The response to a successful "erasure" is the typeball moving over six spaces. If we now try to display $STAT$ (or any other function), we get an error message:

```
       ∇STAT[□]∇
DEFN ERROR
       ∇STAT
              ∧
```

Can you think of a way to get $STAT$ back without retyping it?

Editing the header

In our discussion thus far we have neglected the header. It is possible to change the header itself in exactly the same way as any line by using [0] as the line number:

```
       ∇STAT[0□]
[0]    STAT X
[0]    STATE X
[1]    ∇
       ∇STAT[□]∇
DEFN ERROR
       ∇STAT
              ∧
```

Since $STAT$ has been renamed $STATE$, we get an error message when we call for $STAT$, which no longer exists. Just remember that any changes in the header must be consistent with what is in the body of the function itself, unless of course the corresponding changes are made in the rest of the function as well.

Locked functions

You can *lock* a function in *APL ★PLUS* ® by closing it with the ⍢ character (formed by overstriking ∇ and ~) instead of ∇. In *APLSV* you can use ⍢ for either starting or ending functions to be locked. Once a function is locked, it cannot be edited or displayed (although it can be executed), so make sure you keep a reference version as a base for future work. Locking is useful for protecting proprietary algorithms or things like classroom exercises which a teacher may not want students to see.

Review

Here is a summary of the function editing capabilities of *APL*:

∇ *FN*	open fn, control directed to first available line
∇ *FN*[3]	open fn, control directed to line 3
∇ *FN*[3☐]	open fn, display line 3, control directed to line 3
∇ *FN*[☐]	open fn, display all lines, control directed to first available line
∇ *FN*[☐3]	open fn, display line 3 and all following, control directed to first available line
∇ *FN*[3☐10]	open fn, detailed editing at print position 10 of line 3
∇ *FN*[3☐0]	open fn, add onto end of line 3
∇ *FN*[3]	ATTN RETURN, delete line 3
∇ *FN*[3]*X*←2+*A* ∇	open fn, rewrite line 3 as shown, close fn
∇ *FN*[☐]∇	display entire fn, return to execution mode
∇ *FN*⍢	lock fn
∇ *FN*[Δ4]	open fn, delete line 4 (*APLSV*)
∇ *FN*[~4]	open fn, delete line 4 (*APL ★PLUS* ® System)
) *ERASE FN*	delete fn from active workspace

Besides the editing techniques described here, Chapter 33 will discuss a method of capturing the text of a function as a variable, altering it, and reconstituting it as a function.

PROBLEMS

Execute $)LOAD$ 1 $CLASS$ and enter the following program to calculate the standard deviation of a set of numbers (see problem 6, Chapter 10):

```
      ∇ STD N
[1]     R←AVG N
[2]     R←R-N
[3]     R←AVG R*2
[4]     ANS←R*0.5
      ∇
```

1.   Display the function and direct control to line 5.

2.   Use detailed editing to change ANS on line 4 to R.

3.   Edit the header to return an explicit result R.

4.   Eliminate line 2.

5.   Display the function and remain in function definition mode.

6.   Change line 3 to $R←AVG$ ($R-N$) $*2$.

7.   Display lines 3 and 4.

8.   Close out the function.

9.   Use a single expression to open up the function again and reinsert the former contents of line 2.

10.   Change line 3 back to its original form with detailed editing.

11.   Insert just prior to line 1 a command that will print the number of elements in N. Then close out the function.

12.   Delete the function from the active workspace.

Chapter 13:
Types of variables

All the variables that we have encountered so far have been considered by us to be alike in their behavior. In this chapter we will see that this isn't quite true, and that **APL** has two very useful built-in features. One of these provides protection for variables against their being accidentally respecified as a result of a function execution, while the other enables the same variable name to be used repeatedly in different functions without the possibility of their being confused.

In the workspace 1 $CLASS$, which you should now load,

```
      )LOAD 1 CLASS
SAVED   15.02.39 04/15/74
```

there are five functions, $AVG1$, $AVG2$, $AVG3$, $AVG4$, $AVG5$, which are quite similar and which are all intended to calculate averages. It is the small but significant differences between them that we will use as a vehicle to study the different kinds of variables that exist in **APL**.

Dummy variables

First, display $AVG1$:

```
      ∇AVG1[□]∇
    ∇ R←AVG1 X
[1]   N←ρX
[2]   R←(+/X)÷N
    ∇
```

From the appearance of the header it is a monadic function that returns an explicit result. The first line gives the number of elements in X and stores that value in N, while the second divides the sum of the elements by N and stores it temporarily in R for printing the average when the function is executed.

Let's give X and N values,

```
      X←3 4
      N←3.1415
```

and now calculate

$$AVG1\ \ 2\ \ 1\ \ 2\ \ 1\ \ 2\ \ 1$$
1.5

On checking the values of X and N, we get

$$X$$
3 4
$$N$$
6

    Something seems to be wrong here. We put in 3.1415 for N and got back 6 On the other hand, X was set at 3 4, and apparently wasn't affected, although we used the vector 2 1 2 1 2 1 for the argument X in the header of $AVG1$. According to what was presented in an earlier chapter, the latest value of X is supposed to supersede a previous value. So why didn't we get 2 1 2 1 2 1 when we called for X?

    As a start on some answers to these questions, look at the function header. There is an X in it as the argument. Apparently this isn't the same variable as the X we set before (3 4), even though the symbols are the same. When we executed this function for 2 1 2 1 2 1, *for the time being* X inside the function must have had the value 2 1 2 1 2 1. The X outside (3 4) was not affected, since we were able to retrieve it afterwards unaltered. Are there then really two X's?

    This can be clarified by reference to an interface diagram for $AVG1$:

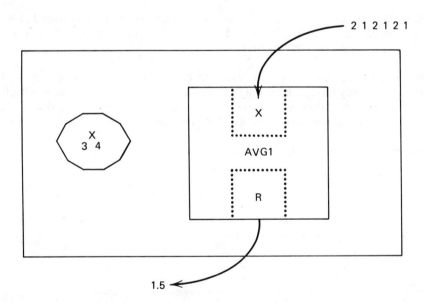

    The X in the header is a temporary storage box for the argument (dotted box). It is filled in this case by the vector 2 1 2 1 2 1, while the variable X previously assigned the value 3 4 is sitting elsewhere in storage (oval box).

    If, however, we failed to specify another argument for $AVG1$, and simply called for $AVG1\ X$, then the data flow would look like this:

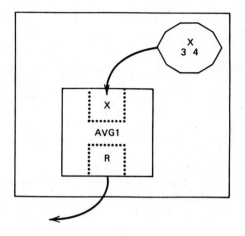

```
        AVG1  X
3.5
        X
3  4
        N
2
```

The system looked around for an X in storage to use as an argument and found 3 4. This situation is exactly the same as though we had called for $AVG1$ A for some A in storage. What may be confusing is the use of the same name at two different levels here.

The variables used in the argument and resultant of the header are in a very real sense "dummy" variables. This means that they have values assigned to them only inside the function itself, and we can find out what these values are only when we ourselves are "inside" the function, that is, when execution is suspended part way through because we interrupted it or because of an error.

To illustrate the point further, imagine we have a function

```
        ∇Z←A  FN  G
[1]     Z←A+G
[2]     ∇
```

and we call for 3 FN 4 to be executed:

```
        3  FN  4
7
```

After execution, if we ask for A and G, we get $VALUE$ $ERRORs$:

```
        A
VALUE ERROR
        A
        ^
        G
VALUE ERROR
        G
        ^
```

A and G have been relegated to limbo.

Interface diagrams of the situations during execution and after show this graphically:

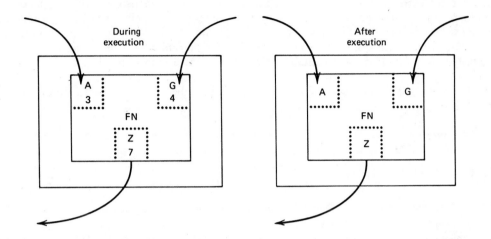

Since the A and G boxes are empty after execution, the *VALUE ERROR* messages received above should be understandable. However, now let's set A as 1 and G as 2, and then display A and G after execution:

```
      A←1
      G←2
      A FN G
3
      A
1
      G
2
```

Again, let's use an interface diagram to clarify the point:

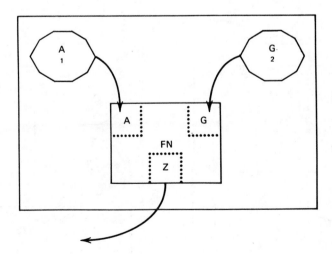

The values of A and G stored outside the function (oval boxes) were not affected by the execution, even though copies of their contents were fed into the A and G dotted boxes.

It should be dawning on you by this time that it ought not to make any difference what names we use for the arguments of FN. They serve only to indicate that two arguments are called for, and in this sense they act very much like the zeros in a number of the form .00032. All the zeros do is fill up space, but you need them to read the numbers correctly. This is why the arguments associated with the function name are sometimes called *dummy variables* and have values only within the function, acquired during execution, and disappearing when execution is complete. They are specific examples of a more general class of variables behaving similarly within functions, and called *local variables*. More about this later.

As the interface diagrams show, we can make similar points about the resultant R in the header. It too is a dummy variable,

```
      AVG1  3  5  10
9
      R
VALUE  ERROR
      R
      ^
```

and acquires a unique value during execution as soon as we get to that part of the function which determines what R will be. As in the case of the arguments, once execution is finished, the value is lost.

Global variables

There is still a little more juice to be squeezed out of our original function $AVG1$. We have answered the question of why calling for X returned the value 3 4. But what about N?

Notice that N, in contrast to X, doesn't appear in the header, but only in the body of the function. Lacking any instructions from us to the contrary, it ought to behave the same way all of our variables had been behaving up to the time when we started to get involved in function definition. That is to say, whenever the system encounters an instruction respecifying a variable whose value has been previously set, it changes that value accordingly. In our case, N was originally set at 3.1415, but as execution proceeded it was reset to 6 as a result of the instructions contained in line 1 of $AVG1$. Interface diagrams would show N as follows:

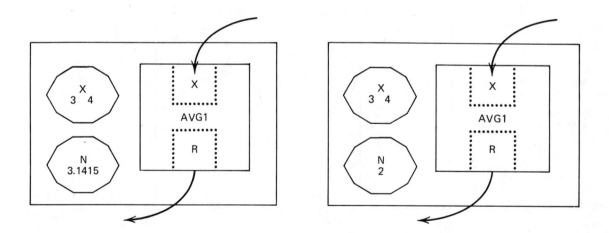

When the variable N is given a value during execution, that new value replaces any existing value of N outside $AVG1$; or if N didn't exist, N is created for the first time (again outside $AVG1$). The key word here is *outside*, with variables like N, appearing in the executable lines of a function (but not in the header), ending up outside the function once a value has been assigned to them. In this sense, they behave exactly like the variables you worked with in Chapter 3, and are called *global variables*.

The next section will describe how these variables can be protected from surprise replacement by having the names appear in the header of the function.

Local variables

Let's look at another way in which variables can be used in function definition. For this, display $AVG2$:

```
      ∇AVG2[□]∇
   ∇  R←AVG2  X;N
[1]     N←ρX
[2]     R←(+/X)÷N
   ∇
```

This time something new has been added - a variable N in the header, preceded by a semicolon. When a variable is used in the header in this fashion, it is also a local variable, whose values are set and used only within the function itself, and behaving like the dummy variables we discussed previously.

To restore the values of the variables to what they were before we first executed $AVG1$ for comparison purposes, we'll have to reset N:

```
      N←3.1415
      X
3  4
```

Using the same argument as before, let's execute $AVG2$ and then call for X and N:

```
      AVG2  2  1  2  1  2  1
1.5
      X
3  4
      N
3.1415
```

As you might have expected, X hasn't changed, but this time N also returns the original value set when we made it a global variable. The instructions for N on line 1 now refer to a *local* N, within the function itself, it being only an accident of choice that we used the same name for both a local and a global variable.

In the following interface diagrams for $AVG2$ we see an example of how local variables such as N, in a very real sense shield or protect previously defined names.

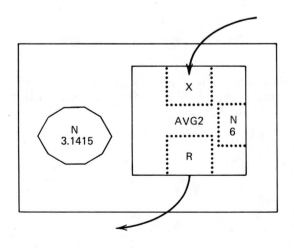
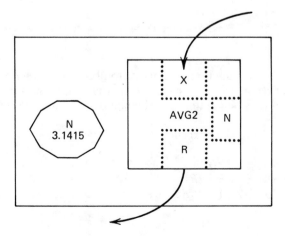

It should now be clear that the **APL** system has the ability to keep the record straight for variables used in these different ways. This is fortunate for us because we may have used the same variable name previously for something entirely different and may want to preserve it. To prevent accidental respecifying of the variable, it would seem wise to make it local by putting it in the header preceded by a semicolon. If more than one variable is to be localized, they can be strung out, separated from each other and the rest of the header by semicolons.

$AVG3$ is another example of the use of a local variable. It has a local variable P and is a niladic function returning an explicit result:

```
        ∇AVG3[☐]∇
     ∇  R←AVG3;P
[1]     P←ρX
[2]     R←(+/X)÷P
     ∇
        AVG3
3.5
        X
3 4
```

By this time you ought to be able to figure out for yourself why the result 3.5 was returned. (HINT: is X a local, global or dummy variable?)

Let's reset X and execute $AVG3$ again. Clearly, the X being averaged is from the most recent global assignment:

```
        X←2 1 2 1 2 1
        AVG3
1.5
```

Before going on to the next section, one more point, somewhat specialized, should be made. If $AVG3$ had called for a subfunction, say $AVG10$, on some step, then the same variables which were local to $AVG3$ (R and P) may also be referred to in $AVG10$, unless they are shielded by the occurrence of the names R and P in the header of $AVG10$.

Global variables as counters

$AVG4$ adds a new twist:

```
        ∇AVG4[☐]∇
     ∇  R←AVG4 X
[1]     R←(+/X)÷ρX
[2]     COUNT←COUNT+1
     ∇
```

This function is intended to illustrate a practical reason to change the value of a global variable inside a function, and is designed so that each time it is used a counter (called $COUNT$) goes up by one. A record can thus be kept of the total number of times the function is executed.

Here is an execution of $AVG4$:

```
        AVG4 2 1 2 1 2 1
VALUE ERROR
AVG4[2] COUNT←COUNT+1
        ^
```

Why do we get an error message? If you think about it, you will see that we goofed and failed to specify the initial value of $COUNT$. So naturally the system didn't know where to start counting, and was unable to execute line 2. This is confirmed by asking for the value of $COUNT$:

```
        COUNT
VALUE ERROR
        COUNT
        ^
```

Setting $COUNT$ to 0 and reexecuting $AVG4$ twice, we get

```
        COUNT←0
        AVG4  2  1  2  1  2  1
1.5
        COUNT
1
        AVG4  5  4  3  2  1
3
        COUNT
2
```

$COUNT$ now behaves as we had intended. It is a global variable because it doesn't appear in the header. Now display $AVG5$:

```
        ∇AVG5[□]∇
     ∇  R←AVG5 X;COUNT
[1]     COUNT←COUNT+1 .
[2]     R←(+/X)÷ρX
     ∇
```

This time $COUNT$ is a local variable in this monadic function. Let's execute $AVG5$:

```
        AVG5  2  3  2  3
VALUE ERROR
AVG5[1]  COUNT←COUNT+1
                ^
```

What's wrong? $COUNT$ was set earlier to 0, so why the error message? True, $COUNT$ was set, but as a global variable, and the set value can't be used in $AVG5$ because we said in the header that $COUNT$ was local. This function just won't work because the local $COUNT$, as mentioned previously, effectively shields the global $COUNT$.

Suppose we put a line before line 1 which sets $COUNT$ to 0. Then each time we executed it, the local variable $COUNT$ would be reset to 0. It would never get beyond 1. Furthermore, because it would be local, all trace of it would be lost once we exited the function.

This means that if we have a global variable (name *not* in the header), we can reset it from within the function and obtain its last value, as in $AVG4$. If we make it local (by preceding it with a semicolon in the header), there is no chance for confusion or destruction of values set previously.

Let's finish up this discussion by pointing out a limitation on the use of local variables. It is not possible to use a subfunction by the same name as a local variable. For example, if $COUNT$ were also a function, we couldn't ask for it to be executed in $AVG5$ and still retain $COUNT$ as a local variable.

By this time you should be getting an appreciation of the usefulness of local variables, as well as an awareness (we hope) of some of their pitfalls. It is not only variables that can be localized; functions can be made local to functions. This advanced concept is treated in Chapter 33.

Suspended functions

We had a couple of executions that resulted in functions being suspended at some point because of errors. The system commands $)SI$ or $)SIV$ allow us to find out what functions are suspended, and where:

```
      )SI
AVG5[1]  *
AVG4[2]  *
      )SIV
AVG5[1]  *              R              X              COUNT
AVG4[2]  *              R              X
```

SI stands for *state indicator* and the results tell which functions are suspended ($*$) and just prior to what step. The most recent suspension is listed first. The command $)SIV$ gives the same information as $)SI$ but adds the names appearing in the header as local or dummies. If the $*$ is missing, it means that the function is held up because of a suspension elsewhere. For example, let's define an arbitrary function $AVG6$,

```
      ∇AVG6  X
[1]    AVG1  X
[2]    AVG5  X∇
```

and execute it with

```
      X←2  1  2  1  2  1
      AVG6  X
1.5
VALUE ERROR
AVG5[1]  COUNT←COUNT+1
              ∧
```

When we now call for the state indicator, our display looks somewhat different:

```
      )SI
AVG5[1]  *
AVG6[2]
AVG5[1]  *
AVG4[2]  *
```

Here $AVG6$ is said to be *pendent*. Functions can't be edited or displayed while pendent, a restriction which doesn't apply to suspended functions.

The interface diagram on the next page illustrates the behavior of a suspended function.

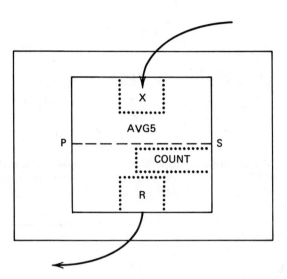

Upon suspension, we are able to look into the function from the outside and access its contents. In the case of $AVG5$, our vision does not extend past the line PS, representing the point of suspension, letting us examine the contents of the local variable X, but not R and $COUNT$, which haven't yet acquired values in the partial execution that has taken place. Here is an example:

```
        AVG5   7  4  2  4
VALUE  ERROR
AVG5[1]  COUNT←COUNT+1
                 ∧
        X
7  4  2  4
        R
VALUE  ERROR
        R
        ∧
```

It isn't good practice to leave functions suspended, since this clutters up the available space. They should be removed as soon as possible from the suspended state. Each time a function is suspended, you should find out what's wrong. For the time being, without further explanation, the instruction →, followed by RETURN will exit you from the most recently suspended function. This instruction should be repeated until $)SI$ yields a list with no functions in it:

```
        )SI
AVG5[1]  *
AVG6[2]
AVG5[1]  *
AVG4[2]  *
        →
        )SI
AVG5[1]  *
AVG4[2]  *
        →
        →
        )SI
        @
```

Of course, any future executions of $AVG5$ will build up our list again:

```
      AVG5 4 2 1
VALUE ERROR
AVG5[1]  COUNT←COUNT+1
              ∧
      )SI
AVG5[1]  *
      →
      )SI
      @
```

Occasionally it happens that a function is suspended not because it is unexecutable, but because we have deliberately interrupted it with ATTN. For example, say $AVG2$ has been interrupted just prior to line 2. The instruction $→2$ will then cause execution to be resumed on line 2 just as though nothing had happened. Chapter 22 will discuss this further.

PROBLEMS

1. After executing the command $)LOAD\ 1\ CLASS$,

    (A) Specify a global variable $C←53\ 78\ 90$ and account for the result.

    (B) Enter the following function F:

    ```
              ∇F
    [1]    Z←(A*2)+B*2
    [2]    Z←Z*.5∇
    ```

    After specifying values for A and B, execute $T←F+7$ and $T←Z+7$. Explain your results.

2. Below are several functions. Execute the command following each and give the values of the variables. Reset these variables to their initial values before each function is executed:

R	B	C	M	S
3	2	5	7	1

```
        ∇PERIM1                 ∇R←B PERIM2 C              ∇R←PERIM3 C
[1]    R←2×B+C∇          [1]    R←2×B+C∇            [1]    R←2×B+C∇
        PERIM1                   S←M PERIM2 R               S←PERIM3 R
```

3. Redefine the second function of problem 2 to include a local variable P in the header. Make line 1 the sum of B and C, the result to be stored in P. The second line is to finish the algorithm for the perimeter.

4. Write a function $MARGIN$, which returns an explicit result, to solve the following problem: Experience show that the sales S of a toy depends on the price, P, as $S←40000-5000×P$. The total cost C of production is $C←35000+2×S$. For each price P, $P←1\ 2\ 3\ 4\ 5\ 6\ 7$ (in dollars), what is the profit margin?

Chapter 14:
Workspace movement

In the previous chapters all the work you placed in storage, both variables and defined functions, was lost when you signed off. The only recoverable work was in 1 *CLASS* and in 1 *APLCOURSE*. And the only reason you could still access it was that when you loaded one of these workspaces into your own active workspace, you were actually taking an exact *image* of the original, not the original itself. Although you lost the image in signing off, you could always obtain another in the same manner.

We need to know how to preserve what we do for posterity. Therefore, in this chapter we will go through a series of exercises designed to show how workspaces can be manipulated by you, the **APL** user. To insure continuity, you should repeat the entire sequence of commands exactly as they are given in this chapter.

Workspace contents

We will start off by typing

```
    )CLEAR
CLEAR WS
```

As we pointed out earlier (page 75), this is one of a family of so-called system commands, like the sign-on and sign-off. It has the effect of wiping out all the work done in the active workspace and replacing it with a clean workspace, such as is normally obtained at the sign-on. Remember that the active workspace is the one that you have currently available to you, in which all your work is now being done.

To show that this workspace is now empty as a result of the *CLEAR* command, we can use the commands

```
    )FNS
@
    )VARS
@
```

and we see there isn't anything in the active workspace.

Since the purpose of this chapter is to teach you how to save functions and variables for future use, we'll need some example functions. For this, let's enter the function *HYP*:

```
        ∇R←A HYP B
[1]     R←((A*2)+B*2)*.5
[2]     ∇
```

Our listing of functions now shows

```
        )FNS
HYP
```

Let's set a couple of variables,

```
        PI←3.14159
        V←1 2 3 4 5
```

and the command

```
        )VARS
PI      V
```

now shows that PI and V are in storage.

For a second function, enter

```
        ∇TOSS
[1]     ?2∇
```

and then obtain a new listing of functions

```
        )FNS
HYP     TOSS
```

to confirm that $TOSS$ has indeed been stored.

Saving and recovering a workspace

We could continue entering material and checking on it, but for purposes of illustration let's pretend that we are through with our work at this point and want to preserve these functions and variables.

The system command $SAVE$ does this. However, since users are normally assigned more than one workspace, even though only one is being used at any one time, we have to assign a name to the workspace we are saving. This is so that we'll know what to ask for when we call for it again. Only the first eleven characters of a workspace name are recognized by the **APL** system.

For the work previously entered we'll use the name $FIRST$:

```
        )SAVE FIRST
15.52.19 05/22/74
```

We get a message back giving the time and date. This means that the $SAVE$ was successful and an image of the workspace is now in storage with the name $FIRST$.

There is a command which lists all the saved workspaces so that we know what we have in our own **APL** library. ("Library" in **APL** refers to a collection of workspaces associated with a single identification number.) This command is LIB. It lists the names of your saved workspaces:

```
        )LIB
FIRST
```

Only one workspace is listed because that's all we have saved so far. $)FNS$ shows that HYP and $TOSS$ are still around:

```
      )FNS
HYP      TOSS
```

Remember we saved an *image* of the active workspace. Let's now get a fresh workspace:

```
      )CLEAR
CLEAR WS
```

Imagine that it is the following day and we are ready to do some work with HYP and $TOSS$. They were lost from the active workspace when we cleared, but there is an exact image stored in our library with the name $FIRST$. To recover this image, execute the command

```
      )LOAD FIRST
SAVED  15.52.19 05/22/74
```

If a lock was originally associated with the name when it was saved, it must be included here, separated from the name by a colon. The response indicates that it was saved most recently at a certain time and date, which, you will note, is identical with what appears under the original $SAVE$ command on page 114.

Our functions and variables are available to us once again:

```
      )FNS
HYP      TOSS
      )VARS
PI      V
```

Let's check on V to see whether it's still what it's supposed to be:

```
      V
1  2  3  4  5
```

Most people have more than one project cooking at any one time, and usually save a separate workspace for each project. How is this done? To illustrate the procedure, type

```
      )CLEAR
CLEAR WS
```

and enter the function $SQRT$:

```
      ∇R←SQRT X
[1]    R←X*.5∇
```

We then save an image of the active workspace (which contains only the function $SQRT$) with the name $SECOND$:

```
      )SAVE SECOND
 15.55.10    05/22/74
```

Before going on, let's be sure we understand what we have immediate access to at this point, namely a single workspace with only the function $SQRT$ in it, an image of which exists also in storage with the name $SECOND$.

```
      )FNS
SQRT
```

If we want to use any of the functions or variables in $FIRST$ now, we must execute

```
        )LOAD FIRST
SAVED   15.52.19 05/22/74
```

and we see that HYP and $TOSS$ are back in the active workspace:

```
        )FNS
HYP     TOSS
```

Now we'll load $SECOND$ and look at its contents. We don't need to clear between loadings because the act of loading replaces the contents of the active workspace with the material in the workspace being loaded.

```
        )LOAD SECOND
SAVED   15.55.10 05/22/74
        )FNS
SQRT
```

It should be obvious to you that we can access only one workspace at a time using the $LOAD$ command.

Let's save still another workspace with the name $THIRD$. This time, just to be different, we'll clear, load 1 $CLASS$, and get a list of the functions:

```
        )CLEAR
CLEAR WS
        )LOAD 1 CLASS
SAVED   15.02.39 04/15/74
        )FNS
ADD     AGAIN   AREA    AUTO    AVG     AVG1    AVG2    AVG3
AVG4    AVG5    C       CHARMAT CMP     CMPN    CMPX    CMPY
COMPINT COS     CP
```

We have cut off this lengthy printout by pressing ATTN. The contents of 1 $CLASS$ (or perhaps we should be more precise and say an *image* of the contents) will now be saved as $THIRD$:

```
        )SAVE THIRD
 15.58.27 05/22/74
```

Our listing of saved workspaces has grown:

```
        )LIB
FIRST
SECOND
THIRD
```

Although the listing is in the order in which we saved the workspaces, the LIB command ordinarily produces an alphabetized list. Furthermore, just as with FNS and $VARS$, a partial listing can be obtained:

```
        )LIB S
SECOND
THIRD
```

Let's clear again, define a couple of variables, and save them in $FOURTH$:

```
        )CLEAR
CLEAR WS
        X←4 6 8 10
        Y←2 5 8
        )SAVE FOURTH
NOT SAVED, WS QUOTA USED UP
```

We are told, in effect, that we have only three workspaces allotted to us and they are used up, so we're out of luck. Actually it is possible to have more workspaces assigned, but this is a decision which depends on the total amount of available storage in the **APL** system you are using and whatever arrangements you have with the computer center management for obtaining more storage.

Dropping a saved workspace

If X and Y were really some big functions or tables of data and we wanted desperately to save them, then our question is: Which of the three workspaces in our library can we afford to sacrifice? Again look at the list:

```
      )LIB
FIRST
SECOND
THIRD
```

Assuming we don't need $THIRD$, let's try to save X and Y, which are still in the active workspace, in $THIRD$:

```
      )SAVE THIRD
NOT SAVED, THIS WS IS CLEAR WS
```

We are prevented from saving it in $THIRD$ because we already have stored a workspace with the name $THIRD$. Again **APL** keeps you from inadvertently destroying a saved workspace by replacing it with another workspace with the same name. As we'll soon see, there is a way to include X and Y in $THIRD$ without destroying what is already there.

Suppose we really wanted to get rid of $THIRD$. The command

```
      )DROP THIRD
16.01.03 05/22/74
```

does this, the response giving the time and day when the workspace was dropped. $THIRD$ is now gone, as shown by

```
      )LIB
FIRST
SECOND
```

We have no functions in the active workspace, but it still contains the two variables X and Y:

```
      )FNS
@
      )VARS
X       Y
```

This shouldn't surprise us, since we haven't done anything to the active workspace yet. Now that an available slot exists, let's save these variables in a workspace simply called XY for the sake of variety,

```
      )SAVE XY
16.01.34 05/22/74
      )LIB
FIRST
SECOND
XY
```

and XY is added to our library.

Altering a saved workspace

What if we wanted to merge the variables X and Y into $FIRST$? Here is what happens when we try this:

```
      )SAVE FIRST
NOT SAVED, THIS WS IS XY
```

What this means is that the contents of our active workspace have already been saved with the name XY and therefore can't be saved also with the name $FIRST$. To save the material in the active workspace into $FIRST$, we would have to drop $FIRST$ and then save the active workspace with the name $FIRST$. Later we'll see how the $COPY$ command can be used to merge two workspaces.

Another way to change the status of a saved workspace is illustrated by the following sequence:

```
      )LOAD FIRST
SAVED  15.52.19 05/22/74
```

It currently has

```
      )FNS
HYP    TOSS
```

Let's define the function $SIGN$:

```
      ∇R←SIGN X
[1]    R←(X>0)-X<0∇
```

Now our list includes the new function:

```
      )FNS
HYP    SIGN    TOSS
```

Here is what happens when we try to save this into $SECOND$:

```
      )SAVE SECOND
NOT SAVED, THIS WS IS FIRST
```

We are again prevented from doing so because the active workspace already contains an image of $FIRST$, not $SECOND$. However, we can save into $FIRST$, since an image of $FIRST$ exists in the active workspace as a result of the previous loading. Since the active workspace has the name $FIRST$ already associated with it, when we now save, it isn't necessary to repeat the name $FIRST$ (though it wouldn't hurt matters any):

```
      )SAVE
 16.09.07 05/22/74 FIRST
```

The response returns the name of the saved workspace as a reminder.

$FIRST$ is now updated. This can be shown by clearing and reloading it:

```
      )CLEAR
CLEAR WS
      )FNS
@
      )LOAD FIRST
SAVED 16.09.07 05/22/74
      )FNS
HYP    SIGN    TOSS
```

Notice that the time and day given after the $LOAD$ command is that associated with the most recent save.

Our library once more consists of

```
    )LIB
FIRST
SECOND
XY
```

but the contents of $FIRST$ have been updated.

The workspace *CONTINUE*

There is one more workspace in the user's personal library that needs discussion. It is called $CONTINUE$. Should you lose your telephone connection with the **APL** system before signing off, everything in your active workspace would be available automatically to you when you sign back on. This is because the system plunks an image of your active workspace into a workspace named $CONTINUE$, and reloads it at the next sign-on, as indicated by the response $SAVED$ right after the system identification message.

$CONTINUE$ is really an extra workspace that is not part of the regular user allotment, and can be used for emergencies if the other workspaces aren't available. However, you have to be very careful with it. Each time there is a phone line failure, the contents of $CONTINUE$ are replaced by whatever is in the active workspace. So if you must, you can save work into $CONTINUE$, since it is always available to you. But it isn't a wise move for long-term storage because of the danger posed by the possible replacement of its contents.

Summarizing, we can (1) preserve all storable material in the active workspace by saving it; (2) recall material from a saved workspace into the active workspace just as it was when it was last saved; (3) delete a workspace with the $DROP$ command; and (4) feel secure that our work will be saved should the phones fail.

PROBLEMS

Carry out the following instructions and *APL* system commands in the order given:

Define a number of arbitrary functions and variables. Then enter

```
)SAVE WORKONE
)CLEAR
```

and repeat these instructions several times until your workspace quota is used up. Use workspaces named *WORKTWO, WORKTHREE*, etc.

```
)LIB
```

How many workspaces can you save in your *APL* system?

```
)DROP WORKONE
)LIB
)LOAD WORKTHREE
)FNS
)VARS
```

Define additional functions and variables.

```
)SAVE WORKTWO
```

Why wasn't the material saved?

```
)SAVE WORKTHREE
)CLEAR
)LOAD WORKTHREE
)FNS
)VARS
```

Has *WORKTHREE* been updated?

Delete several functions and variables from *WORKTHREE*.

```
)ERASE FN1 FN2 V1 V2 ...
)SAVE
)LIB
)FNS
)VARS
```

Chapter 15:
Managing the active workspace

In the last chapter you learned to use the LIB command to get a listing of the saved workspaces in your personal library. Someone else may have saved workspaces in his personal library with the same names as yours, but there is no confusion, since each user's workspaces are associated with his own user identification number (same as sign-on number).

You can load an image of someone else's workspace into your active workspace like this:

```
      )LOAD 78974 INTERACT
SAVED  8.23.17 09/18/73
```

Here we are loading the workspace named $INTERACT$ that is stored in user 78974's personal library. Since you can't execute $)LIB$ on anyone else's personal library (for reasons of privacy), user 78974 would have had to tell you which workspace names he is using for you to load them.

The libraries with numbers between 1 and 999 are intended to hold workspaces of general or common interest, and are called *common libraries*. The contents of any of these can be displayed using the LIB command followed by the library number, as for example, library 1. As discussed on page 116, a partial listing beginning, say, with N, can be obtained by $)LIB$ 1 N:

```
      )LIB 1
APLCOURSE
CLASS
FILEAID
FILEPRINT
FILES
FORMAT
NEWS
TYPEDRILL
WSFNS
∆FD∆WS
```

The list you get may differ from what is shown here because common library contents are not static; they will be different on each *APL* system, and they change from time to time. Notice that *CLASS* and *APLCOURSE*, which have been used before, are in the list. Ordinarily, individual *APL* users cannot save material into a common library, or drop any workspaces from it. If you were to try to save 1 *CLASS* you would not be permitted to because yours was not the user number that saved it the first time:

```
      )SAVE 1 CLASS
IMPROPER LIBRARY REFERENCE
```

Library 1 is a general interest library on most *APL* systems. Other common libraries may or may not be present on a given system. Let's now explore the contents of library 10:

```
      )LIB 10
EDIT
FPLOT
FULLTEXT
PLOT
```

These lists may seem meaningless to you, but there is a practical way to find out what is in a strange workspace. As an example, type

```
      )LOAD 1 NEWS
SAVED  15.10.12 03/12/75
```

You have probably noticed that the load commands are slightly different for one's own workspaces as compared to those in the common libraries. As a matter of fact, for any library other than your own, it is necessary to include the library number. Its use is optional for one's own library. The complete command has the syntax

```
      )LOAD LIB NO. WSNAME:LOCK  (if required)
```

Having loaded the workspace 1 *NEWS*, the best thing to do next is to get a list of the functions.

```
      )FNS
ADDNEWS ALL      DATEOUT DESCRIBE       GETNEWS GOON
HEADLINES        LASTREAD       MAINHELP       MOREΔDETAILS
NEWS    NEWSHELP        NEWSITEM       OFFICES PBS
PHONES  PROMPT  SCHEDULE       THRU    TIENEWS TIME
UNTIENEWS        UPDATE
```

By convention, if there is a function that contains the word *HOW* or *DESCRIBE* or something similar, then executing it will generally give information about what is in the workspace:

```
      DESCRIBE
          APL*PLUS WORKSPACE 1 NEWS

THE PURPOSE OF THIS WORKSPACE IS TO DISTRIBUTE
INFORMATION WHICH MAY BE OF INTEREST TO APL*PLUS USERS.
THIS INFORMATION INCLUDES OPERATING SCHEDULE, TELEPHONE
ACCESS NUMBERS, A LIST OF STSC OFFICES AND NEWS ITEMS.  ALL
OF THIS INFORMATION IS AVAILABLE THROUGH THE MAJOR FUNCTION
('NEWS') IN THIS WORKSPACE.

THE FOLLOWING INFORMATION IS USEFUL WHEN RUNNING 1 NEWS:
A) ENTERING A TAB,CARRIAGE RETURN WHEN ASKED FOR INPUT WILL
UNTIE THE FILES AND TERMINATE THE FUNCTION.
```

```
B) ENTERING JUST A CARRIAGE RETURN WILL LIST YOUR OPTIONS.
C) ALL OUTPUT, WITH THE EXCEPTION OF NEWS ITEM DETAILS, IS
INTERRUPTABLE.  THAT IS, HITTING ATTENTION WHILE OUTPUT
IS BEING TYPED WILL UNLOCK THE KEYBOARD FOR INPUT.
HITTING JUST A CARRIAGE RETURN AT THIS POINT (SEE B
ABOVE) WILL LIST YOUR OPTIONS FOR YOU.
D) IF FOR ANY REASON THE FUNCTION IS INTERRUPTED AND DOES
NOT AUTOMATICALLY CONTINUE (FOR EXAMPLE, HITTING
ATTENTION WHILE NEWS DETAILS ARE PRINTING), JUST TYPE
'→GOON' TO CONTINUE.

THE FUNCTIONS IN THIS WORKSPACE KEEP TRACK OF HOW MANY
NEWS ITEMS HAVE BEEN ENTERED SINCE YOU LAST CHECKED THE
NEWS, AND TYPE OUT THIS NUMBER WHEN THE FUNCTION 'NEWS' IS
EXECUTED.  ASKING FOR NEWS AUTOMATICALLY PRINTS THE
HEADLINES OF THESE NEWS ITEMS; AND THEN ALLOWS YOU TO ASK
FOR MORE HEADLINES OR DETAILS OF ANY NEWS ITEM.  FOR
INFORMATION ON SUBFUNCTIONS WHICH CAN BE USED APART FROM THE
MAIN FUNCTION 'NEWS', EXECUTE 'MOREΔDETAILS'.
```

Even if there is no description of the contents of a workspace, you can often gain some information by displaying functions with interesting names. In particular, looking at the header will tell you how many arguments the function has, and whether it returns an explicit result.

Some workspaces require so much description that complete documentation in the workspace would take up too much space (and take a lot of time to print out). For many of these, separate instruction manuals may be available. For example, let's explore workspace 10 *PLOT* of the **APL ★PLUS** ® system:

```
      )LOAD 10 PLOT
SAVED   14.13.12 05/29/73
      )FNS
ABSCISSA      ALL      AUTOMATIC      AXES     BLANK
BROAD         COLUMN   DEFAULT        DESCRIBE
FINE      (display interrupted by ATTN)
      DESCRIBE
THIS WORKSPACE COPYRIGHT 1972 BY SCIENTIFIC TIME SHARING THIS
WORKSPACE COPYRIGHT 1972 BY SCIENTIFIC TIMESHARING
CORPORATION.  SEE 'APL★PLUS PLOT INSTRUCTION MANUAL' FOR
FULL DETAILS.
```

Workspace descriptions are very important. You'll realize just how important the first time you have to use someone's workspace which is not adequately described. Furthermore, you should always prepare descriptions for your own workspaces. It makes it much less painful to use the functions after the contents (and you) have lain fallow for a while.

The *COPY* command

We already know how to define the cosine and sine functions (see page 66), but suppose we'd like to have the cosine function available in our workspace called *SECOND*. There is one in 1 *CLASS*, but we don't need the whole workspace for this. Can we select just what we want and transfer it from 1 *CLASS* to *SECOND*? The diagram which follows shows how material can be moved around.

Each saved workspace may have many functions and variables. The active workspace may get its contents by your having loaded a saved workspace (your own or from another library) as well, of course, as from what you may be entering at the keyboard. In the diagram the arrows show the paths by which material can be transferred to your active workspace by the *LOAD* and *COPY* commands, the latter to be discussed next.

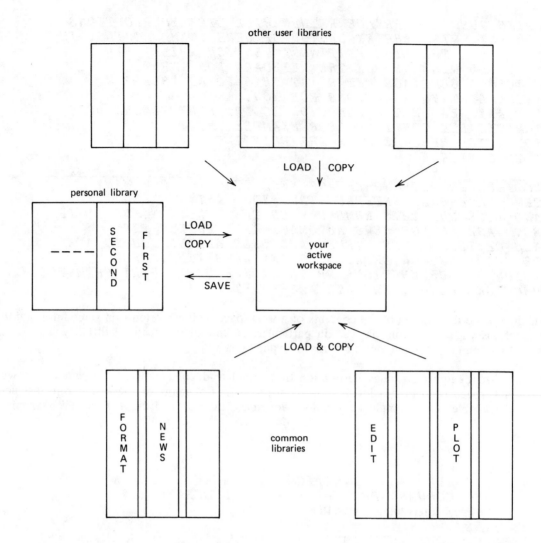

Our task will be to load *SECOND*, which isn't exactly bursting at the seams at the moment,

```
      )LOAD SECOND
SAVED  15.55.10 05/22/74
      )FNS
SQRT
```

and place the function *COS* and an accurate value of π (also in 1 *CLASS* under the name *PI*) in it. Note from the arrows on the diagram that all copying takes place in the active workspace. We cannot copy from one saved workspace into another saved workspace except by loading the latter into the active workspace, copying in the desired objects and then resaving the workspace.

The sequence of steps is not too complicated. We have just moved an image of *SECOND* into the active workspace by loading it. To include *COS* and *PI*, the *COPY* command is used as follows:

```
      )COPY 1 CLASS COS PI
SAVED  15.02.39 04/15/74
      )FNS
COS    PI     SQRT
```

The proper syntax for the *COPY* command is

```
      )COPY LIB NO. WSNAME:LOCK  (if required) LIST OF GLOBAL OBJECTS
```

COPY, like *ERASE*, lets you name several objects in one command. The response to a successful copy is the time and date that the workspace from which the copied objects were taken was last saved.

Our active workspace now contains all the objects we had planned to collect. We must remember to save the workspace or it will be lost when we sign off:

```
      )SAVE
16.54.23 05/22/74 SECOND
```

When we try to copy something that doesn't exist, the response is self-explanatory.

```
      )COPY 1 CLASS SIN
OBJECT NOT FOUND  SIN
```

A command like `)COPY 1 CLASS` causes everything in 1 *CLASS* to be copied into the active workspace. This is useful when you really want to merge the contents of two workspaces, but should not be used as an alternative to loading a workspace. A *COPY* takes much more computer resources than a *LOAD* does.

When you copy an object with the same name as an object already in the active workspace, the one that you copied replaces the one in the active workspace. So long as this is what you intended to do, fine (or even if you didn't intend to do that, but by chance the functions are identical, it's still OK). However, if you are copying and want the version in the active workspace to remain intact in case of name duplication, use the *PCOPY* command instead of *COPY*. It works in exactly the same way, except that for duplicated names, the version that was already in the active workspace is not replaced. In this event, you'll get the report *NOT COPIED*, followed by a list of those objects that were not replaced.

When you copy, the name associated with the active workspace is not changed, as shown by

```
       )LOAD SECOND
SAVED   16.54.23 05/22/74
       )COPY XY
SAVED   16.01.34 05/22/74
       )SAVE XY
NOT SAVED, THIS WS IS SECOND
       )SAVE SECOND
19.02.12 05/22/74
```

The *WSID* command

After an hours-long session at the keyboard, with your fingers worn down to the bone, you can't be blamed for having forgotten the name of the workspace you started out with. If you aren't sure, the *WSID* command will tell you.

WSID stands for *workspace identification*. When followed by a name, it renames the active workspace as shown:

```
       )WSID
SECOND
       )WSID SMITH
WAS SECOND
       )WSID
SMITH
       )SAVE
19.09.23 05/22/74 SMITH
```

Groups of objects

So far, we've learned how to copy selected objects into the active workspace by naming each object we want (or, by not naming any objects, copying the entire contents of a workspace). The *GROUP* command allows us to set up a collection of global objects, which may then be copied (or erased) by referring to the collection by a single name. Any objects, including names of other groups and even nonexistent global objects can be members of a group. A group is formed by

$$)GROUP \ GROUPNAME \ OBJECT1 \ OBJECT2 \ ...$$

GROUPNAME follows the same rules for naming variables and functions. However, *GROUPNAME* can't be the same as that of any other global object in the workspace. You can get a listing of the groups in your active workspace by the command *)GRPS* or *)GRPS N* (for a partial listing) where *N* is any alphabetic character. The command *)GRP GRPNAME* gives you a listing of the objects in any group. An already existing group can be enlarged as follows:

$$)GROUP \ GROUPNAME \ GROUPNAME \ NEWOBJECT1 \ NEWOBJECT2 \ ...$$

When you copy a group from a saved workspace what actually gets copied is everything in the group, along with the group name (except that if another group name is a member of the copied group, the latter's constituent objects are not copied). If you erase a group from the active workspace, all the objects named in the group are erased. This feature is a mixed blessing, so be careful when you use it. Sometimes you may simply need to remove the group name (disperse the group) without erasing the individual objects. To do this, enter *)GROUP GROUPNAME* (without any objects following). The group commands are not implemented on the IBM 5100.

The symbol table

A workspace has certain finite limits to its capacity to store information. One of these limits is the number of names, or symbols, that can be stored. Normally, space for 256 symbols (variables, functions and groups) is provided (125 in the IBM 5100 and 512 on the *APL ★PLUS* ® system). When that number has been exceeded you will get a *SYMBOL TABLE FULL* message. You can change the allotment of symbol space by executing the command *)SYMBOLS NNN*, where *NNN* is some integer. This command can be executed only in a clear workspace. When you get a *SYMBOL TABLE FULL* error, you should save the workspace somewhere, clear, execute *)SYMBOLS NNN*, and then copy the workspace you just saved. Having done all this, it would be a shame if you forgot to save the corrected active workspace when you're finished.

You may be surprised to find occasionally that you'll get *SYMBOL TABLE FULL* even though the listings of *)FNS*, *VARS* and *)GRPS* show just a handful of names. The reason for this is that any time a name is mentioned, it goes into the symbol table and the trace of the name is not removed by the *ERASE* command. In fact, whenever you attempt to execute a nonexistent function, the name you type is recorded in the symbol table. Likewise, local variable names are in the symbol table. The reason for this is to increase efficiency in processing your work in normal use. In practice, *SYMBOL TABLE FULL* errors are relatively rare, but it's worth knowing that there is a way to get around the problem when it occurs.

Just as the size of the symbol table can be increased to provide more symbols (at a slight reduction of working space for computations), the size of the symbol table can also be adjusted downward, and doing so provides a slight increase in working space. The normal allowance of symbols is a practical compromise. You can find what the present symbol table allocation is by executing *)SYMBOLS* (without a number). The result is the present capacity.

Sign-off commands

Besides the sign-off command $)OFF$ introduced in Chapter 1, there are three others which are available (except on the IBM 5100) to the *APL* user. These are

$$)OFF\ HOLD$$
$$)CONTINUE$$
$$)CONTINUE\ HOLD$$

The effect of the "$HOLD$" is to keep your line open for about a minute after sign-off so that someone else may sign on at your terminal without having to redial. This is a time-saver when a single terminal is shared by a number of eager beaver users or when the *APL* system is being used at capacity.

When signing off with $)CONTINUE$, the active workspace is first automatically saved in $CONTINUE$. The same happens in the case of a disconnect.

Security features for user protection

APL has many ways to protect you from careless or malicious users. One of these has already been introduced, the lock associated with a user number. It can be changed at sign-off by

$$)SIGN-OFF\ COMMAND:NEWLOCK$$

or simply discontinued by following the sign-off command with a colon.

Another is a workspace lock, which follows the workspace name and is separated from it by a colon. This lock must be included with the workspace when loaded. The lock remains in effect unless it is changed when the workspace is saved again. As with the sign-off command, a $SAVE$ followed only by a colon removes the lock. Workspaces which are locked are listed when $)LIB$ is called for, but the locks aren't shown (for obvious reasons), and locked workspaces aren't identified as such in the listing. The $WSID$ command can be used to give the active workspace a new lock as well as a new name as shown here:

$$)WSID\ NEWNAME:NEWLOCK$$

Should you be so unfortunate as to forget what the lock name is, there isn't any way for you to retrieve the workspace in question yourself. It requires the assistance of the computer center staff to retrieve it. If your work has security or privacy implications, take the proper precautions to make sure your locks are not available to other people. Change them frequently, and don't leave any printouts lying around with locks showing. On the *APL★PLUS*® System, the system command $)BLOT$ will produce a smudged line of typing, over which you can type your locks. Similar practices may exist on other *APL* systems.

Lengths of names and locks

Earlier we touched on how names of functions and variables can be made up. There is considerable freedom in choosing such names; any sequence of letters (including underlined letters) and numbers can be used, as long as the first character is alphabetic. *APL* recognizes only the first 11 for workspace names and the first 77 for all others, which is hardly likely to cramp any user's style Some *APL* systems let you abbreviate system commands to the first four letters. Locks can be any combination of letters and numbers, but only the first eight are recognized.

Other system commands

The rest of this chapter deals with topics specific to the IBM 5100. If you don't use a 5100, you should jump ahead to the problems at the end of the chapter. There are still more system commands for all *APL* users, but they will be taken up in subsequent chapters as needed.

The IBM 5100 tape cartridge (stand-alone)

The tape cartridge of the IBM 5100 serves a similar purpose to that part of the computer where the libraries (yours, others and common) are stored, making the 5100 self-contained. Each cartridge may be considered as a library, with different cartridges used for different users on the same machine, as well as common library workspaces. The tape cartridges have a small switch with two positions, one of which is marked SAFE. This is used when a cartridge has data on it that is not to be erased. For writing on a tape, the switch should *not* point to SAFE.

Many of the system commands used in the 5100 are similar to those for *APL* time-sharing systems (and you also have convenience keys for selected commands to be used with CMD).

While *APL* time-sharing systems have the size and number of workspaces allocated users predetermined, the 5100 cartridge has a blank "library". In effect, you are the system manager, with the ability and responsibility to lay out the library to suit your own needs.

The tape is marked off into *files* with the $MARK$ system command. Your first step is to determine how big to make them. If this is a problem, you may want to refer to Chapter 32, where there is a brief discussion of *APL* storage requirements.

Having decided on the number of files and their size, you are now ready to mark the tape (which, incidentally, doesn't have to be done all at once), remembering that you have 204,000 bytes of storage available. The $MARK$ command takes as its argument a three-element vector consisting of the *size* (in 1024-byte chunks), *number of files* and *starting file number*. For example,

```
        )MARK  30  4  1
MARKED  0004  0030
```

marks off four 30,000-byte files starting with file number 1. You may then mark off an additional section of the tape by entering a command like

```
        )MARK  10  3  5
MARKED  0007  0010
```

Notice that the response indicates the last file number used and its size. Should you inadvertently use a file number which was already marked, you will get an $ALREADY$ $MARKED$ message. To re-mark it, enter GO and press EXECUTE. However, data in any files after the last re-marked one will no longer be available. One final point: marking a tape will not affect the existing contents of the active workspace.

Now for the commands which move data between the active workspace and the tape:

```
        )SAVE  device/file number   file name : lock  (if any)
        )CONTINUE  device/file number   file name : lock  (if any)
```

These two commands write the active workspace on tape in two different forms, and each form has certain restrictions. The $SAVE$ command cannot be used for a clear workspace or one which contains suspended functions. The $CONTINUE$ command must be used in these cases. However, the $CONTINUE$ command has its drawbacks. Objects cannot be copied from a $CONTINUE$d workspace; a $CONTINUE$d workspace cannot be loaded into a 5100 with a smaller active workspace than the 5100 on which it was originally created; and when a $CONTINUE$d workspace is loaded into a machine with a larger active workspace, the additional space is unusable. If either a $CONTINUE$ or a $SAVE$ is interrupted by ATTN, the referenced file is set to UNUSED.

One advantage of the $CONTINUE$ command is that it takes less time than a $SAVE$ of the same workspace, and a $CONTINUE$d version of a workspace will load much faster than a $SAVE$d version.

The built-in tape unit is device 1. Thus, the command

>)*CONTINUE* 1003 *THIRD*
CONTINUED 1003 *THIRD*

saves an image of the workspace on device 1, file 003, with the name *THIRD*. The file number and workspace name may be omitted if the active workspace already has had them assigned from a previous loading or the use of *WSID*.

Here are more system commands used on the 5100:

>)*DROP* device/file number file name : lock   marks the file unused.
>)*COPY* device/file number file name : lock objnames
>)*PCOPY* device/file number file name : lock objnames   operates as in **APL** time-sharing, except that no copying takes place if there are suspended functions in the active workspace, or if the file is a *CONTINUE*d workspace.
>)*LIB* device/starting file number gives file header information, in this order: *file number, file name, file type, file size, available storage* and *number of defective records*.

File types of interest to the **APL** user are

type	description
00	unused
01	shared (see Chapter 31)
02	shared
06	continued
07	saved
08	internal data format (see Chapter 31)

For example, the file header 003 *THIRD* 06 030,020 0 tells you that file number 3 is called *THIRD*, was written by the *CONTINUE* command, has 30 1024-byte blocks of storage (in which 20 contiguous blocks are unused), and contains no defective "records" (512-byte blocks).

All file headers from the starting file number to the end of the tape will be displayed. If)*LIB* alone is entered, the list contains information about all files after the one where the tape is currently positioned.

>)*REWIND*   rewinds the tape.

The following commands are similar to their time-sharing counterparts:

>)*LOAD* device/file number file name:lock
>)*SI*
>)*SIV*
>)*WSID* device/file number file name:lock
>)*VARS*
>)*FNS*
>)*SYMBOLS*
>)*ERASE*
>)*CLEAR*

Besides the commands shown in this section, there are still others which are used to put the 5100 in COMMUNICATE mode (Chapter 1), select and use auxiliary I/O devices like the printer and the second tape unit, and apply an internal machine fix to the system or get data back when there is a tape error. Only those needed for communicating with a remote **APL** system will be discussed in the next sections. You should consult the IBM 5100 APL Reference Manual SA21-9213 for details on the others.

Transferring information to the cartridge

When the 5100 is used as a terminal, you can transfer data from a remote system onto the tape cartridge and vice versa. Following a discussion of the commands which make this possible, we display a sample terminal session showing how this is done.

To store on the tape data which appears in the extended display, you must have a *marked* tape. In the home state (CMD and alphanumeric 8) enter the command <u>&</u> OPEN OUT file number. This will store transmitted data starting at the beginning of the specified file. If there is any data on the file already, it is destroyed. The command <u>&</u> OPEN ADD file number works similarly, except that the new data transmitted is stored right after existing data on the file.

Now there's a catch to this. You will be entering *APL* instructions at the keyboard to read or get the remote data that you wish to store on the tape. Once the file is opened, *all* the information transferred, including your instructions to the remote *APL* system, will be written on the tape. To avoid this, enter the command <u>&</u> OUTSEL SYS. This causes only those lines transmitted by the remote system to be written on the tape, while the lines that you enter will not be so written.

You aren't out of the woods yet. Successful transfer of the information requires certain enabling functions to be present in the remote system. These do two necessary jobs: They convert any functions to be sent to canonical (character) form, using the $\square CR$ system function described in Chapter 33; and they write all the variables, including the converted functions, to a file using a shared variable (Chapter 31), preparatory to being sent out.

So much for the transmittal. But since any functions transmitted will still be recorded on the tape as character variables, another function must be present on the receivng end to convert them back into usable form. Examples of the functions needed may be found in the IBM 5100 Communications Reference Manual SA21-9215.

The last step that needs to be taken is to enter the command <u>&</u> CLOSE, to "close" the tape and prevent further data transfer. Failure to do so before removing the cartridge may result in loss of data not only from the cartridge being removed, but also from the next one you insert in the built-in unit.

Here are the steps required to transfer information from the *APL* ★*PLUS* ® system to the 5100. The communications tape referred to in this section and the next can be obtained from Scientific Time Sharing Corporation. It holds the functions to make the 5100 convenient for transferring information.

1.   Sign on the *APL* ★*PLUS* ® system with the 5100, using the communications tape in the built-in unit.
2.   )*LOAD* the workspace to be transferred.
3.   )*COPY* 11 *WSTOFILE*   (Brings *WSTOFILE* into the active workspace.)
4.   *WSTOFILE*   (Writes workspace to an *APL* file, using tie number 90.)
5.   )*LOAD* 510 *TO*5100   (Gets functions to convert the file to transferrable form.)
6.   *TABS* 6   (Sets the 5100 tabs at every 6 positions.)
7.   *CONVERT* 90   (Makes conversions to variables and functions on the file.)
8.   *BUILDTRFILE* 90   (Builds specially formatted transfer file.)
9.   <u>&</u> OUTSEL SYS
10. <u>&</u> OPEN OUT 6   (Opens a receive file on the special communications tape.)
11. *TO*5100   (Writes transfer file on receive file of the 5100.)
12. <u>&</u> CLOSE   (Closes the receive file.)
13.)*OFF*   (End session with the time-sharing system.)
14. RESTART   (Return to 5100 *APL* mode.)
15.)*COPY* 5 *TRANSFER FILETOWS*   (Read from special communications tape.)
16. *FILETOWS*   (Builds an active workspace from the receive file.)
17.)*ERASE FILETOWS*   (Removes *FILETOWS* function from the workspace.)
18.)*WSID* new workspace name   (Assign name to transferred information.)
19. Save or use workspace as required.

The auxiliary functions needed and access method used will be different on other *APL* systems, but in general will follow the above scheme conceptually.

Transferring information from the cartridge

Sending data from the 5100 to a remote system is the reverse in many respects of the procedure discussed in the previous section. In this case two actions are necessary on the part of the user: a "local" file must be created on tape with the data to be transmitted; and the tape contents must then be transmitted to the remote system.

Again, appropriate auxiliary functions must be present in the workspace with the data to be sent. They perform the same two jobs described before, that is, convert any functions present to canonical form and write the data on tape using a shared variable. The receiving end again should contain an auxiliary function to convert the character representation to a useable form.

The following example shows a transfer of information from the 5100 to the *APL ★PLUS* ® system:

1.   )*LOAD* the workspace to be transferred.
2.   Insert the communications tape.
3.   )*COPY 5 TRANSFER WSTOFILE*   (Bring *WSTOFILE* into the active workspace.)
4.   *WSTOFILE*   (Writes workspace to a special file on the communications tape.)
5.   )*LOAD 5 TRANSFER*   (Gets functions to convert file to transferrable form.)
6.   *CONVERT* 6   (Makes conversions to variables and functions on the file.)
7.   *BUILDTRFILE* 6 7   (Builds a transfer file (7) containing all data needed to transfer the workspace.)
8.   Sign on to the *APL ★PLUS* ® system, using the communications tape.
9.   )*LOAD 510 FROM*5100   (Gets functions to receive the information.)
10.   *FROM*5100
11.   & OPEN IN 7   (Opens the transfer file on tape.)
12.   &TAPEIN   (Begins actual transfer of information to a file on the time-sharing system.)
13.   )*CLEAR*   (Prepares to reconstitute the information.)
14.   )*COPY 510 FROM*5100 *FILETOWS*
15.   *FILETOWS*   (Reads the file and builds active workspace.)
16.   )*ERASE FILETOWS*   (Removes *FILETOWS* function from the workspace.)
17.   )*WSID* new workspace name   (Assigns name to transferred workspace.)
18.   Save or use workspace as required.

As was pointed out in the last section, some of the individual steps and auxiliary functions used will be somewhat different on other *APL* systems.

PROBLEMS

1. Follow the instructions given and carry out the indicated system commands:

    ```
    )LIB  1
    )LOAD  1  ADVANCEDEX
    )FNS
    )VARS
    ```

    If there is a function or variable named $DESCRIBE$ or HOW, execute it.

    ```
    )WSID
    ```

    Define a function $RECT$ which gives only the area of a rectangle of length L by W. Display it after executing.

    ```
    )COPY  1  CLASS  RECT
    ```

    Was your own defined function $RECT$ unchanged?

    ```
    )ERASE RECT
    ```

    Redefine $RECT$ as above to give only the area of a rectangle.

    ```
    )PCOPY  1  CLASS  RECT
    ```

    Does this command behave the same as $)COPY$?

    ```
    )SAVE JONES
    ```

    If the workspace was not saved, drop one of those in your library and then save it. Then change the name of your active workspace to $SMITH$.

    ```
    )WSID SMITH
    )SAVE
    )CLEAR
    )LOAD 1 NEWS
    )SAVE 1 NEWS
    ```

    Why couldn't $NEWS$ be saved?

    ```
    )CONTINUE  HOLD
    ```

    Now sign on again.

    ```
    )LIB
    )FNS
    )VARS
    ```

2. You have saved your work in a workspace called $GOOD$ and have just developed a function OK in your active workspace. Write out a sequence of commands which will get OK into $GOOD$ without carrying with it any unwanted "trash" which may be in the active workspace.

3. Compose a group $\underline{A}$ consisting of the variables $TAB0$, $TAB1$, $TAB2$, $TAB3$, and a group $\underline{B}$ consisting of functions $AVG1$, $AVG2$, $AVG3$, $AVG4$, $AVG5$ of workspace 1 $CLASS$. Enlarge group $\underline{A}$ by including the variable PI. List the groups, list the members of group $\underline{A}$, and then disperse group $\underline{A}$.

Chapter 16:
Mixed functions

Thus far we have worked mainly with primitive scalar dyadic and monadic functions. One of their characteristics is that the shape of the result is the same as that of the argument. For example, if the arguments are vectors, so is the result. If the arguments are scalars, then the result is a scalar. In this and subsequent chapters, additional functions will be introduced in which the shape of the result is not related to those of the arguments in such a consistent way. Appropriately, these are called *mixed* functions. The dyadic and monadic ρ, introduced earlier in Chapters 3 and 7, are examples of mixed functions.

Index generator

To start off, let's consider a familiar algorithm: our earlier investigation of the cosine function, (the Maclaurin's series used in Chapter 9). Here is a review of the steps involved, the last being a one-line *APL* expression equivalent to the preceding three lines:

$$\cos x = \frac{x^0}{0!} - \frac{x^2}{2!} + \frac{x^4}{4!} - \frac{x^6}{6!} + \frac{x^8}{8!} - \cdots$$

It would be nice to have a way to generate regular sequences like these so as to eliminate the monotony of typing. What's more, the only way now that we can change the length of the sequence is to type in more or fewer numbers.

In *APL* the mixed function ι, which is upper shift I on the keyboard, solves all your problems - or at least some of them, if you don't like exaggeration. When used monadically with nonnegative integer arguments, it is called the *index generator*.

We can see how it works by entering $\iota 5$ and noting the vector of integers that results:

```
      ι5
1  2  3  4  5
```

Here is another:

```
      ι10
1  2  3  4  5  6  7  8  9  10
```

Now we're ready to use this function to produce the sequence needed for calculating the cosine. We know that multiplying any integer by 2 produces an even integer. Since our desired sequence is 0 2 4 6 8..., this suggests that we need

```
      2×ι6
2  4  6  8  10  12
```

Almost, but not quite there, 0 being omitted. The correct expression should be

```
      ¯2+2×ι6
0  2  4  6  8  10
```

and we have it. Incidentally, we can get something else out of this for free. If adding ¯2 gives an even sequence, then adding ¯1 should result in a sequence of odd integers:

```
      ¯1+2×ι6
1  3  5  7  9  11
```

Getting back to our cosine function, we can now incorporate ιN for a variable number of terms. First execute

```
      )CLEAR
CLEAR WS
```

and we are ready to define the function. Since N, the number of terms, is now a variable, we ought to make the cosine function dyadic. We may want to use the result for other calculations, so the header should be set to return an explicit result:

```
      ∇R←N COS X
[1]   V←¯2+2×ιN
[2]   R←-/(X*V)÷!V∇
```

Here is cos π/3 evaluated for a varying number of terms,

```
      2 COS 0÷3
0.4516886444
      4 COS 0÷3
0.4999645653
      6 COS 0÷3
0.4999999964
      8 COS 0÷3
0.5
```

and for comparison, the primitive function

```
      2○0÷3
0.5
```

Even though the last result from the defined function *COS* is shown as .5, it is still approximate, .5 being the best value to ten places.

Our ι function is good for all kinds of sequences. Suppose we want a multiple of the first five integers. Try

```
      ι5×2
1  2  3  4  5  6  7  8  9  10
```

We forgot parentheses. Clearly it should be

          (ι 5) × 2
2   4   6   8   10

or better still

          2 × ι 5
2   4   6   8   10

   Powers of 2 can be obtained with an expression like

          2 * ι 5
2   4   8   16   32

which can be easily modified to include 2 raised to the 0 power:

          2 * ‾1 + ι 5
1   2   4   8   16

   Now look at the following sequences:

          ι 5
1   2   3   4   5
          ι 4
1   2   3   4
          ι 3
1   2   3
          ι 2
1   2

   So far, they seem straightforward.   ι N obviously generates a vector of N elements. Well, if you're so sure, what do you suppose ι 1 is?

          ι 1
1

   Carrying the analogy along, ι 1 has to be a vector of length 1 containing the single element 1. Is it the same as this 1 generated simply by entering it on the keyboard and following with RETURN?

          1
1

   They look the same, but in **APL** as in love, looks aren't everything. The 1 we typed is a scalar. The result of ι 1 is a vector. In mathematics there is a term which is associated with the difference - *rank*, which we introduced earlier and will have more to say about later.

   One (?) down, one to go. What about

          ι 0
          @

   This must be a vector of *no* elements, and the system in its response is trying to print a vector of length 0, but there just aren't any elements to put on the paper !

   What good is a vector of length 0? A good question. One might as well ask, "What good is an empty warehouse?" The warehouse represents a place in which goods can be stored. An empty vector (you should pardon the comparison) is somewhat analogous. Think about this: if you needed to generate vectors of varying length and you were looking for a starting place to store elements as they were accumulated, what better place to start with than a vector of no elements, an empty "warehouse," the vector ι 0? You can't really appreciate its many uses until you begin to get more deeply involved in function definition in **APL**. A number of examples of empty vectors will be introduced in this and subsequent chapters.

Shape

In Chapter 7 the shape function ρ was discussed and used to give information on the sizes of arrays. Actually ρ isn't quite as limited in its applicability as would appear from the few examples cited previously.

It was stated in Chapter 7 that ρ could be applied to *any* array. Let's explore this by using some sample arrays put in 1 *CLASS* for illustrative purposes. Bring copies of these arrays, called *TAB*0, *TAB*1, *TAB*2 and *TAB*3 into your active workspace with the *COPY* command:

```
      )COPY 1 CLASS TAB0 TAB1 TAB2 TAB3
SAVED  15.02.39 04/15/74
```

Display *TAB*0:

```
      TAB0
4.1
```

It's just the scalar number 4.1. Look at ρ*TAB*0:

```
      ρTAB0
@
```

*TAB*0, a scalar, has no dimensions. It doesn't "extend out" any distance in any direction, unlike a vector or a matrix. In this sense it's like an idealized geometric point, which is also considered to be dimensionless.

Let's now investigate *TAB*1:

```
      TAB1
1.414213562 1.732050808 2 2.236067977
      ρTAB1
4
```

ρ*TAB*1 yields a single number, which tells us that it is one-dimensional (a vector), with four elements along that dimension.

Now for *TAB*2:

```
      TAB2
   3  1  7
   7 10  4
   6  9  1
   1  6  7
      ρTAB2
4 3
```

Here we have a two-dimensional array (matrix), with four elements along one dimension (number of rows) and three elements along the other (number of columns).

Finally, display *TAB*3:

```
        TAB3
 111  112  113
 121  122  123
 131  132  133
 141  142  143

 211  212  213
 221  222  223
 231  232  233
 241  242  243
        ρTAB3
2  4  3
```

This may look peculiar, but remember that we are restricted to two-dimensional paper to depict a three-dimensional array. The result of $\rho TAB3$ indicates that we do indeed have a three-dimensional array, two elements deep (number of planes), four elements down (number of rows), and three elements across (number of columns).

If you are wondering how $TAB3$ was constructed, this is how it was done. Try the following algorithm, which uses the outer product:

```
        100  200∘.+10  20  30  40  ∘.+ι3
 111  112  113
 121  122  123
 131  132  133
 141  142  143

 211  212  213
 221  222  223
 231  232  233
 241  242  243
```

Rank

Earlier in this chapter, as well as in Chapter 7, *rank* was mentioned as a distinguishing description of the number of dimensions of an array. Let's see how this is handled in **APL**. First consider

```
     ρρTAB0
0
```

An unexpected response? Not really, when you think about it. Let's see if we can construct a plausible explanation. First we'll line up the responses from $\rho TAB0$, $\rho TAB1$, $\rho TAB2$ and $\rho TAB3$.

```
        ρTAB0
        @
        ρTAB1
4
        ρTAB2
4  3
        ρTAB3
2  4  3
```

What do you see? The shape of ρ applied to an array of N dimensions is itself a vector of N elements. So $\rho TAB0$ must really be a vector with no elements ($\iota 0$), and $\rho\rho TAB0$ is equivalent to

```
      ρ ι 0
0

      ρ ρ TAB 0
0
```

The number of elements in a vector of length 0 is 0. There just aren't any.

Similarly, we get

```
      ρ ρ TAB 1
1
      ρ ρ TAB 2
2
      ρ ρ TAB 3
3
```

Thus, ρ ρ of any array gives the number of dimensions of the array. The name *rank* is attached to this concept. A scalar is of the rank 0; a vector, rank 1; and a matrix, rank 2. Arrays of rank 3 and higher don't have generally accepted names.

At last we are ready to tell the difference between

```
      1
1
```

and

```
      ι 1
1
```

which distinction was left unanswered when it was introduced on page 135. They have different ranks:

```
      ρ ρ 1
0
      ρ ρ ι 1
1
```

Catenate

In our work with vectors, we haven't yet said anything about how we might increase the length of the vector by putting more elements in it. This would certainly be desirable if the vector represented, say, the bills run up by a single customer in a department store. Our only recourse thus far has been to respecify the vector by retyping it with the new values which, you'll agree, isn't very satisfactory.

APL does have a function which allows us to enlarge a vector. To illustrate how it can be done, let's design a memory calculator capable of summing a list of numbers. Here is its description:

key	purpose/action
C	clears accumulator
E	allows entry of values and prints number of values accumulated since last entry
S	prints sum of accumulated numbers

A simulation of this calculator is provided in 1 *CLASS*:

```
     )LOAD 1 CLASS
SAVED  15.02.39 04/15/74
```

First, we clear the "memory":

```
     C
     @
```

Next, type E followed by the data as shown:

```
     E 5  3  1
3
```

The system responds with a 3, indicating that three values have been entered. Again make an entry:

```
     E 5  6
5
```

Typing S gives the sum of the values accumulated:

```
     S
20
```

We can continue to enter values and get the sum:

```
     E 2
6
     S
22
```

Now clear the memory again:

```
     C
     @
     S
0
     E 1  2  3
3
     S
6
```

What do the functions look like that comprise this simple calculator? First let's display C:

```
     ∇C[□]∇
   ∇ C
[1]    VECT←ι0
   ∇
```

It is niladic and doesn't return an explicit result, which is reasonable enough since its purpose is only to set the accumulator $VECT$ to $ι0$ each time it is executed. $VECT$ is a global variable and in C is an empty vector, a good place to start.

Here is E:

```
     ∇E[□]∇
   ∇ E X
[1]    ρVECT←VECT,X
   ∇
```

It has one argument, X, and takes the elements in X and tacks them on to the back of $VECT$. This result is stored in $VECT$ and the number of elements resulting is printed. In effect we update $VECT$ and print information about its elements at the same time.

A new dyadic function is introduced in E. It is called *catenate*, the symbol for which is the comma, and its job is to join or chain together its two arguments.

Next, we'll display S to complete the picture of our calculator:

```
      ∇S[□]∇
    ∇  S
[1]    +/VECT
    ∇
```

All S does is print the sum of the accumulated values in $VECT$.

The catenate function has a number of characteristics worth noting. For example, if we make the assignments

```
      J←ι3
      K←9  8  7  6
```

and catenate J and K putting the result in Y,

```
      Y←J,K
```

then there are seven elements in Y:

```
      ρY
7
      Y
1  2  3  9  8  7  6
```

Two vectors can be catenated. What about a scalar? Can it be catenated to a vector? Consider

```
      J,6
1  2  3  6
```

For purposes of catenation, the 6 is regarded as a vector of length 1. If this is so, we ought to be able to catenate two scalars to make a vector:

```
      X←3,5
      X
3  5
```

X is now a vector of length 2, containing a 3 and a 5.

Catenating ι0 to a vector gives the same vector, as we would expect:

```
      J,ι0
1  2  3
      (ι0),J
1  2  3
```

What about catenating a vector of length 0 to a scalar?

```
      R←6
      ρρR
0
      T←R,ι0
      T
6
      ρT
1
      ρρT
1
```

T is a vector of one element, as shown by the last two results. Clearly the result of catenation of vectors and/or scalars is always a vector.

When applied to matrices, catenation allows us to increase the number of rows or columns. This extension of the function, along with another interesting use of the comma (called *lamination*) which creates a new array of greater rank than that of the arguments, will be taken up in Chapter 24.

Ravel

If we're not careful, this distinction between vectors and scalars can cause difficulties. Sometimes it is advantageous to have a vector of length 1 instead of a scalar. As an example, look at AVG in 1 $CLASS$, which you should still have in your active workspace:

```
      ∇AVG[□]∇
    ∇ R←AVG X
[1]   R←(+/X)÷ρX
    ∇
```

It appears to be in working order:

```
      AVG 2 3 4
3
```

or is it?

```
      AVG 4
@
```

Something must be wrong. One check is to see what $ρAVG$ 4 is:

```
      ρAVG 4
0
```

which means that AVG 4 must result in a vector of length 0. Why should this be? Again let's display the function:

```
      ∇AVG[□]∇
    ∇ R←AVG X
[1]   R←(+/X)÷ρX
    ∇
```

Working from right to left on line 1, if X is a scalar, then $ρX$ is an empty vector. But the algorithm calls for dividing $+/X$ (a scalar) by $ρX$ (in this case a vector of length 0). Dividing a scalar by a vector gives a result which has the same shape as the vector argument. Need we say more?

Interesting though all this may be, it doesn't solve our problem. Our function, to be consistent, should return a result of 4 in this case. We have to make the argument X a vector if it isn't one already. The monadic *ravel* is used for this. It employs the same symbol, the comma, as the dyadic catenate. Let's insert this between ρ and X in AVG:

```
        ∇AVG[1□10]
[1]     R←(+/X)÷ρX
                   1
[1]     R←(+/X)÷ρ,X∇
```

Now executing $AVG\ 4$, we get the anticipated result:

```
      AVG 4
4
```

The ravel function has some interesting uses. $TAB2$ is a good example.

```
        TAB2
    3   1   7
    7  10   4
    6   9   1
    1   6   7
        ρTAB2
4 3
        ,TAB2
3 1 7 7 10 4 6 9 1 1 6 7
```

Notice that the last coordinate is raveled first, and that there are as many elements in the result as in the original array:

```
      ×/ρTAB2
12
      ρ,TAB2
12
```

Raveling proceeds similarly on a three-dimensional array like $TAB3$:

```
        TAB3
    111 112 113
    121 122 123
    131 132 133
    141 142 143

    211 212 213
    221 222 223
    231 232 233
    241 242 243
```

Again, the last coordinate is raveled first:

```
      ,TAB3
111 112 113 121 122 123 131 132 133 141 142 143 211 212 213 221
      222 223 231 232 233 241 242 243
```

Thus, no matter what the rank of the array with which we start, ravel converts the array to a vector.

Reshape

This function was introduced in Chapter 3. By way of review, specify

      $U \leftarrow 4 \quad 3 \quad 5 \quad 7 \quad 8 \quad 9$

Suppose we want to build a two-dimensional table with the first row 4 3 5 and the second row 7 8 9. The reshape function rearranges the elements in the right argument to have the shape of the left argument:

```
      2  3ρU
4  3  5
7  8  9
```

Here is an example where the left argument contains a single element:

```
      3ρU
4  3  5
```

The number of elements in the left argument gives the rank of the resulting array.

Here are some additional examples:

```
      5ρ3
3  3  3  3  3
      5ρ0  1
0  1  0  1  0
```

So far our right arguments have been vectors or scalars. What happens when we have a matrix on the right?

```
      A←2  3ρ2  3  4  5  6  7
      A
2  3  4
5  6  7
      3  4ρA
2  3  4  5
6  7  2  3
4  5  6  7
      A←2  3  4  5  6  7
      3  4ρA
2  3  4  5
6  7  2  3
4  5  6  7
```

From this we can conclude that whatever the shape of the right argument A, for reshaping purposes it is in effect $,A$. This is perfectly reasonable, since raveling an array of rank 2 or more before reshaping is just what most people would do if they had to do it by hand.

Finally, what if the right argument contains no elements, i.e., is an empty vector?

```
      3ρι0
LENGTH ERROR
      3ρι0
      ∧
```

There are no elements on the right on which to perform the desired reshaping, so the instruction can't be carried out. But now try

```
          0ρι0
          @
          (ι0)ρι0
LENGTH ERROR
          (ι0)ρι0
          ∧
```

Can you explain these results?

PROBLEMS

1.   DRILL. Specify $A \leftarrow 0\ 8\ ^-3\ 4\ 6\ 10$

ρA	$\iota 10$	$+/\iota 15$
$\rho \rho A$	$(\iota 5)+3$	$\div \iota 5$
$\rho \rho \rho A$	$^-7 \times \iota 1$	$\iota 28 \div 3 + 1$
$A \lceil 0.8 \times \iota 6$	$\iota \lceil /A$	$\iota 10000$

Now specify $M \leftarrow 2\ 4 \rho \iota 8$ and $V \leftarrow 3\ 3 \rho \iota 9$ and execute

ρM	$5\ 4 \rho V$	$3\ 3 \rho 1, 3 \rho 0$
$(^-2)\ 1\ 2$	V, M	$5\ 4 \rho 0$
$^-2, 1\ 2$	$6 \rho 12$	$5, 4 \rho 0$
$\rho \rho V$	$10 \rho 100$	$\rho \rho 0 \rho 9\ 10\ 11\ 12$

2.   What is the difference in meaning of the two expressions $\rho A = 6$ and $6 = \rho A$?

3.   Load 1 *CLASS* and execute each of the following:

$\times / \rho TAB0$ $\times / \rho TAB1$ $\times / \rho TAB2$ $\times / \rho TAB3$

What information is gained from these instructions?

4.   For the vector A (problem 1) execute $\iota \rho A$ and $\rho \iota \rho A$. What meaning can be assigned to each of these expressions?

5.   Write one-line monadic functions returning an explicit result to give

A) the sum of the square roots of the first N positive integers
B) the square root of the sum of the first N positive integers
C) the geometric mean of the first N positive integers (the Nth root of the product of the N numbers)

6.   Construct each of the following sequences using ι :

$$1 \quad 3 \quad 5 \quad 7 \quad 9 \quad 11 \quad 13 \quad 15$$

$$^-7 \quad ^-2 \quad 3 \quad 8 \quad 13$$

$$0 \quad 0.3 \quad 0.6 \quad 0.9 \quad 1.2 \quad 1.5$$

$$^-250 \quad ^-150 \quad ^-50 \quad 50 \quad 150 \quad 250$$

$$5 \quad 4 \quad 3 \quad 2 \quad 1$$

$$1 \quad 0 \quad 1 \quad 0 \quad 1 \quad 0$$

7.   Enter $\iota 3 \star \iota 3$. Account for the error message.

8.   Write an *APL* expression to generate a vector of fifty 1's.

9.   Rewrite each of the following statements without parentheses:

$$^-1 + (- / (\iota 5)) \times 2$$

$$+ / (\iota 5) - 1$$

$$+ / ((\iota 5) + 1) = 5$$

$$+ / 0 = (\iota 5) = 6$$

10.   Write functions that would approximate each of the following series to N terms:

A) $1 \; - \; \dfrac{1}{2} \; + \; \dfrac{1}{3} \; - \; \dfrac{1}{4} \; + \; \cdots$

B) $\dfrac{1}{0!} \; + \; \dfrac{x^1}{1!} \; + \; \dfrac{x^2}{2!} \; + \; \cdots$

11.   Write an *APL* expression that yields 1 if the array A is a scalar, 0 otherwise.

12.   What is the difference between $\rho A , \rho B$ and $(\rho A) , \rho B$ for two vectors A and B?

13.   Write an *APL* instruction to cause three 2's to be printed out in a vertical column.

14.   Select 100 random positive integers, none of which is greater than 10.

15.   A) Construct a matrix whose shape is always random and not greater than 8, made up of elements which are random positive integers not greater than 150.
B) Modify your result for A) to make the upper bound for the elements itself a random number less than 300.

16.   Use the ravel, reshape and catenate functions to reshape a 5   4 matrix A and a 4   7 matrix B into a 1 2 4 result R such that the first five rows of R contain A and the last seven rows contain B.

17.   This chapter introduces the function E as part of a simulated calculator. Suppose the function E were dyadic. How could you tell the difference between it and, say, $6E8$ in scaled notation?

18. Make the scalar S a vector without using the ravel function.

19. Construct a table of sines of angles from 0 to $\circ \div 2$ radians in steps of $\circ \div 2\,0$ radians.

20. Show how to find, in **APL**, the sum of the alternate elements in ιN, beginning with the second.

21. How do you set up an "empty" matrix with, say, 5 columns?

22. Express each of the following numbers in **APL** and determine which is the smallest:

A) $\dfrac{321{,}400}{\sqrt{27.8}} - \dfrac{17}{.00065}$

B) $\log_5 \dfrac{1}{\sqrt[4]{.0000068}}$

C) $\sqrt[9]{(32{,}200)^2}$

23. Find the sum of the first 30 terms in the series $1 - \frac{1}{2} + \frac{1}{4} - \frac{1}{6} + \frac{1}{8} - \ldots$

24. Create an $N \times N$ matrix with an arbitrary vector of elements V along the major diagonal and 0's elsewhere.

25. Use the outer product to form the $4\ 4$ matrix

$$
\begin{array}{cccc}
1 & 1 & 1 & 1 \\
2 & 2 & 2 & 2 \\
3 & 3 & 3 & 3 \\
4 & 4 & 4 & 4 \\
\end{array}
$$

26. You owe a kind-hearted loan shark $10,000 and are required to pay as interest 1/2 of this sum the first year. Because of the lender's generosity, the second year you pay only 1/2 of the first year's repayment, and during the third year, only 1/2 of the second year's payment, etc. in perpetuity. There being no discount for prepayment, how much would you have to repay to wipe out the debt?

Chapter 17:
Character data

Have you noticed that except for variable and function names the input and output that we have been working with has been entirely numerical? You have undoubtedly observed that when by mistake you enter alphabetic characters without a specification you get a *VALUE ERROR*. It hasn't been a real problem up to now, but what if we want to label our results or associate some message with them? We need a way to have such *literal* or *character* output alone or mixed with numeric information. This chapter will introduce you to **APL**'s methods of handling such nonnumeric data.

Some examples

In 1 *CLASS*, which should now be loaded,

```
      )LOAD 1 CLASS
SAVED  15.02.39 04/15/74
```

the function *RECT* shows the need for some kind of identification for the output:

```
      ∇RECT[☐]∇
    ∇ L RECT H
[1]    2×L+H
[2]    L HYP H
[3]    L×H
    ∇
      3 RECT 4
14
5
12
```

The three lines of output are the perimeter, diagonal and area (in that order) of the rectangle whose sides are 3 and 4. But we had to look back at the function to see what each of the numbers represented. Even if you had used comment statements, they wouldn't help identify the printed results.

You should now turn to the function *GEO2* in 1 *CLASS*, which is similar to *RECT*. Try

```
      3 GEO2 4
PERIMETER IS:
14
AREA IS:
12
DIAGONAL IS:
5
```

This is more like it, so let's open up the function and look at it:

```
      ∇GEO2[□]∇
   ∇ L GEO2 H;X
[1]   X←' IS: '
[2]   'PERIMETER',X
[3]   2×L+H
[4]   'AREA',X
[5]   L×H
[6]   'DIAGONAL',X
[7]   L HYP H
   ∇
```

Line 1 looks like nothing we've done so far. It introduces a new use for the quote sign, namely, to enclose characters. As a matter of fact, not only are there obvious alphabetic characters I and S, but also a colon used as a punctuation mark, and even blank spaces at either end.

APL interprets each of these, including the blanks, as a character of literal information. But it does more than that. Since in line 2 catenation is used between the set of characters on the left and those on the right (stored in X), there is a strong suggestion that such characters are elements of an array, in this case of rank 1. It's a fancy way of calling what is between the quotes a vector. However, since we could conceivably have a table of characters, the rank will depend, as with numerical information, on the shape. X here is a vector of length 5.

Continuing down the function, lines 4 and 6 catenate the words $AREA$ and $DIAGONAL$, respectively, to X, which consists of the characters forming the word IS and the colon. Since even the spaces are counted as elements of the literal vector, you should be able to see why at least the one before IS was necessary.

You don't have to be in function definition mode to use literals. For instance:

```
      A←'HELLO '
```

Again, notice the space after the O. Counting the space, it's a vector of length 6:

```
      ρA
6
```

We can do some rather cute things with these literals. As an example, if we specify

```
      B←'HOW ARE YOU'
      B
HOW ARE YOU
```

then catenation forms the message

```
      A,B
HELLO HOW ARE YOU
```

Now back to business. Suppose we had a family of rectangles we wanted information about:

```
      1 3 GEO2 1 4
PERIMETER IS:
4 14
AREA IS:
1 12
DIAGONAL IS:
1.414213562 5
```

Our answers are OK, but the grammar is a little peculiar. What would be nice to have is identification to match the output. Specifically, the labels should be followed by ARE or IS, depending on the number of elements in the arguments. Let's therefore explore the function $GEO3$:

```
      1 3 GEO3 1 4
PERIMETERS ARE:
4 14
AREAS ARE:
1 12
DIAGONALS ARE:
1.414213562 5
```

If we give only a single rectangle to this function, we obtain

```
      3 GEO3 4
PERIMETER IS:
14
AREA IS:
12
DIAGONAL IS:
5
```

$GEO3$ does exactly what we want it to, and changes the alphabetic information to fit the conditions of the problem:

```
      ∇GEO3[□]∇
    ∇ L GEO3 H;X;FLAG
[1]   FLAG←((ρ,L)>1)∨(ρ,H)>1
[2]   X←((4×~FLAG)ρ' IS:'),(6×FLAG)ρ'S ARE:'
[3]   'PERIMETER',X
[4]   2×L+H
[5]   'AREA',X
[6]   L×H
[7]   'DIAGONAL',X
[8]   L HYP H
    ∇
```

The first thing to note is the presence of the two local variables X and $FLAG$. Looking at line 1, if the number of elements in either L or H is greater than 1, then the variable $FLAG$ is set to 1. Otherwise it is 0. If the result of line 1 is 1 (i.e., we ask for information about more than one rectangle), $6 \times FLAG$ is 6 and 6ρ 'S $ARE:$ ' is simply the characters S $ARE:$. At the same time $\sim FLAG$ would be 0 and 4×0 is 0, so that 0ρ ' $IS:$ ' results in an empty vector and thus no characters are printed. When catenated, the effect is just S $ARE:$. You should be able to figure out for yourself what happens in this line if $FLAG$ is 0. Line 2 tells the system to pick up $IS:$ or S $ARE:$, depending on the length of the arguments. The rest of the function is like $GEO2$. Finally, here is some food for thought before leaving this function: Why must the arguments L and H in line 1 be raveled before ρ is applied to them?

Mixed output

You have probably wondered by now why in both *GEO2* and *GEO3* the numeric and alphabetic information was placed on separate lines when a more natural format would call for them to be on the same line, as, for example, *PERIMETERS ARE:* 4 14.

However, when we try to catenate characters and numeric values, we run into trouble, as seen in the following illustration:

```
      A←'GIVE '
      F←' DOLLARS'
      B←15
      B,F
DOMAIN ERROR
      B,F
      ∧
```

Since the comma is useless for this purpose, we need another mechanism for putting together mixed output. The semicolon is used for this. It has already been introduced in Chapter 13 to separate local variables in the header of a function. For mixed output, the semicolon again serves in effect as a separator:

```
      A;B
GIVE 15
      A;B;F
GIVE 15 DOLLARS
```

Since practice makes perfect, as an exercise you should now go back and modify *GEO2* and *GEO3* to contain lines of mixed output as appropriate.

Mixed output is useful for printing only. The results cannot be assigned to a variable or used as arguments. Compared to commas, semicolons are strong separators, that is, expressions between semicolons are executed independently. Note the following statement:

```
      10ρ'X';'TEST'
XXXXXXXXXXTEST
```

and contrast it with

```
      10ρ'X','TEST'
XTESTXTEST
```

Complete *APL* expressions can be executed between semicolons. This includes the assignment of variables, but the order of execution may differ from implementation to implementation. You should therefore avoid such uses of mixed output.

The concept of mixed output has numerous ramifications which will be explored in depth in Chapter 21, at which time new *APL* primitives will be introduced to make many formatting problems more tractable.

Specifying character variables

It is important that when literal information is entered, *both* quotes appear. Otherwise you have an open quote, not unlike the problem we faced before on page 32 where in forming the symbol for the combination function we failed to line up the quote and period.

To review this point, let's look at the following examples. Make the assignment

        D←'ENGINE   (RETURN)
'@

Here the ***APL*** system supplied the closing quote on the next line and unlocked the keyboard. If we press RETURN again, we will find that *D* has been assigned the literal vector *ENGINE*.

How many characters are in *D*?

        ρ*D*
7

Since *ENGINE* has only six characters, where did the seventh come from? A display of *D* may help us answer this question:

        D
ENGINE

        @

A little thought should convince you that the carriage return was entered (automatically) as a character, accounting for the extra blank line in the display. This closing carriage return, which was supplied by the ***APL*** system, is treated just as though the user had entered it.

Here is an example:

        H←'ENGINE   (RETURN)
'
v   (BACKSPACE and ATTN)
ERING'   (entered at keyboard)
        H
ENGINE
ERING
        ρ*H*
12

Occasionally a word to be entered has an apostrophe in it. Since this is the same character as the quote, how can it be handled? For example, look at the following attempted assignment:

        W←'ISN'T'   (RETURN)
'@   (RETURN)
SYNTAX ERROR
        '
        ^

Since this doesn't help us at all, ***APL*** uses a double quote to get the apostrophe in:

        W←'ISN''T'
        W
ISN'T

Functions that work with characters

What about all the functions we've studied so far? Do they work with literals? Let's try some and see:

```
      A←'X'
      B←'Y'
      A+B
DOMAIN ERROR
      A+B
      ^
      A<B
DOMAIN ERROR
      A<B
      ^
```

These functions make no sense operating on literals because literals aren't orderable. Indeed, most of the primitive functions would behave similarly. But consider

```
      A=B
0
      A≠B
1
```

Here we are asking the system to compare each element of the left argument A with the corresponding element of B. There is only one element on each side, and they don't match, so we get the responses shown.

A more sophisticated way in which = can be used is shown in the following example, which asks how many occurrences of the letter E there are in the vector D:

```
      D←'ENGINEERING'
      'E'=D
1 0 0 0 0 1 1 0 0 0 0
      +/'E'=D
3
```

Another function which works with a literal argument is the dyadic ρ, which isn't surprising since all it does is reshape the argument:

```
      ALF←'ABCDEFGHIJKLMNOPQRSTUVWXYZ'
      4 6ρALF
ABCDEF
GHIJKL
MNOPQR
STUVWX
```

We can create all kinds of interesting literal arrays this way. Here is another example in which the nonblank contents of the lines are of varying lengths:

```
      FURN←4 6ρ'DESKS CHAIRSTABLESFILES '
      4 6ρFURN
DESKS
CHAIRS
TABLES
FILES
```

In such cases you should be extra careful to pad each prospective line with the correct number of blanks to insure a proper display. Otherwise the consequences can be ludicrous:

```
      4 6ρ'DESKSCHAIRSTABLESFILES'
DESKSC
HAIRST
ABLESF
ILESDE
```

In workspace 1 *CLASS*, you will find the function *ROWNAMES* convenient for making character matrices without having to count the number of characters between words. *ROWNAMES* makes use of a number of **APL** features to be described later, but because it is so handy for building matrices of names or titles, we are introducing it here.

```
        )COPY 1 CLASS ROWNAMES
SAVED   15.02.39 04/15/74
        ∇ ROWNAMES [□]∇
    ∇ Z←S ROWNAMES T;A;B;R
[1]    B←T=1↑T←,T
[2]    A←(+/B)↑▼B ◊ R←⌈/A←(1↓A,(?1)+ρT)-1+A
[3]    Z←((ρA),R)ρ(,A∘.≥(~?1)+ιR)\(~B)/T ◊ R←ρZ
[4]    →BY×R∨.≠S←2↑(2× 3 2 ⊥(ρ,S),0=¯1↑S)↓((¯2↑0,S),R,-R)
       [2 3 2 3 2 1 2 5 0 1 0 5 +?1]
[5]    BY:Z←(X×1 ¯1 ⌈×S)↑Z ◊ →OUT×0>¯1↑S
[6]    OUT:Z←(1-(Z=' ')⊥1)⌽Z
    ∇
        FURN2←(ι0)ROWNAMES '/DESKS/CHAIRS/TABLES/FILES'
        ρFURN2
4 6
        FURN2
DESKS
CHAIRS
TABLES
FILES
```

The right argument is a character vector. Its first character is arbitrary (we used the /) and is called the *delimiter* (separator). The resulting matrix will have as many rows as there are delimiters. The left argument can be a variety of things. If it is an empty vector, as above, the result contains as many columns as the longest character sequence between delimiters. If it is a scalar positive integer, then the number of columns is chopped (or extended with blanks):

```
        4 ROWNAMES '⌿DESKS⌿CHAIRS⌿TABLES⌿FILES'
DESK
CHAI
TABL
FILE
```

If the left argument is a scalar zero, each column is as long as the longest character sequence between delimiter characters (here a blank is used), but each row is *right-justified*:

```
        0 ROWNAMES ' DESKS CHAIRS TABLES FILES'
 DESKS
CHAIRS
TABLES
 FILES
```

If the left argument is a negative number, then that sets the number of columns with each row again right-justified:

```
        ¯9 ROWNAMES '/DESKS/CHAIRS/TABLES/FILES'
    DESKS
   CHAIRS
   TABLES
    FILES
```

Finally, if the left argument is a two-element vector, the first element sets the number of rows (positive from the top or negative from the bottom), while the second element controls the configuration of the columns, as in the scalar left arguments described above:

```
      ‾3 5 ROWNAMES '/DESKS/CHAIRS/TABLES/FILES'
CHAIR
TABLE
FILES
```

More hints about literals

Up to this point we have used only alphabetic characters, punctuation marks, spaces and the carriage return as literals. Actually, any keyboard character, including overstruck ones, can be employed in this manner. This can lead to some mystifying situations with numbers:

```
      T←'10'
      T
10
```

But T doesn't have the value 10:

```
      T=10
0 0
```

Neither element of T matches the 10 on the right! If this is puzzling to you, remember that T is a *vector* of two elements, 1 and 0, neither of which obviously is equal to 10.

One other point about character entry. Look at

```
      ρ'ABC'
3
      ρ'AB'
2
      ρ'A'
@
```

This means that a single character in **APL** is considered to be a scalar, and to make it a vector we would have to ravel it:

```
      ρ,'A'
1
```

Don't make the common mistake of putting the comma inside the quotes. Why?

And finally, look at

```
      ρ''
0
```

'' is an empty character vector, just as ι0 is an empty numeric vector.

PROBLEMS

1.   DRILL. Specify $X \leftarrow 'MISSISSIPPI'$ and $Y \leftarrow 'RIVER'$

$'ABCDE' = 'BBXDO'$	$1 \ 2 < 'MP'$	$\rho\rho AL \leftarrow 3 \ 3\rho 'ABCDEFGHI'$
$\rho V \leftarrow '3172'$	$\rho X, Y$	$X = 'S'$
$(\rho V)\rho V$	$+/X = 'S'$	$+/'P' = X$
$3172 = V$	$+/X \neq 'S'$	$+/(X,' ',Y) \neq 'S'$
X, Y	$X,' ',Y$	$\vee/X = 'R'$

2.   Here is a record of executions with an unknown vector D:

```
        D
        @
       ρD
15
        5×D
DOMAIN ERROR
        5×D
        ^
        ' '=D
1 1 1 1 1 1 1 1 1 1 1 1 1 1 1 1
```

What is D?

3.   Define a function F which takes a single argument A and prints its shape, rank and number of elements with appropriate descriptive messages. Assume rank $A \geq 1$.

4.   Show how to print 1- and 2-digit positive integers I so that 1-digit integers are indented one space and the 2-digit integers begin at the left margin.

5.   Copy the functions HYP and $GEO3$ in $1 \ CLASS$. Open up the function and direct control to line $[0.5]$. Use the comment symbol ⍝ on this line and the next to write a message describing what the function does. Then close out the function, display it and execute it. Do comments introduced in this manner affect execution?

6.   The matrix $GR3$ contains the grade records (A, B, C, D and F) of 25 students in a class, with the first row listing the number of A's received by each student, the second row the number of B's, etc. Each course represented in the is three credits. A similar similar matrix $GR2$ records grades for two-credit courses, and $GR1$ for one-credit courses. Write a program to calculate the grade point average for each student and for the class. (The grade point average is computed by multiplying 4 times the number of A credits, 3 times the number of B credits, etc., adding them up and dividing by the total number of credits earned.)

Chapter 18:
Mixed functions for ordering and selecting

Ranking

One of the points stressed at the end of the last chapter was that literal characters are unorderable, that is, it makes no sense to say, for example, that the letter X is less than the letter Y. Yet there are clearly times when ordering is desirable, primarily for sorting and selection purposes. Dictionaries and telephone books would be impossible to use if words or names weren't listed in some order.

To see how this can be done in **APL**, let's first get a clean workspace and specify X as shown:

```
      )CLEAR
CLEAR WS
      X←'ABCDEFGHIJK'
```

Now try

```
      Xι'CAFE'
3  1  6  5
```

This dyadic use of ι (called *ranking* or *index of*) is an interesting one. The result has four elements, the same as the length of the right argument, and it isn't too hard to tell what they stand for. C is the *third* character in X , A the *first*, F the *sixth*, and E the *fifth*.

Suppose there is no match, as in

```
      Xι'CAFYE'
3  1  6  12  5
```

All the characters except the Y can be matched. For that the system returns 12. But since there are only 11 characters in the left argument,

```
      ρX
11
```

then it should be clear that the function returns a value one greater than the number of characters in the left argument. If we were to try

```
        Xι'CAXYXE'
3  1  12  12  12   5
```

we see that this time both the X 's and the Y result in 1 2. This returning of an index number one greater than the number of elements on the left is characteristic of the dyadic iota when there is no match.

It is important to note that when characters are repeated in the right argument, the index numbers aren't used up. The *first* occurrence in the left argument is returned, with the index values of subsequent occurrences not appearing in the result. For example, let's make the assignment

```
        W←'AARDVARK'
        ρW
8
```

and we ask where in W is W found:

```
        WιW
1  1  3  4  5  1  3  8
```

The first letter in $AARDVARK$ is matched against the left argument and A is found first in position 1, so that 1 is recorded. Then the second A is matched and is found on the left again in position 1, giving us a second 1 in the result. R is found in position 3 on the left and 3 is recorded, etc. From this you can infer that a sequence like 1 2 3 4 5 6 7 8 would be returned only if no letters were repeated.

What if the right argument happens to be a matrix?

```
        A←3  2ρ10×ι6
        A
10  20
30  40
50  60
        B←30  10  40  20  50
        BιA
2  4
1  3
5  6
```

The shape of the result is the same as that of the right argument, but the left argument must be a vector.

Indexing

Back now to X. If for

```
        X
ABCDEFGHIJK
        Xι'CAFE'
3  1  6  5
```

converts the characters $CAFE$ into the integers 3 1 6 5 (called a *mapping*), it is perfectly reasonable to ask if there is any way we can change the integers back into characters. In **APL** this is done by the *indexing* function, also referred to as *subscripting*:

```
        X[3  1  6  5]
CAFE
```

This expression is usually read as "X sub 3 1 6 5." Note that the brackets, not parentheses, are used.

Any valid **APL** expression can be used for subscripting. For instance, execute

```
      X[X⍳'CAFE']
CAFE
      X[2 5⍴3 1 8 9 4 2 10 6 7 5]
CAHID
BJFGE
      X[4⍴3]
CCCC
```

The result has the shape of the expression in the brackets. But if we try to execute the following, we get an *INDEX ERROR*:

```
      X[X⍳'CAFYE']
INDEX ERROR
      X[X⍳'CAFYE']
      ∧
```

To avoid an error message, the expression in brackets must refer only to left argument indices that exist. In the last example, the character *Y* is not found in the variable *X*. *X* has 11 characters, and if we were to ask for

```
      X[12]
INDEX ERROR
      X[12]
      ∧
```

the **APL** system can't answer the question because there is no twelfth position. This isn't quite the same situation we had in ranking, where the result returned for an unidentifiable right argument element was one more than the number of elements in the left argument. In that case the response is the system's way of telling us that the character in question was not to be found on the left. Thus, indexing and index of, are inverse operations, provided that each element on the right is also to be found in the left argument.

Not only does indexing have a different form from the other functions, it is also unique in being the only function that can appear on the left side of the specification arrow. For example, suppose we want to change the character *D* in *X* above to the character *?*:

```
      X[4]←'?'
      X
ABC?EFGHIJK
```

The substitution has taken place. More generally, elements can be rearranged by indexing. The following illustration shows such a change:

```
      X[5 6]←X[6 5]
      X
ABC?FEGHIJK
```

If no indices are entered, every element of the array is respecified:

```
      X[]←'T'
      X
TTTTTTTTTTT
```

Both ranking and indexing can be used with numerical as well as literal arrays. For instance, say we are given the heights (in inches) of five students:

```
      L←51 63 60 62 59 62
```

What is the position of the student who is 63 inches tall?

        $L \iota 63$
2

If the third student's height had been entered incorrectly, and should have been 61 instead of 60 inches, the change can be made easily by

        $L[3] \leftarrow 61$
        L
51 63 61 62 59 62

The height of the *first* student (why only the first?) who is 62 inches tall can be changed to 65 inches:

        $L[L \iota 62] \leftarrow 65$
51 63 61 65 59 62

Indexing matrices

To illustrate indexing on a two-dimensional array, we'll first define a matrix M:

        $M \leftarrow 2\ 4 \rho 2\ 5\ 6\ 1\ 4\ 2\ 9\ 3$
        M
  2   5   6   1
  4   2   9   3

To specify any element of this array requires two numbers, one to tell the row and the other the column in which the element is located. Suppose we want the element in the second row and fourth column. The expression

        $M[2\ 4]$
RANK ERROR
        $M[2\ 4]$
          ∧

doesn't work because the two elements of the expression in the brackets refer to two different coordinates of the array M. We get a *RANK ERROR* message because we have failed to take into account that M is of rank 2, not rank 1.

What is needed here is a separator for the row number and column number. You'll not be surprised to find that very handy symbol, the semicolon, again used for this purpose:

        $M[2;4]$
3

More than one element can be specified at a time, like the second and fourth elements of the second row or the first and second elements of the second column:

        $M[2;2\ 4]$
2 3
        $M[1\ 2;2]$
5 2

There is a shorthand way of specifying all the elements along a particular coordinate, namely, by not typing any indices of the coordinate in question. This is an extension to two dimensions of a previous example, $X[\ ] \leftarrow 'T'$. Our last problem could have been written more compactly as

```
      M[;2]
5  2
```

which selects all the elements of the second column. To select all the elements of the first row, type

```
      M[1;]
2  5  6  1
```

This implies that to get all of *M*, we could use

```
      M[;]
2  5  6  1
4  2  9  3
```

which is perhaps a bit wasteful, but consistent.

We have mentioned that subscripting could be used on the left of the specification arrow. This works with matrices as well as vectors, as shown by the following examples:

```
      M
2  5  6  1
4  2  9  3
      M[2;3]←90
      M
2   5   6   1
4   2  90   3
      M[1;]←M[1;]×2
      M
4  10  12   2
4   2  90   3
      FURN←4 6ρ'DESKS CHAIRSTABLESFILES '
      FURN
DESKS
CHAIRS
TABLES
FILES
      FURN[3;]←'LAMPS '
      FURN
DESKS
CHAIRS
LAMPS
FILES
```

Now for some miscellaneous but useful observations about indexing. When indexing a matrix, there must be one semicolon to separate the row and column indices. Since vectors are one-dimensional, no semicolon is needed. Scalars, being dimensionless, cannot be indexed. And the shape of the result in indexing is the same as the shape you would get by taking outer products among the indices. This may not seem significant to you, but it does explain the following:

```
      X←2 3ρι6
      X[1 2;3]
3  6
      ρX[1 2;3]                          ρ1 2∘.+3
2                              2
      X[1 2;,3]
3
6
      ρX[1 2;,3]                         ρ1 2∘.+,3
2  1                             2  1
```

Previously you saw that *APL* permitted multiple assignments. If you are using this feature extensively, you should observe and remember this example:

```
X←5ρ0
Z←X[2 3 4]←1
X
0 1 1 1 0
Z
1
```

The result may differ, depending on the implementation.

Compression

Another *APL* function used for selecting specific elements of an array is *compression*. Given the previously defined vector *L*,

```
L
51 63 61 65 59 62
```

we could find the heights of the second and third students with the expression

```
L[2 3]
63 61
```

We can also select with the following operation:

```
0 1 1 0 0 0/L
63 61
```

which can be read as the "0 1 1 0 0 0 compression of *L*." The same symbol, the slash /, is used for both compression and reduction, but the difference is that instead of having a function symbol before the slash, the left argument consists entirely of 0 's and 1 's. Where there is a 0 in the left argument, the corresponding element on the right isn't picked up. The only elements returned are in those positions where there is a 1 to match it on the left. This means that for vector arguments the lengths of both must be the same.

To illustrate a practical use of compression, here is a bank account problem similar to one introduced at the beginning of Chapter 6. For *A*, a vector of accounts in dollars,

```
A←3 ¯4 5 0 ¯6
```

the instruction

```
A<0
0 1 0 0 1
```

produces a vector with 1's in the positions of the offenders and 0's elsewhere. This is made to order for compression,

```
(A<0)/A
¯4 ¯6
```

and we have extracted from *A* only the negative elements.

We can squeeze even a little more information out of this. For instance, the instruction

```
        (A<0)/ιρA
2  5
```

tells us that accounts 2 and 5 are the guilty parties and should be flagellated, dunned or whatever, depending on the circumstances.

Keep in mind that the left argument must contain 0's and 1's only:

```
        2 3/5 6
DOMAIN ERROR
        2 3 / 5 6
              ∧
```

Both arguments normally must have the same length, unless all or none of the elements are desired. In this case we need only a single 1 or 0:

```
        A←'ABCDEF'
        1/A
ABCDEF
        0/A

        @
```

If the lengths don't agree, an error message results:

```
        1 0 1 0/A
LENGTH ERROR
        1 0 1 0 /A
              ∧
```

In 1 *CLASS* the function *CMP* uses compression to compare two scalar arguments for size and prints a message stating whether the left argument is less than, equal to or greater than the right argument. Use the *COPY* command to get it into your active workspace:

```
        )COPY 1 CLASS CMP
SAVED   15.02.39 04/15/74
```

Let's try it out on a few examples:

```
        3 CMP 5
LESS
        5 CMP 3
GREATER
        5 CMP 5
EQUAL
```

Here is what *CMP* looks like:

```
        ∇CMP[□]∇
    ∇ A CMP B
[1]    ((A>B)/'GREATER'),((A=B)/'EQUAL'),((A<B)/'LESS'
    ∇
```

It doesn't return an explicit result (since we wouldn't be apt to have any further use for the result). Notice the practical use for catenation here operating on literals, not unlike line 2 of the function *GEO3* on page 149. Starting from the right on line 1, we pick up either all of the literal vector *LESS* or none of it, depending on whether *A* is less than *B*. The vectors *EQUAL* and *GREATER* are treated similarly and catenated. Since only one of the three conditions can possibly hold at any one time, we are actually catenating two empty vectors to a nonempty literal vector to produce the desired result.

There are other ways of doing this, two of which will be considered in Chapter 22. The function $CMPN$ (also in 1 $CLASS$) uses indexing and avoids compression altogether. It is further evidence that the richness of the **APL** language is reflected in the wealth of different algorithms to do the same thing:

```
      ∇CMPN[□]∇
    ∇ A CMPN B
[1]   (3 7ρ'LESS   EQUAL   GREATER')[2+×A-B;]
    ∇
      3 CMPN 5
LESS
      5 CMPN 5
EQUAL
      5 CMPN 3
GREATER
```

When using compression with two-dimensional arrays, you have to keep one additional piece of information in mind: the left argument must have as many elements as the number of elements in the coordinate across which compression occurs. Here is an example in which the third element of the second coordinate (columns) is elided:

```
      X←3 4ρ'ABCDEFGHIJKLM'
      1 1 0 1/X
ABD
EFH
IJL
```

To remove a row, compress the first coordinate using $/$:

```
      FURN
DESKS
CHAIRS
LAMPS
FILES
      1 1 0 1/FURN
DESKS
CHAIRS
FILES
```

The use of compression here parallels that of reduction on matrices (Chapter 7).

Formally, the conditions for compression of matrices are as follows:

If $C←A/B$, then

1. A must be a vector or a scalar consisting of all 0's and 1's.
2. $ρA$ must be $(ρB)[1]$ for $/$, or $(ρB)[2]$ for $/$.
3. $ρρC$ is $ρρB$.

Expansion

Just as compression gives us a way to get a subset of an array, so there exists also in **APL** a function called *expansion*, which allows us to insert additional elements. To illustrate its use, specify

```
      A←'ABCDEFG'
```

It has 7 elements:

```
      ρA
7
```

The symbol for expansion is \, the backward pointing slash, on the same key as the compression symbol in the lower right corner of the keyboard. Here are some examples:

```
      1 0 1 0 0 1 1 1 1 1\A
A B  CDEFG
      1 0 0 1 0 1\323
323 0 0 323 0 323
      1 0 0 1 0 1\3 2 3
3 0 0 2 0 3
```

The examples show that where 0 appears in the left argument, a blank (for literals) or 0 (for numeric arrays) is inserted in the result, which otherwise is identical to the right argument. A scalar right argument is extended to match the length of the nonzero part of the left argument. Note also that the number of 1's in the left argument must be the same as the dimension of the right argument, i.e., we have to pick up *all* of the right argument.

With two-dimensional arrays, the treatment is similar to that for compression. For the X previously defined,

```
      1 1 1 0 1\X
ABC D
EFG H
IJK L
```

will insert a column of blanks between the third and fourth columns of the original array, while to make room for an additional row between the existing first and second rows of $FURN$, execute

```
      FURN←1 0 1 1 1\FURN
      FURN
DESKS

CHAIRS
LAMPS
FILES
```

The expression

```
      FURN[2;]←'TABLES'
```

replaces the second row with nonblank characters as shown:

```
      FURN
DESKS
TABLES
CHAIRS
LAMPS
FILES
```

Finally, here is a summary of the conditions governing the use of the expansion function on matrices:

If $C \leftarrow A \setminus B$, then
1. A must be a vector consisting of all 0's and 1's.
2. $(+/A)$ must be $(\rho B)[1]$ for ⍀ or $(\rho B)[2]$ for \.
3. (ρC) is $(\rho A),(\rho B)[2]$ for ⍀ and $(\rho B)[1],\rho A$ for \.

PROBLEMS

1. DRILL. Specify $A \leftarrow 0\ \ ^-5\ \ ^-8\ \ 6.2\ \ 15\ \ ^-2\ \ 25$
   $B \leftarrow 1\ \ 0\ \ 0\ \ 1\ \ 0\ \ 1\ \ 1$
   $C \leftarrow {}'ABCDEFGHIJKLMNOPQRSTUVWXYZ\ ?'$
   $M \leftarrow 3\ \ 4 \rho \iota 12$

$(2 < \iota 5)/\iota 5$	$M[2;3\ 1]$	$1\ 0\ 1 \neq M$
B/A	$\rho A[2\ 4\ 7]$	$A[1] + A[2\ 3\ 4] \times A[7]$
$A[\rho A], B[\ ^-2 + \rho B]$	$1\ 1\ 0\ 1 \backslash 'TWO'$	$1\ 0\ 0\ 1\ 1\ 1 \backslash M$
$(3\ 2\ 7)[2\ 1\ 3]$	$A[8]$	$A[0 \rho 3]$
$A[3\ 6] \leftarrow 2E5\ \ 4E^-4$	$A \iota \lceil /A$	$B \backslash 2\ 3\ 4\ 5$
$C[1\ 16\ 12\ 27\ 9\ 19\ 27\ 1\ 12\ 7\ 15\ 18\ 9\ 20\ 8\ 13\ 9\ 3]$		

2. Specify $D \leftarrow {}^-2.1\ 4\ 1.9\ 0\ ^-1\ ^-4\ ^-1.4\ .7\ 2.5\ 2$. Select those components which are

   A) less than .5
   B) positive
   C) equal in magnitude to 4

   D) negative and greater than $^-1$
   E) equal to 2
   F) less than 1 and greater than or equal to $^-2$

3. Define a monadic function to insert the character $\circ$ between each pair of adjacent elements in vector V.

4. For any arbitrary vector V write a function $INCR$ to compute increments between adjacent elements.

5. For mathematicians only: Obtain the area under the curve $Y = 3X^2$ between X_1 and X_2 by breaking it up into rectangles of width I in that interval. Hint: First define F to compute $3 \times X * 2$.

6. Write a program $WITHIN$ to select from a vector W those elements which lie within an interval R on either side of the average of W.

7. Write an **APL** expression to select those elements in a vector which are integers.

8. Define a function IN to tell what percent of the elements in a vector A lie within the interval B±C.

9. Construct an expression that selects the largest element in a three-element vector V and prints a 1 if it exceeds the sum of the remaining two elements, 0, otherwise.

10. Show how to select the elements with even indices in a vector Y.

11. You are given a vector X whose components are all different and arranged in ascending order. Write a program to insert a given scalar S into the appropriate place in the sequence so that the result is still in ascending order. Be sure that your function is able to handle the case where S is identical to some element in X.

12. What is the difference between

   A) $\iota A[2]$ and $(\iota A)[2]$ for some integer A
   B) $\rho M, \rho N$ and $(\rho M), \rho N$ for $M \leftarrow 1\ 2$ and $N \leftarrow 3\ 4$

13. Write an **APL** expression to pick up the last element of a vector V.

14. Why is $V[\ ^-1 + \iota \rho V]$ not executable?

15.   Write an **APL** expression which returns the index of the largest element in a vector W.

16.   Define a function to remove all duplicate elements from a vector.

17.   Write an **APL** expression to calculate the sum of the first eight elements of a vector Q (or all of them if the number of elements is less than eight).

18.   Write a program $SELECT$ which takes two arguments and will print that element in the left argument X whose position corresponds to the position of the largest element in the right argument Y.

19.   Construct **APL** expressions to insert for $V \leftarrow \iota N$ a zero

   A) between each two adjacent components of V
   B) before each even component of V
   C) after each odd component of V

20.   Write a function whose explicit result is all the factors of a given integer N (i.e., the integers which divide evenly into N).

21.   Write a program to convert a numeric literal with less than ten digits to a number, so that, for example, '1456' becomes 1456, and can be used like an ordinary number for further calculations.

22.   Define a function $COMFACT$ to print a list of common factors, if any, of two integers A and B.

23.   Define a monadic function which takes a literal argument and selects the longest word in it. Hint: look for the longest set of consecutive nonblank characters.

24.   What is the difference between $M[1;2]$ and $M[,1;,2]$?

25.   Write an **APL** expression to delete all occurrences of the letter A from a literal vector W.

26.   Show how to pick out the elements of a vector X which are A) divisible by 2 and/or 3, and B) divisible by neither 2 nor 3.

27.   A vector A contains the ages of all the employees of the Zee Manufacturing Company. Define an **APL** function that will yield the two ages which are closest to one another.

28.   For an arbitrary matrix, $M \leftarrow 5\ 5 \rho \iota 25$, show how to obtain

   A) the first three rows of M.
   B) the four elements in the upper left corner.
   C) the last two columns of M.
   D) the four corner elements.

29.   As production and sales manager for one of your company's products, you must decide how much to produce and what to charge for it. Your compensation is a salary plus 2% of the total receipts from the sale of the product. The company will not sell the product for less than $7.00. At the same time, if the price goes above $7.50 then the company's facilities are liable to be picketed by local consumer groups. The demand function for this product is Q=600-3.7P², where Q is the quantity sold and P the price charged. What price should you charge and how much should you produce to maximize your personal income? Assume you produced only enough to cover sales, and can vary the price only in 1¢ increments.

30.   The auditors of a progressive company find in a study of the cost of sampling information for accounting purposes that the total cost can be described by the expression $(.08 \times N) + 10.24 \div N \star .5$ where N is the number of items to be sampled, $.08 the unit cost of sampling an item and $10.24 the cost of a unit error in estimation. How many items should be sampled to minimize the total cost? Assume $N \leq 50$.

Chapter 19:
Still more mixed functions

We continue the discussion of the last chapter, covering several more mixed functions that alter the order of the elements of an array and let us make selections from among the elements.

Reversal

This mixed monadic function, the symbol for which is ϕ (upper shift O overstruck with upper shift M), *reverses* the order of the elements of an array:

```
      φ1 2 3 4
4 3 2 1
      φ'ABCDEFG'
GFEDCBA
```

Reversal of a scalar results in the same scalar:

```
      φ4
4
```

and, like logical negation, reversal is its own inverse:

```
      φφ'ABCDEFG'
ABCDEFG
```

When we come to reversal of matrices, it is sometimes easier to see what is happening with characters, so we'll specify a matrix X as follows:

```
      X←3 4ρ'ABCDEFGHIJKLM'
      X
ABCD
EFGH
IJKL
```

The reversal of this matrix is

```
      φX
DCBA
HGFE
LKJI
```

It reverses the order of the columns (i.e., acts across the last coordinate).

To reverse the first coordinate, the symbol ⊖ is used. This is formed by overstriking the large circle with the subtract sign (analogous to the use of the symbols ≠ and ↖ for reduction, compression and expansion):

```
      ⊖X
IJKL
EFGH
ABCD
```

Rotate

The symbols φ and ⊖ also have a dyadic use, and are called *rotate* or *rotation* when so employed. To get a feel for what they do, try

```
      2φ'ABCDEFG'
CDEFGAB
      4φ1 2 3 4 5 6 7
5 6 7 1 2 3 4
      0φ34 56 78
34 56 78
```

All the elements are rotated or shifted to the left by the number of places specified in the left argument.

Since we will be using the same vector of literals repeatedly, let's represent it by H. It has seven elements:

```
      ρH←'ABCDEFG'
7
```

What happens if we rotate H seven places?

```
      7φH
ABCDEFG
```

The result is H itself, which shouldn't surprise you at all. How about rotation by a number greater than the number of elements in the right argument, say eight?

```
      8φH
BCDEFGA
```

which is equivalent to

```
      1φH
BCDEFGA
```

and, in fact, 7 | 8 gives the number of places shifted. In general, if H is the right argument and L is the left argument, the shift is (ρH) | L places.

Can the left argument be negative? It would seem reasonable that a negative left argument ought to produce a shift to the right:

```
      ¯2φH
FGABCDE
```

The characters are moved to the right two places. Since 7 | ¯2 is 5, then ¯2φH should be the same as

```
      5φH
FGABCDE
```

To illustrate rotation on matrices, we'll use the same array *X* as before:

```
      X                        1φX                        1⊖X
ABCD                      BCDA                      EFGH
EFGH                      FGHE                      IJKL
IJKL                      JKLI                      ABCD
```

There is a more general way to use rotation, in which we can specify in vector form in the left argument how we wish to rotate each slice of a given coordinate. For example, suppose we want to move the first row rightward one position, the second row leftward three positions and the third row two positions to the left. This can be done with

```
      ¯1 3 2φX
DABC
HEFG
KLIJ
```

To rotate across the first coordinate of our matrix *X*, we need four elements in the left argument. The following example leaves the first column alone, moves the second column up one position, the third up two positions and the last up three positions:

```
      0 1 2 3⊖X
AFKD
EJCH
IBGL
```

Thus, if the right argument is a matrix, the left argument is either a scalar or a vector whose shape is the same as the number of elements in the coordinate over which the rotation is to take place.

Take and drop

Besides compression and indexing, there are two other versatile functions which help the user select portions of an array. Their behavior and syntax are best explained with a few well-chosen examples.

First let's examine the *take* function, ↑, (upper shift *Y*), with vector and scalar right arguments:

```
      V←8 5 3 9 ¯1 ¯4
      4↑V
8 5 3 9
      0↑V
@
      8↑V
8 5 3 9 ¯1 ¯4 0 0
      ¯1↑V
¯4
      ¯8↑V
0 0 8 5 3 9 ¯1 ¯4
      2 3↑5
5 0 0
0 0 0
```

If A is the left argument and is positive, $\uparrow$ selects the first A elements from the right argument. If A is negative, the last $|A$ elements are taken. When $|A$ is greater than ρV the result is V with sufficient 0's (or blanks for literals) on the right or left to make a vector of length A. A must be an integer or a vector of integers. With a vector left argument and a scalar right argument, $\uparrow$ returns an array whose shape is determined by the left argument and whose elements consist of zeros, except for the [1;1] element.

In the case of two-dimensional arrays, the elements of the left argument refer to what is to be taken across each coordinate as shown:

```
      M←3 4ρι12
      M                    2 3↑M             ¯2 3↑M            ¯4 ¯5↑M
  1   2   3   4        1 2 3            5   6   7        0   0   0   0   0
  5   6   7   8        5 6 7            9  10  11        0   1   2   3   4
  9  10  11  12                                         0   5   6   7   8
                                                        0   9  10  11  12
```

Drop, $\downarrow$, (upper shift U) behaves in much the same way, except that if A is the left argument, A elements are dropped instead of selected. As with *take*, A must be an integer or a vector of integers.

```
           0↓V
  8  5  3  9  ¯1  ¯4
           2↓V
  3  9  ¯1  ¯4
           8↓V
           @
          ¯3↓V
  8  5  3
```

Here are some illustrations with the matrix M defined earlier. The cross-hatched area shows what is dropped:

```
        M
  1  2  3  4
  5  6  7  8
  9 10 11 12
     2 3↓M
  12
```

```
        M
  1  2  3  4
  5  6  7  8
  9 10 11 12
     ¯2 1↓M
  2  3  4
```

Generally speaking, if A is the left argument and B the right, then the result C is such that (ρC) is $(\rho B)-|A$.

Membership

Earlier we encountered a number of functions (logicals, relationals) that yield only 0's and 1's as results. Another function that behaves similarly is *membership*, represented by the symbol ϵ (upper shift E). To see how it works, we'll ask the following question: Given a set of numbers, 3 1 6 1, which of these are members of the set 1 2 3 4 5?

What we are really asking is a series of questions which in **APL** could be stated as

```
      (∨/3=ι5),(∨/1=ι5),(∨/6=ι5),∨/1=ι5
  1 1 0 1
```

or, put more succinctly,

```
      ∨/3 1 6 1∘.=ι5
  1 1 0 1
```

The net result is the logical vector 1 1 0 1. Using the membership function on the terminal this is

          3 1 6 1ϵ1 2 3 4 5
1 1 0 1

Clearly the shape of the result must be the same as that of the left argument. Both arguments may be arrays of any rank whatever with this function, which is one less problem for you to worry about. Here are some examples with M as defined earlier:

          M
    1   2   3   4
    5   6   7   8
    9   10   11   12
          A←2 2ρ4 15 2 ¯3
          A
    4   15
    2   ¯3
          AϵM
    1 0
    1 0
          3 40 4ϵM
1 0 1

Next is a useful defined function employing expansion, compression and membership to automatically make a matrix of words from a literal vector, using either commas or blanks as delimiters. The right argument V is a literal vector. The function is a simpler version of $ROWNAMES$ on page 153.

```
      ∇  Z←CHARMAT V;A
[1]      V←(~A←Vϵ'  ,')/V←V,'  '
[2]      Z←(ρA)ρ(,A←A∘.≥ι⌈/0,A←(A≠0)/A←A-1+0,¯1↓A←A/ιρA)\V
      ∇
```

We have here deliberately violated our earlier warnings about incomprehensible lines so that it might serve as an object lesson to you not to sin likewise. You should try to rewrite the function in 3 to 5 lines to gain some insight into how it works.

Grade up and grade down

These two functions by themselves give the indices according to which we would have to select elements of a numeric vector to place them in order: ascending (*grade up*) or descending (*grade down*). The symbols used are the upper shift H and G overstruck with upper shift M, for grade up and grade down, respectively. Here are some examples:

          V←8 5 3 9 ¯1 ¯4
          ⍋V
6 5 3 2 1 4
          ⍒V
4 1 2 3 5 6

In the grade up of V the first element, 6, tells us that the sixth element of V should be taken first; the second element, 5, tells us to take the fifth element of V next, etc., to reorder V in ascending fashion.

If the elements happen to be duplicates, the indices of the duplicates are treated in the same way as the vector is searched from left to right:

```
        W←3  2  4  6  3  3
        ⍋W
2  1  5  6  3  4
```

Since the result tells us the order of the indices that should be chosen to sort out the elements ascending or descending, these functions give us a handy, quick way to produce an actual reordering:

```
        V[⍋V]
⁻4  ⁻1  3  5  8  9
        V[⍒V]
9  8  5  3  ⁻1  ⁻4
```

In present implementations of **APL**, grade up and grade down operate only on vectors. Hence, to reorder, say, the columns of a matrix, one of the selection functions (indexing, take, drop, compression) would have to be used to pick and sort each column in turn. More about the general technique in Chapter 22, since the procedure involves an iterative process.

Deal

The last mixed function to be considered in this chapter is the dyadic query, $?$, called *deal*, a few examples of which follow:

```
        3?8
3  7  4
        6?10
10  6  3  8  1  9
        6?6
3  5  2  4  1  6
        ⁻2?6
DOMAIN ERROR
        ⁻2?6
        ∧
        8?6
DOMAIN ERROR
        8?6
        ∧
```

The result is a vector which has the same length as the magnitude of the left argument. If A is the left argument and B the right, $A?B$ generates a random selection of A integers with *no duplication* from the population ιB. Both arguments must be positive scalars or vectors of length 1, with $A \le B$.

Some applications to cryptography

Because of the ease with which vectors of all sizes can be operated on, **APL** is quite suitable for the development of schemes for coding information (cryptography). We will explore some of these to illustrate a few practical uses of the functions introduced here and in Chapter 18.

Since we will need the alphabet repeatedly throughout this section, let's store it:

```
    ALF←'ABCDEFGHIJKLMNOPQRSTUVWXYZ'
```

To start, here's a function which makes a simple random letter substitution for a message M:

```
      M←'TOBEORNOTTOBETHATISTHEQUESTION'
   ∇ C←P SUBST M
[1]   ALF
[2]   ALF[P]
[3]   ' '
[4]   M
[5]   C←ALF[P[ALFιM]]
   ∇
      P←26?26
      P SUBST M
ABCDEFGHIJKLMNOPQRSTUVWXYZ
WGMKRUYTBZHCNXFDJLPEVOAQSI

TOBEORNOTTOBETHATISTHEQUESTION
EFGRFLXFEEFGRETWEBPETRJVRPEBFX
```

Grade up can be used to improve on the letter substitution by transposing the letters according to the following scheme:

```
   ∇P TRANSP M
[1]   T←⍋(ρM)ρP
[2]   M
[3]   M[T]
   ∇
      M←'SENDSUPPLIESTONEWLOCATIONATONCE'
      P TRANSP M
SENDSUPPLIESTONEWLOCATIONATONCE
ILSECNEOEAWDCLNNTTOOSENPUASTOPI
```

We now introduce a further complication by using a "key" to be added to the indices resulting from $ALF\iota M$, thus generating a new set of indices for application to ALF:

```
   ∇ K VIG M;C
[1]   N←ALFιM
[2]   M
[3]   C←1+26|N+(ρN)ρK
[4]   ALF[(ρN)ρK]
[5]   (ρM)ρ'‾'
[6]   ALF[C]
   ∇
      K←1 2 3
      M←'ENEMYWILLATTACKATDAWNWITHTENDIVISIONS'
      K VIG M
ENEMYWILLATTACKATDAWNWITHTENDIVISIONS
BCDBCDBCDBCDBCDBCDBCDBCDBCDBCDBCDBCDB
-------------------------------------
FPHNAZJNOBVWBENBVGBYQXKWIVHOFLWKVJQQT
```

Our last illustration catenates an arbitrary string of literal characters P onto the front end of a message M and drops off the excess characters from the back end, so that the resulting character string Q is the same length as M. The indices produced by $ALF\iota Q$ are added to those from $ALF\iota M$ and the results reduced with the residue function as before:

```
      ∇  P AUTO M;Q;R;S
[1]      R←ALFιQ←P,((ρM)-ρP)↑M
[2]      S←1+26|R←ALFιM
[3]      M
[4]      Q
[5]      (ρP)ρ'*'
[6]      ALF[S]
      ∇

      P←'GYLTZZY'
      P AUTO M
ENEMYWILLATTACKATDAWNWITHTENDIVISIONS
GYLTZZYENEMYWILLATTACKATDAWNWITHTENDI
*******
KLPFXVGPYEFRWKVLTWTWPGIMKTAAZQOPLMBQA
```

Another prepared drill exercise

In Chapter 9 the tutorial exercise *EASYDRILL* was introduced to give you practice in the **APL** functions discussed up to that point. We haven't yet exhausted all the functions so far implemented in the language, but, as before, it's worth taking a breather at this point to review what has been done. In the workspace 1 *APLCOURSE* there is another drill exercise called *TEACH*, which contains a larger variety of more difficult problems for you to work on.

Load this workspace now and execute *TEACH*. Indicate which functions you want practice in. Be sure at least this first time to include exercises in vectors of length 0 and reduction. Especially note the instructions pertaining to your responses for vectors of length 0 or 1. The format and way in which the problems are generated are the same as in *EASYDRILL*. You get three tries, then the answer is furnished and you are given another problem of the same kind. Typing *PLEASE* gives you the answer and another, similar problem. Typing *CHANGE* gives you the answer, followed by another problem, generally of a different type. Both *STOP* and *STOPSHORT* get you out of the exercise, but *STOP* gives you a record of your performance. Continue practicing at this point and at any subsequent time as your needs require and your schedule permits.

Below is a short sample practice session with *TEACH*.

```
      )LOAD 1 APLCOURSE
SAVED  11.07.53 09/01/69

      TEACH
ANSWER THE FOLLOWING QUESTION WITH Y FOR YES OR N FOR NO.
ARE YOU ALREADY FAMILIAR WITH THE INSTRUCTIONS FOR THIS
EXERCISE?
N
THIS IS AN EXERCISE IN SIMPLE APL EXPRESSIONS.
YOU WILL FIRST HAVE THE OPPORTUNITY TO SELECT THE FEATURES
YOU WISH TO BE DRILLED IN.  THE EXERCISE THEN BEGINS.  FOR
EACH PROBLEM YOU MUST ENTER THE PROPER RESULT.  ANSWERS
WILL CONSIST OF SCALAR INTEGERS IF EXERCISES WITH VECTORS
ARE NOT DESIRED; OTHERWISE ANSWERS WILL CONSIST OF
SCALARS OR VECTORS.  A VECTOR OF LENGTH ZERO REQUIRES THE
RESPONSE ι0, A VECTOR OF THE LENGTH ONE REQUIRES THE RESPONSE
,X WHERE X IS THE VALUE OF THE ELEMENT.  YOU HAVE THREE
TRIES FOR EACH PROBLEM.  TYPE STOP AT ANY TIME TO TERMIN
ATE THE EXERCISE AND PRODUCE A RECORDING OF YOUR PERFORM
ANCE.  TYPING STOPSHORT WILL TERMINATE THE EXERCISE BUT
WILL NOT PRODUCE A RECORD OF PERFORMANCE.  TYPING PLEASE OR
CHANGE FOR ANY PROBLEM WILL LET YOU PEEK AT THE ANSWERS.
TYPE Y UNDER EACH FUNCTION FOR WHICH YOU WANT EXERCISE:
```

```
SCALAR DYADIC FUNCTIONS
+-×÷*⌈⌊<≤=≥>≠!|∧∨⍟⍱⍲
       YY        YY
SCALAR MONADIC FUNCTIONS
+-×÷⌈⌊!|~
    Y   Y
TYPE Y IF EXERCISES ARE TO USE VECTORS, N OTHERWISE
Y
TYPE Y IF REDUCTION EXERCISES ARE DESIRED, N OTHERWISE
Y
TYPE Y IF VECTORS OF LENGTH ZERO OR ONE ARE DESIRED,
N OTHERWISE.
Y
MIXED DYADIC FUNCTIONS
ρ⍳,∊⊥⊤/↑↓\⌽
YYY
MIXED  MONADIC FUNCTIONS
⍳ρ,⌽
YY
                        ⌈/ ¯2 ¯5 4
⎕:
      4
                        ≠/,¯5
⎕:
       ,¯5
TRY AGAIN
⎕:
      ¯5
                        10>7
⎕:
      1
                        ⌊/,¯6
⎕:
      ¯6
                        6 4 ⌊ 3 ¯9
⎕:
      6 9
TRY AGAIN
⎕:
       PLEASE
ANSWER IS  3  ¯9
                        (⍳0)⌊⍳0
⎕:
      ⍳0
                        ! 1 4
⎕:
      1 24
                        7 1 5 ⌊ 7 1 5
⎕:
      7 1 5
                        ! 0 4
⎕:
      1 24
                        >/,¯1
⎕:
      ¯1
                        ÷⍳0
⎕:     STOPSHORT
```

PROBLEMS

1. DRILL. Specify $A \leftarrow 3 \ 2 \ 0 \ ^-1 \ 5 \ ^-8$ and $M \leftarrow 3 \ 4\rho\iota12$

$3\phi A$	$\phi0,\iota3$	$A[\psi 0 \ 1 \ 0 \ 1 \ 0 \ 1]$
$2\phi A[\iota4]$	$2\phi\phi\iota7$	$(\iota4)\epsilon A$
$4\uparrow A$	$^-3\downarrow A$	$(3\uparrow A)\epsilon\iota4$
$2\uparrow^-3\phi A$	$A[\blacktriangle\blacktriangle A]$	$(\iota6)=\blacktriangle A[\blacktriangle A]$
$^-2 \ 1 \ 3\phi M$	$1 \ 2\downarrow M$	$A\epsilon M$

2. Use the membership function to identify and select the one-digit integer elements of a vector V.

3. Write an **APL** expression to determine if two sets of numbers, $S1$ and $S2$, have identical elements, except possibly for order.

4. You are given a vector of characters $S \leftarrow$ 'WE ARE ALL GOOD MEN'. Write an **APL** expression to determine how many occurrences of the letters $ABCDEFGHIJKL$ are in S.

5. Use **APL** to rearrange the above character vector S so that the letters (including duplicates and blanks) are in alphabetical order.

6. Define a function to remove the extra blanks in S where they occur.

7. For an arbitrary numerical vector V which has been sorted in ascending order, show how to insert another vector $V1$ so as to preserve the ordering.

8. For a given numeric vector V of length N, write an **APL** expression that tests whether V is some permutation of the vector ιN (i.e., every element of V is in ιN and vice versa).

9. Let C be a vector of characters. Construct an expression which replaces every X in C with a Y.

10. For a vector of eight elements, construct two expressions for selecting the last three elements. Use the compression function in one and the take function in the other.

11. Write a program to find the median of a set of numbers. (The median is defined as the scalar in the middle of the list after it has been sorted. When the number of elements is even, the arithmetic mean of the two middle elements is defined to be the median.)

12. Explain what each of the following expressions does:

$$A[\blacktriangle\blacktriangle(\rho A)\rho 0 \ 1] \qquad (A \text{ a vector})$$
$$A \uparrow \blacktriangle?B\rho \lfloor/\iota0 \qquad (A \text{ and } B \text{ scalars})$$

13. Write a program to decode the message resulting from execution of the function $SUBST$ on page 173.

14. Modify the function VIG on page 173 to require two keys, KA and KB, of varying length, to be restructured and added on line 4. Let the function now take only the single argument M.

15. Define a function $VERNAM$ that modifies the indices resulting from $ALF\iota M$ (M is the message to be coded) by adding to them a vector V of M random numbers from 0 to 25. Reduce the result, as in VIG and $AUTO$, and apply it to ALF.

16. Write an **APL** expression to select N random elements from a matrix M.

17.   Show how to add a scalar N to each element in the even columns of a matrix M.

18.   You are given five vectors $V1 - V5$ of invoices from fifteen customers. The first represents bills under 30 days old, the second 30-59 days old, the third 60-89 days, etc. All entries with a given index are associated with the same customer. Write a program that will (1) construct a matrix of these invoices with each vector $V1 - V5$ occupying a single row; (2) print the total amount of receivables in each category and separately for each customer, with an appropriate message; (3) print the grand total of all receivables with an identifying message; and (4) identify which customers are deadbeats (have invoices outstanding more than 59 days).

19.   A magic square of order n is one made up of the integers 1 through n. The sums over each row, column and diagonal are the same. One way to construct the squares of odd order is to start with a matrix of the right size, made up of the successive integers ordered rowwise. Then set up a vector of n successive integers with 0 in the middle to rotate the matrix successively over the last and first coordinates. Define a monadic function MS to do this.

20.   Using *only* the take ($\uparrow$) function, select from the literal vector $V \leftarrow 'INDUBITABLY'$ the characters DUB. Ditto for drop ($\downarrow$).

21.   You are given a vector D which may be literal or numeric (nature unknown). Write an **APL** function that will distinguish the two *without* generating an error message.

22.   Write an **APL** expression to compare two sets of 50 random integers each (generated without duplication from $\iota 100$) and select those integers common to both.

23.   Construct a function LOC that locates all occurrences of a word or phrase W in a literal vector V.

24.   The vector G contains the grade point averages of all the seniors in a certain college. Find the two highest grades.

25.   Given $V1 \leftarrow 2\ 3\ 4\ 5\ 6\ 9\ 15$ and $V2 \leftarrow 4\ 9\ 15\ 6\ 20\ 25\ 40$, write **APL** expressions to find

      A)   those elements in both $V1$ and $V2$
      B)   those elements in either $V1$ or $V2$
      C)   those elements of $V1$ not in $V2$.

26.   Write an **APL** expression that simulates the dealing of four bridge hands. Let the numbers 1-52 stand for the cards in the deck.

27.   The vector S lists the amounts of individual holdings of shares of stock in the Squeaky Wheel Company. Show how to find the smallest number of individuals who together control 50% of the shares.

28.   You are given a vector V of scholastic grades. Write an expression to drop off the lowest four and find the average of the rest.

29.   Using *only* four characters, construct an expression that returns 1 if the first element in a given vector V is the largest, and 0 otherwise.

30.   Write an **APL** expression that returns the index of the rightmost nonzero element in a vector V, that is, we get 5 for $V \leftarrow 3\ 2\ 0\ 0\ 8\ 0\ 0$.

31.   Write an expression to delete a specified row R from a matrix M, storing the result in $M1$.

Chapter 20:
Number systems

It is a fact of life in our language that it is impossible to conceive of a number in the abstract without associating it with some concrete representation. Take the number 3, for instance. Can you think of the concept of "threeness" without imagining three objects or visualizing the number 3 in some system of notation, be it Roman numerals, scaled notation, base-2 notation or whatever?

No matter how many different ways of depicting the number 3 we may come up with, they all stand for the same thing - this abstract notion of threeness. Yet most of the time, we have no difficulty recognizing the number if it is embedded in a context which conditions our thinking along the right lines:

$$0.03E2$$
$$003$$
$$3.000$$
$$EXACTLY***\$3*DOLLARS*AND*00*CENTS$$
$$\square\square\square$$
$$00011$$

The last line above could be eleven in decimal notation, but because of the other more familiar ways of expressing 3 that preceded it, we would quite likely accept it as 3 in the binary system.

What it all boils down to is this: Just as a rose by any other name is still a rose and smells just as sweet, so in mathematics there are many ways to express the same number, and their value to us depends on what we are most used to and what form is most useful to us.

Thus far in all our **APL** work we have been using ordinary decimal notation. But many other systems are in common use. Mixed systems like clock time and number systems to the bases 2, 8, 16 are examples. In this chapter we will be examining how **APL** makes it possible for us to switch conveniently from one system to another. For this, two powerful functions, *decode* and *encode*, will be introduced.

Decode

Suppose we are in a room whose length is 3 yards, 0 feet and 1 inch. How could we reduce this example of the English system of measurement at its worst, to a single unit, say, inches? If we were to do it by hand, we would probably set up something like the following:

$$\begin{array}{ccccc} 3\,yds & & 0ft & & 1\,in \\ \underline{\times(12\times3)} & & \underline{\times12} & & \underline{\times1} \\ 108 & + & 0 & + & 1 & = 109\,in. \end{array}$$

There is a dyadic function in **APL** that will make this conversion for us. It is called the *base value* or *decode* function, and its symbol is the upper shift B, $\bot$. The right argument of $\bot$ is the array to be converted, while the left argument is a vector whose elements are the increments needed to make the conversion from one unit to the next. Since each of the elements on the left can be thought of as acting somewhat like the base of a number system (called a "radix" by mathematicians), the left argument is usually referred to as the *radix vector*.

In a *mixed number system* like the one involving our length measurements of the room, the syntax of the $\bot$ function requires that the number of elements in both arguments be the same. There is one exception to this, namely, that either argument may be a scalar or vector of length 1, a case which will be considered shortly. For our particular problem, we'll use 1760 (the number of yards per mile) as the multiplying factor for the next increment, even though it won't be used specifically in the conversion:

```
      1760 3 12⊥3 0 1
109
```

As a matter of fact, any number will do in that position, as long as there is something there:

```
      0 3 12⊥3 0 1
109
      3 1⊥3 0 1
LENGTH ERROR
      3 1 ⊥ 3 0 1
         ^
```

Here is another example, converting 2 minutes and 10 seconds to seconds:

```
      60 60⊥2 10
130
      0 60⊥2 10
130
```

We can formalize the action of the radix vector on the right argument concisely by letting $W[J]$ be the weighting factor that tells us what the increments should be from one unit to the next in our reduction. In our example of the room size, if A is the radix vector and B is the right argument, then $W[3]$ is 1, $W[2]$ is $A[3]\times W[3]$ or 12, $W[1]$ is $A[2]\times W[2]$ or 3×12. This is equivalent to $+/36\ 12\ 1\times3\ 0\ 1$, or $+/W\times B$.

Ordinary length and time measurements are examples of mixed number systems. The decode function, however, works equally well for decimal or other fixed base number systems. For instance, suppose the following is a picture of the odometer reading (in miles) of a car:

3	5	2	1

This can be regarded as a scalar 3521 or a vector $3\ 5\ 2\ 1$. If it is a vector and we want to convert it to the scalar number 3521, then we can execute

```
      10  10 10 10⊥3 5 2 1
3521
       0 10 10 10⊥3 5 2 1
3521
```

The decode function can be applied to number systems other than decimal. Here is a binary counter:

1	0	1	1	0

This can be converted to a decimal number by

```
      2 2 2 2 2⊥1 0 1 1 0
22
```

But if the counter were to be interpreted as readings on an odometer, our result will be different:

```
      10 10 10 10 10⊥1 0 1 1 0
10110
```

Obviously, we need to know what the representation is to tell what a particular number stands for.

It may help in understanding how the decode function works if we diagram the last three problems in parallel fashion, showing the radix and weighting vectors:

	room length	odometer	binary counter
radix vector	1760 3 12	10 10 10 10	2 2 2 2 2
weighting vector, W	36 12 1	1000 100 10 1	16 8 4 2 1
array to be decoded, B	3 0 1	3 5 2 1	1 0 1 1 0
result ($+/W \times B$)	109	3521	22

This function extends to two-dimensional arrays as well, as shown by the following example using the arrays B and X. The diagram which follows it will help you keep track of what is going on.

```
        B
  0  0  1  1  2  2
  0  1  0  1  0  1
  0  0  0  0  0  0
           3  2  2⊥B
  0  2  4  6  8 10
```

```
      X←2 3ρ3 2 2 2 4 2
      X
3  2  2
2  4  2
      X⊥B
   0   2   4   6   8  10
   0   2   8  10  16  18
```

radix vector	weighting array W						array to be decoded B					
3	4	4	4	4	4	4	0	0	1	1	2	2
2	2	2	2	2	2	2	0	1	0	1	0	1
2	1	1	1	1	1	1	0	0	0	0	0	0

The result is $+ / W \times B$.

Note from the diagram that the decode function acts across the first coordinate of the matrix. More generally, for $R \perp B$, where R and B may be scalars, vectors or matrices, the decode function will work if (a) R or B is a scalar, or (b) $(\rho R)[2]$ equals $(\rho B)[1]$, or (c) $(\rho R)[2]$ or $(\rho B)[1]$ equals 1.

Case (a) can be illustrated by the following:

```
      10⊥3 5 2 1
3521
      2⊥0 1 0 1
5
      10 10 10 10⊥5
5555
      2⊥B
0 2 4 6 8 10
```

One final illustration that may be of interest. Suppose you have an "irregular" matrix of characters M (the irregularity is really illusory since the apparently ragged edges are padded with blanks that don't show):

```
      M
 DOG
   CAT
TIGER
                        (fourth row of M is blank)
CHICKS
      ρM
5 6
```

The problem is to "right justify" the matrix. (See also the defined function $ROWNAMES$ in Chapter 17.) We first identify the location of the blanks with $M = ' '$. This logical matrix, used as the left argument of the decode function with 1 as the right argument, results in a vector whose elements are related to the number of blanks to the right of the first nonblank character in each line of M (why?):

```
      Q←(M=' ')⊥1
      Q
2 1 2 6 1
```

Subtracting Q from 1 should tell us how much to shift each line to the right (with the fourth line it is, of course, immaterial what number we put down:

```
      QS←1-Q
      QS
⁻1 0 ⁻1 ⁻5 0
```

```
      QSφM
  DOG
  CAT
TIGER

CHICKS
```

Our completed algorithm thus looks like this:

$$(1 - (M = ' \quad ') \bot 1) \phi M$$

Encode

Like so many of the other functions we've encountered so far in **APL**, there is a function that "undoes" the work of the decode function, i.e., converts from a value to some predetermined representation. Appropriately, it is called *representation* or *encode*, and its symbol is ⊤ (upper shift *N*). Thus, if we execute

```
      2 2 2 2⊥0 1 0 1
5
```

then the function ⊤ brings back our initial argument:

```
      2 2 2 2⊤5
0 1 0 1
```

Here are our room length and odometer problems in reverse:

```
      1760 3 12⊤109
3 0 1
      10 10 10 10⊤3521
3 5 2 1
```

This latter example describes how 3 5 2 1 would appear on a 4-position odometer. How would 1 3 5 2 1 appear on the same odometer?

```
      10 10 10 10⊤13521
3 5 2 1
```

We can draw an analogy here. It's like an odometer which reads only up to 9999 and then starts over from 0 again. In fact, in this case the right argument has been reduced by 10 * 4:

```
      (10*4)|13521
3521
```

What happens when we're not sure how many elements are needed in the radix vector, yet we don't want to lose anything, as was unfortunately the case in the example above? Using zero as the first element of the left argument puts everything remaining in the first element of the result, as shown below:

```
      0 10 10 10⊤43521
43 5 2 1
      0 60⊤130
2 10
```

The encode function also operates on arrays. For example:

```
        A←2 2ρ27 15 12 48
        B←2 3ρ2 2 2 6 6 6
        C←2 3 4
        10 10⊤A
2 1
1 4
```
              (This result has three dimensions.)
```
7 5
2 8
        B⊤2
0 0 0
2 2 2
        B⊤C
0 0 0
0 0 0
0 0 0
```
              (This result has three dimensions.)
```
2 3 4
2 3 4
2 3 4
```

In general, if $R \leftarrow A \top B$, then ρR equals $(\rho A), \rho B$.

Both encode and decode yield some rather interesting results when used with negative numbers and nonintegers. Here are a few illustrations, but you are advised to explore their uses on your own. You may find drill problem 1 at the end of the chapter helpful in this regard.

```
        ¯2 3 ¯6⊥2 7 9
¯69
        ¯2⊥6 7 8
18
        5 2 ¯6⊤487
4 0 ¯5
        2.167⊥5 4 2
34.147445
        16.21 32.68⊤4 29
   0   0
   4  29
        (3ρ2.5)⊤(3ρ2.5)⊥1 1 1
1 0.05 2.25
```

To aid in understanding the above results, bear in mind that representation is a sequential process that operates in a right-to-left manner on the elements of the radix vector.

Applications of decode and encode

An obvious application lies in the conversion of decimally represented information to another numbering system. Since the bases 2, 8 and 16 have been used for computers, for our first illustration let's build an algorithm to convert from the decimal to the *hexadecimal* (base-16) system.

Just as in our ordinary decimal (base-10) system, we require ten distinct symbols 0123456789, so in the base-16 system, 16 symbols are needed. Larger values in the base-10 system are represented by adding positions on the left (provided, of course, we are talking about whole numbers and not fractions). For example, 10 is a two-position number, 9 being the largest number that can be represented by a single symbol.

In the hexadecimal system the symbols are 0123456789ABCDEF. If you were to ask why the letters ABCDEF, the most appropriate response would be "why not?" We need some single symbol for each of the numbers 10 through 15. New symbols could be invented or old ones used differently (like upside down or with a bar across them), but it really doesn't matter as long as they are distinct from one another and are used consistently.

A decimal system number can be represented in so-called expanded notation as follows:

$$\text{Number: } 6325$$
$$\text{Decimal expansion: } 6\times10^3 + 3\times10^2 + 2\times10^1 + 5\times10^0$$

We can define a hexadecimal number in exactly the same way, except that powers of 16 instead of powers of 10 are involved. Here is an example using the hexadecimal number $1AF2$:

$$\text{Hexadecimal Expansion: } 1\times16^3 + 10\times16^2 + 15\times16^1 + 2\times16^0$$

which is equivalent to 6898 in decimal form.

In 1 $CLASS$ there is a dyadic function $HEXA$ which makes the conversion for us. The left argument is the number of positions we want to see represented; the right argument is the number to be converted:

```
        )LOAD 1 CLASS
SAVED  15.02.39 04/15/74
        3 HEXA 254
0FE
        2 HEXA 254
FE
        1 HEXA 254
E
```

Let's look at $HEXA$:

```
        ∇HEXA[□]∇
    ∇ R←N HEXA X
[1]    R←'0123456789ABCDEF'[1+(Nρ16)⊤X]
    ∇
```

$N\rho16$ generates a vector of N elements, each of which is 16. If, for example, N is 3 and X is 254, $(N\rho16)\top X$ is

```
        (3ρ16)⊤254
0 15 14
```

In expanded notation this is the same as

$$0\times16^2 + 15\times16^1 + 14\times16^0$$

On looking through the vector of characters $0123456789ABCDEF$, we see that since the 0 is in the first position, 1 in the second position, etc., it is necessary to add 1 to $(3\rho16)\top254$ to pick up the subscripts for the proper characters:

```
        1+(3ρ16)⊤254
1 16 15
```

257 is a number which needs at least three positions in hexadecimal notation:

$$1\times16^2 + 0\times16^1 + 1\times16^0$$

Let's execute $HEXA$ for this number, specifying first four and then two positions:

```
      4  HEXA  257
0101
      2  HEXA  257
01
```

We get a false result if we don't specify sufficient positions. Incidentally, `0101` is a vector of characters:

```
      ρ4  HEXA  257
4
```

Do you see why?

Hexadecimal to decimal conversion

What about the reverse operation, converting from hexadecimal to decimal representation? Such a function, called DEC, exists already in 1 $CLASS$. We'll use it before displaying it. It is monadic and requires quotes for the argument:

```
      DEC  'OFE'
254
```

It seems OK in this example, so let's display it:

```
      ∇DEC[□]∇
    ∇   R←DEC  H
[1]     R←16⊥¯1+'0123456789ABCDEF'ιH
    ∇
```

H represents the vector of literals in hexadecimal notation. The dyadic iota with H on the right picks up the positions of the corresponding characters in the left argument. Trying this out with OFE, we get

```
      '0123456789ABCDEF'ι'OFE'
1 16 15
```

which is one position too high to use as the right argument of ⊥. Hence `¯1` is added before the decode function is applied:

```
      16⊥0 15 14
254
```

It should be clear why no left argument is needed in DEC. The decode function will automatically extend the scalar `16` in length to match the length of the right argument.

If we were to try DEC with undefined characters, say, WER, we still get a result,

```
      DEC  'WER'
4336
```

but it is meaningless. To find out why, remember what the dyadic iota does for an element in the right argument not found on the left. It will produce the vector `17 15 17`, and after adding `¯1` to each element we have

```
      16⊥16 14 16
4336
```

Now try

```
      DEC 5 HEXA 321
321
      DEC 2 HEXA 321
65
```

and we see that DEC and $HEXA$ are inverse functions, provided that sufficient positions have been allowed.

Numeric coding

In the last chapter we experimented with cryptographic techniques by converting readable messages into "scrambled" characters. Using $\top$ and $\bot$ we can now code several characters into a single number.

The following function, $NUMCODE$, takes a character vector M, breaks it up into groups of four characters each and codes each group into a single numerical value:

```
      ∇  Z←B NUMCODE M
[1]      M←(4×⌈.25×ρM)↑M
[2]      M←(4,.25×ρM)ρM
[3]      Z←B⊥ALFιM
      ∇
```

ALF is specified as the letters of the alphabet, with a blank character included,

```
      ALF←'ABCDEFGHIJKLMNOPQRSTUVWXYZ '
```

and B is a scalar which must be at least one greater than ρALF. The key to this function is line 3 which takes the four-row character matrix into which M has been transformed (lines 1 and 2), converts it into indices ($ALFιM$) and then changes each column into a unique number in base B. There is an upper limit on the value of B which depends on the way in which numbers are represented in the computer. More about this in Chapter 32.

Decoding can be done similarly, provided that one knows the base B:

```
      ∇  Z←B DENUMCODE MESSAGE
[1]      MESSAGE←(4ρB)⊤MESSAGE
[2]      Z←,ALF[MESSAGE]
      ∇
```

Here is an example:

```
      M←'REBELS ADVANCING ON ALL FRONTS'
      MESSAGE←30 NUMCODE M
      MESSAGE
490416 155268 55335 148424 326750 521479 741987 34137
      30 DENUMCODE MESSAGE
REBELS ADVANCING ON ALL FRONTS
```

Check protection

Another practical application is demonstrated by the function CP, which fills in the space before a number with stars up to a predetermined position. Its use for check protection should be evident. CP, which is in 1 $CLASS$, is dyadic. The left argument is the total number of places to be filled up, including the dollar amount, and the right argument is the amount of the check. Here are a few examples:

```
      5  CP 301
**301
      5  CP 12345
12345
      5  CP 00301
**301
```

Let's look at CP:

```
      ∇CP[□]∇
    ∇ R←N CP X;P
[1]   R←'0123456789'[1+(Nρ10)⊤X]
[2]   P←¯1+(R≠'0')ι1
[3]   R←(Pρ'*'),P↓R
    ∇
```

Line 1 makes a vector of characters out of X, the argument, and adds enough 0's in front to make ρR equal to N. Line 2 sets P as one less than the index of the first nonzero character, while line 3 puts into R, P copies of $*$ followed by all but the first P elements of R.

Check protection is only one of a multitude of often-used commercial representations, or *formats*. The next chapter discusses this topic in detail.

PROBLEMS

1. DRILL

$(3\rho40)\perp8\ 7\ 2$	$2\perp5\ 1\ 9\ 6$	$1\ 4\ 7\perp3\ 5\rho\iota15$
$1\ ^-4.1\ .8\perp1\ 2\ 3$	$7\ 8\ 9\perp7\ 8\ 9$	$3\top5217$
$3\ 3\top5217$	$3\ 3\ 3\top5217$	$(5\rho3)\top5217$
$(4\rho8)\perp^-14$	$1\ 4\ 6\top345$	$2\ 4\ 6\top\iota10$

2. Write **APL** expressions: A) to convert 2 gallons, 8 quarts and 1 pint to pints;   B) to find the number of ounces in 3 tons, 568 pounds and 13 ounces.

3. Find the

    A) base-8 value of 2 1 7 7
    B) base-2 value of 1 0 1 1 0 1
    C) base-3 representation of 8933
    D) base-5 representation of 4791

4. Write expressions that will show that $\perp$ and $\top$ are inverses of each other (not, however, for all arguments).

5. Define a function to remove commas from a character vector consisting of digits and commas, and convert the result to a numerical vector.

6. Write an **APL** expression which determines whether or not, for a given three-digit number N, N is equal to the sum of the cubes of its digits.

7.   For $M \leftarrow$ '1234583', what are the differences between each of the following expressions?

  A) $M \leftarrow {}^-1 + '0123456789' \iota M$
  B) $M \leftarrow 10 \perp {}^-1 + '0123456789' \iota M$
  C) $M \leftarrow 10 \perp 0\ 1\ 2\ 3\ 4\ 5\ 6\ 7\ 8\ 9['0123456789' \iota M]$

8.   It is a fact that a number N is divisible by 11 if the alternating sum of its digits is divisible by 11. Construct an expression that uses the encode function with this condition to test for divisibility by 11.

9.   Write an **APL** function to illustrate the following well-known arithmetic "trick": Given any 3-digit number N whose first and last digits are different, reverse the digits and subtract the smaller number from the larger. Reverse the digits in the answer and add this value to the original difference. The sum will always be 1089.

Problems 10-14 are designed to show you a little of the often unappreciated power of the decode and encode functions.

10. Earlier in the text the residue and floor functions were used to separate the integer and fractional parts of a number. Show how this separation can be done in a single step by using the encode function.

11. Use $\perp$ to write a dyadic function $EVAL$ to evaluate at the point X a polynomial with coefficients C (descending powers of X). Compare with pages 53 and 54.

12. Use $\perp$ to obtain the last element of a vector V.

13. Simulate $+/V$ and $-/V$ using $\perp$.

14. With the decode function, convert a vector V of integers in the range 0 through 9 into a number whose integral part is the first element of the vector and whose decimal part consists of the remaining elements of the vector taken in order from left to right, i.e., 4 2 8 7 becomes 4.287.

15. Array C contains the costs for various items of clothes purchased by Abigail Adams for Polly Jefferson and her maid in 1787. (First column is pounds, second column shillings and the third is pence). The total submitted to Thomas Jefferson was 10 pounds, 15 shillings, 8 pence. Jefferson changed this to 11 pounds, 16 shillings and 2 pence. Which sum is correct? (Pound = 20 shillings; shilling = 12 pence.)

```
C←0  5  6  3 10  0  0 15  0  1 10  0  0  6  6  0  5  0  0  7  6  0 13  0
C←C,0  2  4  0  5 10  0 13  6  0  3  0  0  5  6  0  1  6  1  5  6  0  7  4
C←20 3ρC,0  6  0  0  2  0  0  4  6  0  6  8
```

Chapter 21:
Report formatting

You have probably observed by now that you haven't been able to exercise much control over the way *APL* prints a numeric result on the terminal. If this limit on your options for formatting output doesn't bother you, skip this chapter. If, on the other hand, you have developed some concern (or consternation) over this, then you should find the additional *APL* features described in this chapter helpful.

Thus far it would appear that *APL* decides how output numbers will be formed, how they will be spaced, and how many significant digits will be shown. However, while you can always get the answers out in an understandable form, they may not necessarily be in the proper shape to hand to your boss, who may have a preference for reports with such features as all negative numbers in parentheses, and commas separating each group of three digits, and with column headings and row names, and perhaps with exactly two decimal positions shown for the fractional part.

In the last chapter, you saw how you could write programs (using ⊤) to achieve some format control, but those programs are relatively tough to write and not as efficient as what will be covered here.

Printing precision

Suppose you want to prepare a table of compound interest (on one dollar) for interest rates 2, 4, 6, 8, 10 and 12 percent and for years 1 through 5. That suggests an outer product. Ordinarily the output will not fit on this page. However, use of the $\Box PP$ (*p*rinting *p*recision) system variable helps us in this respect. Use it to set the number of printing positions for numeric output to some number between 1 and 16.

```
      □PP
10
      □PP←5
      1÷7
0.14286
      □PP←10
      1÷7
0.1428571429
      □PP←16
      1÷7
0.1428571428571428
      □PP←20
DOMAIN ERROR
      □PP←20
      ^
      □PP
```

16

The actual calculations aren't affected, only the printed output. Notice that the normal value of $\Box PP$ is 10 (5 on the 5100), and the response is the previously set value. If you just enter $\Box PP$ without any number, you get the present digit setting without changing anything.

Getting back to our compound interest problem, let's set $\Box PP \leftarrow 7$ so that the display can be accomodated in the width available:

```
      □PP←7
      TABLE←((1+.04×ι3)∘.*ι5)-1
      TABLE
0.04          0.0816        0.124864      0.1698586     0.2166529
0.08          0.1664        0.259712      0.360489      0.4693281
0.12          0.2544        0.404928      0.5735194     0.7623417
```

Now it's obvious that by showing even seven digits we confuse the issue somewhat, the missing decimal places in the display being, of course, zeros. So we try again with

```
      □PP←3
      TABLE
0.04       0.0816     0.125      0.17      0.217
0.08       0.166      0.26       0.36      0.469
0.12       0.254      0.405      0.574     0.762
```

This still isn't satisfactory because we'd like the trailing zeros to show in such a commercial display. At this point we're ready to explore the formatting facilities of **APL**.

The formatting operator

The symbol ⍕ is the formatting operator. It is formed by typing ⊤ overstruck with ∘. The right argument is the data to be formatted, and the left argument holds the format instructions. For example, suppose you type

```
      6 3⍕TABLE
.040   .082   .125   .170   .217
.080   .166   .260   .360   .469
.120   .254   .405   .574   .762
```

What you are doing is asking that each column of *TABLE* be formed into a *field* six characters wide, with three decimal places.

In the above example the left argument 6 3 was (conceptually) repeated for each column of *TABLE*. On the other hand, if you enter

```
      (10ρ8 3 7 4)⍕TABLE
.040    .0816      .125   .1699    .217
.080    .1664      .260   .3605    .469
.120    .2544      .405   .5735    .762
```

you get a pattern of alternating field specifications. Note that ⍕ applies each pair of numbers in the left argument to a column of the right argument. ⍕ returns an explicit result which is a character representation (in this case a matrix) of the right argument.

```
      ρ(10ρ8 3 7 4)⍕TABLE
3 38
```

The shape of the result is the same as the shape of the right argument, except that the last dimension of the result is the sum of the field widths. Thus, if the right argument is a (numeric) vector, the result is a (character) vector. Of course, if the right argument is a scalar, you'll still get a vector as a result. If you want a complete table with row and column headings, the following program will do it:

```
      ∇ RATES COMPINT TIMES
[1]    (4ρ' '),6 0⍕TIMES
[2]    (4 2,(2×ρTIMES)ρ6 3)⍕RATES,((1+RATES)∘.*TIMES)-1 ∇

      (.04×⍳3) COMPINT ⍳5
          1      2      3      4      5
 .04    .040   .082   .125   .170   .217
 .08    .080   .166   .260   .360   .469
 .12    .120   .254   .405   .574   .762
```

Note in line one that if the number of decimal positions is given as zero, then the decimal point itself is suppressed. As you might expect, the result is always rounded.

If the second number of the pair is negative, then the corresponding field will be printed in scaled notation. Most commercial reports have no need for scaled notation, so unless you are making reports involving very large or very small numbers, skip the rest of this paragraph. If in spite of this warning you're still interested, the first number in the pair still dictates the field width, but the second number controls the minimum number of significant digits of *mantissa* (the number before the E) that will be produced. The absolute value of this number must be at least six smaller than the field width to allow for a negative sign and the characters of the exponent itself. For example:

```
      10 ¯4 20 ¯3 10 ¯4⍕12345 .000001234567 ¯1
1.23450E4          1.235E¯6 1.00000E0
```

To recap, so far we have seen that the shape of the left argument must either be a vector with two elements (implied replication) or with one pair of elements for each column. The first element of the pair gives the field width, and the second gives the number of digits after the decimal point (or the number of significant digits for scaled notation). If the second element of the pair is zero, the result appears as an integer.

Now suppose the first element of the pair is zero. The width is then automatically taken to be whatever is required to represent the value, allowing for one blank space in front. Look at this example:

```
      0 5 0 0⍕2ρ101.49
101.49000 101
```

If you format a matrix, and use zero (automatic) width specification, the resulting width is whatever is needed to cause each column of the result to line up properly, and yet not run together, as shown by

```
      X←2 2ρ1.5 1234567 ¯79.68 ¯.9
      0 3 0 0⍕X
   1.500 1234567
 ¯79.680       ¯1
```

When using implied replication and automatic widths (that is, formatting several columns of the right argument using a pair of elements the first of which is zero in the left argument), the width is based on the number of characters required to represent the largest value in the right argument, rather than dealing with it on a column-by-column basis. Observe the difference in these two examples:

```
      0  2  0  2⍕X
    ¯1.50 1234567.00
  ¯79.68        ¯.90

      0  2⍕X
      1.50 1234567.00
   ¯79.68        ¯.90
```

As a special case, the left argument can be a single element. If it is a positive value, the result has automatic width, with the number of decimal positions taken from the left argument:

```
      5⍕Y←20 .012345 ¯7.2
 20.00000    .01235 ¯7.20000
```

This means that if the left argument is a single zero, the result will be formed with automatic width and no decimal positions:

```
      0⍕Y
 20    0  ¯7
```

When the left argument is a negative integer, the result is formed in scaled notation, as discussed previously. For example:

```
      ¯3⍕Y
 2.0000E1  1.235E¯2 ¯7.2000E0
```

Lest you have any doubts, a character array as the left argument is a *DOMAIN ERROR*, and left arguments that aren't scalars or vectors give *RANK ERROR*s. A vector left argument must be the proper length (2 or 2×¯1↑ρ*ARRAY*) to avoid a *LENGTH ERROR*.

⍕ also can be used as a monadic function. The result is a character array that, if printed, looks exactly like what would be printed by typing in the name of the expression itself:

```
      CTABLE←⍕TABLE
      CTABLE
0.04       0.0816    0.125    0.17      0.217
0.08       0.166     0.26     0.36      0.469
0.12       0.254     0.405    0.574     0.762
      ρCTABLE
3 45
      □PP
3
      □PP←7
      ρ⍕TABLE
3 65
      ⍕TABLE
0.04          0.0816     0.124864    0.1698586    0.2166529
0.08          0.1664     0.259712    0.360489     0.4693281
0.12          0.2544     0.404928    0.5735194    0.7623417
```

As you can see, monadic ⍕ uses the present □*PP* setting in determining the width. The rules for spacing with monadic ⍕ (and *APL* raw output as well) differ from system to system, and are subject to change. For this reason, do not use monadic ⍕ in applications where the result must be aligned with other printing, such as headings and titles. Rather, use dyadic ⍕ or □*FMT* (next section) for these applications.

APL ★PLUS ® **formatting**

In addition to ⍕, the dyadic *system function* □*FMT* is used to do formatting in the *APL ★PLUS*® system. It produces most common printed representations of values. The left argument is always a character vector with its own set of rules to determine how the right argument will be formed. Regardless of the nature of the data to be formatted, the result is always a character matrix.

We'll call the left argument the *format string* and the right argument the *data list*. Going over the examples given previously, we first format the variable *TABLE* so that each field is six characters wide, with three digits after the decimal point:

```
      'F6.3' □FMT (TABLE)
0.040 0.082 0.125 0.170 0.217
0.080 0.166 0.260 0.360 0.469
0.120 0.254 0.405 0.574 0.762
```

Parentheses aren't really needed around the right argument. However, since you'll need the parentheses later to format several data items at the same time, you might as well form the habit now. One difference from ⍕ is that leading zeros are produced in the result for all numbers smaller than 1. This is a stylistic difference in the two formatting facilities.

Let's now examine the format string. The character *F* indicates that this is to be produced in *fixed point*, in other words, a decimal point will be present. The 6 indicates the fields are to be six characters wide, and the 3 calls for three positions after the decimal point. In effect, the *format phrase F*6.3 is replicated once for every column in the data list.

To produce fields of varying width, you can make up format strings composed of several format phrases, with each phrase set off by a comma:

```
      'F8.3,F7.4,F8.3,F7.4,F8.3' □FMT (TABLE)
0.040 0.0816    0.125 0.1699    0.217
0.080 0.1664    0.260 0.3605    0.469
0.120 0.2544    0.405 0.5735    0.762
```

For that matter, since □*FMT* will cycle through the list of format phrases and start again at the front (much like the dyadic ρ) '*F*8.3,*F*7.4' could have been used just as well.

Integer formatting is done using the letter *I* in place of *F*, followed by the desired width. If the value to be formatted by an *I*-code is not an integer, it is rounded to the nearest integer. Look carefully at the next example, because we're sneaking in yet another new feature:

```
      'I4,2F10.5,I4' □FMT ((⍳4)∘.*1 .5,(÷3),2 3)
   1    1.00000    1.00000    1    1
   2    1.41421    1.25992    4    8
   3    1.73205    1.44225    9   27
   4    2.00000    1.58740   16   64
```

The above table of numbers, square roots, cube roots, squares and cubes has two main formats. The *I*4 produced fields one, four and five, and the *F*10.5 produced fields two and three. The new feature we introduced was the explicit *replication factor*, namely the 2 that comes before the *F*10.5. Its meaning is straightforward: you could just as well replace the phrase 2*F*10.5 by the two phrases *F*10.5,*F*10.5.

Replication factors can be made to apply to several format phrases by using parentheses. For example,
$$'2(I4,2F10.3)'$$
is the same as
$$'I4,F10.3,F10.3,I4,F10.3,F10.3'$$
and
$$'I4,2(F6.2,2(I3,I2),I5),F10.6'$$
is the same as
$$'I4,F6.2,I3,I2,I3,I2,I5,F6.2,I3,I2,I3,I2,I5,F10.6'$$

You can express results in scaled notation using a format phrase of the form $'E14.8'$. The 14 stands for the field width, and the 8 stands for the number of significant digits in the mantissa that will be represented. The *APL ★PLUS*® system requires that the number of significant digits requested must always be at least six less than the width to allow for the letter E, the decimal point, possible negative signs in the mantissa and exponent, and the two-digit exponent itself. To give you the flavor of the E-format code, try some variants of this example:

```
      'I4,E10.3,E20.12' ⎕FMT (2 ¯5 10∘.*1 ¯4 15)
  2   6.25E¯2    3.27680000000E4
 ¯5   1.60E¯3   ¯3.05175781250E10
 10   1.00E¯4    1.00000000000E15
```

So far every illustration we have used as the right argument to $⎕FMT$ has been a matrix. When the data list contains a vector, it is treated as though it were a one-column matrix, as in

```
      'I1' ⎕FMT (!ι4)
1
2
6
*
```

*   (Stars are produced whenever the value is too big for the field width.)

which produces a character matrix with four rows and one column. This is particularly advantageous because a very common use of $⎕FMT$ is to list several data items side-by-side.

Here is an example which displays the first five integers, their factorials, reciprocals, exponentials and natural logarithms:

```
      '2I4,F10.7,2E14.6' ⎕FMT (ι5;!ι5;÷ι5;*ι5;⍟ι5)
   1   1 1.0000000    2.71828E0      0.00000E0
   2   2 0.5000000    7.38906E0      6.93147E¯1
   3   6 0.3333333    2.00855E1      1.09861E0
   4  24 0.2500000    5.45982E1      1.38629E0
   5 120 0.2000000    1.48413E2      1.60944E0
```

Since semicolons are used to separate items in the data list, parentheses aren't needed for any of the expressions.

Now suppose you really wanted the example $'I5' ⎕FMT (!ι6)$ to produce a one-line result. You could do it either by making the data items into a one-row matrix or by raveling the result:

```
      'I5' ⎕FMT (1 6ρ!ι6)
    1    2    6   24  120  720
      ,'I5' ⎕FMT (!ι6)
    1    2    6   24  120  720
```

The shape of the first result is a matrix with one row and 30 columns, and the shape of the second result is a character vector with 30 elements. Can you explain the difference?

Working with alphabetic data

Most business reporting has character information (such as names of items or people) shown next to whatever numbers apply to them. For example, with this data

```
NAMES←4 6ρ'NUTS  SCREWSBOLTS NAILS '
  COSTS←.05 .03 .20 .01
  QUANT←150 200 4 1000
```

you might want a report (or invoice) that looks like this:

```
NUTS        0.05   150       7.50
SCREWS      0.03   200       6.00
BOLTS       0.20     4       0.80
NAILS       0.01  1000      10.00
TOTAL                       24.30
```

The first four lines above can be obtained by executing

```
'6A1,F10.2,I5,F10.2' □FMT (NAMES;COSTS;QUANT;COSTS×QUANT)
```

The point of interest here is the format phrase $6A1$. The A-code is used to format literal or character data items. Its width specification is usually 1, and it almost always has a replication factor of the same value as the column dimension of the character matrix you are formatting. But width factors other than 1 can be useful, as shown by the following:

```
   '6A2' □FMT (NAMES)
N U T S
S C R E W S
B O L T S
N A I L S
```

Note that each character position in the variable $NAMES$ produces two positions in the result. In a sense, this is a very limited way to perform an expansion on the second dimension of a character matrix. However, it is introduced here because reports can sometimes be made more attractive by spreading out the text a bit.

It is easy to get messed up when using the A-code if you forget that each column of a character array is a separate entity. We will emphasize that point by this example:

```
   '2A1,A4' □FMT (NAMES)
NU   TS      
SC   REW    S
BO   LTS     
NA   ILS     
```

```
       2A1   A4   2A1   A4
```

Dotted lines have been drawn in to emphasize the result produced by each part of the format string. Notice that the monadic A-code incorporates the proper number of leading blanks to complete the column width specification.

The picture code

By using the G-code, you are able to do very detailed formatting with numeric data. Embellishments such as placing slashes between the day, month and year in a date, separating the parts of a Social Security number, or "dressing up" a telephone number are easily accomplished. To use it, the letter G is followed by a *picture pattern*. The pattern starts and ends with the character ⌷, and the field width is the number of characters between pairs of ⌷'s. The characters between the ⌷'s determine how the result appears: a character 9 says "put a digit here," and the character Z says, "if this position would have been a leading or trailing zero, put a blank here, otherwise, put in the appropriate digit character." Any other character that appears between the ⌷'s is literally placed in the result in that position. Some examples follow:

```
          X←72.71  0  ‾12  .026
          'G⌷9999⌷' ⌷FMT (X)
0073
0000
‾012
0000
        ,'G⌷ZZZ9⌷' ⌷FMT (X)
     73     0 ‾12     0
        ,'G⌷ZZZZZ⌷' ⌷FMT (X)
     73    ‾12
```

Note that only the integer part of the values are taken, as for an I-code. In the last example, the values that would have printed as all zeros have disappeared and have been replaced by blanks.

```
          'G⌷ZZ9.ZZZ⌷' ⌷FMT (1000×1 100.2 0 123.456)
    1.
100.2
    0.
123.456
```

Here we multiplied the argument by 1000 to scale it properly, since the G-code takes only the integer parts of the values. A decimal point appearing in the pattern is merely a character to be inserted and has nothing to do with aligning the value or scaling it. Some additional examples:

```
          'G⌷DATE IS 99/99/9999⌷' ⌷FMT (03051974)
DATE IS 03/05/1974

          'G⌷999-99-9999 SOCIAL SECURITY NUMBER⌷' ⌷FMT (245444440)
245-44-4440 SOCIAL SECURITY NUMBER

          'G⌷PHONE (999) 999-9999⌷' ⌷FMT (9144286910 3016578220)
PHONE (914) 428-6910
PHONE (301) 657-8220

          'G⌷$ZZZZZZZ.99 REFUNDED⌷' ⌷FMT (100×1063.24 .87 123456.78)
$     1063.24 REFUNDED
$         .87 REFUNDED
$   123456.78 REFUNDED
```

The characters Z and 9 are "reserved" in their use in the G-picture code. If you ever had to use them literally (for example, to include the word '$FRAZZLE$' or '$MODEL\ X9$' in a picture), you'd be in trouble without the S-qualifier. It works this way: if you put $S⌷9⊛Z\underline{Z}⌷$ in front of the G, then for that picture, ⊛ now has the meaning "put a digit here" and $\underline{Z}$ has the meaning that Z used to have, so that 9 and Z are released from their regular duties, as shown below:

```
          'S⌷9⊛Z\underline{Z}⌷G⌷ZZZ⊛ UNITS OF PRODUCT Z9R⌷' ⌷FMT (73)
 73 UNITS OF PRODUCT Z9R
```

Filler and positioning codes

So far we've covered the F-, I-, E- and G-codes for formatting numeric values, and the A-code for formatting character values. The remaining **APL ★PLUS** ® formatting codes don't associate with any data in the right argument, but rather are used to supply filler spaces or text between fields. The X-code supplies blanks:

```
     'I4,X3,6A1'  ⎕FMT (ι4;NAMES)
1    NUTS
2    BOLTS
3    SCREWS
4    NAILS
```

Can you think of an alternate way of producing the display without using the X-code?

Fields of literal constants can be sandwiched between data fields in the result by placing the literal text between two ⍛'s:

```
       '⍛PRODUCT⍛,I2,⍛ IS ⍛,6A1'  ⎕FMT (ι4;NAMES)
PRODUCT 1 IS NUTS
PRODUCT 2 IS BOLTS
PRODUCT 3 IS SCREWS
PRODUCT 4 IS NAILS
```

The last of the codes is the T-code (for horizontal tabbing). It is used to specify in which visible column of the result the next characters will be placed. For example,

```
     'I3,T20,I1'  ⎕FMT (ι3;2×ι3)
1                  2
2                  4
3                  6
```

starts the second field in column 20 of the result.

T and X are quite similar. The major difference is that X positioning is relative to the present position, while T positioning is relative to the left margin. These two codes may be used to position back. For instance, assume you are presently at print position 50. The phrase $T40$ will cause the characters that were in print position 40 and beyond to be replaced by any following formatted characters. X^-10 moves backward 10 print positions.

The T-code, when used without a number following it, moves the print element over to the right to the first "unused" position. You'd use it in a very complicated formatting job in which backspacing is needed.

Qualifiers

If you are warming up to the idea that the **APL** language can do commercial formatting, you should be convinced after being introduced to the use of *qualifiers* and *decorations*. They are used with format codes F-, I- and G-, and further tailor the report to specific needs. All qualifiers and decorations come before the format codes and after the replication factor (if there is one). Here is an example using two qualifiers:

```
     'BCF13.2'  ⎕FMT (10 ‾4 0 1234567.9 ‾.004 ‾1000)
        10.00
        ‾4.00


 1,234,567.90

     ‾1,000.00
```

The B-qualifier says, "if the number would have been represented as a zero, make the field all blanks." Notice that since we're showing only two decimal positions, the result is rounded to the nearest whole number, and hence the value ‾.004 is rounded to zero and subsequently blanked. The C-qualifier simply inserts commas separating the digits of the integer parts in groups of three.

The Z-qualifier is used to insert leading zeros in a field (instead of leading blanks). It would ordinarily be used when preparing output destined for punched card transfer to another (non-*APL*) computer as shown:

```
      'ZI9,⎕/⎕'  ⎕FMT ( 3 4ρι12)
000000001/000000002/000000003/000000004/
000000005/000000006/000000007/000000008/
000000009/000000010/000000011/000000012/
```

In the following illustration, the L-qualifier is used to *left-justify* the represented values within the field:

```
       ∇FACTORIALS
[1]    28ρ14↑' N  !N'
[2]    'I2,X2,LI10,I2,X2,LI19'  ⎕FMT ( ι10;!ι10;10+ι10;!10+ι10)
    ∇

       FACTORIALS
  N  !N              N   !N
  1  1              11   39916800
  2  2              12   479001600
  3  6              13   6227020800
  4  24             14   87178291200
  5  120            15   1307674368000
  6  720            16   20922789888000
  7  5040           17   355687428096000
  8  40320          18   6402373705728000
  9  362880         19   1216451004088320__
 10  3628800        20   2432902008176640___
```

Note the dashes at the lower right of the display. They appear because the *internal* value stored in *APL* is accurate only to approximately 16 decimal places, and the positions shown as dashes indicate that there is no accuracy in those positions.

Results can be scaled using the K-qualifier. For example,

```
      'K‾2F6.2'  ⎕FMT (17620)
176.20
```

could be used when data is stored in cents, but displayed as dollars and cents. The number following K can be positive or negative, and is the power of 10 by which the argument is scaled. It's often easier than multiplying the right argument by a power of 10. The example on page 196 could have been written `'K2G⎕$ZZZZZZZ.99 REFUNDED⎕'  ⎕FMT ( 1063.24  .87  123456.78 ).`

Substitution of standard symbols

The previous discussion introduced some characters with special meaning in ⎕FMT left arguments and results. Here is a summary of them:

character	code	meaning
9	G	digit selector
Z	G	zero-suppress digit selector
*	F G I	overflow indicator
.	F	decimal point
,	C	comma insert
	F G I	insignificant digit marker
$\bar{0}$	Z	fill character
(blank)	G	lead zero fill character

For special effects, any of the above can be replaced by a different character through use of the *S*-qualifier. The following expression replaces commas by dashes and the star by a question mark:

```
      'S⎕,-*?⎕CI10' ⎕FMT (1234567 123456789)
 1-234-567
?????????
```

The first character in each pair is the standard symbol, and the second is the substitute.

Instead of ⎕, the characters < and > can be used to enclose text in ⎕FMT left arguments. Thus, '*G*<999*Z*>' is the same as '*G*⎕999*Z*⎕'.

Decorations

The codes *MNPQR*, each followed by a string of text enclosed between ⎕'s or < >, are used to inject that text into the field according to these rules:

> *M*⎕ text ⎕ places text to left of negative result
> *N*⎕ text ⎕ places text to right of negative result
> *P*⎕ text ⎕ places text to left of nonnegative result
> *Q*⎕ text ⎕ places text to right of nonnegative result
> *R*⎕ text ⎕ fills in "unclaimed" spaces with text.

Since some people still aren't accustomed to the way negative numbers are shown in **APL**, you can use the *M*-decoration to replace the **APL** overbar by the dash:

```
      'M<->P<$$>F10.2' ⎕FMT (¯79.32 10000 0 ¯123.45)
    -79.32
$$10000.00
   $$0.00
  -123.45
```

Besides using the *M*-decoration to get the minus sign in the above example, *P* was used to place two dollar signs before each nonnegative value. This is often called a "floating currency symbol" because it is placed adjacent to the first visible digit.

Business reports often indicate losses or decreases by placing the negative values in parentheses, rather than prefixing them with a negative sign. This can be accomplished on the **APL ★PLUS** ® system with the following combination:

```
     'MⒾ(ⒾNⒾ)ⒾQⒾ ⒾCI10' ⎕FMT ( ¯79 1000 0 ¯123.45)
     ( 79)
 1,000
     0
 (123)
```

Do you know why the QⒾ Ⓘ decoration is used?

The next illustration shows a typical "check protection" application in which the field is protected against someone tampering with the printed value. Compare the following with the defined function CP on page 187.

```
     'PⒾ$ⒾCRⒾ*⊛ⒾF14.2' ⎕FMT (7932.56)
*⊛*⊛*$7,932.56
```

Here is a way you can replace zeros by a literal indicator:

```
     'BRⒾ         NONEⒾF10.2' ⎕FMT ( ¯79.32 10000 0 ¯123.45)
   ¯79.32
10000.00
    NONE
 ¯123.45
```

Note that six blanks are required in front of the characters $NONE$ to match the given field width of 10.

These decorations and qualifiers consume additional character positions, and the field width must be sufficient to hold them all. If you try to put more characters in a field than will fit, the field will be entirely filled with the * character, but there is no other error indication given. This is so that in an involved commercial format, you can see what field caused the problem and revise your format string.

The most frequent cause of *'s appearing is the attempt to format literal data with an F-, I-, E- or G-code, or conversely, trying to format numeric data with the A-code. This often happens when you haven't counted the number of columns carefully in a literal matrix, so that there is no correlation between the format phrases and the columns of the data items in the right argument. For example, if you used the format

```
     '5A1,F10.2,I5,F10.2' ⎕FMT (NAMES;COSTS;QUANT;COSTS×QUANT)
NUTS **********        0    150.00*
SCREW**********        0    200.00*
BOLTS**********        0      4.00*
NAILS**********        0   1000.00*
```

you get the stars in the second field because the matrix $NAMES$ has six columns instead of five. The remaining data items are displaced one field to the right, with the consequences as shown.

One last fact about ⎕FMT: it really doesn't care whether all of the data items occupy the same number of rows or not; it simply fills in any "ragged edges" with blank fields. Note how we can produce the whole report, including a total line at the bottom:

```
     QC←COSTS×QUANT ◊ NAMT←5 6ρ( ,NAMES),'TOTAL '
     '6A1,F10.2,I5,F10.2' ⎕FMT (NAMT;COSTS;QUANT;QC,+/QC)
NUTS        0.05   150     7.50
SCREWS      0.03   200     6.00
BOLTS       0.20     4     0.80
NAILS       0.01  1000    10.00
TOTAL                     24.30
```

PROBLEMS

1. Using the numeric array $TABLE$ (page 190), format the array according to each of the following specifications: A) field width 10, 4 decimal places; B) field width 10, E-notation, 3 mantissa places; C) automatic width, 3 decimal places; D) columns 1 and 3 having 3 decimal places and field width 8, columns 2, 4, 5 having 5 decimal places and width 10.

2. You are given a logical matrix Q. Use ⊤ to display Q more compactly.

3. Without using the semicolon, form a line of mixed output from a literal vector L and a numeric vector N.

Chapter 22:
Branching

One of the more prominent features of most programming languages is the concept of program flow and control, commonly referred to as *branching*. If you are familiar with other languages, you may be wondering why this notion, which involves selection of only some of the steps of a function or causes repeated execution under specified conditions, hasn't yet been presented in this text. The reason is due to the nature of *APL*, which makes it possible to solve many problems in a more straightforward way without branching.

The branch instruction

Whenever an algorithm requires a decision to be made as to what the next step should be, based on the results of some previous step, a branch is generally called for. This is nothing more than an instruction to alter the regular sequence of steps.

We can demonstrate how this can be done by using a function called *SORT* in 1 *CLASS*. The problem which *SORT* is designed to handle is a very simple one: Rearrange the elements of a vector in ascending order. Actually there isn't any need to write a function to do this, since ▲ (grade up) can be used with subscripting to accomplish the same thing very concisely (see page 172). The function, however, is an easily understood example of how to control the sequencing of the steps in a program.

Let's talk ourselves through the algorithm needed to solve the problem. The first and most obvious step is to start with a clean sheet of paper.

Don't laugh. Try doing a large sorting problem by hand without it (or its equivalent). And as we'll see when we "translate" the steps required into their *APL* equivalents, this part of the algorithm really does have an *APL* analogue.

Next we pick out the smallest value in the vector, see how many times it occurs, and write it down that number of times. Then we cross these off the original vector, go back and pick out the smallest value from what's left and repeat the process above until all the numbers are used up.

It isn't any great challenge to design a machine to go through the repetitive steps, but it would need a safeguard built into it. *We* know when to stop, but a machine would have to be explicitly instructed; otherwise it would continue to cycle through the sequence of steps indefinitely. This means that our algorithm needs a step which says in effect, "Look each time through to see if any numbers are left in the vector. If there are any, go on; if not, stop."

Now we are ready to build the function $SORT$. Since only one argument is required, make it monadic, with an explicit result. Here is the header:

$\nabla R \leftarrow SORT\ X$

To start with, R has nothing in it. (Remember the clean sheet of paper?) Thus, line 1 should be

[1] $R \leftarrow \iota 0$

The next step is to look for the smallest number in X, which is $\lfloor / X$. But we need as many copies of it as there are in X. So what we require is really $(X = \lfloor / X) / X$ to pick them out. Since these are to be put into R, we can set line 2 as follows:

[2] $R \leftarrow R, (X = \lfloor / X) / X$

We then look at what's left, which is the new X, namely

[3] $X \leftarrow (X \neq \lfloor / X) / X$

This is as far as we can go, and now we have to repeat the process. In **APL** the instruction which directs the system to a step out of the normal sequence is the right-pointing arrow $\rightarrow$, found on the same key as the specification arrow $\leftarrow$. The arrow, which may be read as "go to" or "branch to," has to be followed by some value to complete the instruction. In this case the obvious step is

[4] $\rightarrow 2$

Unfortunately, we have neglected to tell the system when to stop, so it will loop around steps 2, 3 and 4 forever! One logical place for a checkpoint is just before step 2. What should it be? $0 = \rho X$ will yield 1 if X is empty, or 0 if X is not. Our problem is how to write the complete statement so that this extra line will cause execution to fall through to the next line (i.e., continue cycling) or cease, depending on the state of X. An instruction which does this is

[1.5] $\rightarrow 0 \times \iota 0 = \rho X$

Assuming that X is not a scalar to start with, here is how this works: If ρX is 0 (X is empty), then the instruction reads "branch to 0" ($0 \times \iota 1$ is 0). But there is no line 0 in the function, and we are in effect asking the system to leave the function and await your next entry from the keyboard.

Branching to *any* line number which isn't in the function will do the same thing, namely, result in an exit from the function. Branching to line 0 is guaranteed to work, however, because no function, no matter how big, has a line 0. The header doesn't count as a line here, even though we refer to it as [0] in function editing.

What if X isn't empty? Then $0 \times \iota 0$ is a vector of length 0, and the instruction reads "branch to an empty vector." A reasonable interpretation might consider this to be no branch at all, and indeed this is the way it is used in **APL**. It simply causes execution to continue with the next statement.

$\times \iota$ is an interesting combination of **APL** functions. Its action is such that when it occurs it can be read as "if," so that our line above reads "branch to 0 if X is empty; otherwise continue with the next statement."

APL interprets a branch to a vector as applying only to the first element of the vector, ignoring any others. In the case of a branch to an empty vector, there is no first element since there aren't any elements at all. Hence there is no branching, and the next statement in the function is executed.

Getting back to our algorithm, all the steps have been incorporated into the function $SORT$, and the lines renumbered. Load 1 $CLASS$, display $SORT$, and try it on a couple of vectors:

```
      )LOAD 1 CLASS
SAVED  15.02.39 04/15/74
      ∇SORT[☐]∇
  ∇ R←SORT X
[1]   R←ι0
[2]   →0×ι0=ρX
[3]   R←R,(X=⌊/X)/X
[4]   X←(X≠⌊/X)/X
[5]   →2
  ∇

      SORT 5 3 2
2 3 5
      SORT 5 3 1 5 4 2
1 2 3 4 5 5
```

It seems to work satisfactorily, so we'll go on to a second example, the function CMP, introduced earlier on page 162. Here is the original version, which doesn't contain any branches and prints $GREATER$, $EQUAL$ or $LESS$ after comparing the right and left arguments:

```
      ∇CMP[☐]∇
  ∇ A CMP B
[1]   ((A>B)/'GREATER'),((A=B)/'EQUAL'),(A<B)/'LESS'
  ∇
```

Comparing 3 and 5, we get

```
      3 CMP 5
LESS
```

Labels

An equivalent function which uses branching is $CMPX$:

```
      ∇CMPX[☐]∇
  ∇ A CMPX B
[1]   →BIGGER×ιA>B
[2]   →SMALLER×ιA<B
[3]   'EQUAL'
[4]   →0
[5] BIGGER:'GREATER'
[6]   →0
[7] SMALLER:'LESS'
  ∇
```

The colon on lines 5 and 7 of $CMPX$ is a separator. The name immediately to the left of the colon is a *label*. In $CMPX$ the label $BIGGER$ appears on line 5. Branching to $BIGGER$ is equivalent to branching to line 5, the value of the label being set at the beginning of function execution.

Why use a label? Because it is a convenient way to branch if there is any possibility that the function is to be later edited and lines added or deleted. For example, if line 1 were [1] →5 and we were to insert a line between 1 and 2, line 5 would then be what line 4 is now, namely, a command to exit the function. So labels direct us to specific points in the function, rather than specific line numbers.

Labels are local objects and hence not known outside the function, as can be seen by inspection of the following list of variables, which is from 1 $CLASS$:

```
      )VARS
CIRCUIT D          HELP      MILEAGE SPL      STOP      TAB0      TAB1
TAB2      TAB3      X
```

Having labels local instead of global avoids confusion among labels in different functions, and prevents the user from accidentally resetting the label outside the function. However, unlike local variables, they do not have to be listed in the header of the function. Also, as mentioned above, they are automatically respecified each time the function is executed.

CMPX, which has the two labels *BIGGER* and *SMALLER*, will be used to show these features. To illustrate the behavior of the label when the function is suspended, let's edit *CMPX* to include a variable *R* which has no value assigned:

```
      ∇CMPX[5.1]R∇
```

Now we'll execute the function for given values of *A* and *B*:

```
      3  CMPX  2
GREATER
VALUE ERROR
CMPX[6]  R
         ∧
```

BIGGER has a value (the line number) assigned to it within this suspended function:

```
      BIGGER
5
```

Suppose we try to assign a value to *BIGGER*:

```
      BIGGER←3
SYNTAX ERROR
      BIGGER←3
            ∧
```

The **APL** system prevents us from assigning a value to a label.

Labels as well as local variables are shown in the list of suspensions when the *SIV* command is used:

```
      )SIV
CMPX[6]  *         A         B         BIGGER  SMALLER
```

Editing of a suspended function contains a few pitfalls, as can be seen from the following display:

```
      ∇CMPX[1□6]
[1]     →BIGGER×ιA>B
        //////6
[1]     →LARGER×ιA>B
[2]     [5□6]
[5]    BIGGER:'GREATER'
        //////6
[5]    LARGER:'GREATER'
[6]     ∇
SI DAMAGE
```

The message *SI DAMAGE* is a warning that continued execution (without removing the suspensions) could produce erroneous results. Note that *CMPX*[6] is missing from the following)*SIV* display. When you get a *SI DAMAGE* message, you should enter → (alone) to remove the suspension.

```
      )SIV
*         A         B         BIGGER    SMALLER
      →
      @
      )SIV
      @
      3  CMPX 2
GREATER
VALUE ERROR
CMPX[6] R
      ∧
      )SIV
CMPX[6] *         A         B         LARGER    SMALLER
      →
```

An $SI\ DAMAGE$ message also results when a function in the state indicator list is erased or replaced by recopying it. The result of such replacement or removal makes it impossible for the execution to be resumed. In any event, the SI display generally marks the damage by omission of the function name.

Finally, here is another version (the last!) of the same function. This one is called $CMPY$:

```
      ∇CMPY[□]∇
    ∇ A CMPY B
[1]   →4+2××A-B
[2]   'LESS'
[3]   →0
[4]   'EQUAL'
[5]   →0
[6]   'GREATER'
    ∇
```

Line 1 is the key here. It subtracts B from A and uses the monadic signum to return 1, $^-1$ or 0 depending on what comes out of the subtraction. Thus, if A is greater than B, $A-B$ is positive and line 1 causes a branch to line 6. If A is less than B, we branch to line 2, while if A and B are equal we go to line 4, which is pretty sneaky, albeit an effective way to go about it.

If you haven't been asleep during the first part of this chapter, you already may have thought about still other ways to branch. Besides $×ι$, compression is frequently used in *conditional* (i.e., where there is a choice) branch statements. Here is an example of a function which locates the line(s) in a literal matrix corresponding to a given name:

```
    ∇ R←X FINDROW STRING;HOLD;I
[1]   R←ιI←0
[2]   STRING←(¯1↑ρX)↑STRING
[3] LOOP:I←I+1
[4]   →(I>1↑ρX)/OUT
[5]   HOLD←X[I;]
[6]   →(~∧/HOLD=STRING)/LOOP
[7]   →LOOP,R←R,I
[8] OUT:→(0≠ρR)/0
[9]   'NAME NOT FOUND'
    ∇

      X←4 5ρ'JOHN MARY JAMESJOHN '
      X FINDROW 'JOHN'
1  4
```

```
      X FINDROW 'JOHNNIE'
NAME NOT FOUND
      X FINDROW 'JAMESIE'
3
```

Here line 1 sets up a counter I and the resultant (to receive the proper row numbers as they are generated). Line 2 pads out or truncates $STRING$ for later comparison. It is not foolproof, as will be seen from the third example. (Do you see a way to correct this?) Line 3 increments the counter I while line 4 is a checkpoint to get us out (via line 8) when we have cycled through every row of the matrix X, printing an appropriate message if the name represented by the right argument $STRING$ is not in X (line 9.) Next, the row of the matrix represented by the counter I is stored in $HOLD$ (line 5) and compared with $STRING$ (line 6). If there is a match, the result of line 6 is a fall-through to line 7, where the row number is catenated to the contents of R. The program cycles back to line 3, where the counter is incremented. If there is no match on line 6, there is no updating of line 7.

In Chapter 32 the *index origin* feature will be introduced, at which time it will be possible to change the starting point for indexing, ranking, sequence generation, etc., from its normal 1 to 0. One nice feature about the use of compression for branching is that, unlike $\times \iota$, it is independent of the origin, a point to be kept in mind as you begin to define your own functions with branching. For a start, you might go back and use compression to rewrite line 2 of $SORT$.

Compression is also a bit faster that $\times \iota$. It doesn't matter much if you are only executing the expression a few times, but the saving can be considerable for highly iterative functions.

Iteration

The function $FINDROW$ in the last section illustrates one of the most common uses of the branch in computer programming: to cause repeated execution of a set of statements while incrementing a counter or until some condition is reached. This type of branching, called *iteration* or *looping*, occurs less frequently in **APL** than in other languages because of **APL**'s powerful array handling operations, but it still merits discussion.

Here is another example of an algorithm using loops: a simulation of the dyadic iota (index of) function. Each element of the right argument must be compared to each element of the left argument until a match is found.

```
       ∇ R←A DIOTA X;RX;I;J                      ∇ R←A DIOTA2 X;RX;I;J
 [1]     RX←ρX                            [1]     RX←ρX
 [2]     X←,X                             [2]     X←,X
 [3]     R←ι0                             [3]     R←ι0
 [4]     I←1                              [4]     I←0
                                    →  [5]     LPI:I←I+1
                                    * [6]     →(I>×/RX)/DONE ──┐
                                      [7]     J←0              │
 →  [5]     LPI:J←1               →  [8]     LPJ:J←J+1         │
                                    * [9]     →(J>ρA)/HIT ──┐  │
 ┌→* [6]  LPJ:→(A[J]=X[I])/HIT─┐   *[10]     →(A[J]=X[I])/HIT─┤  │
 │   [7]     J←J+1             │    [11]     →LPJ         │  │
 └ *[8]     →(J≤ρA)/LPJ        │    [12]  HIT:R←R,J  ←────┘  │
 │   [9]  HIT:R←R,J      ←─────┘                            │
 │  [10]     I←I+1                  [13]     →LPI  ←──────────┘
 └ *[11]   →(I≤×/RX)/LPI            [14]  DONE:R←RXρR  ←──────┘
    [12]     R←RXρR
       ∇                                    ∇
```

The loops are bracketed, with decision points marked with a ✱. Note that $DIOTA$ has a series of steps followed by a logical test (*trailing decision*) while in $DIOTA2$ the test is placed first (*leading decision*). If you are inclined to view this as nit-picking, you should observe the following difference: $DIOTA2$ will accept and properly handle empty left and right arguments while $DIOTA$ will not (why?). It is true that both forms are equivalent in most cases, but in general you'll be better off with leading decisions.

Examples of branch instructions

For the benefit of the reader, here is a list of some of the different ways of writing branch instructions in **APL**. Labels may be used in place of line numbers. Also, the membership function and any appropriate logical or relational function may be used in place of those listed.

(1) Branch unconditionally to a fixed point in the program:

```
→5
→LABEL
```

(2) Branch unconditionally out of the program:

```
→0  (or  any  nonexistent  line  number)
```

(3) Branch to one of two possible lines:

```
→(L1,L2)[1+X≥Y]
→((X≥Y),~X≥Y)/L1,L2
→(1 0≠X≥Y)/L1,L2
```

(4) Branch to one of several lines:

```
→(L1,L2,L3)[2+×X-Y]
→((X>Y),(X<Y),X=Y)/L1,L2,L3
→IϕL1,L2,L3,...        ( I  is  a  counter)
```

(5) Branch to a given line or drop through to the next line:

```
→(X≥Y)/L1
→(X≥Y)ρL1
→(×X-Y)↑L1,L2
→L1×ιX≥Y
→L1⌈ιX≥Y
→(L2,L3,L1)[I]×ιX≥Y
→L1×ιX≥I←I+1
→((A<0),A>0)/L1,L2
→L1 IF C
```

where IF is defined as follows for those users who prefer English in their instructions (C is a logical scalar or vector of length 1):

```
        ∇A←L1 IF C              ∇A←L1 IF C
[1]     A←C/L1∇        or   [1]     A←CρL1∇
```

(6) Branch out of the program or drop through to the next line:

```
→(X≥Y)/0
→(∨/,X≥Y)/0
→0×ιX≥Y
```

(7) Branch out of the program or to a specific line:

$$\rightarrow((X \geq Y), X < Y)/L1, 0$$
$$\rightarrow L1 \times X \geq Y$$

(8) Branch to a given line or the line following it:

$$\rightarrow L1 + X \geq Y$$

Finally, as a reminder, to remove a suspension, execute $\rightarrow$, and to branch to a particular point in a suspended program,

$$PROGRAM~[9]$$
$$\rightarrow 12$$

Rules for branching

We may summarize the rules for branching in function definition as follows:

$$\rightarrow \quad (\text{any } \textbf{\textit{APL}} \text{ expression})$$
is

(1)   INVALID if the expression results in other than an integer or a vector whose first element (the only one which can cause a branch) is an integer or a valid label.

(2)   VALID if the expression results in

   (a)   an empty vector, which causes a branch to the next statement.
   (b)   an integer outside the range of statement numbers of the function, which causes an exit from the function.
   (c)   an integer inside the range of statement numbers of the function, which causes a branch to that line number.
   (d)   a label, which causes a branch to that line of the function on which the label is to be found.

Branching is a powerful programming tool. Branch if you must, but with a little extra care and ingenuity on your part, you will often find a way to eliminate the need for it and probably use less computer time.

Some thoughts on programming style

From time to time in the text we have commented on nonsyntactical do's and don'ts in writing **_APL_** instructions. Now that branching has been introduced, it is appropriate to summarize these and other observations that may be of help to you:

Names - mnemonic identifiers whenever possible
Documentation - comment statements to define the purpose of the function, global variables used, environmental assumptions made, appropriate credits and references
Readability - short, concise statements (using ◊ if available)
Branching - avoidance of absolute and relative branches, using labels instead
Variables - localized in the header if assigned in the function, or clearly documented if globals are set or changed
Restartability - avoidance of lines that require undoing something that was done prior to the error
Normal function flow - downward, with error processing proceeding to the right
Input - flexible in form, with error messages containing enough information to allow the user to correct mistakes.

We would be less than candid if we attempted to dictate by fiat what "good" programming style is. Whatever good style is, it certainly changes with time and depends on the features available on the system being used.

"Good" can probably be best translated as "readable." It should be pointed out, however, that readability is not necessarily synonymous with efficiency of execution and effective use of storage. We would hope that **APL** systems with many large applications where execution time and storage limitations are concerns, would provide appropriate software tools to make readable functions more efficient or more compact.

PROBLEMS

1. Tell what each of the following does:

   A) $\rightarrow((5<W),5>W)/3\ 2$

   B) $\rightarrow 3\times\iota A=8$

   C) $\rightarrow END\times Y>,R\leftarrow 1\ 1\rho 1$

   D) $\rightarrow(\vee/,B\epsilon C)/7$

   E) $\rightarrow 5\ 0[1+A>C]$

   F) $\rightarrow\bar{\ }1\uparrow\phi 3\ 4\ 7\ 9$

   G) $\rightarrow 8\times\iota 0\neq J\leftarrow J-1$

   H) $\rightarrow 4\times(|X)\geq I\leftarrow I+1$

   I) $\rightarrow AGAIN\times\iota N=2\times 1\rho R\leftarrow 2\ 4\rho 5\ 7\ 1\ 8$

2. Let T be a vector of "trash" characters, some of which may occur in the literal vector V. Define an **APL** function that will eliminate the trash from V.

3. Write a program to determine all three-digit numbers between P and Q such that if the final digit is eliminated, the result divides the original number.

4. Use branching to find the median of a set of numbers. (See problem 11, Chapter 19 for more information about the median.)

5. Define a dyadic function $DUPL$ that will locate all occurrences of some scalar N in a vector V and print an appropriate message if the desired scalar is not present.

6. Design an **APL** function so that it ignores all nonscalar input and takes the square root of any scalar argument. Assume all input is positive.

7. Take the opening two sentences of this chapter, eliminating all punctuation, underlining and blanks, and define a function to arrange the characters in alphabetic order.

8. Write an **APL** program to find the *mode* (most frequently occurring number) of a set of data.

9. The Fibonacci series is of the form 1 1 2 3 5 8 13 ..., where each term after the first two is the sum of the preceding two terms. Define a function which prints N terms of the series.

10. Define a function which will produce a histogram of a vector A of nonnegative integers, i.e., the height of the histogram for $A[1]$ is $A[1]$, the height for $A[5]$ is $A[5]$, etc. Show how the histogram can be "cleaned up" by replacing the 0's with blanks and the 1's with *'s.

11. Use branching to construct a function which prints an annual compound interest table. Design your function to produce three columns, the first to be the year, the second the value of the principal at the beginning of the year, and the third the interest accumulated during the year. Include appropriate column headings and round off each figure to the nearest cent.

12. Estimate the odds that 3 or more cards of any one suit will appear in a 5-card poker hand from a well-shuffled deck.

13. Define a dyadic function $PICT$ that will "draw" a picture of any matrix M consisting of 0's and 1's. Each of the two scalars used is to be converted to a separate character as specified in the vector A, one of the arguments of $PICT$.

Chapter 23:
Diagnostic aids

Until the chapter on branching, execution of defined functions was relatively straightforward, proceeding from one line to the next in order. With the introduction to branching, it is possible for the sequence of steps to become quite intricate. At such times it is often desirable to be able to follow what is happening on certain lines during execution. And, if problems arise, knowledge of what occurs at each step may be a definite help to us in debugging the program.

APL provides controls for tracing and stopping execution of defined functions. These will be examined and illustrated in the following sections.

Trace and stop controls

Our guinea-pig function will be $SORT$, which is in 1 $CLASS$:

```
      )LOAD 1 CLASS
SAVED  15.02.39 04/15/74
      ∇SORT[□]∇
   ∇  R←SORT X
[1]    R←ι0
[2]    →0×ι0=ρX
[3]    R←R,(X=⌊/X)/X
[4]    X←(X≠⌊/X)/X
[5]    →2
   ∇
```

The interesting lines here are 3 and 4. We can trace execution on them to see what has been put into R (line 3) and X (line 4) by the command

```
      TΔSORT←3  4
```

$TΔSORT$ is called the *trace control* for the function $SORT$, and is set to trace lines 3 and 4. It will remain set to these lines in $SORT$ until we remove it or change it. The trace lets us execute $SORT$ and follow the progress of its execution. Here is an example:

```
        SORT 3 2 4 3 2 5
SORT[3]  2 2
SORT[4]  3 4 3 5
SORT[3]  2 2 3 3
SORT[4]  4 5
SORT[3]  2 2 3 3 4
SORT[4]  5
SORT[3]  2 2 3 3 4 5
SORT[4]
2 2 3 3 4 5
```

The first time through, R starts as $\iota 0$ and then the vector 2 2 is catenated to it. X becomes 3 4 3 5, which is what's left. The second time through 3 3 is catenated to R, and X has just 4 5 in it, etc.

If the next time we execute $SORT$ we want to change the trace vector, all that is necessary is to respecify $T\Delta SORT$. Without actually doing it at this point, what do you think should be specified if we want to drop the trace altogether?

Now let's look at the action of the *stop control* on $SORT$. It operates in much the same way as the trace, but has the effect of suspending the function just prior to the lines specified. For example, set

```
    S∆SORT←ι5
```

and execute

```
    SORT 3 2 3 2
SORT[1]
```

The response tells us where in the function we are suspended, the number being the line to be executed next. This is confirmed by the state indicator:

```
    )SI
SORT[1] *
```

Once inside the function we can take a look at the values of the local variables, which are otherwise inaccessible to us. For instance, here is R:

```
    R
VALUE ERROR
    R
    ^
```

We get a $VALUE\ ERROR$ since $SORT$ is suspended just prior to line 1 and R hasn't been set yet. But X has already received a value:

```
    X
3 2 3 2
```

If we wanted to do so, X could be changed at this point by respecifying it. However, we'll continue with the execution of this function by using the branch command:

```
    →1
SORT[2]
```

There is a stop on line 2 also, and in fact on every line in this function. Now we can get R:

```
        R
        @
        ρR
0
```

Since R was specified to be an empty vector on line 1, no $VALUE\ ERROR$ occurs. Remember, we're still inside the function. Continuing, we get the following display:

```
        →2
SORT[3]
        →3
SORT[3]  2  2

SORT[4]
```

The new value of R, 2 2, is printed here because the trace is still set on lines 3 and 4. We could go on, but this should be enough to demonstrate how the stop works.

To remove the stop, we reset it as follows:

```
        SΔSORT←ι0
```

However, we are still suspended on line 4 of $SORT$:

```
        )SI
SORT[4]  *
```

Branching to line 4 continues the execution without any further suspensions but with the trace still on (we haven't taken it off yet):

```
        →4
SORT[4]  3  3
SORT[3]  2  2  3  3
SORT[4]
2  2  3  3
```

Now we'll turn the trace off in the same manner as the stop, and then try the state indicator:

```
        TΔSORT←ι0
        )SI
        @
```

We see that by having resumed execution in a function ($SORT$) which is completely executable and doesn't have any stops on it, we have removed the suspension. $SORT$ can now be executed normally:

```
        SORT  2  3  4  1  2
1  2  2  3  4
```

A word of advice: It pays to be selective in setting the trace vector. For instance, suppose we set

```
        TΔSORT←ι5
```

and execute $SORT$. Little useful information is obtained by tracing lines 1, 2 and 5.

```
        SORT  2  3  2  1  4  5
SORT[1]
SORT[2]  →3
SORT[3]  1
```
(display continued on next page)

```
SORT[4]  2 3 2 4 5
SORT[5]  →2
SORT[2]  →3
SORT[3]  1 2 2
SORT[4]  3 4 5
SORT[5]  →2
SORT[2]  →3
SORT[3]  1 2 2 3
SORT[4]  4 5
SORT[5]  →2
SORT[2]  →3
SORT[3]  1 2 2 3 4
SORT[4]  5
SORT[5]  →2
SORT[2]  →3
SORT[3]  1 2 2 3 4 5
SORT[4]
SORT[5]  →2
SORT[2]  →0
1 2 2 3 4 5
```

Both the trace and stop control vectors can be used as a line or part of a line in a defined function, since they are valid **APL** instructions. Also, the trace and stop vectors are *not* variables and are deleted when the function for which they are set is erased. They are saved and loaded along with the workspace containing them, but they do *not* copy. As an incidental observation, it is advisable to avoid names beginning with $T\Delta$ or $S\Delta$. (Try it to see what happens.)

Recursion

Sometimes it is necessary for a function to appear on one of the lines of its own definition. When this happens, it is said to be *recursively defined*. Here is an example, a defined function to calculate factorials, and found in 1 $CLASS$. The function is called $FACT$, but before displaying it, let's look at the definition of N! in conventional notation:

$$N! \text{ is } \begin{cases} \text{undefined for N not a positive integer or zero} \\ 1 \text{ if N is zero} \\ N \times (N-1)! \text{ if N is a positive integer.} \end{cases}$$

By this definition 5! would be figured as

$$\begin{aligned} 5! \quad &= 5 \times 4! \\ &= 5 \times (4 \times 3!) \\ &= 5 \times (4 \times (3 \times 2!)) \\ &= 5 \times (4 \times (3 \times (2 \times 1!))) \\ &= 5 \times (4 \times (3 \times (2 \times (1 \times 0!)))) \\ &= 5 \times (4 \times (3 \times (2 \times (1 \times 1)))) \\ &= 120 \end{aligned}$$

Now for the function $FACT$, which carries out a recursive calculation of a factorial:

```
      ∇  R←FACT N;NM1
[1]      →0×ιN≠⌊N
[2]      →BOTTOM×ιN=0
[3]      NM1←N-1
[4]      R←N×FACT NM1
[5]      →0
[6]      BOTTOM:R←1 ∇
```

The local variable $NM1$ stands for $N-1$ and is useful for tracing the function. Line 1 causes a branch to 0 if N is not a positive integer or 0. Line 2 branches to 6 if N is 0, at which point R is set to 1 (since $!0$ is 1). If N isn't 0, line 3 sets $NM1$. Line 4 sets R to $N \times FACT\ N-1$, which will itself result in execution of $FACT$. Each time the function comes to line 4, it gets deeper and deeper into successive levels of execution until N works its way down to 0. Then the function begins to work its way out to the surface again and finally exits on line 5.

Let's execute $FACT\ 4$:

```
      FACT  4
24
```

This gives the same answer as $!4$ (since we set it up that way), but takes longer to execute:

```
      !4
24
```

If we set a trace on $FACT$, we can see how it develops. Lines 3, 4 and 6 are our best bets here for tracing:

```
      TΔFACT←3  4  6
      FACT  4
FACT[3]  3
FACT[3]  2
FACT[3]  1
FACT[3]  0
FACT[6]  1
FACT[4]  1
FACT[4]  2
FACT[4]  6
FACT[4]  24
24
```

The first time through, line 3 sets $NM1$ to be 3. But when execution drops through to the next line to execute $FACT\ 4$, $FACT\ 3$ has to be calculated first. So the function cycles through the first three steps again, and this time the trace on line 3 shows that $NM1$ is 2. This will continue until $NM1$ is 0. When the system tries to calculate $FACT\ 0$ it loops through steps 1 and 2 and branches to 6, yielding a 1.

Meanwhile, back on line 4 there finally is a value to put in R, namely, 1, which is followed by 2, 6 and 24 in succession as the function works its way out.

Now let's turn the trace off and set the stop control at 6 to explore what's happening near the end of the function:

```
      TΔFACT←ι0
      SΔFACT←6
      FACT  4

FACT[6]
```

We are suspended just prior to line 6. The state indicator shows some interesting results:

```
      )SI
FACT[6]  *
FACT[4]
FACT[4]
FACT[4]
FACT[4]
```

Line 4 is listed four times as pending, which isn't surprising since we are held up on that line that many times, each time getting deeper into the function while waiting for $NM1$ to reach 0.

We can get out by branching to line 6, which our previous trace shows we won't encounter again:

```
        →6
24
```

If this is what we get into with 4 for an argument, what do you suppose would happen if we ask for $FACT$ 50? This will take quite a while, and we may want to interrupt execution with ATTN before line 6 is reached:

```
        FACT 50

FACT[2]
```

We get a suspension on line 2. Let's see what the state indicator shows:

```
        )SI
FACT[2]  *
FACT[4]                 (Execution of this list has been interrupted
FACT[4]                 by the use of ATTN, since otherwise it would
FACT[4]                 be apt to run on for some while.)
FACT[4]
```

What happens if we try to get out of this mess? If we branch to line 6, it might go on a lot longer while the system worked its way out. Branching to 0 will get us out, as indeed will typing → alone:

```
        →0
VALUE ERROR
FACT[4] R←N×FACT NM1
         ∧
```

We get a $VALUE\ ERROR$ because at line 2, R (the resultant) hasn't been set yet. At this point the function is in a pretty sad state. We are suspended at great depth. There are two ways to get out of a dilemma like this: you could type → alone; that will reduce the state indicator to the last suspended function as discussed in Chapter 13; or use the $)COPY$ system command to help clear things up.

What to do when the state indicator is cluttered

The sequence of commands that will get us out is to first save the active workspace, then clear and copy the saved workspace. $CONTINUE$ is always available to us (CAUTION! don't use for long term storage), so we'll save into $CONTINUE$:

```
        )SAVE CONTINUE
  2.32.13 03/11/74
        )CLEAR
CLEAR WS
        )COPY CONTINUE
  SAVED   2.32.13 03/11/74
```

The $COPY$ command copies all the global objects in $CONTINUE$, but won't copy suspensions. However, loading $CONTINUE$ will bring along all the suspensions associated with the functions in $CONTINUE$. If we don't want to keep the function, the easiest way out would be to delete it with the $ERASE$ command, or drop the entire workspace without saving it. These alternatives may be unacceptable if the workspace and function are important to the user. Just remember that copying an entire workspace uses up a considerable amount of CPU time, compared to loading it.

The line counter

The niladic system function $\square LC$ returns a numeric vector of pending and suspended lines of functions. The numbers in the result are the as what that you would get from $)SI$ at the same point. For example, if you had executed $\square LC$ at the point of the display in the middle of the last page, the result would have been 6 4 4 4 4 . Whenever the state indicator is empty, $\square LC$ is an empty vector. Otherwise, the first element of $\square LC$ is the line presently being executed (or suspended). On earlier systems, $\text{I}26$ or $\text{I}27$ ($\perp$ overstruck with $\top$) was used instead of $\square LC$.

When resuming execution of a suspended function, $\rightarrow\square LC$ causes resumption at the suspended line (see page 317 for an example). $\rightarrow\square LC[1]+4$ causes the line which is 4 lines from the present line to be executed next.

$\rho\square LC$ is a useful diagnostic to build into application programs. It can be used to measure the depth of the state indicator, and take appropriate actions (usually a prompt to the user to clear his suspensions).

PROBLEMS

1. Trace the execution of each of the functions developed in the problem section at the end of Chapter 22, problems 2, 7 and 8.

2. The function below uses the Euclidean algorithm to get the greatest common divisor of the two arguments:

```
        ∇  Z←A  GCD  B
   [1]     Z←A
   [2]     A←A|B
   [3]     B←Z
   [4]     →A≠0
        ∇
```

Enter the function GCD in your workspace and trace its execution for $A\leftarrow75$ and $B\leftarrow105$.

3. ACK is a function constructed for the purpose of proving that nonprimitive recursive functions do exist, and is named after its creator (see Communications of the ACM, page 114, Vol. 8, No.2, February, 1965.) Use *small* integers for I and J. Follow the execution of ACK with the trace and stop controls:

```
        ∇  R←I  ACK  J
   [1]     →(0=I,J)/4  3
   [2]     →0,R←(I-1)  ACK  I  ACK  J-1
   [3]     →0,R←(I-1)  ACK  1
   [4]     R←J+1
        ∇
```

4. Redo problem 9, Chapter 22 and define a dyadic recursive function $FIB1$ whose right argument A specifies the first two terms of the series, with the left argument N the number of terms desired.

Chapter 24:
Multidimensional arrays

Thus far the functions introduced have been illustrated with examples of scalars, vectors and matrices. Except for a few illustrations earlier in the text, three- (and higher-) dimensional arrays have not been used.

APL can handle arrays of up to rank 63, which should be enough to satisfy the most ambitious among you. The subject of this chapter is how the functions you have already worked with operate with these arrays. The examples will be primarily three-dimensional, most people's minds having some difficulty visualizing what is happening for more complex arrays. Besides the functions used up to this point, two new ones, *transpose* and *laminate* will be examined.

For purposes of illustration, let's define several arrays of rank greater than 1:

```
A←2 3 4ρι24
B←2 3 4ρ2×φι24
C←2 2 3 4ρι50
```

Many of the functions previously introduced with two-dimensional arrays are easily extendible to A, B and C:

```
          A
  1   2   3   4
  5   6   7   8
  9  10  11  12

 13  14  15  16
 17  18  19  20
 21  22  23  24
          B
 48  46  44  42
 40  38  36  34
 32  30  28  26

 24  22  20  18
 16  14  12  10
  8   6   4   2
```

```
      A+B
49 48 47 46
45 44 43 42
41 40 39 38

37 36 35 34
33 32 31 30
29 28 27 26
     ÷A
 1               0.5             0.3333333333     0.25
 0.2             0.1666666667    0.1428571429     0.125
 0.1111111111    0.1             0.09090909091    0.08333333333

 0.07692307692   0.07142857143   0.06666666667    0.0625
 0.05882352941   0.05555555556   0.05263157895    0.05
 0.04761904762   0.04545454545   0.04347826087    0.04166666667
     2×C
 2   4   6   8
10  12  14  16
18  20  22  24

26  28  30  32
24  36  38  40
42  44  46  48
```

(Note the varying amount of space used by **APL** as a separator between those parts of C representing the different dimensions.)

```
50   52 54 56
58  60 62 64
66  68 70 72

74  76 78 80
82  84 86 88
90  92 94 96
     B[2;2 3;3 4]
12 10
 4  2
```

In fact, the rules for primitive scalar dyadic and monadic functions stated earlier can be boiled down to

$$\text{any-dimensional} \leftarrow \text{any-dimensional} \; f \; \text{any-dimensional}$$
$$\text{array} \qquad\qquad \text{array} \qquad\qquad \text{array}$$

with the array restrictions on dimension and rank previously stated and allowing the combination scalar-higher rank array on the right, f here standing for any primitive scalar dyadic function; and

$$\text{any-dimensional} \leftarrow g \; \text{any-dimensional}$$
$$\text{array} \qquad\qquad \text{array}$$

with g standing for any primitive scalar monadic function.

Operations along a single dimension

In Chapter 7 we saw how reduction could be used along the rows or columns of a matrix. The problem is slightly more complicated with an array of rank greater than 2. For example, consider this problem: A store sells three items, A, B, C, and keeps the following sales record over a two-month period in the array S:

```
                    MONTH 1                                    MONTH 2
           ITEM | A   B   C                          ITEM | A   B   C
          ------+--------                           ------+--------
           WEEK 1| 1   2   0                          WEEK 1| 2   4   7
           WEEK 2| 1   3   2                          WEEK 2| 1   0   8
           WEEK 3| 3   4   2                          WEEK 3| 4   1   6
           WEEK 4| 3   3   0                          WEEK 4| 1   2   3
```

```
        S←2 4 3ρ1 2 0 1 3 2 3 4 2 3 3 0 2 4 7 1 0 8 4 1 6 1 2 3
        S
  1  2  0
  1  3  2
  3  4  2
  3  3  0

  2  4  7
  1  0  8
  4  1  6
  1  2  3
```

Executing $+/S$ results in

```
      +/S
   3   6   9   6
  13   9  11   6
```

which represents the total number of items purchased for each week of month 1 (first row of the result) and month 2 (second row). However, $+/S$ does *not* give us what you might expect from our earlier work in Chapter 7, namely the total number of items 41, 65 and 44 purchased over each month:

```
      +⌿S
   3   6   7
   2   3  10
   7   5   8
   4   5   3
```

Instead, the result appears to be a combined sales record by item and week which lumps together both months.

The problem here is that the expression $+/$ operates across the *last* coordinate of an array. Since S has the dimensions 2 4 3, the operation is carried out along the rows, the coordinate represented by the 3. Similarly, $+⌿$ operates across the *first* coordinate, here the planes.

To get at any coordinate other than the first or the last, it is necessary to specify the coordinate. In the above example, to sum over the second coordinate of S, execute

```
      +/[2]S
  8  12   4
  8   7  24
```

Of course it is possible (though somewhat superfluous in the above calculations) to use the same syntax to operate over coordinates 1 and 3:

```
      +/[1]S
   3   6   7
   2   3  10
   7   5   8
   4   5   3
```

```
        +/[3]S
    3   6   9   6
   13   9  11   6
```

The coordinate selector in all cases must be a scalar or a 1-element vector.

To carry our illustration one step further, suppose we wish to compute row, column and plane averages. This would require our dividing the sums over each coordinate by the respective lengths of the array along each coordinate. There is a function called $MEAN$ in 1 $CLASS$ that will compute these averages for us. Let's first copy it and then display it:

```
        )COPY 1 CLASS MEAN
SAVED   15.02.39 04/15/74
        ∇MEAN[□]∇
    ∇ R←K MEAN X
[1]     R←(+/[K]X)÷(ρX)[K]
    ∇
```

It is dyadic, the left argument K being the coordinate of the array X across which we are averaging. The function takes a given coordinate of X and divides the sum across that coordinate by the number of elements comprising that sum, as explained above.

Let's try it on S. Here are the averages across the three coordinates:

```
        1 MEAN S
   1.5              3              3.5
   1                1.5            5
   3.5              2.5            4
   2                2.5            1.5
        2 MEAN S
   2                3              1
   2                1.75           6
        3 MEAN S
   1                2              3              2
   4.333333333      3              3.666666667    2
```

The overall average is

```
        1 MEAN 2 MEAN 3 MEAN S
2.625
```

Can you think of why 3 $MEAN$ 2 $MEAN$ 1 $MEAN$ S won't work?

The same coordinate selection scheme outlined above for reduction applies to other functions as well. Here are a number of representative examples using $TAB3$:

```
        )COPY 1 CLASS TAB3
SAVED   15.20.39 04/15/74
        TAB3                          +\[2]TAB3
   111 112 113                   111 112 113
   121 122 123                   232 234 236
   131 132 133                   363 366 369
   141 142 143                   504 508 512

   211 212 213                   211 212 213
   221 222 223                   432 434 436
   231 232 233                   663 666 669
   241 242 243                   904 908 912
```

```
        1ϕTAB3
112  113  111
122  123  121
132  133  131
142  143  141

212  213  211
222  223  221
232  233  231
242  243  241
```

```
        (A←2 3ρ1 2 3 2 1 3)ϕ[2]TAB3
121  132  143
131  142  113
141  112  123
111  122  133

231  222  243
241  232  213
211  242  223
221  212  233
```

The last illustration needs careful examination to see what is happening. Note that the left argument is itself a matrix:

```
        A
1  2  3
2  1  3
```

To see what is happening, look at $A[1;2]$. It contains a 2 and therefore rotates $TAB3[1;;2]$ two positions. Can you describe the result of $(4\ 3\rho\iota12)\ominus TAB3$?

Here are some additional examples:

```
        1 0⌿TAB3
111  112  113
121  122  123
131  132  133
141  142  143
        1 1 1 0 1\[2]TAB3
111  112  113
121  122  123
131  132  133
  0    0    0
141  142  143

211  212  213
221  222  223
231  232  233
  0    0    0
241  242  243
        1 2 ¯2↑TAB3
112  113
122  123
        1 ¯1 2↑TAB3
213
223
233
        R←2 4ρTAB3
        R
111  112  113  121
122  123  131  132
        R∈TAB3
1 1 1 1
1 1 1 1
        TAB3[2;;2]
212  222  232  242
        TAB3[1;2 4;3]
123  143
```

Note that (+\[2]TAB3)[;4;] is the same as +/[2]TAB3. Can you generalize this?

```
      ( ,TAB3)ιTAB3
  1  2  3
  4  5  6
  7  8  9
 10 11 12

 13 14 15
 16 17 18
 19 20 21
 22 23 24
```

Catenation and lamination

Two variables whose shapes are *conformable* (i.e., the "right size") can be joined along an existing coordinate. If no coordinate is specified, the catenation is over the last coordinate. The character arrays P, Q, R, S and T will be used here for illustration:

```
         P                          Q                      R                  S                 T
∇ ∇ ∇ ∇ ∇ ∇ ∇        □□□□□□□        ○○○○○○○        * * * * * * *      Δ Δ Δ Δ
∇ ∇ ∇ ∇ ∇ ∇ ∇        □□□□□□□        ○○○○○○○                ρS              ρT
                     □□□□□□□               ρR       7               4
∇ ∇ ∇ ∇ ∇ ∇ ∇        □□□□□□□         2  7                                       .
∇ ∇ ∇ ∇ ∇ ∇ ∇               ρQ
         ρP          4  7
 2  2  7
```

```
         Q,[1]R                          Q,[1]S                          Q,T
□□□□□□□                        □□□□□□□                        □□□□□□□Δ
□□□□□□□                        □□□□□□□                        □□□□□□□Δ
□□□□□□□                        □□□□□□□                        □□□□□□□Δ
□□□□□□□                        □□□□□□□                        □□□□□□□Δ
○○○○○○○                        * * * * * * *                          ρQ,T
○○○○○○○                              ρQ,[1]S                  4  8
       ρQ,[1]R                 5  7
 6  7
```

A scalar argument is extended for purposes of catenation:

```
      W←'*'
      Q,W                   Q,[2]W                   Q,[1]W                  W,[2]P
□□□□□□□*        □□□□□□□*        □□□□□□□        * * * * * *
□□□□□□□*        □□□□□□□*        □□□□□□□        ∇ ∇ ∇ ∇ ∇ ∇ ∇
□□□□□□□*        □□□□□□□*        □□□□□□□        ∇ ∇ ∇ ∇ ∇ ∇ ∇
□□□□□□□*        □□□□□□□*        □□□□□□□
      ρQ,W             ρQ,[2]W        * * * * * *        * * * * * *
4  8            4  8                            ρQ,[1]W        ∇ ∇ ∇ ∇ ∇ ∇ ∇
                                      5  7               ∇ ∇ ∇ ∇ ∇ ∇ ∇
                                                               ρW,[2]P
                                                        2  3  7
```

You can also join two variables along a new coordinate. The *laminate* function, which also uses the comma, does this:

```
        Q,[.5]W                      Q,[1.4]W                    R,[2.3]W
□□□□□□□                      □□□□□□□                    ○*
□□□□□□□                      *******                    ○*
□□□□□□□                                                 ○*
□□□□□□□                      □□□□□□□                    ○*
                             ******                     ○*
******                                                  ○*
******                       □□□□□□□                    ○*
******                       *******
******                                                  ○*
        ρQ,[.5]W             □□□□□□□                    ○*
 2  4  7                     ******                     ○*
                                     ρQ,[1.4]W          ○*
                              4  2  7                   ○*
                                                        ○*
                                                        ○*
                                                              ρR,[2.3]W
                                                         2  7  2
```

Here is a way to think about laminating arrays. Suppose we wish to laminate two matrices of shape 3 by 5. The result will, of course, have three dimensions, and the shape will be 3 5 2, 3 2 5 or 2 3 5. The only question is "where will the 2 go?" Much like inserting a line in a function, to squeeze the 2 between the existing dimensions, use a value between 1 and 2; in the third position, use a number between 2 and 3.

As in catenation, scalars are extended. By the way, the catenation of two scalars to form a vector (page 140) is really an example of lamination.

Decode and encode

Decode and encode also extend to arrays of rank greater than two:

```
      5  7⊤TAB3                          (2 2ρ3 5 7 8)⊥TAB3
 0  1  1                            766    772    778
 2  2  2                            826    832    838
 3  3  4                            886    892    898
 0  0  0                            946    952    958

 0  0  0                           1099   1108   1117
 1  1  1                           1189   1198   1207
 3  3  3                           1279   1288   1297
 4  4  4                           1369   1378   1387


 6  0  1
 2  3  4
 5  6  0
 1  2  3

 1  2  3
 4  5  6
 0  1  2
 3  4  5
```

Each row of the left argument of the decode function acts across the first coordinate of $TAB3$.

Encode can generate very large arrays as results. Its action can be summarized by pointing out that for left and right arguments L and R, with result RES, $RES[\;;I\;;J\,]$ encodes the element $R[\,J\,]$ in base $L[\;;I\,]$. This means that for $R \leftarrow TAB3$, as above, and L a two-dimensional array, the result is a five-dimensional array. You should try a few examples yourself.

Transposition

Transposition is the interchanging of elements along two or more coordinates. It wasn't introduced earlier mainly because it operates meaningfully on multidimensional arrays only. The transpose function may have one or two arguments. These will be considered separately.

Monadic transpose

If X is the matrix specified below,

$$X \leftarrow 3\ 4\rho\,'ABCDEFGHIJKLMN'$$

then the transposition of X is an interchange of rows and columns such that the element whose indices are $[\,J\,;K\,]$ ends up in the $[\,K\,;J\,]$ position of the result for all J and K values possible. The **APL** function which does this is the monadic *transpose*, formed by overstriking the large circle with the backward pointing slash:

```
        X                              ⍉X
ABCD                           AEI
EFGH                           BFJ
IJKL                           CGK
                               DHL
```

The first *row* of X has become the first *column* of the transpose of X, etc.

What happens when we apply the transpose function to a vector?

```
     ⍉2 5 1
2 5 1
```

Nothing has changed. The same is true for a scalar, incidentally. But we see something a little more interesting when we work with a three-dimensional array. Our old standby, $TAB3$, is still handy:

```
     TAB3
111 112 113
121 122 123
131 132 133
141 142 143

211 212 213
221 222 223
231 232 233
241 242 243
     ρTAB3
2 4 3
```

Note the dimensions of $TAB3$: two planes, four rows, three columns. Here is what the transpose does to $TAB3$ and $TAB2$:

```
      ⍉TAB3
111 211
121 221
131 231
141 241

112 212
122 222
132 232
142 242

113 213
123 223
133 233
143 243
      ρ⍉TAB3
3 4 2
      )COPY 1 CLASS TAB2
      TAB2                        ⍉TAB2
  3   1   7              3   7   6   1
  7  10   4              1  10   9   6
  6   9   1              7   4   1   7
  1   6   7
```

The coordinates are reversed. As a matter of fact, this is always the case for all multidimensional arrays. Formally, for $B \leftarrow \⍉A$, then ρB is $\phi \rho A$.

Dyadic transpose

The monadic transpose doesn't help us to interchange coordinates other than in the manner described above. The dyadic transpose is used for this. Its left argument is a vector specifying the new positions of the original coordinates. Here are 6 transpositions of $TAB3$:

```
    1 2 3⍉TAB3              1 3 2⍉TAB3              2 3 1⍉TAB3
111 112 113           111 121 131 141         111 121 131 141
121 122 123           112 122 132 142         211 221 231 241
131 132 133           113 123 133 143
141 142 143                                   112 122 132 142
                      211 221 231 241         212 222 232 242
211 212 213           212 222 232 242
221 222 223           213 223 233 243         113 123 133 143
231 232 233                                   213 223 233 243
241 242 243              3 1 2⍉TAB3
                      111 211                    3 2 1⍉TAB3
                      112 212                 111 211
    2 1 3⍉TAB3         113 213                 121 221
111 112 113                                   131 231
211 212 213           121 221                 141 241
                      122 222
121 122 123           123 223                 112 212
221 222 223                                   122 222
                      131 231                 132 232
131 132 133           132 232                 142 242
231 232 233           133 233
                                              113 213
141 142 143           141 241                 123 223
241 242 243           142 242                 133 233
                      143 243                 143 243
```

1 2 3⍉TAB3 is identical to TAB3, and 3 2 1⍉TAB3 is identical to ⍉TAB3. Those two cases are easy to see. Now consider 2 1 3⍉TAB3. The dimensions of the result are 4 2 3. The third coordinate, representing the number of columns, is unchanged. The elements in each of the original columns remain in the same column but not necessarily in the same order row-wise and plane-wise after transposition. More formally, if an arbitrary element in TAB3 has indices $[I;J;K]$, then its new position in the result is $[J;I;K]$ for the example above. For instance, the indices of the value 232 in TAB3 are $[2;3;2]$, and they are $[3;2;2]$ in the result of 2 1 3⍉TAB3.

Let's apply dyadic transposition to a two-dimensional object, the matrix T:

```
      T←3 5ρι15
      T                        1 2⍉T                          2 1⍉T
   1  2  3  4  5           1  2  3  4  5                 1  6 11
   6  7  8  9 10           6  7  8  9 10                 2  7 12
  11 12 13 14 15          11 12 13 14 15                 3  8 13
                                                         4  9 14
                                                         5 10 15
```

The 1 2 transpose of a matrix doesn't change it at all, and the 2 1 transpose is the same as the monadic transpose.

What about

```
      1 1⍉T
1 7 13
```

It gives the elements on the major diagonal of T:

```
      T
   1  2  3  4  5
   6  7  8  9 10
  11 12 13 14 15
```

The result is made up of those elements of T whose row and column indices are the same.

Here are some more examples using TAB3. Each result is an array of reduced rank.

```
      1 1 1⍉TAB3
111 222
```

```
      1 1 2⍉TAB3            1 2 1⍉TAB3                 1 2 2⍉TAB3
111 112 113          111 121 131 141           111 122 133
221 222 223          212 222 232 242           211 222 233
```

```
      2 1 1⍉TAB3            2 1 2⍉TAB3                 2 2 1⍉TAB3
111 211              111 212                   111 221
122 222              121 222                   112 222
133 233              131 232                   113 223
                     141 242
```

```
      1 3 3⍉TAB3
DOMAIN ERROR
      1 3 3 ⍉TAB3
      ∧
```

The example 1 2 1⍉TAB3 selects from TAB3 these elements whose first and third coordinate indices are the same, giving us a diagonal slice of TAB3. Elements along the main diagonal are obtained with 1 1 1⍉TAB3, while the last example resulted in a $DOMAIN$ $ERROR$. Do you see why?

Here is an application which uses dyadic transpose to reformat a character matrix (each row representing a word) into several columns of words, so that the order is preserved by reading down the first column, then the second, etc. Our sample matrix is SPL in workspace 1 $CLASS$.

```
        )LOAD 1 CLASS
SAVED  15.02.39 04/15/74
        ρSPL
10 5
        SPL
ZERO
ONE
TWO
THREE
FOUR
FIVE
SIX
SEVEN
EIGHT
NINE
```

Suppose you wanted it to appear as follows, with two words across:

```
ZERO    FIVE
ONE     SIX
TWO     SEVEN
THREE   EIGHT
FOUR    NINE
```

A general function to do this is

```
      ∇ R←F SPRED X
[1]      R←⌈(ρX)[1]÷F
[2]      X←((R,1)×ρX)↑X
[3]      X←2 1 3⍉(F,R,1↓ρX)ρX
[4]      R←(×/2 2ρ1,ρX)ρX
      ∇
```

where the left argument is the number of words to be printed across, and the right argument is the data matrix. Do you know why the blank is catenated to SPL in the following execution?

```
        2 SPRED SPL,' '
ZERO    FIVE
ONE     SIX
TWO     SEVEN
THREE   EIGHT
FOUR    NINE
        ρ2 SPRED SPL,' '
5 12
        3 SPRED SPL,' '
ZERO    FOUR    EIGHT
ONE     FIVE    NINE
TWO     SIX
THREE   SEVEN
```

We took care (in lines 1 and 2) to pad in extra blank rows if F is not a factor of the number of rows in the original argument.

The dyadic transpose is useful in many types of transformations, one example of which is the function *SPRED*. Its action on arrays of rank greater than 2 is sometimes difficult to see. For that reason, the function is not among the more popular with many **APL** users.

If you need dyadic transpose, there are two ways to approach it. One is to use any of the following relationships,

ρ right argument is (ρ result)[left argument]
left argument is (ρ,result) $\iota \rho$ right argument
ρ result is (ρ right argument)[left argument $\iota \iota \rho$ left argument]

which are applicable only when the elements of the shape of the right argument are all different. And if you're confused by all this, you can't go wrong by trying some permutations of the left argument until you get the result you want.

A transformation mnemonic

You have probably noticed by this time that the appearance of the symbols ϕ, $\ominus$ and $\lozenge$ is related to the kind of transformation which results when they are applied to certain arrays. Specifically, let's use them with a matrix $M \leftarrow 3 \quad 4 \rho \iota 12$:

```
        M                   φM                    ⊖M                  ⍉M
   1   2   3   4       4   3 ¦ 2   1        9  10  11  12        1   5   9
   5   6   7   8       8   7 ¦ 6   5       -5--6--7--8-         2   6  10
   9  10  11  12      12  11 ¦10   9        1   2   3   4        3   7  11
                                                                4   8  12
```

In each case the overstruck line, | , – or \ , represents the axis (shown as a dotted line) about which the transformation occurred.

PROBLEMS

1. DRILL. Specify $S \leftarrow 4 \quad 5 \rho \phi \iota 20$, $T \leftarrow 4 \quad 5 \rho \iota 20$, $U \leftarrow 2 \quad 3 \quad 4 \rho \iota 24$

$S+T$	$S \leq T$	$\lceil / \lceil / \lceil / U$
$2 \times S + T \div 2$	$+/[2]T$	$\lceil /,U$
$S \lfloor T$	$+ \neq T$	$\times \neq U$
$3 \mid T$	$4 + T$	$+ / + / [1] T$

Now specify $A \leftarrow 3 \quad 5 \rho \iota 15$, $B \leftarrow 3 \quad 3 \rho 'ABCDEFGHI'$, $C \leftarrow 2 \quad 3 \quad 4 \rho , A$

$A[;2 \ 5]$	$+ \neq C[1 \ 2;2;3]$	$B[1;2 \ 3]$
$C[1;2 \ 3;]$	$A[1 \ 3;\iota 4]$	$2 \ 2 \ 2 \uparrow \phi C$
$^-1 \ 1 \ 2 \downarrow \ominus C$	$1 \ 0 \ 1 \ 1 \backslash [2]C$	$1 \ 0 \ 1 \neq B$
$1 \ 1 \ 1 \ 1 \ 0 \ 1 \backslash A$	$0 \ 1 / [1] C$	ϕA
$\ominus A$	$3 \ 1 \ 2 \phi A$	$^-1 \ ^-2 \ 2 \phi B$
$^-1 \ ^-2 \ 2 \ 1 \ 1 \ominus A$	$, \phi B$	$1 \ 3 \ 3 \phi (-\iota 5) \phi [1] A$

And finally specify $M \leftarrow 3 \quad 4 \rho \iota 10$ and $N \leftarrow 2 \quad 3 \quad 4 \rho \iota 24$

$1 \ 1 \Qoppa M$	$2 \ 1 \ 3 \Qoppa N$	$\phi 2 \ 1 \Qoppa M$
$1 \ 1 \ 2 \Qoppa N$	$\Qoppa \phi \ominus M$	$\Qoppa M$
$\rho 2 \ 1 \ 3 \Qoppa N$	$1 \ 2 \ 1 \Qoppa N$	$\Qoppa \Qoppa M$

2. Make the first row of B (second segment of problem 1) equal to the third column.

3. Define a function that will delete a given name from a matrix of names A, or print an appropriate message if the name is not in the matrix.

4. Starting with a matrix $M \leftarrow 3 \quad 4 \rho \iota 4$, produce another matrix R whose shape is $3 \quad 3 \quad 4$ and made up of the columns of M. Use only indexing.

5. For the matrix B (problem 1, second segment) write an **APL** expression to obtain the diagonal that runs from the upper right to lower left.

6. Define a function $DIAG$ that takes as its right argument a matrix M whose elements are positive integers, and forms a decimal number out of the diagonal elements, i.e., $3 \quad 2 \quad 2 \quad 9$ becomes 3229.

7. Write a one-line function to produce a table of three columns listing N, the factorial of N, and the reciprocal of N for the integers 1 through N.

8. S is an operation table for some **APL** function f. Write an expression that returns a 1 if the function is commutative, 0 otherwise.

9.   Execute the following instructions and explain in your own words what they do:

$$B \leftarrow \phi A \leftarrow \iota 25$$
$$\Diamond 3 \quad 25 \rho A, B, A \times B$$

What tentative conclusion can be drawn from the data in the table?

10.   Define a recursive function $PERM$ that prints all possible permutations of ιN for some positive integer N.

11.   Construct this matrix using the monadic transpose.

```
0  3  2  1
1  0  3  2
2  1  0  3
```

12.   The XYZ advertising agency currently has 10 accounts. Each of these accounts represents an amount of money which is budgeted to be spent over a 12-month period in the following categories: 1) radio, 2) TV, 3) newspapers, 4) magazines, 5) direct mail. Assume the financial data is stored in an array $BUDGET$ whose first coordinate is time (in months), whose second coordinate consists of the cost categories above, and whose third coordinate is the accounts themselves. Write **APL** expressions to answer each of the following:

A)   Find the total yearly cost for accounts 4 and 10.
B)   How much was spent for the year for newspaper advertising in account 6?
C)   What is the total yearly cost by account?
D)   Which account spent the least money on TV during any month? In which month did this occur?
E)   How much was spent each month in accounts 1 and 3 for magazine and direct mail advertising?
F)   Construct a matrix of total monthly costs/accounts. Include appropriate row and column headings.
G)   Enlarge the array $BUDGET$ to include extra planes after the 6th and 12th months that will contain cumulative semiannual or annual costs/account/budget category.

13.   For an arbitrary matrix $M \leftarrow .15 \times \bar{}3000 + ?5 \quad 5 \rho 6000$, use $\overline{\Phi}$ to construct a new matrix $M1$ with column headings 10 through 14, and row headings STORE1 through STORE5.

14.   Develop a function which enumerates all the combinations of N things taken from a population P. If the header is $\nabla R \leftarrow N \quad COMB \quad P$, then the result is a numeric matrix with $N!P$ rows and N columns. Hint: 3 $COMB$ 4 is the same as $\bar{}1 + \bar{}1 \quad 1 \downarrow 4 \quad COMB \quad 5$.

```
        3  COMB  4                          4  COMB  5
    1  2  3                            1  2  3  4
    1  2  4                            1  2  3  5
    1  3  4                            1  2  4  5
    2  3  4                            1  3  4  5
                                       2  3  4  5
```

15.   You are given a long character vector V. Use laminate to follow each character with a semicolon.

16.   A magazine subscription service sells 25 different magazines in 16 cities. The 12 by 25 by 16 array $MAGSALES$ contains a record of the number of subscriptions sold by month, magazine and city. Construct a function that will print in matrix form the name of the leading magazine each month. Assume the names of the magazines are stored in a matrix $MAGNAMES$, with the names of the months in the matrix CAL. Ignore the possibility of a tie for total sales per month to simplify the algorithm.

17.   Define a function $REPEAT$ to replicate each element of the right (vector) argument the number of times indicated by the corresponding element in the left argument. For example, the result of 2 3 2 $REPEAT$ 2 5 8 is 2 2 5 5 5 8 8.

Chapter 25:
Generalized outer product

Multidimensional outer products

In Chapter 4 we introduced the *outer product* as a way to generate operation tables for the primitive scalar dyadic functions. At that time we used vectors as arguments, which gave us two-dimensional results.

More generally, the arguments can be arrays of any rank. The rank of the result is the sum of the ranks of the arguments, and the dimensions of the result the catenation of those of the arguments. Here are a few examples to illustrate these rules:

```
      1 3∘.+ι6
2 3 4 5 6 7
4 5 6 7 8 9
      'HELLO'∘.='LOVE'
0 0 0 0
0 0 0 1
1 0 0 0
1 0 0 0
0 1 0 0
      (2 3ρι6)∘.×1 8 4 1
  1  8  4   1
  2 16  8   2
  3 24 12   3

  4 32 16   4
  5 40 20   5
  6 48 24   6
```

Some of the patterns obtainable are interesting. Here is the *identity matrix* of order 4 (so-called because when matrix multiplication (the definition used in Matrix Algebra) is used with any other 4 4 matrix *M* and the identity matrix, the result is identical to *M*):

```
      (ι4)∘.=ι4
1 0 0 0
0 1 0 0
0 0 1 0
0 0 0 1
```

If = with the outer product gives the identity matrix, can you guess what ≠ will result in? And finally, here are two others that yield matrices of all zeros and ones:

```
        (ι5)∘.<ι5                              (ι5)∘.≤ι5
   0  1  1  1  1                         1  1  1  1  1
   0  0  1  1  1                         0  1  1  1  1
   0  0  0  1  1                         0  0  1  1  1
   0  0  0  0  1                         0  0  0  1  1
   0  0  0  0  0                         0  0  0  0  1
```

Some uses for the outer product have already been explored in the text and exercises. Others will be looked at in the problems at the end of the chapter. Until then, for those of you in whom the gambling instinct runs strong and unrestrained, consider the following "practical" problem: Assume games of chance have been legalized and you wish to use the facilities of **APL** to simulate 20 rolls of a single die. Identify those successive rolls which between them result in a 7.

In solving this problem, we obviously must first generate the 20 rolls by

```
     R←?20ρ6
     R
1 6 4 3 3 2 2 1 6 5 3 5 5 6 1 3 6 3 3 1
```

The corresponding vector of the "neighbors" of these rolls is most easily obtained by

```
     1⌽R
6 4 3 3 2 2 1 6 5 3 5 5 6 1 3 6 3 3 1 1
```

and the sums by

```
     ¯1↓R+1⌽R
 7 10 7 6 5 4 3 7 11 8 8 10 11 7 4 9 9 6 4
```

(Why is ¯1↓ used?)

Those successive rolls adding up to 7 can be identified by

```
     HIT←(7=¯1↓R+1⌽R)/ι¯1+ρR
```

while the rolls represented by HIT are

```
     HIT∘.+0 1
 1   2
 3   4
 8   9
14  15
```

The actual values of R selected with the above can be displayed with

```
     R[HIT∘.+0 1]
1 6
4 3
1 6
6 1
```

As a corollary to the last problem, consider the following question: How many 4's are there in R? Clearly this is $+/R=4$. But suppose we modify the question slightly and ask how many times each of the integers 1 through 6 occurs in R.

Of course, we could repeat the above expression for each integer. But the outer product allows us to do it all at once:

```
      +/R∘.=ι6
4  2  6  1  3  4
```

Our next example is a function $FIND$ designed to locate all occurrences of a given phrase W in some literal vector T of text. There are several ways in which the problem can be approached. The one to be shown here makes use of the fact that an outer product with vector arguments results in a matrix, each of whose rows corresponds to the execution of the given operation between each element of the left argument and the entire right argument. (Compare with $R∘.=ι6$ in the last paragraph.)

With the function =, this will result in a logical matrix, each row of which checks for the presence of one character of the phrase W in the text T. To illustrate, assign

```
      W←'IN'
      T←'IT DOES NOT RAIN IN SPAIN'
      A←W∘.=T
      A
1 0 0 0 0 0 0 0 0 0 0 0 0 0 0 1 0 0 1 0 0 0 0 0 1 0
0 0 0 0 0 0 0 0 1 0 0 0 0 0 0 1 0 0 1 0 0 1 0 0 0 1
```

The interesting thing about this array is the location of the 1's in the rows, corresponding to the occurrences of I and N in T. Note the shift of the 1 corresponding to the location of N in the second row, compared with the location of I in the first row (except the letter N in the word NOT).

One way to distinguish between occurrences of IN and those of isolated I's and N's is to shift the second row one element to the left, which produces columns of all ones, corresponding to the locations of IN:

```
      B←(¯1+ιρW)⌽A
      B
1 0 0 0 0 0 0 0 0 0 0 0 0 0 0 1 0 0 1 0 0 0 0 0 1 0
0 0 0 0 0 0 0 1 0 0 0 0 0 0 0 1 0 0 1 0 0 0 0 1 0 0
```

Next, an easy way to identify these columns is to carry out ∧-reduction across the first coordinate:

```
      C←∧/B
      C
0 0 0 0 0 0 0 0 0 0 0 0 0 0 0 1 0 0 1 0 0 0 0 0 1 0
```

This result can now be used to pinpoint in T the indices representing the locations of the first elements of occurrences of IN in W:

```
      C/ιρT
15  18  24
```

Finally, our completed defined function looks like this:

```
      ∇  R←W FIND T
[1]      R←(∧/(¯1+ιρW)⌽W∘.=T)/ιρT
      ∇
```

What would change if we wanted to locate all occurrences of the *word* IN instead of just the successive characters I and N?

Graphing

Our last topic has to do with the use of the outer product to build up a simple-minded but instructive graphing function. To begin, define

```
      Y←⌽X←¯5+⍳9
      X
¯4 ¯3 ¯2 ¯1 0 1 2 3 4
      Y
 4 3 2 1 0 ¯1 ¯2 ¯3 ¯4
```

Because the middle elements in both X and Y are 0's, their outer product will produce 0's along the "axes" of the matrix:

```
      M←Y∘.×X
      M
¯16 ¯12  ¯8  ¯4   0   4   8  12  16
¯12  ¯9  ¯6  ¯3   0   3   6   9  12
 ¯8  ¯6  ¯4  ¯2   0   2   4   6   8
 ¯4  ¯3  ¯2  ¯1   0   1   2   3   4
  0   0   0   0   0   0   0   0   0
  4   3   2   1   0  ¯1  ¯2  ¯3  ¯4
  8   6   4   2   0  ¯2  ¯4  ¯6  ¯8
 12   9   6   3   0  ¯3  ¯6  ¯9 ¯12
 16  12   8   4   0  ¯4  ¯8 ¯12 ¯16
```

The next step is to replace the 0's with some character, say, +, and everything else with blanks. One way to do this is to use the array to index a suitable character vector:

```
      ' +'[1+0=M]
        +
        +
        +
        +
++++++++
        +
        +
        +
```

Since the horizontal axis looks somewhat out of scale (one character space isn't as wide as a line space), we will adjust our "graph" as follows:

```
      (18⍴1 0)\' +'[1+0=M]
         +
         +
         +
         +
 + + + + + + + +
         +
         +
         +
         +
```

Suppose now we wish to plot on this set of axes a number of points (X, Y), where $Y←X+1$. Our axes are made up of literal characters, so that the points themselves would have to be represented as literals to include them. It is more interesting, however, to go back to our original outer product, which is numeric, and superimpose the desired set of points F on it before converting to characters:

```
        F←Y∘.=X+1
        F
0  0  0  0  0  0  0  1  0
0  0  0  0  0  0  1  0  0
0  0  0  0  0  1  0  0  0
0  0  0  0  1  0  0  0  0
0  0  0  1  0  0  0  0  0
0  0  1  0  0  0  0  0  0
0  1  0  0  0  0  0  0  0
1  0  0  0  0  0  0  0  0
0  0  0  0  0  0  0  0  0
```

F produces a matrix of 1's where the points are. We next add the matrices F and $1+2\times0=M$. You should be able to see why multiplication by 2 is necessary if you execute the next step but without the multiplication by 2:

```
        F+1+2×0=M
1  1  1  1  3  1  1  2  1
1  1  1  1  3  1  2  1  1
1  1  1  1  3  2  1  1  1
1  1  1  1  4  1  1  1  1
3  3  3  4  3  3  3  3  3
1  1  2  1  3  1  1  1  1
1  2  1  1  3  1  1  1  1
2  1  1  1  3  1  1  1  1
1  1  1  1  3  1  1  1  1
```

Finally, our expanded plot is

```
        PLOT←(18ρ1  0)\'  ∘+∘'[F+1+2×0=M]
        PLOT
         +           ∘
         +         ∘
         +       ∘
         +     ∘
+   +   +   ∘   +   +   +   +
       ∘     +
     ∘       +
   ∘         +
             +
```

Now that we have built up the algorithm for the plot routine, we can incorporate it into a defined function, $GRAPH$, and try it out after setting F and X:

```
     ∇  Z←GRAPH
[1]     Z←((2×ρX)ρ1  0)\'  ∘+∘'[F+1+2×0=(ΦX)∘.×X]
     ∇
        X←¯5+ι9
        F←(ΦX)∘.=X+1
        GRAPH
         +           ∘
         +         ∘
         +       ∘
         +     ∘
+   +   +   ∘   +   +   +   +
       ∘     +
     ∘       +
   ∘         +
             +
```

Plotting functions can get quite complex when it is desired to include such amenities as labeling of the axes, provision for changing the scale of the plot, and rounding off the computed values for the coordinates, since the terminal can't type characters between lines and spaces.

APL provides a useful set of prepared plotting routines in the common library. Since instructions for the use of this workspace are quite complete, practice in the functions is left as an exercise (see problem 11). The plotting facilities available may differ somewhat from system to system, so carefully read the instructions for each plot workspace you load.

PROBLEMS

1. DRILL. Specify $A \leftarrow \iota 4, B \leftarrow 2\ 3\rho'ABCDEF', C \leftarrow 'ABD', D \leftarrow 3\ 1\rho\iota 3$

    $C \circ . = B$ $A \circ . + 3 \times D$ $\sim(A \circ . = A) \circ . \wedge 1\ 0\ 0\ 1$

    $D \circ . \times A$ $D \circ . \div A$ $\lozenge D \circ . * A$

    $1\ 3\ 9 \circ . > D$ $B \circ . \neq C$ $A \circ . \lceil \bar{\ }1\ 3\ 2\ 4$

2. What is the shape of the result when the outer product is used to add the elements of a vector of length 4 to the elements of a 2 2 matrix?

3. Define a function $DIST$ that computes the rounded off (nearest integer) distances between any two cities whose X and Y coordinates are given in a matrix L. Assume ρL is $N, 2$ and the cities are all located north and east of the origin of the coordinate system.

4. Write an **APL** expression to find the number of occurrences of each of the letters $ABCDEFG$ in the word $CABBAGE$.

5. Construct expressions which will give the sum and carry digits for addition of two numbers in any number system B (for B less than 10). Write a function to generate an addition table of a set of integers INT in the base B.

6. Write a program to multiply two polynomials together. Assume their coefficient vectors $C1$ and $C2$ are arranged in descending order of powers of X.

7. Use the function $GRAPH$ (page 237) for each of the following:

    A) $Y \leftarrow |X \leftarrow \bar{\ }5 + \iota 9$
    B) $Y \leftarrow \bar{\ }5 + X * 2$
    C) $Y \leq X + 1$
    D) $(Y \leq X + 1) \wedge Y \geq 3 - |X$
    E) $Y \leq 3 | X$

8. Execute the following instructions in order and explain the resulting display.

    $Y \leftarrow \phi \bar{\ }13 + \iota 25$
    $R \leftarrow (0 = (\bar{\ }3 \times Y) \circ . + (2 \times X) - 2) \vee 0 = (2 \times Y) \circ . + X - 8$

9. Modify $GRAPH$ (page 237) to scale down all the data X by a factor S.

10. Define a function $FORM$ that will replace with blanks all zero elements in a matrix M.

11.   After loading the workspace with plotting routines in your **APL** system, execute each of the following. (As pointed out at the end of the chapter, the syntax, name of the function, and auxiliary features may be different, so be sure to call for $DESCRIBE$ or $HOWPLOT$ or $HOWFORMAT$, or whatever instructions are available in your system.)

A) $X \leftarrow \iota 20$
      $Y \leftarrow X \star 2$
      $Z \leftarrow 2 \times X \star 2$
      $20 \ 60 \ PLOT \ X \ VS \ Y$
      $20 \ 60 \ PLOT \ (Y \ AND \ Z) \ VS \ X$

B) $X \leftarrow 1, 50 \times \iota 7$
      $Y \leftarrow 3 \times X$
      $20 \ 60 \ PLOT \ Y \ VS \ X$
      $Y \leftarrow \div X$
      $20 \ 30 \ PLOT \ Y[1+\iota 7] \ VS \ X[1+\iota 7]$

12.   To evaluate the strength of a bridge hand (13 cards dealt from a standard deck), the Milton work-point count is used. This assigns 4 points for each Ace, 3 for each King, 2 for each Queen and 1 for each Jack. Out of a possible 40 points in the deck, a particular hand can have up to 37 high card points (HCP), with the average being 10. Define a function to simulate the dealing of a large number of bridge hands and use a histogram (problem 10, Chapter 22, or in the $PLOT$ workspaces if available) to determine the shape of the HCP distribution.

Chapter 26:
Generalized inner product

None of the *APL* functions introduced so far result directly in what is called ordinary *matrix multiplication* in mathematics. For those not familiar with it, here is an example which illustrates the use of matrix multiplication. We have three men who are engaged in buying four items, A, B, C and D. The cost and tax on each item are given. If we know how much each man bought, what is the total cost and total tax per man? In tabular form:

		cost/unit	tax/unit
	A	4	.05
	B	2	.06
item	C	1	.01
	D	1	.02

		item A	B	C	D		cost/unit	tax/unit
	1	2	3	0	1		[1; 1]	[1; 2]
man	2	0	2	1	4		[2; 1]	[2; 2]
	3	1	1	2	1		[3; 1]	[3; 2]

What we want are the entries to go into the dotted table, whose boxes are numbered as shown above. Let's see how we can figure them out. To get the total cost for each man, we would multiply the numbers of the various items purchased by their respective costs, add them up and put the results in the appropriate boxes. For man 1 this is

$$(2 \times 4) + (3 \times 2) + (0 \times 1) + (1 \times 1) \quad \text{or} \quad 15$$

This will go in box 1-1. The total tax for man 1 can be obtained similarly and placed in box 1-2:

$$(2 \times .05) + (3 \times .06) + (0 \times .01) + (1 \times .02) \quad \text{or} \quad .30$$

What goes in box 3-1, to take one more example, can be gotten by

$$(1 \times 4) + (1 \times 2) + (2 \times 1) + (1 \times 1) \quad \text{or} \quad 9$$

The completed table looks like this:

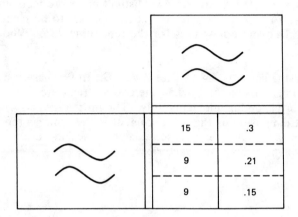

15	.3
9	.21
9	.15

Observe that the first dimension of the result is the same as the first dimension of the left matrix, and the second dimension of the result is the same as the second dimension of the right matrix. The inner two dimensions (second dimension of the left argument and first dimension of the right argument) must be the same. A *LENGTH ERROR* results otherwise.

Inner product

To show how this operation can be performed on the terminal, let's build these matrices from their elements:

```
      A←3 4ρ2 3 0 1 0 2 1 4 1 1 2 1
      A
2 3 0 1
0 2 1 4
1 1 2 1
      B←4 2ρ4 .05 2 .06 1 .01 1 .02
      B
4                 0.05
2                 0.06
1                 0.01
1                 0.02
```

The desired result, which corresponds to matrix multiplication in mathematics, is formed by executing

```
      A+.×B
15                0.3
 9                0.21
 9                0.15
```

Why use three symbols for this common operation? Very simple: any primitive scalar dyadic functions can be substituted for the + and ×. The reason + and × are used here is that these are the two operations needed to get the right result, the products first and then the sums.

There is a definite pattern to the way the elements are combined. For example, the element of the result which goes into box 3-2 (the *third row*, *second column* of the result) is obtained by operating in the fashion described with the *third row* of the left argument and the *second column* of the right argument. Such a sequence of three symbols, *f.g*, *f* and *g* being any primitive scalar dyadic functions, is called an *inner product*.

In present implementations of **APL** there are 441 distinct inner products possible, although most users tend to stay with + . ×, ∧ . =, ∨ . ≠, ∧ . ≠, and ⌈ . +. There appears to be plenty of room for those of you who are adventurous enough to explore new uses for the remaining 436. Who knows? You may become famous!

The inner product is *not* the same as $A \circ .+B$ or $A \circ . \times B$. In this case it can't even be compared with $A \times B$ since the latter operation is possible only when the two matrices are the same size, and the multiplication is carried out between corresponding elements only. The inner product, $Af.g\,B$, operates on any pair of arrays, provided that the last dimension of the left argument is the same as the first dimension of the right argument. The dimensions of the result in each case (except for scalars) are $(^{-}1\downarrow\rho A)$, $1\downarrow\rho B$. Here are some additional examples involving scalars and vectors:

```
      10+.×3 2 8
130
      1 2 3 4+.*0 1 2 3
76
      2 1 6+.×3 2ρι6
35 44
      (3 4ρι12)+.=ι4
4 0 0
      (2 3 4ρι24)+.-4 2ρι8
 ¯6 ¯10
 10   6
 26  22

 42  38
 58  54
 74  70
```

Numerical applications of the inner product

One interesting application involves a pipeline network between cities on a map. The diagram below shows not only the intercity pipeline lengths in miles between A, B, C and D, but also the directions in which they are measured.

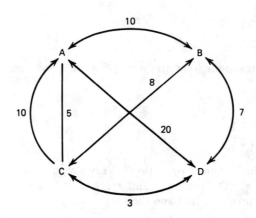

Notice that the distances are not necessarily the same in both directions between any two cities. This is to allow for the most general case where there may be competing pipelines between two cities along different rights of way. We can summarize the diagram in the form of a mileage table:

FROM/TO	CITY A	CITY B	CITY C	CITY D
CITY A	-	10	5	20
CITY B	10	-	8	7
CITY C	10	8	-	3
CITY D	20	7	3	-

Such a table is provided in 1 *CLASS* as the variable *MILEAGE*:

```
      )LOAD 1 CLASS
SAVED 15.02.39 04/15/74
      MILEAGE
  0 10   5 20
 10  0   8  7
 10  8   0  3
 20  7   3  0
```

Believe it or not, a table of the longest pipeline distances from any city to any other city passing through some intermediate city is given by

```
      MILEAGE⌈.+MILEAGE
 40 27 23 20
 27 20 15 30
 23 20 16 30
 20 30 25 40
```

The longest distance from A to B is 27 miles (A-D-B), from B to C 15 miles (B-A-C), etc.

Why does this work? Let's arrange the matrices for the inner product in the same form that our earlier problem was:

				0	10	5	20
				10	0	8	7
				10	8	0	3
			⌈.+	20	7	3	0
0	10	5	20	11	12	13	14
10	0	8	7	21	22	23	24
10	8	0	3	31	32	33	34
20	7	3	0	41	42	43	44

The longest distance from B to C is represented by the contents of box 2-3. This is formed by operating on the second row of the left argument and the third column of the right argument. It requires adding 10 and 5, and taking the greater of that sum and the sum of 0 and 8, which is 15, then taking the greater of 15 and the sum of 8 and 0, which is still 15, and finally taking the greater of 15 and the sum of 7 and 3.

There are many other interesting combinations and possible uses, only a few of which will be considered. For instance, the shortest two-leg pipeline distance is

```
      MILEAGE⌊.+MILEAGE
   0  10   5   8
  10   0   8   7
  10   8   0   3
  13   7   3   0
```

Notice that the shortest distance from A to C is 5 miles, which is A to A to C or A to C to C. We are allowed this possibility because there are entries (they happen to be all 0's) in the mileage table from A to A and C to C on the major diagonal of $MILEAGE$:

```
      MILEAGE
   0  10   5  20
  10   0   8   7
  10   8   0   3
  20   7   3   0
```

One way to be protected from such a sneaky result is to put arbitrarily large numbers along the major diagonal. This can be done as follows without destroying or rewriting $MILEAGE$:

```
      F←MILEAGE+1000×(⍳4)∘.=⍳4
      F
1000    10     5    20
  10  1000     8     7
  10     8  1000     3
  20     7     3  1000
```

Now we get for the shortest two-leg distances

```
      F⌊.+F
  15  13  18   8
  18  14  10  11
  18  10   6  15
  13  11  15   6
```

and this time the shortest such distance from A to C is 18 miles (A-B-C). Application of this operation a second time would give the shortest three-leg distances:

```
      F⌊.+F⌊.+F
  23  15  11  20
  20  18  14  13
  16  14  18   9
  21  13   9  18
```

We can continue this process ad nauseam, but there is a prepared function in 1 $CLASS$ called $AGAIN$ that will do it for us. Let's display it:

```
      ∇AGAIN[⎕]∇
    ∇ AGAIN
[1]   T←T⌊.+F
    ∇
```

It is niladic and simply respecifies T as $T\lfloor.+F$. If we set T equal to F, the first time we execute $AGAIN$ we will get the shortest two-leg distances, the next time the shortest three-leg distances, and so on:

```
     T←F
     AGAIN
     T
15  13  18   8
18  14  10  11
18  10   6  15
13  11  15   6
     AGAIN
     T
15  13  18   8
18  14  10  11
18  10   6  15
13  11  15   6
```

Circuit analysis applications

Imagine a circuit with six functional units connected as follows:

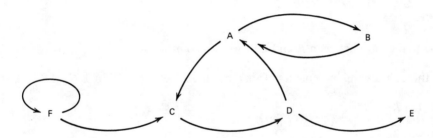

A, B, C, D, E and F are some kind of functional units which can be either energized or not. The circuit works this way: if C is energized, after a certain increment of time D is energized, and after another increment of time E and A are energized; if A is energized, after an increment of time C and B are energized, etc. F is the oddball unit here. Once it is energized it stays on permanently, but unless we start with F on there is no way to turn it on. E is a terminus. It doesn't turn anything on. All this information can be summarized in a matrix, with 1 standing for the existence of a connection from the unit named on the left to the one whose name is on the top:

FROM/TO	A	B	C	D	E	F
A	0	1	1	0	0	0
B	1	0	0	0	0	0
C	0	0	0	1	0	0
D	1	0	0	0	1	0
E	0	0	0	0	0	0
F	0	0	1	0	0	1

This matrix is available as a variable called $CIRCUIT$ in 1 $CLASS$:

```
        CIRCUIT
0  1  1  0  0  0
1  0  0  0  0  0
0  0  0  1  0  0
1  0  0  0  1  0
0  0  0  0  0  0
0  0  1  0  0  1
```

We can set up a vector X with six elements (one for each unit in the circuit) and let 1 signify that the unit is turned on initially. For example, if only A is on, we specify X as

```
    X←1  0  0  0  0  0
```

What units are on after one increment of time? From the matrix it appears that B and C will be turned on and all the others, including A, will be off. The result should therefore be 0 1 1 0 0 0.

This can be achieved by

```
        X∨.∧CIRCUIT
0  1  1  0  0  0
```

(Why is ∨.∧ used?) and after another increment of time,

```
        0  1  1  0  0  0∨.∧CIRCUIT
1  0  0  1  0  0
```

A is back on (due to the loop between A and B) with D also on.

To step this through several increments of time use the function RUN in 1 $CLASS$. Let's display it:

```
        ∇RUN[□]∇
     ∇ NETWORK RUN STATUS;COUNT
[1]    COUNT←0
[2]   LOOP:COUNT
[3]    STATUS
[4]    STATUS←STATUS∨.∧NETWORK
[5]    COUNT←COUNT+1
[6]    →LOOP
     ∇
```

The left argument is $NETWORK$, the matrix which describes the circuit connections. The right argument $STATUS$ represents the initial conditions. $COUNT$ is a local variable which is set to 0 on line 1 and displayed on line 2. Line 3 prints the current status of the circuit elements. This is updated on the next line and the counter upped on line 5. The final line causes a branch to 2.

Does this program look a bit peculiar to you? It should. There is no safeguard in it to turn it off once it starts, and it will run forever! The proper thing to do would be to put a line in it that will cause execution to cease once $COUNT$ reached a certain value. Since there is no such check, we'll let it go and manually interrupt execution with ATTN.

We'll start by turning on only A:

```
    X←1  0  0  0  0  0
    CIRCUIT RUN X
0
1  0  0  0  0  0
1
0  1  1  0  0  0
```

```
2
1  0  0  1  0  0
3
1  1  1  0  1  0
4
1  1  1  1  0  0
5
1  1  1  1  1  0
6
1  1  1  1  1  0
7
1  1  1  1  1  0
RUN[3]
```

Execution has been manually interrupted, as discussed above, and we are suspended on line 3:

```
      )SI
RUN[3]  *
```

F will never turn on no matter how many runs we make.

COUNT is up to 10, the printout having lagged behind execution:

```
      COUNT
10
```

Ordinarily we can't get a value for *COUNT*, it being a local variable, but remember that we are still in the function as a result of the suspension. (Don't forget to remove the suspension by →.)

Character applications

Probably the most frequent application of inner product is finding which row of a character matrix matches a given character vector. For example, if *DATA* is a matrix with each row holding the name of a product,

```
      DATA←5 9ρ'TACO     BURRITO  ENCHALADATOSTADA   TUMS      '
```

then a function like this

```
      ∇HITS←MATRIX FIND VECTOR
[1]      HITS←MATRIX∧.=(1↓ρMATRIX)↑VECTOR ∇
```

returns a bit vector with a 1 corresponding to which row matches the vector.

```
      DATA FIND 'TOSTADA'
0  0  0  1  0
```

The few examples shown barely begin to cover the wide range of possible applications of the inner product. Many of the problems appearing in the previous chapters can be redone more compactly with the inner product. Problem 5 is a representative sampling of these.

PROBLEMS

1. DRILL. Specify $A \leftarrow 3 \quad 4 \quad 5, \quad B \leftarrow 4 \quad 3 \rho \iota 10, \quad C \leftarrow 3 \quad 4 \rho \phi \iota 7$

    $A + . = A$ $\qquad\qquad$ $A \wedge . > C$ $\qquad\qquad$ $B \times . = A$

    $B \times . - C$ $\qquad\qquad$ $A \vee . \neq B$ $\qquad\qquad$ $C \mid . - B$

    $B \vee . < C$ $\qquad\qquad$ $3 + . \times B$ $\qquad\qquad$ $(\lozenge C) \lceil . + A$

2. A) For two vectors A and B of the same length, and the conformable matrices M and U
    $(U \leftarrow (\iota N) \circ . \leq \iota N)$ give a meaning to each of the following:
    $A \wedge . = B, \quad M \wedge . = B, \quad A + . \neq B, \quad (M = 0) \wedge . \geq U, \quad A \times . \star B$
    B) For a logical square matrix N, what is the significance of $R \leftarrow N \vee . \wedge N$?
    C) For the conformable matrices C and D, what is the meaning of $C + . = D$ and $C \lceil . \lfloor D$?

3. Write a program to evaluate at various points X a polynomial with coefficients C. Assume the terms
    of the polynomial are arranged in ascending order of powers of X. Use the inner product in your
    algorithm.

4. The Parochial Computing Systems Corporation reimburses its employees for travel on company
    business at the rate of 14 cents per mile for the first 75 miles, 10 cents per mile for the next 50 miles
    and 6 cents per mile for all mileage in excess of 125. Define a monadic function which uses the inner
    product to compute mileage allowances for employees.

5. Redo using the inner product

    A) problem 6, Chapter 8.
    B) problem 4, Chapter 10.
    C) problem 21, Chapter 18.
    D) problem 5, Chapter 22.

6. The Shallow Water Pump Company manufactures four different sump pumps. Each model requires
    different numbers of five basic parts:

                    PART   TYPE

		1	2	3	4	5
	1	1	2	0	5	2
PUMP	2	0	3	0	1	5
MODEL	3	1	1	4	2	2
	4	1	2	4	5	5

    The company anticipates orders for 300 of model 1, 500 of model 2, 200 of model 3 and 1000 of
    model 4. Assuming no margin for bad parts, how many of each part should be ordered from the
    vendors? These parts cost respectively $32.00, $9.75, $3.20, $.78, $7.20. What is the cost of all the
    parts needed? What is the cost of each pump model?

Chapter 27:
Business and engineering applications

This chapter is optional. It covers, at least superficially, a number of uses of *APL* in matrix algebra, calculus, curve-fitting and splines. If you are a member of that class of users for whom the above topics are esoterica, skip the rest of the chapter. If, however, your curiosity has gotten the better of you, or you have a genuine need for the above, read on.

Linear equations

There are a number of uses for *APL* in the branch of mathematics known as *matrix algebra*. Since this text is a teaching introduction to the language, only a few of these will be considered, the first being the solution of a set of exactly determined simultaneous linear equations.

For those who have forgotten their high school algebra, simultaneous linear equations are of this form in conventional notation,

$$aX + bY + cZ + ... = r$$
$$dX + eY + fZ + ... = s$$
$$\vdots$$

the problem being to find values of the variables X, Y, Z... that satisfy all the equations. a, b, c,... r, s,... are numerical constants.

We will approach it with a numerical example. Suppose that in three successive weeks we bought a number of different items A, B and C, spending the amounts listed:

	TOTAL	A	B	C
WEEK 1	$1.10	4	6	0
WEEK2	$0.59	3	2	2
WEEK 3	$0.78	1	3	4

What are the unit costs of the various items?

The answer happens to be $.05 for A, $.15 for B and $.07 for C. Let's work back from the answer to see how we can solve similar problems. From our previous work with the inner product, we ought to be able to get the vector of total costs from the number-of-items matrix and the unit-costs vector (try this for yourself). We'll call the total-costs vector D, the matrix of the number of each item purchased X, and the unit-costs vector B. Our trouble is that in a real problem we would know X and D but not B.

Before proceeding, here is a quick review of some elementary facts about matrices. M, N, P and R are matrices of the appropriate size. $+.\times$ is ordinary matrix multiplication. All of these facts you may verify on the terminal:

(1) If M equals N, then $R+.\times M$ equals $R+.\times N$
(2) $(M+.\times(N+.\times P))$ equals $(M+.\times N)+.\times P$
(3) If M has an inverse, MI, then $MI+.\times M$ equals I, where I is the identity matrix
(4) $(M+.\times I)$ equals $(I+.\times M)$ equals M

The third point introduces a new concept, that of a *matrix inverse*. This is really not much different from the other kinds of inverses we have encountered thus far. For example, adding the additive inverse to a number resulted in 0, the identity element for addition,

```
    R←ι10
    0=R+-R
1 1 1 1 1 1 1 1 1 1
```

while for multiplication, we get

```
    1=R×÷R
1 1 1 1 1 1 1 1 1 1
```

$-R$ here is the additive inverse and $÷R$ the multiplicative inverse. So the inverse of a matrix M is one which, when it multiplies M (matrix multiplication, not element by element), yields the identity matrix (see page 233).

If $M+.\times MIR$ results in I, then MIR is said to be a *right inverse*. If $MIL+.\times M$ results in I, MIL is a *left inverse*. If the same matrix is both a left and a right inverse of M, then M must be square (why?), and we refer to *the inverse* of M. From this point on, MI will stand for *the inverse* of M.

Now getting back to our problem, with the dimensions underneath as shown, we had

$$D \leftarrow X +.\times B$$
$$(3) \quad (3\ 3) \quad (3)$$

We want to find B. Using a dotted line to indicate that both sides are equivalent statements, the sequence of steps we will take is the following. The rules referred to are those stated above.

$XI+.\times D$	$XI+.\times(X+.\times B)$	rule 1
$XI+.\times D$	$(XI+.\times X)+.\times B$	rule 2
$XI+.\times D$	$I+.\times B$	rule 3
$XI+.\times D$	B	rule 4

The last line is our conclusion, that $B←XI+.\times D$.

To find the inverse of a matrix, **APL** provides a primitive monadic function ⌹, formed by overstriking the quad and divide symbol, and usually called *quad-divide*, *domino* or *matrix divide*. Since the data for this example is stored in 1 $CLASS$, let's copy it and use the inverse of X to solve the unit costs problem at the beginning of this chapter.

```
    )COPY 1 CLASS X D
SAVED  15.02.39 04/15/74
```

```
        X
 4  6  0
 3  2  2
 1  3  4
        D
1.1  0.59  0.78
        ⌹X
 ‾0.03846153846      0.4615384615    ‾0.2307692308
  0.1923076923     ‾0.3076923077     0.1538461538
 ‾0.1346153846      0.1153846154     0.1923076923
        (⌹X)+.×D
0.05  0.15  0.07
```

If the right argument X is scalar, then ⌹X is equivalent to $\div X$, while for X a vector, ⌹X returns a vector result which is a multiple of X.

Use of the inner product can be eliminated by the dyadic matrix divide, $R \leftarrow D⌹X$, instead of (⌹X)$+.\times D$. The right argument is the matrix of coefficients, and the left argument the vector of constants:

```
        D⌹X
0.05  0.15  0.07
```

More generally, for ⌹M to yield a result, the matrix must be invertible, i.e., have at least as many rows as columns. Its determinant must not be zero, otherwise a $DOMAIN\ ERROR$ results. If M is nonsquare, the result is a left inverse,

```
        M←4 2ρ2 1 1 3 4 5 6 7
        ⌹M
  0.3377926421    ‾0.3913043478     0.003344481605     0.1170568562
 ‾0.2575250836     0.347826087      0.05685618729     ‾0.0100334448
2
```

while if the matrix is square, the result is *the inverse* of the matrix:

```
        P←3 3ρ3 4 5 6 7 8 9 10 2
        ⌹P
 ‾2.444444444      1.555555556     ‾0.1111111111
  2.222222222     ‾1.444444444      0.2222222222
 ‾0.1111111111     0.2222222222    ‾0.1111111111
```

In the first case, ρ⌹M equals ρ⍉M. The use of the dyadic ⌹ as in $R \leftarrow B⌹A$, requires that ρρA be 2, with ρρB either 1 or 2. The first dimension of A must be equal to or greater than the second dimension of A, and must equal the first dimension of B. A right argument which is nonsquare (first dimension greater than second dimension) indicates a system of equations with more equations than unknowns, and the solution is a *least-squares* solution (next section). It is also possible for both A and B to be vectors. In this case the result is a scalar. Similarly, if A and B are both scalars, $A⌹B$ is equivalent to $A \div B$.

Least square fits, trend lines and curve fitting

If you wish to fit a straight line of the form $Y = a + bX$ through two points, such as (1.5,2) and (3.5,3), you can use the dyadic ⌹ as shown:

```
        2 3⌹2 2ρ1 1.5 1 3.5
1.25  0.5
```

1.25 is the value of the Y-intercept, and 0.5 is the value for b, the slope. Any predicted Y-value along the line can be found by the defined function $EVAL$:

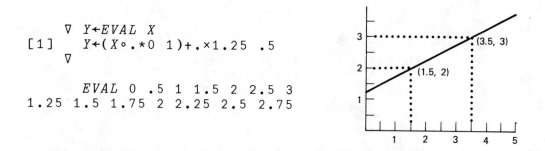

```
     ∇  Y←EVAL X
[1]     Y←(X∘.*0 1)+.×1.25 .5
     ∇

        EVAL 0 .5 1 1.5 2 2.5 3
1.25 1.5 1.75 2 2.25 2.5 2.75
```

Now suppose a business analyst has spent effort, time and funds obtaining the following data, and wishes to find the linear (straight line) relation between X and Y:

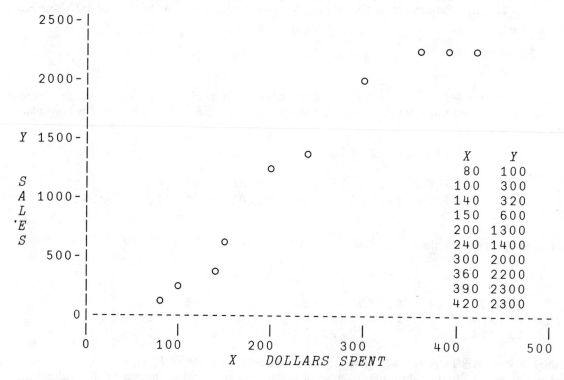

X	Y
80	100
100	300
140	320
150	600
200	1300
240	1400
300	2000
360	2200
390	2300
420	2300

Obviously there is no single straight line which will pass through every one of the points. We are left with the problem of choosing the one particular straight line which is "best" in some sense.

One approach in wide use is to fit a line such that the sum of the squared vertical distances from the line to each point is the smallest possible value. The problem, therefore, is to find the a and b such that $+/(((b,a)+.×X∘.*0 1)-Y)*2$ is the smallest possible value. This is achieved by $Y⌹X∘.*0 1$, and is called a linear *least squares* solution. There is no other set of coefficients you can pick which will get a smaller sum-of-squares of differences, given that you decide a straight line is the right *model*.

The following figures use the function $PLOT$ (workspace 10 $PLOT$ on the **APL★PLUS** ® System), using the "fineplot" option. This requires a Selectric® terminal and a special typing element. PX is a vector of small increments of X.

```
PX←(⌊/X)+0,(ι100)×.01×(⌈/X)-⌊/X
PLOT PX,[1.5](PX∘.*0 1)+.×Y⌹X∘.*0 1
```

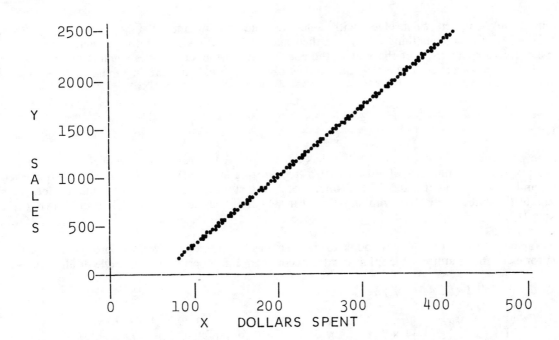

Alternatively, you might want to fit a simple curved line through the points. There is an infinite number of curved lines you could pick, but a typical first choice is to fit a quadratic of the form $Y=a+bX+cX^2$. a, b and c are the three elements of the result of

```
R←Y⊞X∘.*0 1 2
R
```
```
¯996.8729766 13.2153557 ¯0.01230306278
```

There is no other set of three values which will give a smaller result to the expression $+/((R+.\times X\circ.*0\ 1\ 2)-Y)*2$.

```
PLOT PX,[1.5](PX∘.*0 1 2)+.×Y⊞X∘.*0 1 2
```

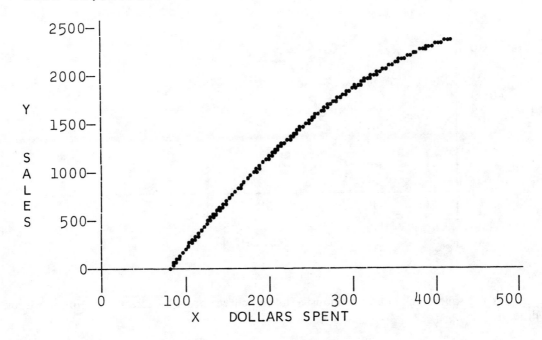

Statisticians concern themselves with selecting the proper model (should it be $A+B\times X$, or $A+(B\times X)+C\times X*2$, or something else?) and then making formal tests of statistical significance. Usually these tests involve comparison of the size of the coefficients to the sum of the squares of the differences. You should *not*, however, conclude that the models used above exhaust the ingenuity of statisticians and mathematicians.

Splines

In the past decade a great deal of effort has been expended in researching models called *splines*. A spline is a mathematical analogue of a draftsman's curve-fitting instrument. Splines have a solid mathematical basis, and they also have the desirable property of fitting curves to a set of points in an esthetic fashion. Their greatest application is for graphing data for which the underlying model is unknown (or even nonexistent!).

It is far beyond the scope of this book to treat splines in any detail. We will present only a working program for evaluating natural cubic splines, with no comment on the programming style or algorithms:

```
      ∇ C←X SPLINECALC Y;N
[1]     N←4×¯2+ρY←0,Y
[2]     C←1 0 0 0 0 0 0 1 1 1 1 0 0 0 0 0 1 2 3 0 ¯1 0 0 0 2 6 0 0 ¯2
[3]     C←((N-2 0)ρ(4+4×N)ρ(5,N)↑4  7ρC),[1]¯1 2φ0 7⊤N↑2 20
[4]     C←X,((ρX),4)ρY[,1⌈(1↓ιρX)∘.+0 1,2ρ-N]⌹C
      ∇
      ∇ R←X SPLINEEVAL C;J
[1]     J←1⌈+/X∘.>R←C[;1]
[2]     R←+/C[J;2 3 4 5]×((X-R[J])÷((1↓R)-¯1↓R)[J])∘.*0 1 2 3
      ∇
      PLOT PX,[1.5] PX SPLINEEVAL X SPLINECALC Y
```

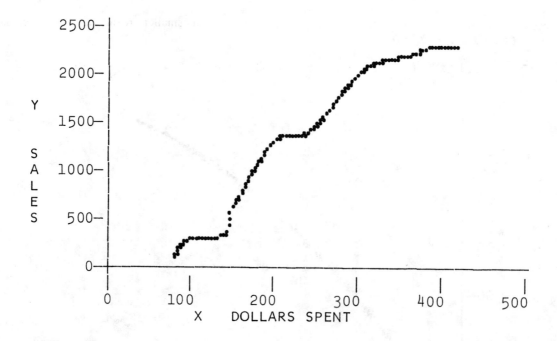

Notice that the spline technique ingeniously fits the curve through each of the points, without any jagged edges.

Some elementary examples from the calculus

The definition of the slope of a straight line (see problem 6, Chapter 7) is of little value if the function we are considering is nonlinear. We can, for example, still use this definition to get an "average" slope over a modest-sized interval, but it is only an approximation.

In calculus courses it is shown that the slope of a function at a particular point P is the limiting value of the average slope over an interval encompassing the given point as the interval shrinks:

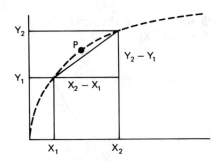

In the figure above, the average slope for the interval shown is $(Y_2 - Y_1) \div (X_2 - X_1)$. By reducing the size of the interval about P, this average approaches the instantaneous value of the slope at the point P, and in the limit is the value of the *derivative* of the function at P.

APL can be used to obtain numerical values for the slopes (derivatives) of functions, provided, of course, that the derivatives exist. As an example, let's define a quadratic function F as follows:

```
     ∇R←F X
[1]    R←2×X*2∇
```

Using our previous definition of the slope, the dyadic function $SLOPE$ allows us to choose intervals of varying size in the computation:

```
     ∇R←I SLOPE X
[1]    R←((F X+I)-F X)÷I∇
```

Here are some executions of $SLOPE$ with different intervals:

```
     X←ι10
     1 SLOPE X
6 10 14 18 22 26 30 34 38 42
     .1 SLOPE X
4.2 8.2 12.2 16.2 20.2 24.2 28.2 32.2 36.2 40.2
     .01 SLOPE X
4.02 8.02 12.02 16.02 20.02 24.02 28.02 32.02 36.02 40.02
     .0001 SLOPE X
4.0002 8.0002 12.0002 16.0002 20.0002 24.0002 28.0002 32.0002
      36.0002 40.0002
     1E⁻6 SLOPE X
4.000001999 8.000001999 12.000002 16.00000199 20.000002
      24.00000199 28.000002 32.00000199 36.00000199 40.000002
```

Those of you familiar with calculus will understand why these last results are nearly identical with

```
     2×2×X
4 8 12 16 20 24 28 32 36 40
```

for the function F defined previously.

Since the result of applying the function $SLOPE$ to F is itself a function namely, $2 \times 2 \times X$, we ought to be able to apply $SLOPE$ again after changing F:

```
∇F[1]R←2×2×X∇
1E¯6 SLOPE X
4 4 4 3.999999997 3.999999997 3.999999997 3.999999997 3.999999997
      3.999999997 3.999999997
```

This execution corresponds to the second derivative of F.

Our final example is one in which we compute the area bounded by the curve, the X-axis and the ordinates at X_1 and X_2 (see problem 5, Chapter 18):

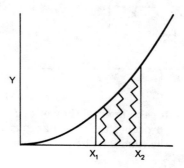

An obvious solution is to break up the cross-hatched area into rectangles of uniform width I,

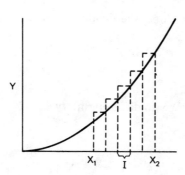

find an expression for the area of the "typical" rectangle, add up the areas and then decrease I to get a better approximation. The defined function $AREA$ does this for us. X is a two-element vector whose elements are X_1 and X_2 in the diagram.

```
      ∇R←I AREA X
[1]   R←I+.×F X[1]+I×ιL(X[2]-X[1])÷I∇
```

Again, those with a calculus background will recognize this as the numerical equivalent of

$$\int_{x_1}^{x_2} f(x)\, dx$$

Before applying the function, let's change F back:

```
    ∇F[1]R←2×X*2∇
    .1 AREA 1 2
4.97
    .01 AREA 1 2
4.6967
    .001 AREA 1 2
4.669667
    .0001 AREA 1 2
WS FULL
AREA[1] R←I+.×F X[1]+I×ι⌊(X[2]-X[1])÷I
                ∧
```

    Sooner or later we'll run out of storage space for the intermediate results in the the algorithm, by continually increasing the number of points used to evaluate the area. This is indicated by the *WS FULL* message. Can you think of a way of rewriting the function to "stretch" your available storage for greater precision?

PROBLEMS

1.   Use the function *SLOPE* to investigate the slope of the curve represented by $Y←*X$ for different points X. Compare your slopes with $*X$.

2.   Find the inverse of the identity matrix.

3.   Use ⊞ to solve the following set of equations:

$$2X + Y + 3Z = 10$$
$$4X + 3Y - Z = 13 \quad \text{(conventional notation)}$$
$$2X + Y - 4Z = 3$$

4.   In algebra it is shown that for the system of equations

$$aX + bY = c \quad \text{(conventional notation)}$$
$$dX + eY = f$$

the application of Cramer's rule gives as solutions

$$X = (ce - bf) ÷ (ae - bd) \quad \text{(conventional notation)}$$
$$Y = (af - cd) ÷ (ae - bd)$$

Write an **APL** program to solve by Cramer's rule a given set of two linear equations and print the message *NO UNIQUE SOLUTION* if ae - bd = 0. Then define a function *SOLVE* which uses ⊞ to solve the equation.

5.   Nearly every calculus book ever printed has a problem similar to the following: A farmer has 300 feet of fencing material which he wants to use to enclose as large a rectangular area as possible. One side of the property to be enclosed is a relatively straight stretch of river, and needs no fencing. How should the fence be put in? (To solve this problem, set up an expression for the area, apply the *SLOPE* function to it, and see where the slope is 0. This corresponds to a maximum point on the graph of area vs the variable representing the length of one side.)

6. Use the function $AREA$ to find the area bounded by the curve represented by $Y \leftarrow \div X$, the X-axis, and the ordinates at X = 1 and X = 2. Compare your answer with $\otimes 2$.

7. Sales forecasters for the Sticky Wicket Company predict the following sales for the next 7 years (in millions of dollars):

year	sales
1975	38
1976	52
1977	64
1978	82
1979	98
1980	128
1981	156

Assuming a linear model, find the equation which best fits this data.

8. (For matrix algebra buffs) A factory makes three finished products, P1, P2, P3. Four subassemblies A1, A2, A3, A4 are involved, along with two detail parts D1, D2. The table below shows how many of each (row) part are used directly in each (column) part:

	P1	P2	P3	A1	A2	A3	A4	D1	D2
P1	0	0	0	0	0	0	0	0	0
P2	0	0	0	0	0	0	0	0	0
P3	0	0	0	0	0	0	0	0	0
A1	1	2	0	0	0	0	0	0	0
A2	0	1	1	0	0	0	0	0	0
A3	0	0	2	1	1	0	0	0	0
A4	0	0	0	1	2	2	0	0	0
D1	3	2	0	0	0	0	1	0	0
D2	0	0	0	0	0	1	3	0	0

What are the total parts required? Hint: if the above matrix is designated as U and the requirements matrix as R, then the following matrix equation (conventional notation) is true: R=UR+I (I is the identity matrix).

9. Recent tests conducted by the U. S. Environmental Protection Agency yielded the following data on fuel economy of 1974 light duty vehicles:

weight class	fuel consumption, gal/100 mi.
2000	4.14
2200	4.67
2500	5.35
2750	5.61
3000	6.77
3500	7.39
4000	9.29
4500	10.45
5000	10.95
5500	12.16

Find the linear least-squares fit of fuel consumption to weight.

Chapter 28:
Input and output

Thus far we have been doing a considerable amount of computing without having to pay too much attention to the problems of input and output. And for a good reason: our work has been of a highly interactive nature. We fed information to the **APL** system and the system either responded or put things into storage for us, to be recalled at some later time.

Nevertheless, there comes a time when we need to take a look at some of the more specialized forms of input and output, especially as they appeared in the drill exercises and some of the prepared functions. These features are the basis for this chapter.

The quad

In 1 *CLASS* there is a function called *SD* which calculates the standard deviation. Here it is:

```
      )LOAD 1 CLASS
SAVED  15.02.39 04/15/74
      ∇SD[▯]∇
    ∇ SD;X;N
[1]   START:'ENTER OBSERVATIONS'
[2]   X←▯
[3]   →0×ι1≥ρ,X
[4]   'NUMBER OF OBS:';▯←N←ρX
[5]   X←X-(+/X)÷N
[6]   'STANDARD DEVIATION'
[7]   ((+/X*2)÷N-1)*0.5
[8]   →START
    ∇
```

It is niladic and does not return an explicit result. Going through the function, we see that line 1 prints the message *ENTER OBSERVATIONS*. This is followed on line 2 by the local variable *X*, which is specified by the quad (upper shift *L*). The effect of this line is that when control is on line 2, ▯: is printed and the system waits until you give it some input and press RETURN. The input is then stored in *X*. Line 3 branches to 0 if you enter fewer than two numbers. It is a signal in this function that we are finished. Line 4 is mixed output. It prints *NUMBER OF OBS*: followed by the number of observations entered (ρ*X* is stored in *N*, put into the box and printed). Line 5 subtracts from each element of *X* the average, and stores it in *X*.

After the message *STANDARD DEVIATION* (line 6), the calculation is carried out on the line 7 and printed, following which control is returned to line 1, and the program loops through the steps once more.

Let's try this a few times to see how it works:

```
     SD
ENTER OBSERVATIONS
☐:
      1 2 1 2 1 2 1 2
8
NUMBER OF OBS:8
STANDARD DEVIATION
0.5345224838
ENTER OBSERVATIONS
☐:
```

Note the 8 just prior to the line giving the number of observations. The reason for this is that on line 4 of the function, in executing from right to left, ρX was put into N and N in turn into ☐. Whenever the quad appears to the *left* of the specification arrow, it is interpreted as a command to print the value of whatever is to the right of the arrow. So the right hand side of line 4 really does two things: It stores the length of vector X in the local variable N for subsequent use on lines 5 and 7 and causes a printout of the length at the same time. Since in going from right to left the box is encountered first, the contents are printed first, before the literal message, and then reprinted following the message. We'll edit the function a little later to remove this undesirable feature.

Any valid *APL* expression can be entered:

```
☐:
      8ρ1 2
8
NUMBER OF OBS:8
STANDARD DEVIATION
0.5345224838
ENTER OBSERVATIONS
☐:
      ☐←8ρ1 2
1 2 1 2 1 2 1 2
8
NUMBER OF OBS:8
STANDARD DEVIATION
0.5345224838
ENTER OBSERVATIONS
☐:
```

Since the quad appears just to the left of the arrow here, it causes an immediate printout of $8\rho1\ 2$ and then proceeds with execution of the function.

The last thing typed above by the system was ☐:, our signal for entering input. The system is very precise about what it judges as valid input. It is seeking a value, and just pressing RETURN will cause it to type another ☐:. (Try it!) By entering an empty vector or a single number, we signal that we want to leave the function:

```
☐:
      ι0
@
```

Let's open up the function to remove the extra quad. We'll use detailed editing on line 4:

```
        ∇SD[4☐10]
[4]     'NUMBER OF OBS:';☐←N←ρX
                         //
[4]     'NUMBER OF OBS:';N←ρX∇
```

Now executing *SD* once more, it appears to be OK:

```
        SD
ENTER OBSERVATIONS
☐:
        10ρ1 2
NUMBER OF OBS:10
STANDARD DEVIATION
0.5270462767
ENTER OBSERVATIONS
☐:
        ' '
        @
```

The last input shows that another way to enter an empty vector is to type `' '`. Do you remember why this works? If you happen to forget what input you've defined to mean "leave the function," or worse, forgot to define an escape, you can always cause an immediate exit by typing → when ☐: appears.

The function *SD* has introduced two new features: (1) the quad to the *left* of the specification arrow, which causes output; and (2) a quad to the *right* of the specification arrow which returns ☐: on the paper, skips a line and waits for any valid **APL** expression to be typed in for evaluation. The contents of the quad in the last case can be put into storage by an expression like $X←☐$, which makes input available for future use in the function (or outside, if X is a global variable).

In a sense, the quad symbol is a mechanism for sharing information between you and **APL**. If you put values into the quad, as in $X←☐$, **APL** uses your values; while if **APL** puts values into the quad, as $☐←X$, you can see them displayed.

SUB is another function that utilizes the quad. Before displaying it we'll try it out a few times:

```
        SUB
3-3
☐:
        0
THATS RIGHT
10-5
☐:
        6
5+☐=10
TRY AGAIN
10-5
☐:
        (RETURN)
☐:
        (RETURN)
☐:
        5
THATS RIGHT
5-0
☐:
        5
THATS RIGHT
14-10
```

```
□:
       HELP
○ ○ ○ ○ ○ ○ ○ ○ ○ ○ ○ ○ ○     TAKE AWAY
○ ○ ○ ○ ○ ○ ○ ○ ○ ○
14-10
□:
       4
THATS RIGHT
19-7
□:
       19-7
THATS RIGHT
11-9
□:
       11-9
THATS RIGHT
1-0
□:
```

Note again that giving no input to the function (just pressing RETURN) won't get you out. Also observe the responses of the function under different conditions, and the fact that any **APL** expression can be used as input.

Let's now interrupt the function to get out. The input quad will even accept some system commands, including)*CLEAR* or)*LOAD*. However, either of these would destroy the active workspace. For the sake of variety, we'll use the stop control and then remove the suspension:

```
□:
       SΔSUB←ι100

SUB[5]
       )SI
SUB[5] *
       →
       SΔSUB←ι0
```

Here is *SUB*:

```
       ∇SUB[□]∇
    ∇ SUB
[1]   L1:P←?20
[2]      P←P,¯1+?P+1
[3]   L3:P[1];'-';P[2]
[4]      A←□
[5]      →OOK×ιA=-/P
[6]      →NP×ιA=HELP
[7]      →0×ιA=STOP
[8]      P[2];'+□=';P[1]
[9]      'TRY AGAIN'
[10]     →L3
[11]  OOK:'THATS RIGHT'
[12]     →L1
[13]  NP:(P[1]ρ'○'),'    TAKE AWAY'
[14]     P[2]ρ'○'
[15]     →L3
    ∇
```

On line 1 a random number from 1 to 20 is generated and stored in P. This is then respecified by catenating to P a second random number from 0 to P. You should be able to see why this guarantees that the second element of P will never be greater than the first, so that no problems requiring negative results will be generated. Line 3 prints mixed output, the first random number followed by the subtract sign and the second random number. Line 4 accepts input, while line 5 causes a branch to line 11 if the answer is correct and prints the message $THATS\ RIGHT$, otherwise it drops us through to line 6. If $HELP$ is typed, line 6 branches us to line 13, and if $STOP$ is typed, we leave the function.

Assuming an incorrect answer and neither $HELP$ nor $STOP$ are entered, lines 8, 9 and 10 restate the problem and tell us to $TRY\ AGAIN$, and we start over on line 3 with the same problem. If the problem is answered correctly this time and we get to line 11, we branch to 1 and get a new problem to do.

Typing $HELP$ brings us to line 13, where $P[1]$ copies of the small circle followed by some spaces and the words $TAKE\ AWAY$ are printed. Then line 14 prints $P[2]$ copies of the small circle on the next line. A branch to line 3 prints a restatement of the problem, and we cycle through the same problem once again.

$HELP$ and $STOP$ in this exercise are global variables with rather unlikely values attached to them:

```
        HELP
2.718281828
       *1
2.718281828
       STOP
15.15426224
      **1
15.15426224
```

Being global they appear on the list of variables for 1 $CLASS$:

```
        )VARS
CIRCUIT D       HELP      MILEAGE SPL      STOP      TAB0      TAB1
TAB2     TAB3   X
```

To see if $STOP$ works, we'll execute SUB again:

```
        SUB
11-1
□:
        10
THATS RIGHT
14-6
□:
        STOP
        @
```

and we get out of the program as expected.

Other uses of the quad

Don't get the impression from the previous illustrations that the quad must be used only within defined functions. Here, for example, are some more ways in which the quad can be utilized for the display and input of information. Keep in mind that a quad at the left of a specification arrow causes printing of a value. No values go into storage as a result of its use in this manner.

```
           □
□:
       15.27×8-42
¯519.18
       A←5 15 ¯2 ¯6 0
       A[□←(+/(A∘.≥A)-□←(X∘.>X)∧□←A∘.=A)ιX←ιρA]
 1 0 0 0 0
 0 1 0 0 0
 0 0 1 0 0
 0 0 0 1 0
 0 0 0 0 1

 0 0 0 0 0
 0 0 0 0 0
 0 0 0 0 0
 0 0 0 0 0
 0 0 0 0 0
 4  3 5 1 2
¯6 ¯2 0 5 15
```

The last example uses the quad to display intermediate results generated in this rather unlikely expression for doing a numerical sort. It suggests that messy one- and two-liners which are incomprehensible to you can be edited to introduce the quad at strategic points to give intermediate results. They are to aid you in understanding what's going on, and should be removed later. On the IBM 5100 an alternative way to examine an expression like the one above would be to enter it on the right side of the input line, one piece at a time, execute it, and scroll down three lines and up one line to remove the result. Then position the instruction already entered so that you can add the next piece at the left and repeat the procedure as often as necessary to execute the whole line.

Here are some additional examples of the quad used as an input indicator on the right of the specification arrow:

```
       R←□
□:
       64
       R
64
       R+□÷10
□:
       16
65.6
       T←□
□:
       'THE CAT IN THE HAT'
       T
THE CAT IN THE HAT
       □ρι8
□:
       2 4
 1 2 3 4
 5 6 7 8
```

The input quad is very handy for coping with a numeric entry that overruns the right margin. Suppose within some function there are lines like

```
[9]    'ENTER DATA'
[10]   'SUM IS ';X←+/□
```

If the number of values being added is large, ☐ can be used in the manner shown below:

```
ENTER DATA
☐:
      5  9  14  6  3  12  15,☐
☐:
      6  2  3,(10ρ21),8  7,☐
☐:
      3  2  1
SUM IS 306
```

It works because the input quad admits any **APL** expression, including the input quad itself. A line of numeric input that ends with a quad has the meaning "to be continued."

The quote-quad

In the function *SUB* we were rather generous in allowing any **APL** expression as input. What if we want an exact answer without allowing just any old expression to be evaluated? An example of such a program is given by *ADD*:

```
        ∇ADD[☐]∇
      ∇  ADD
[1]      ☐←P←? 10  10
[2]   LOOP:→0×ι0=ρA←,▯
[3]      →WRONG×ι~∧/A∈'0123456789'
[4]      A←10⊥‾1+'0123456789'ιA
[5]      →1×ιA=+/P
[6]      'TRY AGAIN'
[7]      →LOOP
[8]   WRONG:'????????????'
[9]      →LOOP
      ∇
```

This contains a quad with a quote overstruck. The effect of this is to make whatever is typed in accepted as a character vector or scalar. This includes even entries like *OFF*, *CLEAR*, etc., so it's important that an appropriate means of escape from the function be planned.

In the program *ADD*, after two random numbers are generated and printed by being assigned to the box, line 2 exits us if an empty vector is entered. There is a branch to line 8 if the input is any character other than 0 through 9. Line 4 converts the character representation of the input to a numeric value which is assigned to *A*. This is then matched against the correct answer on line 5. If correct, we get another problem; if not, the message *TRY AGAIN*. Here is a sample execution:

```
      ADD
8  10
18
8  3
8+3
????????????
R E W
????????????
11
```

```
1  8
)CLEAR
????????????
```
                                    (RETURN)
              @

Note that no quad is printed on the paper. The typeball simply moves over to the left margin when literal input is called for, and the keyboard is unlocked.

Another function that accepts literal input is *SPELL*:

```
        SPELL
3
THREE
THATS RIGHT
5
FIV
TRY AGAIN
5
FIVE
THATS RIGHT
8
STOP
        ∇SPELL[□]∇
    ∇ SPELL
[1]   START:N←¯1+?10
[2]   RE:N
[3]     ANS←⍞
[4]     →0×ι∧/(4↑ANS)='STOP'
[5]     →CORRECT×ι∧/(5↑ANS)=SPL[N+1;]
[6]     'TRY AGAIN'
[7]     →RE
[8]   CORRECT:'THATS RIGHT'
[9]     →START
    ∇
```

On lines 1 and 2, a random number from 0 to 9 is selected, assigned to *N* and printed. Line 3 accepts the input and puts it in *ANS*. The next line compares the first four characters of the input with *STOP*. If they match, we're out. If not, we drop through to line 5 where the first five characters of *ANS* are compared with the (*N*+1)th row of *SPL*:

```
        SPL
ZERO
ONE
TWO
THREE
FOUR
FIVE
SIX
SEVEN
EIGHT
NINE
```

If they match, we branch to line 8, where *THATS RIGHT* is printed and followed by another problem. Otherwise we get the message *TRY AGAIN* and recycle through the problem.

SPL is a character matrix of shape 10 5 with blanks on the end where needed to pad out the five columns. The function *SPELL*, as defined above, does not check beyond the first five characters that are typed in. This leads to anomalies like

```
      SPELL
7
SEVENTY
THATS RIGHT
3
STOP
```

Can you devise a scheme to prevent this?

Extensions of the quote-quad

As with the quad, the quote-quad can also be used by itself:

```
      Z←⍞
SIMON SAYS
      Z
SIMON SAYS
      Z,⍞,'BACKWARD'
TAKE THREE STEPS
SIMON SAYS TAKE THREE STEPS BACKWARD
      ALF←'ABCDEFG',⍞
HIJKLMNOPQRSTUVWXYZ
      ALF
ABCDEFGHIJKLMNOPQRSTUVWXYZ
```


Escape from an input loop

It sometimes happens that in spite of our best efforts, we may be caught in an endless loop and not know how to get out, or, what is worse, the function is poorly designed and has no built-in way to escape. Shutting the terminal off won't help us, since when we sign on again we will be right back where we were before, because the *CONTINUE* workspace is automatically reloaded.

There are two emergency escape mechanisms for such situations. Those functions calling for evaluated input (⎕) can be exited by typing →. Functions calling for literal input (⍞) can be interrupted by entering *O* BACKSPACE *U* BACKSPACE *T*, forming the overstruck symbol *⍝*. This will, however, exit you from the function. It results in an *INTERRUPT* message and an indication of where execution was suspended. Try these escape mechanisms on *SPELL* and *SUB*.

The proper way to handle escape from input loops is to plan that a certain input value is taken as a signal to escape. Examples are found on line 7 of *SUB*, line 2 of *ADD* and line 4 of *SPELL*.

Conversion of literal input to numeric values

A common characteristic of large commercial applications is the need to accept volumes of numeric data from the terminal. Often the people assigned to entering the data are not experienced in the use of computers. It is therefore important that the *APL* programs you write are "forgiving" of input errors. Hence, most applications use ⍞ input instead of ⎕, with the character vector being checked in the program for errors before being converted to numeric values.

The usual means of doing the conversion is to check the input for invalid entries (see Chapter 20) and employ some variant of $10\bot^-1+{}'0123456789{}'\imath INPUT$. Since this may consume a lot of computer time for large amounts of data, the ***APL ★PLUS***® system has a monadic system function $\Box FI$ for doing this efficiently.

$\Box FI$ takes as an argument a character vector (or scalar) and converts it to a vector of numbers, using a subset of the rules for $\Box$ input. For example:

```
      X←□FI '10    25.4 9'
      X
10 25.4 9
      ρX
3
```

If there is anything in the argument which can't be converted, a zero is placed in that position of the result:

```
      □FI '10    23SKIDOO 9 ¯.25'
10  0  9  ¯0.25
```

To distinguish between true and false zeros in the argument, the system function, $\Box VI$, may be used. It accepts the same arguments as $\Box FI$, but returns a vector with 1's in the positions where the result is valid, and 0's where it isn't. Here it is with the above examples:

```
      □VI '10    25.4 9'
1  1  1
      □VI '10    23SKIDOO 9 ¯.25'
1  0  1  1
```

$\Box FI$ and $\Box VI$ are both usually employed in a sequence like this:

```
      INPUT←□
      →(0∈□VI INPUT)/ERRORANALYSIS
      DATA←□FI INPUT
```

More generally, the execute function, $\pmb{\pm}$, described in Chapter 33, can be used to convert literal information to numeric values.

Idiot-proofing

The last section described some techniques for protecting naïve users of ***APL*** from the consequences of their own folly. It is a fact that input and output (I/O) considerations consume a considerable amount of the time and energy of computer people. Perhaps more than any other single factor, properly designed I/O is what lets non-computer people use computers. Imagine the chaos that would result if an online airline reservation system, for example, didn't have built in error checking to exclude unacceptable input!

We've only hinted at some of the difficulties and ways to correct them in this chapter. Those of you who will be designing applications for others to run will find many helpful suggestions and subroutines for prompting, validation of input, and error reporting in a 1976 paper *Writing Interactive **APL** Programs: A Discussion of Techniques*, by Martin A. Zimelis, available from Scientific Time Sharing Corporation.

PROBLEMS

1. Define a function that will give multiplication drill of integers $?N$ for some argument N in the header. Have your function print a message $TRY\ AGAIN$ for wrong answers. Use $STOP$ as a global variable for escape from the function.

2. Modify your answer to the above problem so that three tries are allowed, after which the correct answer is printed and another problem is posed.

3. Add a further refinement to the multiplication drill so that when $HELP$ is typed, the answer to the problem is given as $X[1]$ rows of $X[2]$ stars each, with an appropriate message and a repetition of the problem. X is the vector of random integers generated in the problem.

4. Replace the message $TRY\ AGAIN$ on line 6 of $SPELL$ with a statement which reveals the answer.

5. Define a function $ENTER$ that will take the literal spelling of numbers, like those in SPL, and put them in successive rows of a 20-column matrix. Exit from the function will be effected by entering an empty vector.

6. Define a dyadic function $LIST$ that lets you input and list a specified number of names of specified length.

7. Write a monadic function $LOOKUP$ whose right argument is a list L of names in matrix form, and which asks you to input a name to be looked up by the function, identifies its row location(s), or prints an appropriate message.

Chapter 29:
Introduction to data files

Almost all commercial data processing applications and a good many scientific applications involve more data than can be jammed into a workspace. Even though sophisticated coding and packing techniques may be employed, sooner or later the workspace will fill up. Also, there is a class of applications, typified by an airline reservation system, in which several users must be able to read or update a value almost simultaneously. For example, imagine that your terminal is one of many serving as a reservations station, and you and the other reservation agents are all trying to sell whatever seats are still unclaimed. There would have to be a counter somewhere which holds the remaining number of seats, and is decreased whenever any agent reserves a seat.

Both of these classes of applications can be handled through careful and tedious use of the system commands $)COPY$ and $)SAVE$, but at best they would be prone to error. Furthermore, in the case of a reservation system, you would have the problem of deciding whose saved workspace holds the most recent updating of the counter. There are good odds that you would never resolve the situation of two agents attempting to decrement the counter at the same time.

Large database applications and shared database applications are both properly handled using a file system. In the case of IBM's *APLSV* the file system is called *Shared Variables*, and in Scientific Time Sharing's system it is called *Shared Files*. The two systems differ in approach, but they achieve approximately the same goals: working with data that won't fit in the workspace, and dealing with true real-time applications. In this chapter we'll discuss personal (i.e., nonshared) use of Scientific Time Sharing's files. Subsequent chapters will deal with shared files and shared variables.

A file, as was implied above, is a place to put data so that it is available to the programs in your active workspace, but doesn't take any space away from the active workspace. (You don't have to be concerned with where the data is actually put; it is enough to say that it is stored in the same type of equipment that holds the workspaces of your library.)

Like workspaces, files have names, and data can be stored in them. In fact, the data-items stored in a file have structures that are identical to the variables stored in a workspace. However, unlike workspaces, instead of referring to a data-item by name, you refer to it by a number, that number being the position of that data-item in the file. Each data-item in a file is called a *component* (instead of a variable) and the file itself consists of a sequence of these components. You could have a file with, say, three thousand components, and each component could be a literal matrix of shape 100 by 90. This would amount to nearly three million *bytes* if you had to stuff it into a workspace all at once, which would be impossible anyhow. When using files, you have to contend with only one component at a time in your workspace. The term *byte*, incidentally, is a generally used unit of computer storage. Each **APL** literal character uses up 1 byte, while each integer (up to $2*31$) takes 4 bytes, except for 0 and 1, which require $1/8$ byte. Eight bytes are needed for all other numbers (Chapter 32).

File creation

Now to business. Let's approach learning file use by considering the following "case study." Imagine you are responsible for keeping the medical records of some 5000 patients. When a patient comes in for a visit, a standard set of 23 tests is done on him, and you must keep all 23 test results for future analysis and study. Although the same tests are made for each patient at each visit, some patients may accumulate many more visits than others. Records are kept only for the most recent 100 visits of each patient.

A likely structure for holding this data (if it could fit in the workspace) would be a three-dimensional array of patients by visits and by test results. There would be wasted space, because the second dimension, visits, would either have to be as long as the number of visits accumulated by the biggest hypochondriac or limited to some fixed amount.

In the file we're going to make, the component numbering will correspond to the first dimension of this hypothetical three-dimensional array, and each component will consist of a given patient's data. Each component will be a matrix whose row dimension is the number of visits so far, and there will be 23 columns, for the 23 test results.

First we have to create and name a file. Let's name the file $'MEDICAL'$:

    $'MEDICAL'$ $\Box FCREATE$ 98

The dyadic function $\Box FCREATE$ is used to create the file. The left argument is the name of the file. The naming rules are similar to those of workspaces: names must consist of letters and numbers, and can be up to eleven characters in length. Note that the name is in quotes, which is different from the arguments of conventional functions.

The right argument is called the *file tie number*. It is a unique number for referencing the file while it is in active use. A number is used rather than the file name so that if you have two or more files active (or tied) at the same time, you can "index" from file to file much as you index an array in the workspace. The number you choose doesn't really matter much except that it must be a positive integer, and there must be a different number used for each file in active use at any one time.

You can find out which files are tied at any time by the niladic function $\Box FNAMES$:

    $\Box FNAMES$
    78974 $MEDICAL$

The result is a 22-column character matrix. Columns 1 through 10 hold the user numbers of the owners of the files, column 11 is blank and columns 12 through 22 hold the names of the files. Our particular matrix has only one row, but if you had six files active, the matrix would have six rows. As an aside, the order of the file names in the matrix corresponds to the chronological order in which they were tied.

A listing of file tie numbers in use can be obtained by the function $\Box FNUMS$:

    $\Box FNUMS$
98

The result is a vector holding the file tie numbers in the same sequence as the names in $\Box FNAMES$. Thus, if you already have some files tied, to find a unique file number for activation of another file, execute

```
      1+⌈/0,⎕FNUMS
99
```

In the expression above, the 0 is necessary to cover the case where no files are currently activated. Without it, the result would be ⌈/⍳0, which is ¯7.237005577E75. Of course, 1 added to that is not a positive number. (See the answer to problem 4, Chapter 26.)

Whenever you sign off (or lose your telephone connection) your files are automatically deactivated or *untied*. They are *not* automatically reactivated when you sign back on, even if *CONTINUE* is reloaded. You have to reactivate them with the ⎕*FTIE* function:

```
      'MEDICAL' ⎕FTIE 76
```

The syntax is similar to ⎕*FCREATE*, except that this function is used to tie files that had been created previously. Actually, ⎕*FCREATE* both *creates* and *ties* a file, while ⎕*FTIE* only *activates* a file. Note that in this session, we tied '*MEDICAL*' to the number 76 instead of the number 98. There is no permanent connection between a file name and a file tie number. A file can be tied to whatever number you choose in any session.

To untie a file in midsession, use the monadic function ⎕*FUNTIE*. Its argument is the vector of tie numbers of the files that you want to deactivate. ⎕*FUNTIE* ⎕*FNUMS*[ρ⎕*FNUMS*] would untie the file that was tied most recently in this session.

⎕*FSIZE* is a kind of "shape of" operation applied to a file. It is monadic, and takes a file tie number of an active file as an argument. The result is a four-element vector holding (1) the lowest numbered component in the file, (2) the number of the next available component in the file, (3) the amount of space that you are presently using in the file and (4) the total space available in the file.

```
      ⎕FSIZE 79
FILE TIE ERROR
      ⎕FSIZE 79
      ∧
```

Here we got an error because there are no files tied with 79. But 76 is an active tie number for the '*MEDICAL*' file:

```
      'MEDICAL' ⎕FTIE 76
      ⎕FSIZE 76
1 1 0 50184
```

The lowest component in our file is 1, but the next available component is also 1. This is an indication that the file is empty, which is certainly what we'd expect for a file that we had never put anything into. The third element is zero, again indicating that there is nothing in this file. The last element is 50184, which is the nominal amount of space available for storage in this file. Both the third and fourth elements are expressed in bytes.

It is obvious that our file doesn't have the capacity to hold all the data we intend for it. There are two ways to provide this space. If we had created the file as '*MEDICAL 46200000*' ⎕*FCREATE* 98, then it would have had the required capacity (computed from 4 bytes per integer to be stored, times 5000 patients, times 100 rows, times 23 columns), plus 4 percent overhead. Alternatively, we could have used the dyadic function ⎕*FRESIZE*:

```
      46200000 ⎕FRESIZE 76
```

The right argument is the file tie number, and the left argument is the amount of space to be reserved for the file.

Updating a file

Let's now begin to store some data in the file. We'll use the following variables as data on-hand for two patients:

```
P1←2 23ρι46
P2←(ι4)∘.×⌽ι23
```

We are simulating patient 1 with two visits and patient 2 with four visits. Don't be concerned about our "falsification" of medical records; this is, after all, just an example so that we can have some numbers around to check out our work. In particular, $P1[1;1]$ is 1 and $P2[1;1]$ is 23. Let's put patient 1 on the file, using the dyadic function $\Box FAPPEND$:

```
      P1 □FAPPEND 76
      □FSIZE 76
1 2 1224 46000368
```

$\Box FAPPEND$ puts the value of its left argument as a new component at the end of the file designated in the right argument. The lowest component is still number 1, but the next available component is now number 2. Continuing, we add patient 2:

```
      P2 □FAPPEND 76
      □FSIZE 76
1 3 1224 46000368
```

Note that the space used (third element of the result of $\Box FSIZE$) took a big jump after the first $\Box FAPPEND$ but didn't increase after the second. This is the result of internal tradeoffs for storage and time efficiency in the **APL★PLUS** ® file system. When you make your first append, the system reserves 1224 bytes of storage, keeps it handy, and won't reserve any more until you've used it all up.

Now, we're going to take what looks like a foolhardy action:

```
      )CLEAR
CLEAR WS
```

Before you began using files, doing that operation would have meant permanent loss of the data (unless, of course, you had saved an image of the workspace). However, our patient data is stored safely in our file and isn't affected by clearing the workspace.

We now have to learn how to read information from files. This is accomplished with $\Box FREAD$:

```
      P1←□FREAD 76 1
      ρP1
2 23
      P1[1;1]
1
      ρP2
VALUE ERROR
      ρP2
      ^
      P2←□FREAD 76 2
      ρP2
4 23
      P2[1;1]
23
```

The $\square FREAD$ function is used to bring into the active workspace an image of what's in the file and component you ask for. Note that, as in Chapters 14 and 15, the term *image* is used. The file is no more changed by reading it than a variable in the workspace is changed by using it as part of an expression. Also, while we normally read the values back into the same variables that they came from, there does not need to be this relation. For example, we could have entered $P2\leftarrow\square FREAD$ 76 1 and $P1\leftarrow\square FREAD$ 76 2, which would interchange the data for patients 1 and 2 in the workspace (but *not* in the file).

You may have also observed that the file tie numbers are preserved even though we cleared the active workspace. File tie numbers are not changed during a session except by the functions $\square FCREATE$, $\square FTIE$, $\square FUNTIE$, $\square FSTIE$, $\square FERASE$, (the latter two will be explained subsequently) or signing off.

Here is a simple function to find the total number of visits by all patients (that is, the total number of rows in the file):

```
      ∇ R←TOTVISITS N
[1]    ⍝N IS THE FILE NUMBER
[2]    R←0 ◇ I←(¯1+⎕FSIZE N)[1]
[3]    LOOP:I←I+1 ◇ →(I=(⎕FSIZE N)[2])/0 ◇ R←R+1↑ρ⎕FREAD N,I ◇ →LOOP
      ∇
      TOTVISITS 76
6
```

By this time, you should be catching on how to use files. More file operations will be introduced later in the chapter, along with additional defined functions to utilize our patient data base. There are two operations that are obvious necessities: 1) establishing a new patient in the file by methods a bit more sophisticated than what was done above, and 2) adding the results of a subsequent visit to any individual patient's data already in the file. The first is handled by the defined function $NEWPATIENT$:

```
      ∇ NEWPATIENT N
[1]    ⍝N IS THE TIE NUMBER
[2]    (0 23 ρ0) ⎕FAPPEND N
[3]    'THIS IS PATIENT ';(⎕FSIZE N)[2]-1
      ∇
```

This function simply appends an empty matrix for the new patient and prints the patient number that was assigned.

Here is a defined function for recording the data gathered on a patient's visit:

```
      ∇ P NEWVISIT N;DATA
[1]    ⍝P IS PATIENT NUMBER, N IS TIE NUMBER.
[2]    →((P≥(⎕FSIZE N)[1])∧P<(⎕FSIZE N)[2])/OK
[3]    'NO SUCH PATIENT NUMBER' ◇ →0
[4]    OK:'ENTER 23 VALUES' ◇ →(23=ρDATA←,⎕)/UPDATE
[5]    'INVALID INPUT' ◇ →0
[6]    UPDATE:DATA←(⎕FREAD N,P),[1]DATA ◇ DATA ⎕FREPLACE N,P
      ∇
```

You probably spotted the new file function, $\square FREPLACE$, on line 5. It replaces the P-th file component with new data from the workspace. In our case it's the catenation of what used to be in the component, with another row, $DATA$, on the bottom. There doesn't need to be any relation between what is being replaced and what you're replacing it with, although in the above case there happened to be. The requirement that only the most recent 100 visits are to be kept in the file can be satisfied simply by changing the second statement on line 5 to read $(\overline{\ }100\ 23\uparrow DATA)\ \square FREPLACE\ N,P.$

Getting data from a file

Having written functions to enroll a new patient and enter the data from a visit, we now turn to programs for getting selected data from the file. *Information retrieval* is the computer industry's term for this procedure. Much effort is spent by computer professionals to develop and improve both file design (how the data is laid out in the files) and functions to access the data base. In general, it requires more time to take one value from each of several components than it does to take several values out of one component. And if your data base includes vast amounts of data, you really need to study how the information is to be used before you choose the layout of your file. As you have already seen, the nature of *APL* is such that even if you first happen to choose the wrong layout for your file, it's no great task to revise it. Unfortunately, the limited scope of this text doesn't permit our going into all the fine points of file design.

Complete data on each patient can be obtained by reading his component. Here is a function for obtaining a matrix consisting of data from one or more patient's latest visits:

```
     ∇ R←V LASTVISIT N
[1]   ⍝V IS PATIENT NUMBER;  N IS TIE NUMBER
[2]   R←0 23⍴0
[3]   LOOP:→(0=⍴V)/0 ◊ R←R,[1]¯1 23↑⎕FREAD N,1↑V ◊ V←1↓V ◊ →LOOP
     ∇
```

The following function returns a vector of numbers of all patients who made at least one visit in which the second test (i.e., second column) yielded a result greater than 99:

```
     ∇ R←C2GT99 N
[1]   R←⍳0 ◊ I←(⎕FSIZE N)[1]
[2]   LOOP:→(I=(⎕FSIZE N)[2])/0
[3]   R←R,(∨/(⎕FREAD N,I)[;2]>99)/I
[4]   I←I+1 ◊ →LOOP
     ∇
```

The approach in *C2GT99* can be generalized to produce a function which returns patient numbers all of which satisfy some relation on some column; for example, all patients who ever scored exactly 20 on the fourth test, or all patients who ever scored lower than 19 on test 12:

```
     ∇ R←REL SELECT NCV;N;C;V;COMP;T
[1]   ⍝N IS 3-ELE VECTOR - TIE NUMBER, COLUMN, VALUE
[2]   ⍝REL IS LITERAL RELATION SYMBOL (<≤=≥> OR ≠)
[3]   N←NCV[1] ◊ C←NCV[2] ◊ V←NCV[3]
[4]   R←⍳0 ◊ I←(⎕FSIZE N)[1]
[5]   REL←(LT,LE,EQ,GE,GT,NE)['<≤=≥>≠'⍳REL]
[6]   LOOP:→(I=(⎕FSIZE N)[2])/0 ◊ COMP←(⎕FREAD N,I)[;C] ◊ →REL
[7]   LT: T←∨/V<COMP ◊ →XX
[8]   LE: T←∨/V≤COMP ◊ →XX
[9]   EQ: T←∨/V=COMP ◊ →XX
[10]  GE: T←∨/V≥COMP ◊ →XX
[11]  GT: T←∨/V>COMP ◊ →XX
[12]  NE: T←∨/V≠COMP ◊ →XX
[13]  XX: R←R,T/I ◊ I←I+1 ◊ →LOOP
     ∇

      '=' SELECT 76 4 20
2
      '<' SELECT 76 12 19
1 2
```

We could continue to write functions to get information from the file, but you can generalize from what you've seen so far. Examples of complete information retrieval systems can be found in these publications:

Weaver, Kevin R., *"Information Retrieval System Using One File,"* **APL** Congress 1973, Copenhagen Conference (New York: North-Holland/American Elsevier Publishing Co., 1973), pp. 473-478.

Ravitz, Paul J., *Address Management Package*, (Bethesda: Scientific Time Sharing Corp., 1973).

Rose, Allen J., *Fulltext Users Guide*, (Bethesda: Scientific Time Sharing Corp., 1973).

Robie, Edward A., Jr., *SIMS - Shared Information Management System*, (Bethesda: Scientific Time Sharing Corp., 1974).

More file functions

Some additional useful file functions will now be discussed briefly. First, the $\Box FLIB$ function is used to list the file names in a *library* of files. $\Box FLIB$, with your user number as an argument, produces an explicit result: a character matrix with 22 columns and as many rows as you have different file names. Columns 1 through 10 hold your user number; column 11 is blank; and columns 12 through 22 hold the file name.

To illustrate the next function, $\Box FDROP$, consider a file application involving order entry and invoicing. As each order is received, the pertinent information is appended as a different component on a file. Each order shipped causes an invoice to be produced, and the order information for that order is no longer needed. Most of the time, but not always, orders will be shipped in the order of receipt. It makes sense to let the component number be the order/invoice number, since there will be a different component for each one.

The only fly in the ointment is how to dispose of all the components holding order information that has already been invoiced. For that, we use $\Box FDROP$. It is monadic, and its argument is the file number and the number of sequential components you want to drop from the front end (positive number) or back end (negative number) of the file.

For example, if some file tied to the number 20 presently has 153 components (that is, $\Box FSIZE$ 20 results in 1 154 40028 50184), then dropping 15 components from the front end ($\Box FDROP$ 20 15) leaves 139 components. Then $\Box FSIZE$ 20 would now yield 16 154 35630 50184. Note that component numbering now starts with 16. If you now drop the last nine components, ($\Box FDROP$ 20 ¯9), the result of $\Box FSIZE$ 20 would be 16 145 34918 50184.

An application in which components are appended to the file, and other components are later dropped from the front end is called *FIFO* (first-in, first-out), while an application which appends and drops from the back end is called *LIFO* (last-in, first-out).

Our order/invoice application is a member of the FIFO category. Here is a possible program to process an invoice, the argument N being the invoice number (component number) to be processed:

```
      ∇   INVOICERUN N;ORD;FN
[1]    'ORDERS' ⎕FTIE FN←1+⌈/0,⎕FNUMS
[2]    →(1=+/N<2↑⎕FSIZE FN)/OK1
[3]    'THIS NUMBER NOT IN FILE' ◊ ⎕FUNTIE FN ◊ →0
[4]  OK1: ORD←⎕FREAD FN,N ◊ →(0≠ρORD)/OK2
[5]    'THIS NUMBER ALREADY PROCESSED' ◊ ⎕FUNTIE FN ◊ →0
[6]  OK2: PRINTINVOICE ⍝INVOICE PRINTING PROGRAM NOT SHOWN HERE
[7]    (⍳0) ⎕FREPLACE FN, N ⍝REPLACE WITH EMPTY AFTER PROCESSING
[8]  DROPLOOP:→(=/2↑⎕FSIZE FN)/DONE ⍝ DONE IF FILE IS EMPTY
[9]    →(0≠ρ ⎕FREAD FN, 1↑⎕FSIZE FN)/DONE
[10] ⍝ STOP WHEN FIRST COMPONENT NOT EMPTY
[11]   ⎕FDROP FN, 1 ◊ →DROPLOOP
[12] DONE: ⎕FUNTIE FN
      ∇
```

We have departed from a pure FIFO scheme in using an empty vector to signal that an invoice has been processed. After processing, any empty components on the front end of the file are dropped.

APL limits you to no more than two arguments for a function, but files can be employed as a practical means for using more than two arguments. To use this technique (which is an instance of LIFO), you'll need the functions $PUSH$ and $PULL$ and a "scratch" file to hold the arguments:

```
     ∇ R←VAL PUSH FN                    ∇ VAL←PULL FN
[1]    VAL □FAPPEND FN            [1]    VAL←□FREAD FN,(□FSIZE FN)[2]-1
[2]    R←FN                       [2]    □FDROP FN,¯1
     ∇                                 ∇
```

$PUSH$ appends VAL to a file, while $PULL$ reads the last component from the file and then drops it.

Here is a trivial example of the use of $PUSH$ and $PULL$, along with analogous functions not using files. To keep the analogy accurate (and comprehensible), only two arguments are shown, but the extension to more arguments is straightforward.

| **with files** | **without files** |

```
     ∇ R←HYP FN;A;B                        ∇ R←A HYP B
[1]    B←PULL FN ◊ A←PULL FN       [1]    R←SQRT(A*2)+B*2
[2]    R←SQRT((A*2)+B*2) PUSH FN          ∇
     ∇
     ∇ R←SQRT FN                          ∇ R←SQRT X
[1]    R←(PULL FN)*.5              [1]    R←X*.5
     ∇                                   ∇
     'TEMPORARY' □FCREATE 9999
     HYP 3 4 PUSH 4 12 PUSH 9999          3 HYP 4
5 13                              5 13
```

The components are read and dropped in exactly the reverse order that they were appended. The order of the $PULL$s within any function is critical. Of course, it would be silly to use this technique for the small amount of data in the example, but it is useful for dealing with certain large, complicated problems.

The last file function in this chapter is $□FERASE$. As its name indicates, it is used to *erase* an entire file. The file to be erased must be tied. $□FERASE$ is a dyadic function whose left argument is the file name and whose right argument is the file tie number:

```
     'MEDICAL' □FERASE 76
```

It may seem redundant that both are required, but this is done to protect you from erasing the wrong file by accident.

Chapter 30:
Shared files

The second major area of interest in files is sharing data among several users. To make a file shareable, its owner must overtly arrange for others to share it. For reasons of data security, when a file is first created, it is personal (i.e., not available to anyone other than the owner).

File access

When a file owner decides to share his file, he must determine the type of *access permission* he wants to give others. For example, a bank systems manager may own (and hence control) a file of customer transactions. He might also want to allow the bank tellers to append new transactions on the file, but prevent their reading any of the already filed material. He might also want the bank president to be able to read any transaction, but (because the president has clumsy fingers) might not be willing to let him replace or append any components. And the people in the accounting department may have read, replace and append access, but are not allowed to drop or erase any transactions.

In the **APL ★PLUS** ® file system, all these access rules are determined and recorded in an *access matrix*. Each file has associated with it an access matrix with three columns: the first is the user number of those who have been given access permission of some sort; the second is the sum of *access codes* granted to that individual; and the third is an *access passnumber*, which provides a level of security to be discussed later in this chapter. For the time being the third column will be kept at zero, which means no access passnumber is required.

Here are the codes used to grant accesses to a file:

1	allows	$\Box FREAD$
2	allows	$\Box FTIE$
4	allows	$\Box FERASE$
8	allows	$\Box FAPPEND$
16	allows	$\Box FREPLACE$
32	allows	$\Box FRDOP$
128	allows	$\Box FRENAME$
512	allows	$\Box FRDCI$
1024	allows	$\Box FRESIZE$
2048	allows	$\Box FHOLD$
4096	allows	$\Box FRDAC$
8192	allows	$\Box FSTAC$

The present access matrix of a file is brought into the workspace by an expression of the form $AM \leftarrow \Box FRDAC\ FN$, where FN is the file number. As mentioned earlier, AM will always have 3 columns. For a file which has had no accesses set, AM will be of shape 0 by 3.

Say you wanted user 78975 to be permitted to read components on a file which you own, and user 1729 to be able to append and replace components on your file. You would construct a matrix like this:

```
      X←2 3ρ78975 1 0 1729 24 0
      X
78975       1        0
 1729       24       0
      X □FSTAC 20
```

The $\Box FSTAC$ function is used to reset the accesses for a file. Its left argument will be the access matrix of file 20 in this example. User 78975 has read access to the file because of the 1 in column two, and user 1729 has append and replace access because of the 24 (i.e., 8 for append plus 16 for replace) in $X[2;2]$.

Given that someone has permitted you to access his file, how do you actually do it? You can list the file names to which another user (say 4176382) has given you some kind of access by using $\Box FLIB$:

```
      □FLIB 4176382
4176382 STOCKS
4176382 BONDS
4176382 SHERWOOD
```

Now that you know what files you have access to, you can tie them with $\Box FSTIE$:

```
      '4176382 STOCKS' □FSTIE 90
```

The left argument is the owner's user number and file name, similar to the use of the $)LOAD$ system command for workspaces. $\Box FSTIE$ works much like the function $\Box FTIE$ introduced in the last chapter. Once $\Box FSTIE$ has been executed, you can perform any of the file functions *for which access permission has been granted.*

Any number of users may tie the same file at the same time using $\Box FSTIE$ (called a *shared tie*), while only one person may tie a file using $\Box FTIE$ *(exclusive tie).* Normally, when using someone else's files, you "share-tie" them. In fact, most shared applications don't permit $\Box FTIE$ (as controlled by the access matrix) except for emergency maintenance. $\Box FSTIE$ and $\Box FSIZE$ permission comes along with giving permission to do any of $\Box FREAD$ and $\Box FSIZE$, $\Box FAPPEND$, $\Box FREPLACE$, $\Box FDROP$, $\Box FHOLD$, $\Box FRDAC$, $\Box FSTAC$, $\Box FRDCI$, $\Box FRENAME$ and $\Box FRESIZE$, while the function $\Box FERASE$ requires that the file be exclusively tied.

Here is another example of the use of shared files. Imagine that there is a class of students in a course in computer technology and that the instructor tells them to "mail" their semester project reports as character vectors appended to a file he created, called $PROJECT$. The students' user numbers are 1001, 1002, 1003,...,1020. Since the instructor doesn't want them to read each other's work, the access permissions are set at 8, i.e., append only.

```
      'PROJECT' □FCREATE 90
      ((1000+ι20),20 2ρ8 0) □FSTAC 90
      □FUNTIE 90
```

Each student can either share-tie and append his result, or he can append more than one component. Now there's always one wise-guy in a class of students who figures he can write whatever sort of graffiti he chooses into his instructor's file. But he won't go undetected. The function $\Box FRDCI$ (for *read component information*) is designed to let you know who did what to your file. Its syntax is like $\Box FREAD$. The argument is a two-element vector consisting of the file number and component number, with the result always a three-element vector.

The first element of the result is the number of bytes the component would use up if it were read into the workspace. This gives you the opportunity to bypass reading a large component in a crowded workspace. The second element is the user number of the person who last appended or replaced this particular component. A user who appends or replaces a component cannot suppress this information.

Finally, the third element is the *timestamp* of the component. It is the time when the component was appended or last replaced. This can be very useful when trying to analyze past actions performed on a file. The time is computed in 60ths of a second since midnight, March 1, 1960.

In workspace 1 $FILEAID$ on the **APL★PLUS**® system, you will find the monadic function $TIMEN$. Use the third element of $\Box FRDCI$'s result as its right argument. It will convert the argument into a more readable form, a seven-element vector consisting of the year, month, day, hour, minute, second and 60ths of a second.

```
      )COPY 1 FILEAID TIMEN
SAVED  23.19.18 02/21/73
      ∇TIMEN[□]∇
   ∇ R←TIMEN T;I;PSM
[1]    PSM← 0 31 61 92 122 153 184 214 245 275 306 337
[2]    R←365.2501|+1461|I←⌊T÷5184000
[3]    R(1+12|(~ι1)+(PSM≥R)ι1),⌈R-PSM[¯1+(PSM≥R)ι1]
[4]    R←(1960+⌊(I+60)÷365.25),R, 24 60 60 60 τ''ρ⌊T
   ∇
```

Real-time systems

The $\Box FHOLD$ function is employed in sophisticated real-time systems where it is important that changes to the data base be synchronized among several sharers. For example, suppose you had a shared file in which one component is a character matrix of names and another component is a vector of associated numbers (one number per row of the character matrix), and you did the following update:

```
          NAMES←□FREAD 1 1 ◊ VEC←□FREAD 1 2
          NAMES[K;]←20↑□ ◊ VEC[K]←□
          NAMES □FREPLACE 1 1 ◊ VEC □FREPLACE 1 2
```

There is a risk that some other user might execute

```
          NAMES←□FREAD 1 1 ◊ VEC←□FREAD 1 2
```

and get the data that existed on the file *between* your $NAMES$ $\Box FREPLACE$ 1 1 and your VEC $\Box FREPLACE$ 1 2. If that were to happen, he'd have the new name but the old value.

To prevent this, the $\Box FHOLD$ function is used. It is monadic, its argument consisting of the tie numbers of those shared files for which you want *temporary exclusive access*. The general idea is to bar anyone else from doing anything with the file until you complete whatever critical sequence needs to be done.

Thus, your update section should look like

```
          NEWNAME←□ ◊ NEWVALUE←□
          □FHOLD 1 ◊ NAMES←□FREAD 1 1 ◊ VEC←□FREAD 1 2
          NAMES[K;]←20↑NEWNAME ◊ VEC[K]←NEWVALUE
          NAMES □FREPLACE 1 1 ◊ VEC □FREPLACE 1 2
          □FHOLD ι0
```

and the other user's retrieval section should be

```
          □FHOLD 1 ◊ NAMES←□FREAD 1 1 ◊ VEC←□FREAD 1 2 ◊ □FHOLD ι0
```

What actually happens when you execute $\Box FHOLD$ is that a request for temporary exclusive use of the files is entered. If no one presently has the files in temporary exclusive use, you get them. If someone has a $\Box FHOLD$ active, execution of your function is suspended until his $\Box FHOLD$ is broken (and all users who had executed $\Box FHOLD$ prior to your request have been satisfied). Then it's your turn.

You might think that an uncooperative sharer could hog the file by executing a $\Box FHOLD$ and not breaking it; however $\Box FHOLD$ is broken by any of these actions:

1. An interruption with ATTN
2. Executing another $\Box FHOLD$
3. Any return to execution mode
4. Untying the file
5. Signing off or being bounced

$\Box FHOLD \iota 0$ in the above example relinquishes your hold so that others don't have to wait unnecessarily to use the file. The conversational input $NEWNAME \leftarrow \Box \quad \Diamond \quad NEWVALUE \leftarrow \Box$ was moved outside the domain of $\Box FHOLD$ for a similar reason. It would waste a lot of other users' time waiting for you to input at the keyboard while hogging the file, although in some applications this might be a perfectly valid technique.

Airline reservation system

These ***APL★PLUS*** ® functions provide a framework for developing systems for reservations, inventory control, many-person games, simulation studies and message switching.

The following model of an airline reservation system is typical of many applications in which several people must access and modify a data base in real time. The reservation system consists of a "control center," which makes available an inventory of airplane seats, and any number of "agents" whose task it is to sell the available seats.

To initialize the system, the control center creates two files using the defined function $SETUP$. The first of these files, named $SUPPLY$, holds the currently available number of seats for each of a number of flights. The second file, named $TRANSACT$, is intended to hold a record of each transaction made by the agents.

The control center operator makes more seats available (by simulating departures and arrivals) through the use of the $REPLENISH$ function. The operator enters the flight numbers and the number of additional seats to be made available on those flights.

Agents place orders against the inventory through the use of the defined function $SALES$. An entry here should be a two-element vector consisting of the flight number and the number of seats requested. For purposes of illustration, a reward structure is built into the sales program: orders which can be filled yield the agent one dollar each; orders which cannot be filled cost the agent 50 cents per seat, and invalid entries reduce his earnings by one-half.

Entries of the first two types above are recorded on the transaction file. The defined function $OBSERVE$, which is run by the control center, prints the transactions of the agents in real time, identified by time, city and nature of transaction. When there are more than ten transactions waiting to be printed, $OBSERVE$ blocks further transactions by the agents until printing has caught up again.

Here is a diagram of the information flow, followed by the above-referenced functions and associated variables:

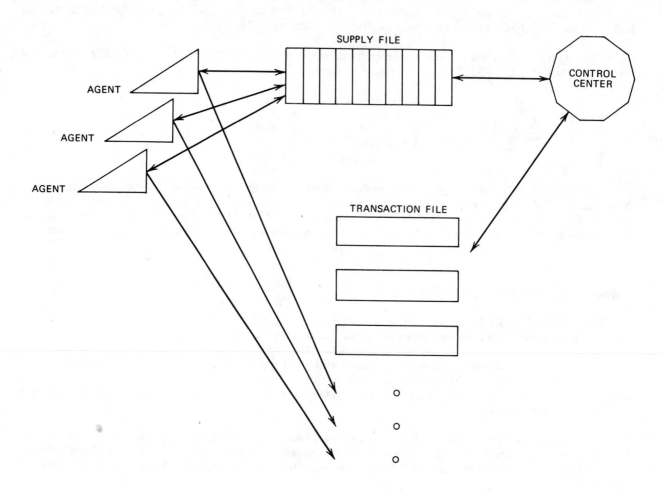

Agent program

```
     ∇ SALES;STOP;B;P;A;INV
[1]    STOP←*1
```
$STOP$ is used as a signal to stop ordering.

```
[2]    →ORD×ι∧/1 2∈FNUMS
```
Bypass if files are already tied.
```
[3]    (OWNER,' SUPPLY')□FSTIE 1
```
Tie supply file.
```
[4]    (OWNER,' TRANSACT')□FSTIE 2
```
Tie transaction file.
```
[5]  ORD:,'⍙EARNINGS: ⍙,F9.2,X3,⍙ENTER ORDER⍙' □FMT EARN
```
Print present amount of earnings, prompt for next order.
```
[6]    →DONE×ιSTOP=1↑P←,□
```
Accept order or stop.
```
[7]    →((0=ρP),(2≠ρP),(~(A←1↑P)∈ι10),B≠|⌈B←1↓P)/ORD,ER,ER,ER
```
Error checking.
```
[8]    □FHOLD 1
```
Request temporary access for inventory file. This causes program to delay if transaction file is being typed out.
```
[9]    INV←□FREAD 1 1
```
Read in inventory.
```
[10]   →NOT×ιINV[A]<B
```
Can order be filled?
```
[11]   INV[A]←INV[A]-B
```
If so, decrement inventory.
```
[12]   INV □FREPLACE 1 1
```
Put updated inventory on file.
```
[13]   □FHOLD ι0
```
Release hold on file.

```
[14]     'ORDER FILLED'                          Report success.
[15]     (1,P,EARN←EARN+B) □FAPPEND 2            Place record of transaction on transaction
                                                     file.
[16]    →ORD                                     Go back to get next order.
[17] NOT:□FHOLD ⍳0                               Release hold on file.
[18]     'ORDER CANNOT BE FILLED'                Report failure to fill order.
[19]     'ONLY ';INV[A];' ON HAND'               Report present status of inventory.
[20]     (0,P,EARN←0⌈EARN-0.5×B) □FAPPEND 2      Place record of attempt to order on file, adjust
                                                     earnings.
[21]    →ORD                                     Go back to get next order.
[22] ER:'INPUT ERROR--ORDER NOT VALID'
                                                 Report failure.
[23]     EARN←EARN÷2                             Adjust earnings.
[24]    →ORD                                     Go back to set next order.
[25] DONE:'YOUR EARNINGS ARE ',,'F10.2' □FMT EARN
                                                 Final report of earnings.
[26]     □FUNTIE □FNUMS                          Untie files.
      ∇
```

Control center programs

```
      ∇ SETUP;A;XX;Y
[1]      'WHO IS TO SHARE?'                      Prompt for agents.
[2]      A←,□                                    Accept user numbers of agents.
[3]      'SUPPLY' □FCREATE 1                     Create file.
[4]      'TRANSACT' □FCREATE 2                   Create file.
[5]      X←(A,[1.5]85),0                         Build access matrix.  Allow read, replace,
                                                     hold.
[6]      X □FSTAC 1                              Set access for SUPPLY file.
[7]      X[;2]←8                                 Rebuild access matrix.  Allow append
                                                     only.
[8]      X □FSTAC 2                              Set access matrix for TRANSACT file.
[9]      □FUNTIE 1 2                             Untie files so they can be shared.
[10]     'SUPPLY' □FSTIE 1                       Share-tie SUPPLY file.
[11]     'TRANSACT' □FSTIE 2                     Share-tie TRANSACT file.
[12]     NEXT←1                                  Set observation counter.
[13]     (10⍴0) □FAPPEND 1                       Install starting inventory.
      ∇


      ∇ REPLENISH;INV;X;Y
[1]  L1:'WHICH ONES?'                            Prompt for agents.
[2]      X←,□ ◊ →ER×⍳~∧/X∊⍳10                    Input airplane numbers, check for invalid
                                                     entry.
[3]      'HOW MUCH EACH?'                        Prompt for quantities.
[4]      →ER×⍳Y∨.≠⌈|Y←,□                         Input; must be a nonnegative amount.
[5]      →ER×⍳(⍴X)≠⍴Y                            Must be one quantity for each airplane.
[6]      □FHOLD 1                                Request hold of SUPPLY file.
[7]      INV←□FREAD 1 1                          Read in present inventory.
[8]      INV[X]←INV[X]+Y                         Update present inventory.
[9]      INV □FREPLACE 1 1                       Replace inventory on SUPPLY file.
[10]     (2,INV) □FAPPEND 2                      Record replenishment information on
                                                     TRANSACT file.
[11]     □FHOLD ⍳0 ◊ →0                          Release hold, leave program.
[12] ER:'INVALID ENTRY, TRY AGAIN.' ◊ →L1
      ∇                                          Error message and return to line 1 for retry.
```

```
       ∇ OBSERVE;Z;MTRX;NA
[1]    MTRX←3 16ρ'< NO >,2I4,F9.2,< YES>,2I4,F9.2,< MORE>,2I4,20I4'
```
Set format pattern for reporting.
```
[2]    →S0×ι∧/1 2∈□FNUMS
```
Bypass if file is already tied.
```
[3]    'SUPPLY' □FSTIE 1
```
Tie *SUPPLY* file.
```
[4]    'TRANSACT' □FSTIE 2
```
Tie *TRANSACTION* file.
```
[5]    S0:SW←0
```
Set holding switch to zero.
```
[6]    S1:→OK×ιNEXT≠(□FSIZE 2)[2]
```
Any more transactions to type out?
```
[7]    'CAUGHT UP'
```
If not, print message.
```
[8]    □FHOLD ιSW←0
```
Release hold, set holding switch to zero.
```
[9]    S5:NA←□DL 2
```
Delay 2 seconds.
```
[10]   →OK×ιNEXT≠(□FSIZE 2)[2]
```
Any more transactions since the delay?
```
[11]   →S5
```
Go to delay again.
```
[12]   OK:Z←(□FRDCI 2,NEXT),□FREAD 2,NEXT
```
Get timestamp and transaction record from file.
```
[13]   NA←,MTRX[1+Z[4];] □FMT (ι1)∘.×4↓Z
[14]   (8↑9↓TIME Z[3]),CITIES[ANUMιZ[2];],NA
```
Format and print this transaction.
```
[15]   NEXT←NEXT+1
```
Increase transaction printing counter.
```
[16]   →S1×ι(SW=1)∨NEXT≥¯10+(□FSIZE 2)[2]
```
If there are fewer than 10 transactions waiting to be printed, go to *S1*.
```
[17]   'HOLDING'
```
Otherwise print message.
```
[18]   SW←1
```
Set holding switch to 1, indicating that printing is more than 10 transactions behind.
```
[19]   □FHOLD 1 2
```
Hold the files. This prevents agents from entering new transactions while printing catches up.
```
[20]   →S1
```
Go to see if there are more transactions to print.
```
       ∇
```

Pertinent global variables at startup time:

```
       EARN
0
       NEXT
1
       OWNER
       78974        (11 character vector)
       SW
0
       '5A1,I6' □FMT (CITIES;ANUM)
N.Y.   1411
L.A.   1412
P.A.   1413
TOR    1414
PHIL   1415
WASH   1416
HQS    78974
DAL    1417
BOS    1418
```

A facility that will be described in Chapter 32 was used above. □DL 2 (line 9 of *OBSERVE*) causes a two-second pause or delay (without using computer time) and then resumes. Its result is the actual delay time (not needed in this application).

Transferring ownership and renaming files

The $\Box FRENAME$ function, as its name suggests, lets you rename a file. The file to be renamed must be exclusively tied. The left argument is the new name, and the right argument is the tie number. If you rename a file belonging to someone else (he would have to have given you access permission to do so), you now own it. Of course, $\Box FRENAME$ can also be used to rename one of your own files if you simply want to change its name.

Access passnumbers and secure applications

Even though you can control what types of file accesses a person can make through the access codes in the second column of a file access matrix, this is usually not enough. For example, you might have a file in which a certain user is permitted to read only the fifth component of a file, or one in which you won't permit him to append a component with more than, say, 500 elements.

Access passnumbers, the third column of the access matrix, are used to gain this level of security control. It works this way: if the access passnumber for a user is *not* 0, then to use the file, that person must supply the identical value in his file functions. Suppose user 78974 has the file '78974 STREAK', with this row in the access matrix: 947394 25 6948520. This means that user 947394 has permission to share-tie, read, append and replace, but he must use expressions like this:

```
'78974 STREAK' ⎕FSTIE 1 6948520
X←⎕FREAD 1 10 6948520
```

The access passnumber, when required, is the last element of the right argument of the file functions. The only exception is for $\Box FHOLD$. For it, use a 2-row matrix. The first row is the tie numbers of the files to be held, and the second row is the corresponding access passnumbers:

```
⎕FHOLD 2 1ρ1 6948520
```

It doesn't make much sense to go through all the bother of setting a passnumber and then telling the user what that number is, so locked functions are employed. In secure applications, the designer or owner of the file usually supplies his correspondents with locked functions to do the file accessing. For instance, the following simple program allows other users to access only the even-numbered components of the file:

```
      ∇R←READ N
[1]  R←⎕FREAD N[1],(N[2]×0=2|N[2]),6948520
      ∇
```

Since the function is locked, there is no way the user can disclose the passnumber. Any attempts to read odd-numbered components will result in a *FILE INDEX ERROR*.

Summary of file functions

Here is a table showing all the file functions. $R \leftarrow$ means that there is an explicit result. *tn, cn* and *pn* mean respectively file tie number, component number and access passnumber. The passnumber is required only if there is a nonzero value in column three of the access matrix. The access codes (column 2 of the access matrix) are shown for your convenience.

	Function		Code
arg	□FAPPEND	*tn,pn*	8
arg	□FCREATE	*tn*	none
	□FDROP	*tn,arg,pn*	32
arg	□FERASE	*tn,pn*	4
	□FHOLD	*tn,tn,...*	2048
$R \leftarrow$	□FLIB	*arg*	none
$R \leftarrow$	□FNAMES		none
$R \leftarrow$	□FNUMS		none
$R \leftarrow$	□FRDAC	*tn,pn*	4096
$R \leftarrow$	□FRDCI	*tn,cn,pn*	512
$R \leftarrow$	□FREAD	*tn,cn,pn*	1
arg	□FRENAME	*tn,pn*	128
arg	□FREPLACE	*tn,cn,pn*	16
arg	□FRESIZE	*tn,pn*	1024
$R \leftarrow$	□FSIZE	*tn,pn*	any
arg	□FSTAC	*tn,pn*	8192
arg	□FSTIE	*tn,pn*	any
arg	□FTIE	*tn,pn*	2
	□FUNTIE	*tn,tn,...*	none

Chapter 31:
Shared Variables

IBM's Shared Variables system (*APLSV*) is intended as a general means of communication. The latter part of this chapter will deal with those general concepts. One of the most important specific things possible with shared variables is communication with a *file processor*. The particular file processor discussed here is the one supplied with *APLSV*, and is roughly analogous to Scientific Time Sharing's *APL ★PLUS* ® Shared Files.

The required functions are found in workspace 1 *APLFILES*:

```
     )LOAD 1 APLFILES
SAVED  15.56.11 01/11/74
```

A file is created by using the dyadic function *CREATE*. The right argument, a character vector, is the name to be associated with the file. The left argument is a three-element vector. Element one contains the maximum number of components available to that file. Element two is the size (in characters) of the chunks of storage set aside for you. A component may use several chunks, but a chunk cannot be used by two components. Therefore, use of many small chunks for a component results in a greater amount of retrieval time, while large chunks mean a lot of wasted storage in your file. The third element consists of the total number of chunks allowed.

For casual use of *CREATE*, you need not worry about all these details. If the third element is not given, 1.1 times the value of element one is supplied automatically. If the second element is not given, a chunk size of 550 is assumed. And if the first element is not supplied (that is, the left argument is ɩ0), then a file with a capacity for 100 components is created:

```
     (ɩ0) CREATE 'SMALLFILE'
```

Here a file named *SMALLFILE* has been created with a capacity of 100 components, a total of 110 chunks, 550 characters each.

Once a file has been created, it can be activated with the *USE* function. *USE* is analogous to □*FTIE* or □*FSTIE* of the *APL ★PLUS* ® file system:

```
     USE 'SMALLFILE'
```

If you are using someone else's files, his user number must precede the file name and be separated by a blank, for example: USE '1234 $DATA$'. *Caution:* The USE function sets three global variables, the first of which begins with the letters $\underline{CTL}$ and is followed by your file name. The second begins with the letters $\underline{DAT}$ and the last begins with $\underline{FD}$. Avoid using these variables directly, as they are a critical part of the operation of the file processor.

Data is put on the file by using the function SET, aided by the function AT, in an expression of the form ($FILENAME\ AT\ COMPONENTNO$) $SET\ DATA$. It is roughly equivalent to $\square FREPLACE$ of the **APL★PLUS**® file system. As an example, let's put the character vector '7 $HOLLAND\ AVENUE$' into the fifth component of the file $SMALLFILE$:

        ('$SMALLFILE$' AT 5) SET '7 $HOLLAND\ AVENUE$'

The fifth component can be set without having set components one through four. However, you can't set any components beyond 100 with this particular file since only 100 were implied when the file was created.

Data is read from the file with the GET and AT functions:

        $R \leftarrow GET$ '$SMALLFILE$' AT 5
        R
7 $HOLLAND\ AVENUE$

GET corresponds to the $\square FREAD$ function of the **APL★PLUS**® file system. If you attempt to GET a component which has not been set, a $FILE\ INDEX\ ERROR$ results.

The function $EXIST$ can be used before GET to determine which components already have values:

        $EXIST$ '$SMALLFILE$' AT 3 4 5 6 100 101 102
0 0 1 0 0 ¯1 ¯1

The result is ¯1 for components out of range, 0 for those components in the range but having no value, and 1 for those that do have values. The closest analogy in the **APL★PLUS**® file system is $\square FSIZE$, but since all active components are consecutively arranged in the **APL★PLUS**® file system, the numbers of the lowest and highest components are all that's needed.

For files shared among users, you can tell who last set a particular component and its timestamp with the $GETL$ function. $GETL\ FILENAME\ AT\ COMPONENTNO$ returns the number of the user who has set the component, and when it was set.

A component can be erased with the $ERASE$ command:

        $ERASE$ '$SMALLFILE$' AT 5
        $EXIST$ '$SMALLFILE$' AT 5
0

This produces the same effect as $\square FDROP$ in the **APL★PLUS**® file system, since it frees up storage. However, the **APL★PLUS**® system permits only end components to be dropped from the file.

When there is only one file for an application, you can omit the AT and its right argument with SET, GET, $ERASE$ and $EXIST$. These functions all use the global variable $FILEID$, which holds the name of the file last used as an argument to USE or AT.

Finally, when access to a file is no longer required, use the $RELEASE$ and $DELETE$ functions:

```
    RELEASE 'SMALLFILE'
1
```

RELEASE returns an explicit result, 1 if the file was in use at the time of release, or 0 if it wasn't. *RELEASE* doesn't destroy the file, but simply retires it from active use, much as □*FUNTIE* does in the *APL ★PLUS* ® file system.

DELETE is used when a file is to be destroyed:

```
    DELETE 'SMALLFILE'
```

This makes its contents permanently unavailable, removes the file name and frees the previously occupied storage space for reuse. □*FERASE* serves this purpose in the *APL ★PLUS* ® file system.

What Shared Variables is really about

The set of functions described in the last section is a specific "cover" for a much more general and powerful facility. Full display of this facility requires dealing with concepts that are not of interest to the typical *APL* user, and are specific to IBM computers. Understanding them is necessary only if you are to be responsible for developing interfaces with other processors, such as OS/360. This work is not usually done in *APL* itself. These topics will not be discussed further in this text. You should consult IBM Publications GC26-3783, "OS/VS Data Management Guide", SH20-1460, "*APL* Shared Variables User's Guide" and SC20-1846, "*APL* \CMS User's Guide" if you need more information.

Nonetheless, the concept of an idealized shared variables facility merits some modest discussion here. For this, consider yourself and the *APL* system as cooperating coworkers in the process of solving some problem. There are certain tasks for which you are better suited, such as those aspects of the problem which require original thought, gathering data to submit to the *APL* system, and interpreting the results. On the other hand, *APL* is better equipped when it comes to adding long vectors of numbers at superhuman speeds, and storing and retrieving information.

Information sharing occurs when you transfer data to your active workspace (by entering it on the keyboard), or when the active workspace transfers data to you (by printing it). These exchanges take place informally whenever you enter information or the computer types out information of any kind.

Formally, the □ used for input (Chapter 28) and the system variables to be described in Chapters 32 and 33 are variables that are shared between you and *APL*. When you input data, as in the expression $X \leftarrow □$, *APL* "knows" as X whatever values you enter. Recall also that *APL* waits at the □ until you supply some data.

Just as you and your active workspace comprise a team to share the work of solving a problem, teams are possible among two *APL* users and their active workspaces. Teams can also consist of an *APL* active workspace and the parent system that lives in the inner depths of the computer, and which controls all *APL* activities. They can further come into being between the parent *APL* system and alien systems running on the same computer, such as FORTRAN, COBOL, Assembly Language and their associated storage mechanisms.

For example, on most *APL* systems you can to print voluminous reports on the high-speed printer attached to the computer, instead of at your terminal. This involves you, your terminal, your active workspace, the parent *APL* system, the system that runs the printer, the printer itself and the person at the computer center who puts the proper paper on the printer and mails the printed results to you.

In actual practice, most *APL* users overlook most of these distinctions as unnecessary philosophy. But the ability to model shared processes is a characteristic of *APLSV*, and well worth an introduction. In this chapter we'll consider only the formal sharing between two active workspaces, thereby avoiding discussion of matters not germane to *APL*. One of the results of this is that you will be able to perform the kind of data sharing available to users of *APL*★*PLUS* ® shared files. We'll use as an example the prototype airline reservation system introduced in Chapter 30.

Any *APL* variable in your active workspace, global or local, can be shared with any other consenting user. Both you and he can give the variable a new value. Then, when either of you uses the variable, you'll be using the most recent value that was given by either. A variable can be shared with the dyadic $\Box SVO$ system function. For example, the expression $78975\ \Box SVO\ 'X'$ is an offer to share your variable X with user 78975.

User 78975 must make a similar offer to share his variable X with you. If your user number is 78974, then he executes $78974\ \Box SVO\ 'X'$. $\Box SVO$ returns an explicit result, called the *degree of coupling*. The result is 1 when the first user has made an offer, and 2 when the second user makes a matching offer. When a result of 2 has been obtained, it's an indication that the sharing arrangement has been consummated. A result of 0 is obtained if no offer has been made.

On the IBM 5100 the left argument of $\Box SVO$ must be a 1 since the 5100 supports only one processor, the I/O processor, which accepts up to 8 offers. A result of 0 for this machine indicates that an invalid variable name for a processor argument was used, or that 8 variables were already being shared. 1 is obtained if the left argument of $\Box SVO$ was not itself a 1, while 2 tells you that the offer was accepted by the I/O processor.

Once a shared variable has been accepted by the 5100 I/O processor, you are ready to communicate with the I/O device, add records to a tape file or send output to the printer attachment. Readers who plan to use the 5100 in this mode should consult the IBM 5100 APL Reference Manual SA 21-9213 and supplements thereto for detailed instructions.

It is not necessary that the two consenting users use the same name to refer to the shared variable. For example, users 78974 and 78975 might agree that 78974's variable $MZ3$ and 78975's variable SX are to be the same thing. Then, after 78974 executes $MZ3\leftarrow'HELLO'$, 78975 would find that his SX is the character vector $'HELLO'$. Any of the following three independent sequences have the same effect:

User 78974	**User 78975**
---------------------------------	---------------------------------
$78975\ \Box SVO\ 'MZ3'$	
1	
	$78974\ \Box SVO\ 'SX\ MZ3'$
	2
---------------------------------	---------------------------------
$78975\ \Box SVO\ 'MZ3\ SX'$	
1	
	$78974\ \Box SVO\ 'SX'$
	2
---------------------------------	---------------------------------
$78975\ \Box SVO\ 'MZ3\ COMM'$	
1	
	$78974\ \Box SVO\ 'SX\ COMM'$
	2
---------------------------------	---------------------------------

The second name mentioned in the right argument is called a *surrogate name*. It serves as a common link to establish the sharing. This is most evident in the third sequence, where both users offer the new name $COMM$ as the surrogate. Surrogate names may not be more than 15 characters long.

You can make several offers to share at the same time. The right argument is then a matrix of names (one row per name, and if there is to be a surrogate it must be separated from the name by a blank). The left argument is a vector of user numbers, one for each row of the right argument.

To determine whether a variable has been offered for sharing, is shared or hasn't been offered, use the monadic $\Box SVO$ system function. Its argument is a character vector (or matrix) holding the names of the variables you are inquiring about. The result is a scalar (or vector) holding the degree of coupling: 0 if the variable has not been offered, 1 if it has been offered, and 2 if it is presently being shared with someone. For those cases where the degree of coupling is 1 or 2 the dyadic $\Box SVO$ may also be used for inquiry, since a repeated offer under those conditions has no implicit result.

There are several possible error conditions that may occur. Attempts to exceed the quota of shared variables assigned by the system management result in *INTERFACE QUOTA EXHAUSTED* messages. Unavailability of the shared variable facility itself causes the report *NO SHARES*.

A variable need not have been assigned to share it. It is also possible that both users have assigned a value to it prior to sharing. Here is how potential conflicts are resolved. If neither sharer has assigned it, an attempt to use it results in the normal *VALUE ERROR*. If only one user has assigned it, that value is taken. If both have assigned values prior to sharing, then the value taken is the one set by the first person to make the offer to share.

For the lonely hearts among our readers, an offer to share a variable with the user number 0 means you're willing to share it with any user who happens to be signed on at that time. Such unbounded generosity, however, can be reciprocated only with a counter-offer that specifically identifies the user making the original general offer.

When a variable is offered for sharing, specifying it and reading its value are completely unconstrained, i.e., either sharer may respecify it or read it at any time. Most applications benefit from a more controlled situation, such as prohibiting your sharer from respecifying a variable until you have had a chance to read the last value he gave you.

The dyadic system function $\Box SVC$ is used to define the accessing protocol. Its right argument is a vector (or matrix) of the names of the variables whose access protocol is to be changed, while the left argument is a four-element vector (or matrix with four columns) whose values can be only 0 or 1 as specified below:

If the first element is 1	Your sharer must read or assign a value to the shared variable before you can reassign it.
If the second element is 1	Your sharer cannot reassign the shared variable until you either read or assign a value to it.
If the third element is 1	You cannot read the shared variable twice unless your sharer has reassigned it.
If the fourth element is 1	Your sharer cannot read the shared variable twice unless you have reassigned it.

It would appear that you can control your sharer's every move. That's not exactly the case, however, since he can make similar restrictions apply to your use of the shared variable. In fact, the resulting access protocol is determined by the logical OR ($\vee$) of both of your access requests. Hence the effect is always to become more restrictive. In one sense this is good, because there is no way that an uncooperative sharer can negate restrictions you have set. As a by-product, dyadic $\Box SVC$ returns an explicit result which is the new setting of the access protocol combining your specifications with those of the sharer. It is the same shape as the left argument. On the 5100, $\Box SVC$ always returns 1 1 1 1 if the coupling state is 2, and 0 0 0 0 if not.

The monadic $\square SVC$, whose argument is a character vector (or matrix) holding names of shared variables, returns the present access protocol as seen by the user, but doesn't change any of the control settings.

In actual operation, when one of the sharers is inhibited from proceeding, and awaits some interlocking action on the part of the other sharer, his execution is held up until the action is performed. As soon as the conditions are satisfied, his execution continues. Pressing ATTN will cause an interrupt, but at the risk of possibly disturbing the sharing aspects of a particular system.

An existing sharing arrangement can be retracted or nullified by the monadic system function $\square SVR$. The argument is a character vector (or matrix) holding the names of the variables you wish to stop sharing. The explicit result returned is the degree of coupling that the variables had prior to being nullified. Thus, you can nullify an offer to share even before a prospective sharer had consummated the sharing arrangement.

A variable also ceases to be shared if you sign off, are disconnected because of a telephone failure, load or clear a workspace, or if the shared variable was local to some function which has completed execution, or if you erase the variable.

Once a variable has been offered for sharing, its access protocol does not have to be respecified. That is to say, after a nullification and subsequent offer to share again, its access protocol is whatever it was the last time it was set with $\square SVC$.

You can find out what variables are presently being offered for sharing with the $\square SVQ$ monadic system function. It has two modes of operation. If the argument is an empty vector, the result is a vector holding the user numbers of all people offering to share something with you. And if the argument is one of those numbers, the result is a character matrix holding the names of the variables that user is offering to you. This matrix holds only the names that are offered for sharing, and not those which are presently being shared. The $\square SVQ$ command on the 5100 will always return an empty vector since the I/O processor accepts offers only from **APL**.

A variable can be shared with only one other person at any time. However, polygamous sharing of information can be done by having one of the people serve as a steward, or "communication center." By sharing at least one variable with each of the other people, the communication center can mediate and route information among any of the people with whom he shares a variable.

Airline reservation system

Here are the airline reservation system functions, employing shared variables:

```
    ∇ SETUP
[1]    CONEX←MSGCNT←0ρINV←10ρ10
[2]    VARBS←0 5 ρ''
    ∇
```

In $SETUP$, $CONEX$ will hold the user numbers of the agents in the order that they offer to share variables with the controller. $VARBS$ is the three-dimensional array that will hold what amounts to five variable names (each up to 11 characters long, counting user numbers) for as many agents as there will be. $MSGCNT$ is a vector, one element per agent holding. The inventory, INV, is set to ten airplanes each with ten seats available.

In the **APLSV** version, the control center must run the control program continuously for the agents to make sales.

```
      ∇ OBSERVE
[1]    LA: A←□SVQ ι0
[2]    A←(A∈ANUM)/A
[3]    →(0=ρA)/LB
[4]    A←A[1]
[5]    B←□SVQ A
[6]    X←5 ' '↑B,0 1↓⍕ 5 1ρA


[7]    Q← □SVO X' ',B



[8]    CONEX←CONEX,A
[9]    MSGCNT←MSGCNT,0

[10]   VARBS←VARBS,[1]X
[11]   →LA
[12] LB: →(0≥ρCONEX)/IDL
[13] LC: ♠'N←',,',',VARBS[;5;]








[14]   Z←(N≠MSGCNT)/ιρN

[15]   →(0=ρZ)/IDL
[16]   Z←Z[1]
[17]   MSGCNT[Z]←N[Z]
[18]   ♠'A←',VARBS[Z;2;]




[19]   ♠VARBS[Z;1;],'←',INV[A[4]]




[20]   →(INV[A[4]]<A[5])/NOGO

[21]   INV[A[4]]← INV[A[4]]-A[5]
[22]   ♠VARBS[Z;3;],'←',VARBS[Z;3;],'+A[5]'

[23]   B←'0'
[24]   →REPORT
[25] IDL: X←□DL 2
[26]   →LA
[27] NOGO: ♠VARBS[Z;3;],'←',VARBS[Z;3;]-.5×A[5]

[28]   B←'1'
[29] REPORT: ♠VARBS[Z;4;],'←',B
[30]   X←(':',6 0⍕ 100⊥A[2 3 4])[2 3 1 4 5 1 6 7]

[31]   X←X,' ',CITIES(ANUMιCONEX[Z];]

[32]   X,' ',(2 4ρ' YES  NO')[1+B;]
[33]   →LC
      ∇
```

Search for agent wishing to participate.
Cull out unauthorized people.
Branch out if no new requests.
Deal only with the first prospective agent.
Find which agent.
Format the variable names by catenating a character representation of the user number to the 5 variable names.
Consumate the sharing.   Note the use of surrogates. Q is not used; its presence is to avoid printing the $□SVO$ result.
Add this agent to the list of active users.
Provide a slot in $MSGCNT$ for this agent.
Post this agent's stored variables.
Go back to check for new agents.
If no agents are active, delay.
The symbol ♠ here is called *execute*. Its argument is executed as though you had entered it on the keyboard. It will be covered in Chapter 33. The variable N is a vector holding the values of the fifth shared variable (S in the $SALES$ program) for each of the active agents.
Z holds the index numbers of those agents who have a pending transaction.
If no transactions are pending, delay.
Process only the first pending transaction.
Remove this agent from pending list.
See [13] for comment on ♠. A now holds the timestamp and number of seats ordered by this user, and on which airplane (set on line 13 of $SALES$).
See [13] for comment on ♠.   The shared variable corresponding to C in $SALES$ is set to the present number of seats available on the airplane requested.
Check for the agent's order greater than available seats.
Adjust inventory for this airplane.
Increase earnings.
Signal that transaction was successful.
Delay two seconds; throw away result.
See if another agent wants to share.
Decrease earnings.
Signal that transaction was not completed.
Pass status of transaction to agent.
Format the time of the order.
Format the city of the order.
Format success/fail and print on terminal.
Go back to see if another agent has ordered.

Each agent runs the program *SALES*:

```
      ∇ SALES;STOP;P;B;A
[1]      STOP←*1
[2]   L1: →(2∧.=⎕SVO 5 1ρ'CDEIS')/ORD


[3]      A←78974 ⎕SVO 5 1ρ'CDEIS'

[4]      A←0 0 1 0 ⎕SVC 2 1ρ'CI'




[5]      S←E←0




[6]      →L1


[7]   ORD: 'EARNINGS: ';E;' , ENTER ORDER'


[8]      →(STOP=1↑P←,⎕)/DONE
[9]      →(0=ρP),(2≠ρP),(~(1↑P)∈ι10))/ORD,ER,ER

[10]     →(B≠1⌈B←1↓P)/ER
[11]      D←(3↑3↓⎕TS),P


[12]     S←S+1
[13]     'ORDER ',(I/'CANNOT BE '),'FILLED'

[14]     →ORD
[15] ER: 'INPUT ERROR--ORDER NOT VALID'

[16]     E←E÷2
[17]     →ORD
[18] DONE: 'YOUR EARNINGS ARE';E
[19]     A←⎕SVR 5 1ρ'CDEIS'
      ∇
```

	STOP is used as a signal to stop.
	Check that all shared variables are properly shared; if so, go to *ORD*.
	Offer to share the variables with user 78974, the controller. *A* is discarded.
	Variables *C* and *I* offered are given access protocol such that the agent cannot read them twice without the controller having respecified them in between. *A* is discarded.
	The shared variable *S*, which serves as a counter of the number of transactions for this agent, is initialed at zero, as is *E*, which will hold the earnings.
	Cycle back until all the offered variables have been shared by the controller.
	Print present amount of earnings and prompt for next order.
	Accept quantity and airplane number.
	Error checking.
	More error checking.
	Place time of order and order itself in shared variable *D*. ⎕*TS* (Chapter 32) gives present time and date.
	Increment *S*, shared transaction counter.
	Shared variable *I* forms output to agent.
	Go back to place next order.
	Message to agent.
	Earnings cut in half.
	Go back to place next order.
	Final report.
	Retract shared variables.

Chapter 32:
APL internals

We have previously commented that *APL* is a user-oriented language. As such, it wasn't really necessary for you to worry too much over such things as having to define a faster moving function, data organization and storage, and other oddments having to do with the detailed inner workings of the computer.

The point is still valid. You may be a frequent user and responsible for paying the piper for *APL* costs, or, like the majority of *APL* users, your horizons don't extend beyond the terminal keyboard. In either case, some knowledge of the internals of the *APL* system may be of interest to you.

The first part of this chapter gives you some familiarity with the way data is stored in the *APL* system, to aid you in developing applications that run efficiently. The facts presented in the following sections apply to *APL* as implemented on IBM 360 and 370 series computers. Machine architecture differs from computer to computer, but the principles are the same for other computers. We will devote the remainder of the chapter to studying some of the facilities which measure and control your use of resources, and conclude with a short section on direct communication with other users.

How data is stored in *APL*

Ultimately, every numeric or character element that you use in *APL* is represented inside the computer as a sequence of binary (0 or 1) values or *bits*. Each literal character is represented internally as 8 bits, called a *byte*. This implies that *APL* has a maximum of 256 (2 * 8) different characters. Your terminal can represent about 150 of them. These are the printing characters, including the overstruck ones.

Literals

Let's now look at how *APL* stores literals. The system function $\Box AV$ (for *a*tomic *v*ector), gives all 256 character values. Here, for example, are the indices of the letters A, B and C:

```
      □AVι'ABC'
87 88 89
```

$\Box AV$ can be used to "pack" data to economize on storage in the following way. Numeric data, as we will explain later in this chapter, takes 4 or 8 bytes each. Suppose you had a lot of data to deal with, and you know the data won't have more than 256 distinct values. (This is a surprisingly common circumstance in working with data from fields as diverse as experimental physics and market research.) Each distinct data element can be mapped into a character and stored. Information stored in this manner would take only one-quarter or one eighth of the space that the original data took. Here are complementary algorithms to do packing and unpacking. $DIST$ is a numeric vector holding the distinct values and is usually derived by $DIST \leftarrow (((,DATA) \iota ,DATA) = \iota \rho ,DATA)/ ,DATA$.

```
       ∇R←PACK DATA                              ∇DATA←UNPACK R
[1]    R←□AV[DISTιDATA] ∇             [1]       DATA←DIST[□AVιDATA] ∇
```

You can use any of the 256 elements in □AV for internal use, however, attempting to print those which are not intended to be printed may produce strange (and useless) effects on your terminal. Moreover, there is no promise that specific locations of □AV will match from system to system, and they may in fact change from time to time on a given system. Early versions of *APL* did not have □AV, but usually had (somewhere) on the system a 256-character vector named Z or $ZCODE$, with the same contents as □AV. Ask your system management for its location.

Certain characters are useful in producing special visual effects on the terminal. On the *APL ★PLUS* ® system these characters have been given qualified names of their own, while on *APLSV* you'll have to get them by subscripting □AV. The *backspace* character is □$TCBS$ or □$AV[159]$. It causes the carrier to move one position to the left. Among other things, it can be used to underline characters that normally cannot be underlined:

```
       '75.96',(5ρ□AV[159]),5ρ'_'
75.96
‾‾‾‾‾
```

The *linefeed*, □$TCLF$ or □$AV[160]$, causes the paper to advance one line (like the carriage return) but does *not* cause any horizontal motion, as shown in the following:

```
       'THIS',□AV[160],'IS AN EXAMPLE OF', □AV[160],'LINEFEED'
THIS
     IS AN EXAMPLE OF
                      LINEFEED
```

The *null* or *idle* character, □$TCNUL$ or □$AV[158]$, causes no movement whatsoever on the terminal, but takes the same amount of time as printing a character. You'll have to try this one on your terminal to see the full effect. When you execute it, notice where the pauses occur.

```
       'I AM GETTING ',( ,'SLEEP',[1.5]□AV[158]),(10ρ□AV[158]),'Y'
I AM GETTING SLEEPY
```

The *delete* character, □$TCDEL$ or □$AV[2]$, is like the null in that it causes no movement on the terminal. It differs in that it takes *no* time, just as though it isn't there at all! It is occasionally used as a "place holder" in printing and reporting routines, as an alternative to catenation or compression. The function $STATEMENT$ illustrates this last point:

```
    ∇ STATEMENT K;NAMES
[1]    NAMES←'MARGE  KELLEY BARBARACLAIRE SHELLEYJANICE '
[2]    NAMES[(NAMES=' ')/ιρNAMES]←□AV[2]
[3]    'THIS IS ',(6 7ρNAMES)[K;],'''S BIRTHDAY'
    ∇
       STATEMENT 3
THIS IS BARBARA'S BIRTHDAY
       STATEMENT 1
THIS IS MARGE'S BIRTHDAY
```

Integers

Integers in the range ‾2147483648 to 2147483647 are usually stored in 32 adjacent bits, called a *word*. Here is what the number 5 looks like internally:

$$00000000000000000000000000000101$$

Negative numbers are denoted with a 1 in the leftmost position, and the number itself is stored as (32ρ2)$\top$*VALUE*, called *2's complement* form. Here are some examples:

‾2147483648	10000000000000000000000000000000
‾2147483647	10000000000000000000000000000001
‾2147483646	10000000000000000000000000000010
‾2	11111111111111111111111111111110
‾1	11111111111111111111111111111111
0	00000000000000000000000000000000
1	00000000000000000000000000000001
2	00000000000000000000000000000010
2147483646	01111111111111111111111111111110
2147483647	01111111111111111111111111111111

Floating point

Nonintegers, as well as integers smaller than ‾2147483648 or larger than 2147483647, take 64 bits for internal storage, called *double-word floating point*. But the value isn't represented in a straightforward manner like 2's complement. Rather, it is stored as follows:

bit	1	Sign of mantissa (1 if negative, 0 if positive or 0)
bits	2 to 8	Value of exponent, in hexadecimal. Decode as 16*(2$\bot$*STORAGE*[1+ι7])-64
bits	9 to 64	Value of mantissa, as a binary fraction. Decode as (2$\bot$*STORAGE*[8+ι56])$\div$2*56 or .5$\bot$0,*STORAGE*[65-ι56]

The value is assembled by the computer with this algorithm:

$$(1-2\times STORAGE[1])\times(.5\bot0,STORAGE[65-\iota56])\times(16*\bar{}64+2\bot STORAGE[1+\iota7])$$
$$\text{(sign)} \qquad\qquad \text{(mantissa)} \qquad\qquad \text{(exponent)}$$

Positive and negative values within the approximate range 10*‾75 and 10*75 can be accommodated. The internal accuracy of the computer is approximately 16 decimal digits (10*16 is about 2*56). We'll have more to say about internal accuracy in the section on comparison tolerance later in this chapter.

Bit storage

When the values you use in *APL* are only 0 or 1, each is stored as a single *bit*. This is an extremely compact way to store information, and in part explains why *APL* is so well suited for analysis of binary choice data, as, for example, market research studies. You can pack 32 times as much of this kind of information into a workspace as you could if you were using integers, or 64 times as much as when using floating point.

Conversion from one storage type to another

An important point to consider is that if one element of an array requires integer (32 bits) or floating point (64 bits) internal representation, then *every* element in the array is stored in the same manner. Thus, we have

$$
\begin{array}{llll}
0 & 1 & 1 & 0 & 1 & 1 & 0 & 0 & \quad \text{takes 8 bits, or 1 byte.} \\
0 & 1 & 1 & 0 & 2 & 1 & 0 & 0 & \quad \text{takes 256 bits, or 32 bytes.} \\
.5 & 1 & 0 & 1 & 1 & 0 & 0 & 0 & \quad \text{takes 512 bits, or 64 bytes.} \\
\end{array}
$$

```
 0  1  1  0  1  1  0  0     takes  8 bits, or  1 byte.
 0  1  1  0  2  1  0  0     takes 256 bits, or 32 bytes.
.5  1  0  1  1  0  0  0     takes 512 bits, or 64 bytes.
   '01101106'              takes 64 bits, or 8 bytes.
```

Of course, you've already seen that literals and numeric values can't be mixed in the same array.

APL tries to pick the most compact internal representation for your data, but in the interests of practicality, certain types of checking are not done by the computer. For example, when you multiply two integers, the result is integer (32 bits) if it fits; otherwise the result is made floating (64 bits). However, if you multiply .2 by 10, the result is stored as floating, even though it would be expressible as an integer. Likewise, $5 - 4$ results in integer (32 bits) storage, rather than taking only one bit.

You can force *APL* to store data the way you wish as follows: Use $X \leftarrow \lfloor X$ or $X \leftarrow \lceil X$ to convert from floating to integer. The only time it won't work is if the integer part is too large to fit into a 32-bit word. (See problem 8 in Chapter 9.)

To convert integer or floating to bit storage, use $X \leftarrow \sim \sim X$ or $X \leftarrow X = 1$. $\sim \sim X$ gives $DOMAIN\ ERROR$ if any of the values to be converted are neither 0 nor 1, while $X = 1$ will produce 0 for any value not equal to 1.

Finally, use $X \leftarrow 2 \times .5 \times X$ to convert bits or integers to floating point representation. On the *APLSV* system, you can also use $X \div 1$, since on that system the result of any division is always floating. However, on the *APL ★PLUS* ® system, division of integers by integers is floated only if there are noninteger results.

Measuring the amount of storage

The amount of storage available in your active workspace can be measured by the $\square WA$ (for *w*orking *a*rea) system function. Its result is a scalar holding the number of bytes (i.e., multiples of 8 bits) available to you. When you define a variable, you will find that $\square WA$ decreases slightly more than the number of bytes actually taken by the data. This is because its name and its dimensions are also stored with the data. For example:

```
      □WA
84028
      Q←200ρ'A'
      □WA
83812
```

$\square WA$ can be employed in programs which use an alternative algorithm (usually involving looping) to solve some problem when there isn't enough space to do the job directly. The function $AREA$, on page 256, is a perfect candidate for this treatment.

The value of $\square WA$ in a clear workspace varies from system to system, usually between 32000 and 80000, as decided by the system management. In earlier *APL* systems, $I22$ was used instead of $\square WA$. The I symbol is formed by overstriking $\top$ and $\bot$, and is called *I-beam*, because that's what it looks like.

Comparison tolerance

On page 297 we mentioned that only about 16 decimal positions are kept in floating point internal representation. Thus, a rational number like 1⅓ is accurate to approximately 1.333333333333333, which is slightly different from an exact value of 1⅓. If you meditate on it for a while, you'll accept the fact that it would take an infinite number of bits (as opposed to the 56 used for the mantissa in floating point) to represent an exact a value as ⅓.

If you must deal with rational numbers with exact precision, consider representing each value as a numerator and denominator pair of integer elements in an array, and developing a set of *APL* functions to perform rational arithmetic.

If 1⅓ is represented in floating point storage as 1.333333333333333 then $3 \times 1 + \div 3$ should be 3.999999999999999. Why is it that $4 = 3 \times 1 + \div 3$ results in a 1? They aren't *exactly* equal! The reason is that *APL* uses a little 'common sense' when comparing two numeric values. If values differ by no more than about one part in 10000000000000, *APL* judges them equal. This facility is called the comparison tolerance, (or *fuzz*, if you prefer) and is used by *APL* in functions like $<, \le, =, \ge, >, \ne, \iota$ and ϵ.

You can change the comparison tolerance with the system variable $\Box CT$. It can take any value between 0 and just under 1:

```
      □←X←□CT
1E¯13
      4=3×1+÷3
1
      □CT←0
      4=3×1+÷3
0
      □CT←X
```

Early versions of *APL* did not have $\Box CT$. Similar effects were obtained by using the function *SETFUZZ*, found in workspace 1 *WSFNS* on most systems.

Printing precision

You might be led to conclude that the system variable $\Box PP$ of Chapter 21 (or its older forms)*DIGITS* or the function *DIGITS* in workspace 1 *WSFNS*) are related to $\Box CT$. However, they are completely independent. Printing precision applies only to numbers to be printed on the terminal or converted to character arrays using ⍕. $\Box PP$, you may recall, can take an integer value between 1 and 16:

`□CT←0`	`□CT←.9`	`□CT←0`	`□CT←.9`
`□PP←16`	`□PP←16`	`□PP←2`	`□PP←2`
`3×1+÷3`	`3×1+÷3`	`3×1+÷3`	`3×1+÷3`
`4`	`4`	`4`	`4`
`4=3×1+÷3`	`4=3×1+÷3`	`4=3×1+÷3`	`4=3×1+÷4`
`0`	`1`	`0`	`1`

Printing width

Another feature of *APL* which affects the appearance of the printed results on the terminal, but doesn't alter internal calculations, is the printing or display width. Its initial setting is 130 on the *APL ★PLUS* system, 120 on *APLSV*, and 64 on the 5100. Attempting to print lines exceeding those settings prints what's left over on succeeding lines, indented 6 positions, so you can tell if it is a continuation of the previous line.

There are ways to change the width to take advantage of terminals with wider carriages, or to make use of narrow paper. On the *APL ★PLUS* ® system, assign any integer between 30 and 250 to the □*WIDTH* variable. On *APLSV* or the 5100, use □*PW* to change the width to any value between 30 and 390.

```
      □WIDTH←50
      100ρ'1234567890'
1234567890123456789012345678901234567890123 4567890
      1234567890123456789012345678901234567890 1234
      567890
      ÷ι20
1 0.5 0.3333333333 0.25 0.2 0.1666666667
      0.1428571429 0.125 0.1111111111
      0.1 0.09090909091 0.08333333333
      0.07692307692 0.07142857143
      0.06666666667 0.0625 0.05882352941
      0.05555555556 0.05263157895
      0.05
```

Note that *APL* won't break a numeric value in the middle.

The *APL ★PLUS* ® system accounts for backspaces in the print width. An expression like 150ρ'X',□*TCBS*,'_' will fit on one line even with a print width of 50, since the carrier never moves beyond position 50, while on *APLSV* you should set □*PW* to at least 150 to get the desired visual result.

APL ignores the print width for entry of data from the terminal. Even if the print width is set to 50, you are free to enter characters up to the right margin. Similarly, direct messages from other users or the operator ignore the print width.

Finally, the)*WIDTH* system command, or the function *WIDTH* in workspace 1 *WSFNS* can be used if your *APL* system doesn't support □*PW* or □*WIDTH*.

Using ·tabs

In printing reports with a lot of "white space" between the columns of information, you can take advantage of the tab stops to speed up printing, if your terminal is so equipped.

On the *APL ★PLUS* ® system, the tab stops must be equally spaced from one another. Nonuniform tab stops may cause erratic terminal behavior. After you have set the tab stops (say, 5 apart), inform the system what they are:

```
      □TABS←5    (set new value)
      □TABS
5
```

You then proceed without any further consideration of tabs. Whenever it takes less time for *APL* to tab over to the next printed position (rather than spacing over), it will do so automatically. □*TABS* alone gives you the present tabs setting.

For input, the *APL ★PLUS* ® system treats a TAB exactly like the equivalent number of spaces. An interesting application of input tabs is to use ⎕ to build the rows of a character matrix. If the tabs are set to the column dimension of the resultant matrix, then tabbing to the next typed word will ensure that the resulting matrix will have text on each line, left-justified.

Here is an example with tabs set at 10, 20, 30, etc. The symbol @ denotes where the TAB key was pressed:

```
        X←□TABS←10
      ∇ R←INPUT
[1]     R←⎕ ◊ R←(⌈(ρR)÷10),10)ρR
      ∇
        T←INPUT
TABLES@CHAIRS@CABINETS@
        ρT
3 10
        T
TABLES
CHAIRS
CABINETS
        □TABS←X
10
```

In **APLSV**, the system variable $\square HT$ may be given a vector of nonnegative integer values corresponding to physical tab stops on the terminal. The behavior is much like **APL ★PLUS** ® tabs, except that the tab stops need not be uniformly spaced. Also, $\square HT$ is associated with a workspace, while $\square TABS$ is associated with the sign-on session.

Changing the index origin

APL normally operates in index origin 1. This means that the first element of a vector is obtained by $VECTOR[1]$. There are branches of mathematics where, by convention, the first element of a vector is called the zero-th. You can change the index origin to 0 with the system variable $\square IO$, after which the first element of a vector is obtained by $VECTOR[0]$. Affected are the monadic and dyadic forms of ι and ?, ⍋ and ⍒, all forms of indexing, and the left argument of dyadic ⍉:

```
        □IO←0
        ι5
0 1 2 3 4
        'ABCD'ι'CAXB'
2 0 4 1
        ?1
0
        3?3
1 0 2
        X←2 6ρ'KELLEYCLAIRE'
        X[0;0 1 5]
KEY
        +/[0]X='E'
0 1 0 0 1 0
        +/[1]X='E'
2 1
        0 0 ⍉X
KL
        1 1 ⍉X
DOMAIN ERROR
        1 1 ⍉X
        ∧
        X,[0] 'MARGE '
KELLEY
CLAIRE
MARGE
```

These are the only things affected. In particular, the lines of functions still start at [1] and file references are always thought of in origin 1. The origin can be reset with $\square IO \leftarrow 1$, and the present origin determined by

```
      □IO
1
```

Only 0 and 1 are acceptable values for $\square IO$. Early versions of *APL* used the system command)*ORIGIN* or the function *ORIGIN* of workspace 1 *WSFNS* for the same purpose.

Random link

On page 63, the monadic *?*, was introduced. A comment was made that you get the same sequence of random numbers each time you sign on. More accurately, there is a *random link*, $\square RL$, associated with each workspace. Each time you use *?*, a random number is generated based on the present value of $\square RL$, and $\square RL$ itself is changed, ready for the next execution of *?*. Actually, the numbers provided aren't really random; they cycle every 2147483646 numbers, but that's more than sufficient for practical purposes.

The value of $\square RL$ in a clear workspace is 16807 ($7 \star 5$). The random link can be manually reset to any value by $\square RL \leftarrow$ some integer between 1 and 2147483646, while the current random link can be captured by $X \leftarrow \square RL$. Earlier *APL* systems used the function *SETLINK* in workspace 1 *WSFNS* to reset the random link.

There are two main reasons for changing the random link. You might want to reset it to some known previous value if you were rerunning some *simulation* or game to check its computations, or you might want to set it to an arbitrary random starting point, as happens in the exercise programs *EASYDRILL* and *TEACH* of Chapters 9 and 19. This is usually done by basing $\square RL$ on the present time of day, since that value is always changing. The next section explains how to get the time of day.

Accounting information, timestamp and delay

The system function $\square AI$ (*accounting information*) produces a 4-element integer vector consisting of your *user number*, the amount of *computer time* used in this session, the amount of *connect time* since you signed on, and the *typing time* (that part of the elapsed time when it was your turn to type, as opposed to the time *APL* was typing or when the keyboard was locked). The last three elements are in milliseconds. To convert to more comprehensible numbers (like hours, minutes, seconds and milliseconds) use a sequence such as

```
      ⍉0 60 60 1000⊤□←1↓□AI
1517 3809817 3113100
      0    0    1  517     (1.517 seconds of  CPU  time)
      1    3   29  817     (1 hour, 3 minutes and 29.817 seconds of  connect time)
      0   51   53  100     (51 minutes and 53.1 seconds of  open keyboard time)
```

The *t*imestamp system function, $\square TS$, returns a seven-element vector consisting of year, month, day, hour, minute, second and millisecond. For example,

```
      □TS
1974  3  10  21  54  7  867
```

means that this function was executed on March 10, 1974, at 21:54 (i.e., 9:54 p.m.) and 7.867 seconds.

One use of the timestamp is to select an arbitrary starting place for the random link. A good way to do it is $\square RL \leftarrow 0\ 60\ 60\ 1000 \perp \bar{\ }4 \uparrow \square TS$.

On earlier *APL* systems, a variety of I-beams were used instead of $\Box AI$ and $\Box TS$. Here is how they are related:

$\Box AI[1]$	user number	$I29$
$\Box AI[2]$	computer time	$(I21)\times1000\div60$
$\Box AI[3]$	connect time	$((I20)-I24)\times1000\div60$
$\Box AI[4]$	keying time	$(I19)\times1000\div60$
$\Box TS[1]$	year	$1900+100\mid I25$
$\Box TS[2]$	month	$\lfloor(I25)\div10000$
$\Box TS[3]$	day	$\lfloor(10000\mid I25)\div100$
$\Box TS[4]$	hour	$\lfloor(I20)\div60*3$
$\Box TS[5]$	minute	$60\mid\lfloor(I20)\div60*2$
$\Box TS[6]$	second	$60\mid\lfloor(I20)\div60$
$\Box TS[7]$	millisecond	$1000\mid(I20)\times1000\div60$

$\Box DL$ causes a *delay* for a fixed period of time. Its argument is the number of seconds of delay that is desired. The result is the number of seconds that actually transpired, because you may be delayed slightly longer than called for if the system is under heavy use, or less if you interrupted by ATTN. When $\Box DL$ is executed, your terminal keyboard stays locked, as when computing; but it doesn't use any computer time, as opposed to when you are computing. On earlier *APL* systems, the function $DELAY$ in workspace $1\ WSFNS$ was used for this purpose.

None of the previous system functions, $\Box AI$, $\Box TS$, $\Box DL$ and the I-beam functions, are supported by the IBM 5100, which has no internal clock.

Measuring the user load

If you are doing extensive computing on a heavily used *APL* system, you may notice that the elapsed time to complete some computation may vary somewhat from time to time. You may be able to defer the job to some other time (usually at night or on weekends) when the load is lighter. $\Box UL$ allows you to take a rough measure of the *user load*. The result is the number of users presently signed on. On earlier *APL* systems, $I23$ was used to give the user load. $\Box UL$ is not implemented on the 5100 since only one user at a time can be on the machine.

Direct communication with the operator and other users

Most modern *APL* systems, via shared files or shared variables, provide a system to send messages to other users. The messages are kept in a common file until the intended recipient decides to read his "mail." However, there is an occasional need to contact another user immediately, and system commands are provided for this purpose. The system command $)PORTS$ gives a listing of *port numbers* (remember your first sign-on in Chapter 1?) and the three-letter codes for the users presently signed on. This command, as well as the message commands described below, is not supported by the 5100 when used as a stand-alone, since there is no one to send messages to.

```
        )PORTS
OPR  OPE
003  AJR
035  PSA
036  LGI
064  TAV
079  KEI
226  ADF
```

In the interests of privacy, the $)PORTS$ command is usually restricted on commercial *APL* systems. But if you know the three-letter code, say, TAV, for the person ypu want to reach, you can enter

```
     )PORT TAV
064  TAV
```

You can communicate with that person by the $)MSG$ or $)MSGN$ commands. The command consists of $)MSG$ or $)MSGN$, followed by the port number and your one-line message. For example:

```
     )MSG 64   THIS IS AL.  DID YOU FINISH THE ACCOUNTING PROGRAM?
```

The message will not be sent while the other user is typing, and your terminal is locked during that time. As soon as he enters a RETURN, the message will appear on his terminal,

```
003:R THIS IS AL.  DID YOU FINISH THE ACCOUNTING PROGRAM?
```

and you will get the message $SENT$ on your terminal. If you used $)MSGN$ instead of $)MSG$, (i.e., *no* reply expected, as evidenced by the absence of R in the message received), your terminal will be unlocked as soon as the message $SENT$ appears on your terminal. In either case, a lock can be broken at any time by ATTN, but the message may be lost ($MESSAGE\ LOST$ appears on your terminal) if you do so prematurely.

A message can be sent to the computer operator with the command $)OPR$ or $)OPRN$, followed by your message. With $)OPR$, your terminal remains locked, while it becomes available for use immediately after the $SENT$ message if you used $)OPRN$.

```
     )OPR A. J. ROSE HERE; MAY I PLEASE HAVE 2 MORE WORKSPACES?
SENT
OPR:  DONE/Q. C. ROTH
      )OPRN THANKS
SENT
```

Good manners are even more important in the use of *APL*'s message commands than in voice telephone communication. Do not send messages capriciously, as you may disturb some important report being prepared by the other user. Remember also that a one-line printed message cannot carry your voice inflections, so be very explicit when you request something or when you reply to a request for information.

To avoid the intrusion of a message while you are working at the terminal, use the command $)KEYB$ $NOMSG$ on the *APL$\star$PLUS*® system or $)MSG\ OFF$ on *APLSV*. After you've executed either of these, no one (except the operator to advise you of an emergency) can send you a message. The would-be sender is informed (by $INCOMMUNICADO$) that you're not willing to take messages. When you're ready to receive them again, use $)KEYB$ when using the *APL$\star$PLUS*® service or $)MSG\ ON$ on *APLSV*.

On the *APL$\star$PLUS*® system, you can also use $)KEYB\ LOCK$. The effect here is to place your terminal in a permanently locked state, so that messages can be received even if you've stepped away from the terminal. In order to use the terminal, just press ATTN before each line of input. Although system commands cannot be put in defined functions, the system variable $\Box KEYB$ may be given any of the following values:

```
          □KEYB←'NOMSG'
          □KEYB←'LOCK'
          □KEYB←''
```

to obtain the same effects as the system command $)KEYB$.

PROBLEMS

1. Using $\square TS$, construct a niladic function $TIME$ that will result in the current time expressed as, for example, $4:47:22$ PM $EASTERN$. Truncate to seconds.

2. Define an *APL* function that will generate today's date as $MM/DD/YEAR$.

3. It is sometimes useful to know how much computer time is used in the execution of various functions. Define a niladic function $CPUTIME$ which, when called for, will give the amount of time used since the last time it was called for. Use it to find the difference in computing time for calculating $2!10$ and $(!10)\div(!2)\times!8$. Since these times are very small, write a function $CHECK$ that will repeat each calculation 1000 times and call for $CPUTIME$ as needed.

4. Define a niladic function that will, when executed, display a message for only those whose user numbers have been incorporated in the function.

5. Modify the function for problem 3, Chapter 28, so that it prints the amount of time required to get the correct solution.

6. Send a message to your own port number. (This is useful when you want to be assured of getting an intelligent response!)

7. Execute each of the following in turn and observe the behavior of the arrays generated:

```
)LOAD 1 CLASS
Y←ι10
□IO←0
TAB3[0;2;1]
Yι4 5 6
□PP←5
÷TAB3
□PW←50
)FNS J
□WA
B←ι1000
□WA
```

8. Specify $A←9.222222222222222$ and $B←9.222222222222227$ and execute $A=B$, $A\in B$, $A-B$. Repeat after setting $\square CT←0$. Account for the responses.

9. Why is the expression $A[\iota N]$ independent of the index origin?

10. Execute $\iota 0$ and $\iota 1$ after setting $\square IO←0$. Are they vectors? Of what size?

11. Rewrite the function SUB (page 262), resetting the origin before generating the random number on line 2.

12. Define an *APL* function $ALFSORT$ to produce alphabetic sorting over N columns of a matrix M.

13. What *APL* instruction will exit you from a function when a certain amount of CPU time (say, 120 seconds) has been used in the current session?

14. Define a function to identify whether it is morning, afternoon, or evening and print an appropriate message.

15. Use $\square DL$ to write a function that executes $DICE$ (page 85) N times, with a built-in delay of D seconds between repetitions.

16. Write an expression to create a dollar sign character if your system doesn't have one.

Chapter 33:
More tools and techniques

Execute

One of the most powerful features of the ***APL ★PLUS***® system and ***APLSV*** is the ability to build ***APL*** character arrays which can subsequently be converted to defined functions and executed, or can be executed directly. The simplest variant of this concept is the function ♠, formed by overstriking ⊥ and ∘, and called *execute*. It is monadic, and its right argument is a character vector. The result (either explicit or not) is what would have happened if you had typed the character string in execution mode. Here is an example:

```
        A←ι5                                    ♠'A←ι5'
        R←A+2                                   ♠'R←A+2'
        R                                       R
3  4  5  6  7                            3   4   5   6   7
```

When used within a function, statements like [5] $X←♠'3+Y'$ or [8] $→♠'LOOP'$ are equivalent to [5] $X←3+Y$ or [8] $→LOOP$. Here are some examples where the use of ♠ really pays off. The function $SELECT$ on page 275 can be rewritten as follows:

```
        ∇  R←REL SELECT NCV;N;C;V
[1]     ⍝ NCV IS 3-ELEMENT VECTOR: TIE NUMBER, COLUMN, VALUE
[2]     ⍝ REL IS LITERAL RELATION SYMBOL ( <≤=≥> OR ≠ )
[3]       N←NCV[1] ◊ C←NCV[2] ◊ V←NCV[3]
[4]       R←ι0 ◊ I←(⎕FSIZE N)[1]-1
[5]     LOOP:I←I+1 ◊ →(I=(⎕FSIZE N)[2])/0 ◊ COMP←(⎕FREAD N,I)[;C]
[6]       R←R,(∨/♠'V',REL,'COMP')/I ◊ →LOOP
        ∇
```

Line 6 is the interesting one here. For a use like $'<'\ SELECT$ 76 12 19, ***APL*** interprets line 6 as though it were $R←R,(∨/V<COMP)/I$.

A related use for ♠ is supplying the *form* (rather than the *value*) of an argument to a function. The $SLOPE$ function on page 255 required that you redefine the function F each time you wanted to find the slope of a different function. Using ♠, it becomes

```
        ∇  R←IX SLOPE F;X;I;R1;R2
[1]       X←1↓IX ◊ I←IX[1]
[2]       R1←♠F ◊ X←X+I ◊ R2←♠F
[3]       R←(R1-R2)÷I
        ∇
```

```
        (.0001,ι10)SLOPE '2×X*2'
4.0002 8.0002 12.0002 16.0002 20.0002 24.0002 28.0002 32.0002
     36.0002 40.0002
```

In the above example, line 2 would be interpreted as

$$R1\leftarrow2\times X*2 \quad \Diamond \quad X\leftarrow X+I \quad \Diamond \quad R2\leftarrow2\times X*2$$

There are several instances in the **APLSV** version of the airline reservation system (pages 292-294) where ♠ is employed to specify or use any of several variables on a selective basis. The argument to ♠ must represent a valid **APL** expression (but no system commands). Its domain is character vectors and scalars.

The latent expression

This system variable, □LX, causes a workspace to "come out running" in the sense that when it is loaded, a designated **APL** expression begins executing immediately. For example,

```
        )CLEAR
CLEAR WS
        )COPY 1 CLASS SPELL SPL GO
SAVED  15.02.39 05/15/74
     ∇ GO;□RL
[1]     'TIME FOR YOUR SPELLING EXERCISE!'
[2]     □RL←1+60 1000ι□TS[6 7]
[3]     SPELL
     ∇
        □LX←'GO'
        )SAVE SUB
SAVED  14.40.02 06/16/74
```

The *l*atent expression can be any **APL** expression held in a character vector. It is executed only when the workspace is loaded, as seen from the following display:

```
        )LOAD SUB
SAVED  14.40.02 06/16/74
TIME FOR YOUR SPELLING EXERCISE!
5
FIVE
8
EIGHT
3
STOP
```

Besides making the use of application and tutorial workspaces more convenient for non-**APL**ers, the latent expression provides a valuable assist to resumption of execution of critical applications after a telephone failure. Since □LX can be respecified any number of times, you can store anticipatory resumption instructions in it. Particularly in shared file or shared variable applications, you will probably need different resumption actions depending on whether a sequence of file updating statements was completed or not.

The *SALES* program on page 282 would be modified as follows:

```
[1]     □LX←'RETIE ◊ →□LC' ◊ STOP←*1
[6]     □LX←'RETIE ◊ ''REENTER LAST ORDER''' ◊ →(STOP=1↑P,□)/DONE
[13]    □LX←'RETIE ◊ →□LC'
[26]    □LX←'' ◊ □FUNTIE □FNUMS
```

```
      ∇ RETIE
[1]   ⍝ RETIES AIRLINE FILES AFTER CONTINUE WS IS LOADED AT SIGNON
[2]    (OWNER,' SUPPLY') ⎕FSTIE 1
[3]    (OWNER,' TRANSACT') ⎕FSTIE 2
      ∇
```

Thus, when the agent signs on again after a telephone failure, his $CONTINUE$ workspace is loaded for him, and the latent expression executes. It ties the files and branches into the $SALES$ program at whatever line it was interrupted (within noncritical sequences) or forces a complete reentry of the last order (within critical sequences).

Other workspace control and session control features

The facilities of this section are **APL ★PLUS** ® system features, and may not exist for **APLSV**.

In large applications, $\Box LOAD$ and $\Box QLOAD$ are often used in conjunction with $\Box LX$. Each initiates loading of a designated workspace. The argument to either is the name (and number and lock, if necessary) of the workspace to be loaded. An example is $\Box LOAD$ '1 $CLASS$'. $\Box LOAD$ and $\Box QLOAD$ operate identically, except that $\Box LOAD$ prints the $SAVED$ message while $\Box QLOAD$ does not.

Usually, the succeeding workspaces are saved by the author of the application system with a latent expression set. Just prior to executing $\Box LOAD$, all pertinent intermediate data is placed on a file. Then $\Box LOAD$ brings in the next workspace, and the latent expression brings in the data that was placed on the file and executes the main function of that workspace. Using these techniques, very large applications are tackled conveniently and economically.

Conversion between character arrays and *APL* functions

The monadic system function $\Box CR$ (for *c*anonical *r*epresentation) produces a character matrix in which each row is a line of a function. Here is an example:

```
      )COPY 1 CLASS SPELL
SAVED  15.02.39 04/15/74
      ∇SPELL[⎕]∇
    ∇ SPELL
[1]   N←¯1+?10
[2]   N
[3]   ANS←⎕
[4]   →0×⍳∧/(4↑ANS)='STOP'
[5]   →CORRECT×⍳∧/(5↑ANS)=SPL[N+1;]
[6]   'TRY AGAIN'
[7]   →2
[8]  CORRECT:'THATS RIGHT'
[9]   →1
    ∇
      XSPELL←⎕CR 'SPELL'
```

The name of the function to be worked on must be supplied as a character vector argument. There doesn't have to be any relation between the name of the function being converted and the name of the result, but you may find it handy to choose related names.

```
      ρXSPELL
10 29
      XSPELL
SPELL
N←¯1+?10
N
ANS←⎕
→0×ι∧/(4↑ANS)='STOP'
→CORRECT×ι∧/(5↑ANS)=SPL[N+1;]
'TRY AGAIN'
→2
CORRECT:'THATS RIGHT'
→1
```

Notice that the function header line becomes the first row of the result, and that the line numbers themselves and the starting and closing ∇'s are stripped off. Also, each line of the statement is left-justified. The column dimension is determined by the number of characters in the longest line of the function.

When you have a canonical representation of a function, you can apply all the character-manipulating tricks of *APL* to do function editing and searching for patterns. You could, for example, find the positions of each occurrence of the letter S with this sequence:

```
      1+⍉(ρXSPELL)⊤¯1+('S'=,XSPELL)/ιρ,XSPELL
1   1
4   3
5  12
5  16
6  18
6  21
9  14
```

Let's change the message *TRY AGAIN* to *HERE'S ANOTHER CHANCE* by

```
      XSPELL[7;]←29↑'''HERE''''S ANOTHER CHANCE'''
```

We haven't changed the function *SPELL* yet. All we've done is change the variable *XSPELL*. A canonical representation is converted to a function by the monadic system function ⎕*FX*, for *fix*.

```
      ⎕FX XSPELL
SPELL
```

If the canonical representation is proper, ⎕*FX* returns a character vector consisting of the name of the function. That the function has been replaced becomes obvious by displaying it in the normal manner:

```
      ∇SPELL[⎕]∇
    ∇ SPELL
[1]   N←¯1+?10
[2]   N
[3]   ANS←⎕
[4]   →0×ι∧/(4↑ANS)='STOP'
[5]   →CORRECT×ι∧/(5↑ANS)=SPL[N+1;]
[6]   'HERE''S ANOTHER CHANCE'
[7]   →2
[8]   CORRECT:'THATS RIGHT'
[9]   →1
    ∇
```

   The canonical representation you are trying to convert to a function must be properly formed. If the argument is numeric, you get *DOMAIN ERROR*. If it isn't a matrix, you get *RANK ERROR*. With character matrix arguments, you can get *SYMBOL TABLE FULL* or *WS FULL*. Any of these suspend the execution.

   Other errors, such as improperly formed headers, blank rows, single quotes and characters which cannot be entered in normal function definition mode (like backspace) get you an explicit numeric result indicating the row of the matrix that is causing the problem. To help catch these kinds of errors, people frequently use tools like this one to "cover" *□FX*:

```
        ∇ FIX X;Z
[1]     →(' '=1↑0ρZ←□FX X)/0
[2]     'CANNOT CONVERT, ERROR AT ',⍕Z∇
```

   Besides *□CR*, the ***APL★PLUS***® system offers *□VR*, for *v*ector *r*epresentation. Like *□CR*, it is monadic, and its argument is the name of a function as a character vector. The result of *□VR* is a character vector, which when displayed looks exactly as though you had displayed the function in the normal manner. Both the starting and trailing ∇'s are in the vector as well as the line numbers in brackets, and there is a carriage return character at the end of each line. *□VR*'s result usually requires less space than that of *□CR* because there is no "padding" to fill out short lines. Which one to use in a given application depends on space considerations and whether what you want to do is easier with the function in vector form or matrix form.

   Here is the vector representation of the function *FIX* shown above:

```
        Z←□VR 'FIX'
        ρZ
82
        Z
     ∇ FIX X;Z
[1]     →(' '=1↑0ρZ←□FX X)/0
[2]     'CANNOT CONVERT, ERROR AT ',⍕Z
     ∇
```

   □DEF on the ***APL★PLUS***® system is a somewhat more powerful cousin of *□FX*. It can accept matrices and properly formed character vectors as its argument. A vector must be similar to the result of *□VR*. Carriage return characters not contained within quotes are used to mark the lines of the function. The characters up to the first carriage return character make up the function header. Headers must begin with a ∇ or ⍫ (if the latter, then the function is created as a locked function). As in the result of *□VR*, the lines of the argument must be numbered consecutively beginning with 1, and must be contained within brackets. Carriage return characters contained within quotes must be followed by six blanks. These six blanks will not become part of the literal constant, but are required for consistency with the result of *□VR*. A trailing ∇ or ⍫ is required, and it may appear on or after the last numbered line.

   If *□DEF* can't convert a character vector to a function, a two-element numeric vector is returned. The first element is the error code, and the second is the character position in the vector or row number of the matrix where the error was encountered. Here is the interpretation of the error codes:

   1 *WS FULL*: not enough room for the function definition.

   2 *DEFN ERROR*: properly formed header; function name in use; vector argument does not contain both a leading and trailing ∇ or ⍫, or contains an extra one; or is missing a line number in brackets; or contains nonconsecutive line numbers; or a matrix argument contains a carriage return character that is not within quotes.

   3 *CHAR ERROR*: the argument contains a character which can't be entered from the terminal (like a backspace); a vector argument contains, in a literal constant, a carriage return character which is not followed by six blanks; or a comment in a matrix argument contains a carriage return character.

4 *SYMBOL TABLE FULL ERROR*: creating the function would require more symbol table entries than are available.

5 UNMATCHED QUOTES: the argument contains an odd number of quotes (outside of comments).

6 (unused at this writing.)

7 EMPTY LINE: an entire row is blank in a matrix argument; or two carriage return characters have only blanks between them in a vector argument.

When $\Box DEF$ is applied to a matrix argument, the error codes are the same, except that the second element of the result is the row number rather than the character position.

On the **APL★PLUS** ® system, variants of $\Box CR$ and $\Box DEF$ allow convenient display (or capture) and change, insertion or deletion of isolated lines of functions. Where appropriate, these variants are quite economical because the entire function doesn't have to be taken apart and reassembled to make a spot change. $\Box CRL$, used in the form

```
      □CRL 'SPELL[3]'
ANS←□
```

returns an explicit result which is a character vector holding the image of line 3 of the function $SPELL$. An empty character vector is given as the result if the argument consists of anything other than a displayable function and a valid line number.

Lines of a function may be altered with $\Box DEFL$:

```
      □DEFL 'SPELL[5]→(SPL[N+1;]^.=5↑ANS)/CORRECT'
SPELL
```

changes line 5 and returns the name of the function as a character vector if the change was successful.

```
      0 0ρ□DEFL 'SPELL[3.1]''ENTER CORRECT SPELLING'''
```

inserts a line between lines 3 and 4, and

```
      0 0ρ□DEFL 'SPELL[~4]'
```

deletes the line that was just inserted above. $\Box DEFL$ '$SPELL[\sim 3\ 5]$' will delete both lines 3 and 5.

$\Box CRL$ and $\Box DEFL$ behave similarly to $\Box CR$ and $\Box DEF$ for invalid arguments.

Local functions

Look at the following terminal session carefully:

```
      )CLEAR
      ∇R←IX SLOPE F;X;I;F
[1]   X←1↓IX ◊ I←IX[1]
[2]   0 0ρ□FX F
[3]   R←((F X)-F X+1)÷I∇

      (.0001,ι10)SLOPE 2 7ρ'R←F X   R←2×X*2'
4.0002 8.0002 12.0002 16.0002 20.0002 24.0002 28.0002 32.0002
      36.0002 40.0002
      )FNS
SLOPE
```

Line 2 of the function is the critical one here. The character matrix right argument of $SLOPE$, $\underline{F}$, was made into the function F. Then line 3 was executed, and we got the expected result. However, upon displaying $)FNS$ after the execution, we find that the function F isn't there The reason F isn't there is that it was declared to be a *local function* by the presence of F in the header. And like any local variable, when the function $SLOPE$ finishes executing, F disappears and the space it had taken is freed up.

The $SLOPE$ example we used here is a trivial one, because ⍎ does it more directly. But remember that ⍎ can handle only one line at a time, and doesn't do a good job with branching, while $\Box FX$ has no such restrictions.

An important use of local functions is storing functions in their character array representation as components of an **APL** file, and bringing into the workspace only those needed for the particular job at the time they are needed.

Local functions follow the same conventions as local variables. In particular, you can have a global and a local function with the same name. The display of a function using [⎕] discloses the global version, while use of $\Box CR$ or $\Box VR$ displays the local version.

Erasing objects under program control

Functions, variables and groups can, of course, be erased with the $)ERASE$ system command. However, that requires manual intervention, since system commands cannot be included in **APL** expressions, not even through devious use of ⍎. The monadic system function $\Box EX$ (for *ex*punge) is provided to erase functions and variables under program control.

To erase a function named $STAT$ from the workspace, use $\Box EX$ $'STAT'$. You can erase several things at once by making the argument a character matrix with each row an object to be erased.

$\Box EX$ always returns a vector of 1's and 0's whose length matches the number of names in the argument. 1 means that the object either didn't exist in the first place or that it was successfully erased. 0 means that the object either could not be erased ($\Box EX$ won't let you erase a label or group or a function in the state indicator) or that the name you supplied was an impossible one, such as $23SKIDOO$. $\Box EX$ operates on the most local version of the object. Recall that $)ERASE$ operates only on global objects.

Another facility for erasing objects is available on the **APL ★PLUS** ® system. $\Box ERASE$ takes an its argument either a character matrix (each row is an object name) or a character vector (each object is separated by spaces). The result is a character matrix holding the names (in alphabetical order) that couldn't be erased.

Groups can also be erased. If a group was erased, but some of its members were not, then their individual names appear in the result. The result is 0 $0\rho'$ ' if the erasure was entirely successful.

Locking functions

$\Box DEF$ produces a locked function if the argument is in vector form and a ⍢ is used instead of the starting or ending ∇. However, there is no way to contain information in the matrix form to lock the function. For this reason, and for general convenience, the $\Box LOCK$ system function is provided on the **APL ★PLUS** ® system. Its argument is a character vector or matrix holding the names of the functions to be locked. The result is an empty matrix (its shape is 0 0) if all the names were in fact functions; otherwise it is a character matrix holding the names that could not be locked.

Name lists

We have just seen how functions can be created, modified and erased using $\Box CR$, $\Box FX$, $\Box VR$, $\Box DEF$, $\Box CRL$, $\Box DEFL$, $\Box EX$, $\Box ERASE$ and $\Box LOCK$. They wield substantial power over their weaker brothers, the system commands and ∇fn function editing of Chapter 12, particularly because they can be executed under program control.

To complement these system functions, some informational facilities are also provided. The first is $\Box NL$, for *name list*. The argument of $\Box NL$ is the class of the object you are inquiring about. Its result is a character matrix holding names of objects satisfying the inquiry.

$\Box NL$ can be either monadic or dyadic. If monadic, the right argument is a scalar or vector of coded values (1 for labels, 2 for variables and 3 for functions) of the classes of object you are trying to list. For example, to find all function and variable names in the workspace, use $R \leftarrow \Box NL\ 2\ 3$. Th most local definition of the object is used.

When $\Box NL$ is used in dyadic form, the left argument is a character vector or scalar. Only objects whose name starts with a character in the left argument will be returned. Thus, to get a list of all labels starting with P or Q, use $R \leftarrow 'PQ'\Box NL\ 1$.

Name classification

The monadic system function $\Box NC$ is closely related to $\Box NL$. The argument is a character matrix of names, and the result is a numeric vector telling how each of the names is used. The most local use of the names is given.

result value	interpretation
0	The name is not in use at this level of the state indicator, and hence can be used to define a function, label, variable or group.
1	The name is in use as a label.
2	The name is in use as a variable.
3	The name is in use as a function.
4	The name is not available for use (i.e., it is a group, and the state indicator is empty and the name is not shielded, or the name is not properly formed).

More *APL ★PLUS* system functions

To help you write major applications that are secure and convenient to maintain, the *APL ★PLUS*® system provides several system functions that are related to system commands. In some cases they give more information than the system command does. In all cases they can be incorporated in your functions, and they all return explicit results. If you aren't using an *APL ★PLUS*® system, you can skip the rest of this chapter.

Alternatives to name list and name classification

$\Box IDLIST$ is similar to $\Box NL$, in that it returns a matrix of object names. However, it can report group names as well. It has both a monadic and dyadic form. In the dyadic form, the result is restricted to names beginning with characters in the left argument.

In both forms, the right argument is a scalar. Here are the codes for the right argument:

1	Functions
2	Variables
4	Groups
8	Labels

For example, use $\Box IDLIST$ 2 to obtain a matrix holding all the variable names. Add the codes together obtain information on two or more classes simultaneously. Thus $\Box IDLIST$ 5 would produce a list of all function and group names. To obtain a list of all named objects in the workspace, use $\Box IDLIST$ 15 or $\Box IDLIST$ ¯1. The result of $\Box IDLIST$ is in alphabetical order, while the result of $\Box NL$ is in arbitrary or "accidental" order.

$\Box IDLOC$ is a very powerful alternative to $\Box NC$. It takes a vector of names, as well as a matrix of names as its right argument. The result is a numeric matrix telling how each name in the right argument is used at each level of the state indicator. Each row of the result corresponds to a name in the right argument. There is one column for each level of depth in the state indicator. Column 1 is the present level, and the last column is what the situation would be in a nonsuspended workspace (that is, the global use of each name). The elements of the result have the following meanings:

result value	interpretation
¯1	The name is *not localized* at this level. It is impossible to have a ¯1 in the last column, since all names, whether defined or not, are considered local to the workspace.
1	The name appears in the header (and has been declared local) at this level, but has *not been assigned a value nor been made into a function*. Again, since all valid names are considered local to the workspace, any name in the right argument that does not exist in the workspace as a global variable, function or group, will be represented in the last column of the result as a 0.
1	At this level, the name is localized as a *function*.
2	At this level, the name is localized as a *variable*.
4	The name is a *group*. The only place a 4 can appear is in the last column, because groups can never be local objects.
8	The name is in use as a *label* at this level.

The objects comprising a group can be identified using the monadic $\Box GRP$ system function. Its argument is a character vector holding the group name. The result is a character matrix holding the members of the group, in alphabetical order. If the argument isn't a group, then the result is an empty matrix.

Size of objects

$\Box SIZE$ is used to find the amount of space used by objects in the workspace. The right argument is either a character vector with the names separated by blanks, or a character matrix with one name per row. The result is a numeric vector (one element per name holding the number of bytes used). Unused names result in a 0, while for groups the value is the sum of space taken up by the individual objects, plus some overhead for the group name itself.

The following function returns the number of bytes taken per element for any **APL** expression or variable:

```
      ∇R←PEREL X
[1]   X←32↑,X
[2]   R←(¯16+□SIZE 'X')÷32∇
      PEREL 1 0 1 1
0.125
      PEREL 2 5ρ'XYZ ABCDE'
1
      PEREL ι10
4
      PEREL 20.4
8
```

Probing the state indicator

□SI returns a character matrix which holds exactly what you would get by using the system command)SI. You might employ □SI in applications designed for people who aren't proficient users, to protect them from cluttered state indicators by working with additional functions while suspended. Except for recursive applications and certain uses of local names to shield, you'd expect a name to appear only once in the state indicator (or the result of □SI).

Here are some example routines to examine the result of □SI:

```
     ∇ R←NAMESONLY X
[1]  ⍝ X IS A □SI RESULT
[2]  ⍝ R IS A MATRIX HOLDING ONLY NAMES
[3]  ⍝ LINE NUMBERS AND STARS ARE STRIPPED
[4]    R←∧\X≠'['
[5]    R←(ρX)ρR\R/,X
     ∇
      □←X←□SI
STAT[3] *
FIN1[4]
MAIN[10]
STAT[5] *
MAIN[15]
      □←Z←NAMESONLY X
STAT
FIN1
MAIN
STAT
MAIN
     ∇ R←DUPLICATES Z
[1]  ⍝ RESULT IS MATRIX HOLDING EACH DUPLICATED NAME IN Z
[2]    X←(1≠+/X∧.=⍉X)/X
[3]    R←66⊥⍉(,X)ιX
[4]    R←((RιR)=ιρR)/X
     ∇
      DUPLICATES Z
STAT
MAIN
     ∇ SUSPENDED;Q
[1]  ⍝ CHECKS STATE INDICATOR FOR SUSPENSIONS, EXITS IF PRESENT
[2]    →(0=Q←+/+/'*'=□SI)/0
[3]    'ENTER→RETURN ';Q;' TIMES TO REMOVE SUSPENSIONS'
[4]    →
     ∇
```

Other information about the active workspace

$\Box WSID$ returns a character vector holding the workspace name. It is equivalent to the $)WSID$ system command when used for inquiry, but of course $)WSID$, like all system commands, doesn't give an explicit result.

```
      )LOAD 1 CLASS
SAVED  15.02.39 04/15/74
      X←□WSID
      ρX
22
      X
       1 CLASS
```

As you can see above, the result holds the library number in elements 1 through 10, element 11 is a blank and elements 12 through 22 hold the name of the workspace.

One use of $\Box WSID$ is to control other people's use of a workspace. Suppose you have a workspace that is undergoing continual development, and you want to ensure that your fellow users always use the latest version, loaded from your library.

As a case in point, let's assume your user number is 78975 and the workspace is called $FINANCEPAK$. At the beginning of each major function you would use this sequence:

```
[1]    →('    78975 FINANCEPAK '∧.=□WSID)/OK
[2]    'RELOAD FROM 78975 FINANCEPAK' ◊ →
[3]    OK:      (...remainder of function goes here)
```

If the user's active workspace was loaded from $78975\ FINANCEPAK$, the test on line 1 is affirmative; however, if the active workspace was loaded from anywhere else, the test on line 1 fails and the warning message on line 2 is printed, followed by an escape from the function.

The niladic system function $\Box WSSIZE$ gives the active workspace size. Its result is the amount of storage that this workspace will occupy when saved, stated in bytes. Even in a clear workspace this will amount to over 4000 bytes. (That space is needed by the system to store your symbol table, workspace parameters and other information necessary to make your workspace operate correctly the next time you load it.)

$\Box WSOWNER$, as its name implies, gives the user number of the owner of the active workspace. If it was loaded from your own library, it will be your user number. If it was loaded from another user's library, it will hold his number. If it was loaded from a common library, it holds the number of the person who saved it there. For a clear workspace, the value is 0.

$\Box WSTS$ gives the timestamp (in 60ths of a second since midnight, March 1, 1960) telling when this workspace was last saved. For a clear workspace, it shows when the active workspace was last cleared.

$\Box SYMB$ returns a two element vector result holding the present symbol table capacity and the number of symbols already used. In major applications where functions are stored on files as character arrays, and reconstituted in the workspace as needed, $\Box SYMB$ would be used (probably along with $\Box WA$) to ensure that the function will "fit."

PROBLEMS

1. Carry out the following sequence of instructions:

    ```
            )LOAD 1 CLASS
    ```
    Execute $AVG4$ and $AVG5$ several times.
    ```
            )SI
            ⎕LC
    ```
    Set $S\Delta RECT \leftarrow 3$.
    ```
            3 RECT 4
            ⎕LC
    ```
    What relationship do $)SI$ and $⎕LC$ have?
    ```
            →⎕LC
    ```
    What effect does this instruction have?
    ```
            ⎕LX←'→⎕LC'
            S∆SPELL←4
            SPELL            (execute once)
            )SAVE CONTINUE
            )LOAD CONTINUE
    ```
    Explain the result.

2. Identify the type of terminal you are using. Use $⎕TT$. The result is 0 for 1050 terminals, 1 for correspondence, 2 for BCD, 5 for ASCII terminals. This system variable is similar to $I28$ in earlier systems. It does not work on the IBM 5100 or on the **APL ★PLUS** ® system.

3. Use the execute function to replace line 4 of the function ADD (page 265).

4. After loading $CLASS$, define a function $DRILL$ which allows the user to choose between the exercises SUB, ADD and $SPELL$, and automatically initiates execution once a choice has been made.

5. Use execute to define a function with header $A\ CHECK\ B$ that prints $TRUE$ or $FALSE$ for $A > B$.

6. Edit the canonical representation of CMP in 1 $CLASS$ to change $GREATER$ to $MORE$.

7. Make HYP local to the function $RECT$ in 1 $CLASS$.

8. Construct a function $DISP$ to display automatically the canonical representations of lists of objects specified by input through ⍞ and ⎕ (arguments to $⎕NL$).

9. Use $⎕LX$ to automatically display one message for authorized users 1500 and 1600, and another for all others when the workspace is loaded. Assume the messages are lines of a two-row matrix M.

10. Write **APL** instructions that force an absolute branch ($\rightarrow$) whenever there are more than six entries in the state indicator.

11. Rewrite the function ADD (page 265) using the atomic vector to test for suitable characters, check with the correct answer and recycle if unacceptable.

12. Define a function $LIST$ to display all the functions in a given workspace. (Hint: use $⎕NL$ to get the names, and convert them to character representation.)

Appendix
Summary of APL notation

This appendix is a summary of all ***APL*** function symbols with their names and the appropriate references in the preceding pages. Miscellaneous ***APL*** symbols are listed separately, following the primitive functions. System commands and system functions may be found in the Index.

Omission of references to the use of some primitive functions with arrays of various ranks doesn't necessarily mean that the syntax of the function doesn't allow it, but simply that no specific examples or discussions were included. Where they occur, f and g stand for any primitive scalar dyadic function.

Symbol	Monadic or Dyadic	Name	References to arrays of rank 0 or 1	References to arrays of rank 2 or more
<	D	less than	35	35
≤	D	less than or equal	35	
=	D	equal	36	
≥	D	greater than or equal	35	
>	D	greater than	35	
≠	D	not equal	35	
∨	D	logical OR	37	
∧	D	logical AND	36	
⍱	D	logical NOR	37	37
⍲	D	logical NAND	37	37
−	M	arithmetic negation	58	58
−	D	subtraction	8	21
+	M	identity	64	64
+	D	addition	7, 10	21, 220

Symbol	Monadic or Dyadic	Name	References to arrays of rank 0 or 1	References to arrays of rank 2 or more
÷	M	reciprocal	59	59, 220
÷	D	division	8, 12	21
×	M	signum	64	64
×	D	multiplication	8, 12	21, 220
?	M	roll	63	63
?	D	deal	172	
∈	D	membership	171	171, 223
ρ	M	shape	44, 136	44, 136
ρ	D	reshape	20, 143	19,143
~	M	logical negation	60	61
↑	D	take	169	170, 223
↓	D	drop	170	170, 223
ι	M	index generator	133	
ι	D	index of (ranking)	156	157, 224
○	M	pi times	65	65
○	D	circular functions	67	
φ, ⊖	M	reversal	167	168
φ, ⊖	D	rotate	168	169, 223
⍉	M	transpose	226	226, 227
⍉	D	transpose		227
⋆	M	exponential	60	
⋆	D	power	27	27
⊛	M	natural logarithm	60	
⊛	D	logarithm to a base	29	
⌈	M	ceiling	61	
⌈	D	maximum	30	
⌊	M	floor	62	62
⌊	D	minimum	30	30
⍋	M	grade up	171	
⍒	M	grade down	171	
!	M	factorial	58	59
!	D	combinations	32	32
[ ]	D	indexing	157	159, 223
⊥	D	decode	179	180, 225
⊤	D	encode	182	183, 225
I	M	I-beam	218, 298, 303	
⍎	M	execute	306	
⍕	M	formatting		192
⍕	D	formatting	190	190
|	M	absolute value	59	59
|	D	residue	33	
,	M	ravel	142	142
,	D	catenate	140	224
,	D	laminate		224
⌹	M	matrix inverse		250
⌹	D	matrix divide		250
f /, *f* ⌿	M	reduction	42	43, 221
f \, *f* ⍀	M	scan	48	48, 224
/, ⌿	D	compression	161	163, 223
\, ⍀	D	expansion	164	164, 223
∘ .*f*	D	outer product	25	233
f .*g*	D	inner product	242	241

Finally, here is a tabulation of miscellaneous ***APL*** symbols:

Symbol	Name	References	
¯	negative	8	
←	specification	15	
→	branch	111	remove suspensions
		203	
_	underline	17	
∇	del	73	function definition
⍂	locked function	100	
~	tilde	95, 311	line deletion
∆	delta	95	line deletion
		212	trace
		213	stop
'	quote	148	literals
⎕	quad	73, 196	function display
		261	input
		261	output
		193	system functions
		189	system variables
⍞	quote-quad	265	literal input
		197	format codes
[ ]	brackets	77, 93	function editing
		221	coordinate specifier
( )	parentheses	51	grouping
		18	system commands
;	semicolon	107	function header
		150	mixed output
		159	indexing
		194	in ⎕*FMT* right argument
:	colon	3, 115, 127	lock
		204	label
⍝	comment	10	
E	scaled notation	27	
.	period	7	decimal point
		99	editing insertion
,	comma	99	editing insertion
∨	correction indicator	9	
		95	delete function line
∧	error indicator	8	
/	character deletion	97	
◊	diamond	54	
&	underscored ampersand	6, 130	IBM 5100 commands

Answers to problems

Some of the problems will have more than one solution given. This will generally occur when there exist different, but sound alternate approaches to the solution. The proposed solutions, because they are keyed to the operations presented up to that point in the text, will not always be the most concise or elegant possible, with the drill problems occasionally returning error messages. For this reason, an occasional solution will have forward references to simplify the task of defining the expressions needed to solve the problem.

Chapter 2 (page 14)

1.
```
        6  8  2  4+3  9  1  1
 9  17  3  5
        1  0  9  8-4  2  2  3
¯3  ¯2  7  5
        3-¯1  ¯56.7  0  ¯.19
4  59.7  3  3.19
        5  4  3×6
30  24  18
        10÷10  5  2  1
1  2  5  10
        3  4×1  2  3
LENGTH ERROR
        3  4×1  2  3
            ^
        1  2  8÷1  2  0
DOMAIN ERROR
        1  2  8  ÷  1  2  0
                  ^
        ¯2  0  .81+15  6  ¯5
13  6  ¯4.19
        2  ¯  ¯3
SYNTAX ERROR
        2  ¯  ¯3
          ^
```
Reminder: the negative sign is a mark of punctuation, not a function.

3.
```
        155  89  45×1.25  .50  .25
193.75  44.5  11.25
```

4.
```
        59.50  72.50  79.50  83.00÷1263  2016  1997  3028
0.04711005542  0.03596230159  0.03980971457  0.02741083223
```

5. The answer is the same as 3+2, or 5. - overstruck with + still looks like +. This exercise emphasizes again that in *APL* what you see is what you get.

Chapter 3 (page 22)

1. $B←2×A←3$ 4 5 6 7
2. A and D are valid. B,C,E and F are invalid because they contain special characters (blank, +, - in B, C and E) or begin with a digit (as in F).

3. $M \leftarrow 5 \ 3 \rho 7$
     $Q \leftarrow 5 \ 3 \rho 4 \ 9 \ 11$
4. $N \leftarrow M \div 7$
     $N \leftarrow M - 6$
     $N \leftarrow 8 - M$
5. $S \leftarrow 2 \ 3 \rho 8 \ 15 \ 7 \ 12 \ 4 \ 0$
     $P \leftarrow 2 \ 3 \rho 3.10 \ 2.00 \ 4.17 \ 3.50 \ 2.75 \ 4.35$
     $TOTSALES \leftarrow S \times P$
6. $A \leftarrow B \leftarrow 5 \ 3$
           $A \ B$
     $SYNTAX \ ERROR$
           $A \ B$
           $\wedge$
           A , B
     $5 \ 3 \ 5 \ 3$

The ***APL*** system will not allow catenation or chaining together of two variables without a comma between them. More about this in Chapter 16.

Chapter 4 (page 28)

1. $^-2 \ast .5$
     $DOMAIN \ ERROR$
           $^-2 \ast 0.5$
              $\wedge$
           $3 \ast 4 \ 2 \ 1 \ 0 \ ^-5$
     $81 \ 9 \ 3 \ 1 \ 0.004115226337$
           $21.268E1 + 4.56E^-2$
     212.7256
           $2 \ast .5 \ .333 \ .25 \ .2$
     $1.414213562 \ 1.25962998 \ 1.189207115 \ 1.148698355$
           $1 \ast 0 \ 1 \ 10 \ 100 \ 1000$
     $1 \ 1 \ 1 \ 1 \ 1$
           $8.3E0 \times 7.9E^-3 \ 56$
     $0.06557 \ 464.8$
           $^-8 \ast .3333333333333$
     $DOMAIN \ ERROR$
           $^-8 \ast 0.3333333333333$
              $\wedge$

Why the $DOMAIN \ ERROR$ message in this example and the first above? Try adding a few more 3's on the right and reexecuting.
           $^-7.11E4 \div 9.45E^-3$
     $^-7523809.524$
              $346 \times 2E3.7$
     $SYNTAX \ ERROR$
           $346 \times 2000 \ . \ 7$
                      $\wedge$

2. $1E0$ $1E^-1$
     1 0.1
           $1E1$ $1E^-2$
     10 0.01
           $1E6$ $1E^-4$
     1000000 0.0001
           $1E9$ $1E^-5$
     1000000000 $1E^-5$
           $1E10$ $1E^-6$
     $1E10$ $1E^-6$

3.
```
        L←3  7  15  2.7
        F←L*2
        AREA←6×F
        AREA
54  294  1350  43.74
```
4.
```
        A←1  2  3  4
        D←3×A
        A∘.×D
  3   6   9  12
  6  12  18  24
  9  18  27  36
 12  24  36  48
        D∘.*A
     3      9     27     81
     6     36    216   1296
     9     81    729   6561
    12    144   1728  20736
```
5.
```
      1  2  3  4  5∘.*2  .5
  1                   1
  4                   1.414213562
  9                   1.732050808
 16                   2
 25                   2.236067977
```
6. There are 86400 seconds in a day.
```
        86400×365
31536000
```
which is $3.1536E7$ seconds per year.

7.
```
        5280×24
126720
        12÷126720
9.46969697E¯5
```
miles per hour.

Chapter 5 (page 34)

1.
```
        ¯5  0  ¯22  15  3⌈3  7  ¯10.8  2  0
 5  7  ¯10.8  15   3
        2  3  4  5  6  10⍟2
1  0.6309297536  0.5  0.4306765581  0.3868528072  0.3010299957
        1  10⍟1
1  0
        10⍟0
DOMAIN ERROR
        10⍟0
         ∧
        ¯2  4  ¯5|8  13  3.78
0  1  ¯1.22
        ¯2⍟25
DOMAIN ERROR
        ¯2⍟25
          ∧
```
Both arguments must be greater than 0. If the left argument is 1, the right argument must be 1 also.
```
        1|3.4  ¯2.2  .019
0.4  0.8  0.019
        0|1  2  3
1  2  3
        ¯1  9  ¯5  ¯2|0  6  4  3
0  6  ¯5  ¯2
        1  9  8|3  4  6
0  4  6
```

```
              0  1   2   3   4!3  4  5  6  7
     1  4  10  20  35
                  3| ̄3  ̄2  0  1  2  3
     0  1  0  1  2  0
```

2.
```
              15  20  18  32  29⌊18  20  15  10  49
     15  20  15  10  29
```

3. $10\circledast 1\div C$. This is a bit ahead of the game in that we haven't said anything yet about order of execution, where multiple operations occur in a single expression. Problems 6, 9 and 10 also involve more than one function in a single expression. See Chapter 8 for more details. You can, of course, always write this as two steps, $D\leftarrow 1\div C$, followed by $10\circledast D$.

4. The 5-residue of any integer is the set $0\ 1\ 2\ 3\ 4$, which is in S. Note also that the condition $N\geq 4$ given in the problem is unnecessary.

5. If the result of $B\,|\,A$ is zero, then A is divisible by B.

6. Hours: $H-1\,|\,H$; minutes: $60\,|\,H\times 60$. This last solution should be tried for typical values of H. You will see that H is multiplied by 60 first, and then $60\,|\,H$ is obtained.

7. $3!47$ Following the hint, there are three separators, each of which can be in any one of 47 positions. (Why 47?)

8. $4!30$

9. $N-1\,|\,N$ This works only for nonnegative values of N.

10. $1\,|\, ̄1\times N$ or $1-1\,|\,N$

11. $C\leftarrow A\lfloor B$

Chapter 6 (page 39)

1.
```
              0  0  1  1∨0  1  0  1
     0  1  1  1
              1  0  1  0∧1  0  0  1
     1  0  0  0
              2  4  7  ̄2>6  ̄1  0  4
   · 0  1  1  0
              4  ̄5  ̄1  ̄6.8≥4  1  ̄1  2
     1  0  1  0
              8  7  6  5  4  3  2  1≤1  2  3  4  5  6  7  8
     0  0  0  0  1  1  1  1
              2  3  0<5  ̄1  4
     1  0  1
              3  1  2≠1  2  3
     1  1  1
              0  1  2  3=0  1  3  2
     1  1  0  0
              0  0  1  1⍱0  1  0  1
     1  0  0  0
              1  0  1  0⍲1  0  0  1
     0  1  1  1
```

2. The factors of an integer N are those integers which divide N. Hence set $0=1\ 2\ 3\ ...\ N\,|\,N$.

3. $A\geq 0$ or $0\leq A$ yields a logical vector with 1's in those positions corresponding to the accounts not overdrawn.

4. Let $C\leftarrow 0=B$. Then $A\vee C$ works if either or both conditions hold while $A\neq C$ works when only one of the conditions holds, but not both. Later, when the function $\sim$ (logical negation) is introduced, $A\vee\sim B$ will also be a possible solution.

5. EXCLUSIVE NOR or NEXCLUSIVE OR.

6. A)
```
     Z←S×0
     Z←S-S
     Z←S≠S
     Z←S|S
     Z←S>S
     Z←0⋆S
     Z←0⌊S
     etc.
```
B)
```
     W←S⋆0
     W←S=S
     W←S≤S
     W←S÷S
     W←S⊛S
     W←0!S
     W←S!S
```

7. $B \leftarrow 2 \mid A$
     $C \leftarrow 0 = B$
8. $0 \ 1 \circ . = 0 \ 1$
     $0 \ 1 \circ . > 0 \ 1$
     $0 \ 1 \circ . < 0 \ 1$
     $0 \ 1 \circ . \geq 0 \ 1$
     $0 \ 1 \circ . \leq 0 \ 1$
9. $\times$ and $\lfloor$ are equivalent to $\wedge$, $\lceil$ to $\vee$, $*$ to $\geq$, $\mid$ to $<$ and $!$ to $\leq$.

Chapter 7 (page 49)

1.
               $+/3 \ 7 \ ^-10 \ 15 \ 22$
    37
               $\div/3 \ 5 \ 2$
    1.2
               $\wedge/1 \ 1 \ 1$
    1
               $=/3 \ 2 \ 2$
    0
               $\lceil/1 \ ^-14.7 \ 22 \ 6$
    22
               $-/2 \ 4 \ 6 \ 8 \ 10$
    6
               $*/3 \ 2 \ 1$
    9
               $\vee/0 \ 1 \ 0 \ 1$
    1
               $>/1 \ ^-2 \ ^-4$
    0
               $\times\backslash 3 \ 2 \ 7 \ 9$
    3 6 42 378
               $\times/2 \ 4 \ 6 \ 8 \ 10$
    3840
               $\wedge/1 \ 0 \ 1 \ 1$
    0
               $\vee/0 \ 0 \ 0$
    0
               $\lfloor/^-2 \ 4 \ 0 \ ^-8$
    $^-8$
               $\lceil\backslash 4 \ 12 \ 7 \ 14$
    4 12 12 14
2. $\wedge/$ returns a 1 if and only if all the elements are 1, 0 otherwise.
     $\vee/$ returns a 0 if and only if all the elements are 0, 1 otherwise.
     $=/$ (applied to a logical vector) returns 0 if there is an odd number of 0's, 1 otherwise.
3. $+/3 \times AV$
     69 (which is the same as $3 \times +/AV$)
4. $\lceil/Q \leftarrow 1 \ 7 \ ^-2 \ ^-3$
5. $S \leftarrow .5 \times +/L$ After the rules governing the order of execution are introduced in
     $A2 \leftarrow S - L$ Chapter 8, this can be done more compactly as
     $Q \leftarrow \times/A2$ $S \leftarrow .5 \times +/L$
     $R \leftarrow S \times Q$ $AREA \leftarrow (S \times \times/S - L) * .5$
     $AREA \leftarrow R * .5$
6.   Since the X-coordinate of a point is customarily written first, it is not enough to take $\div/Q-P$ since
     this results in the difference in the X-coordinates divided by the difference in the Y-coordinates,
     which is the reciprocal of the slope, according to the definition given. Hence, $A \leftarrow \div/Q-P$ and
     $SLOPE \leftarrow 1 \div A$, or more compactly, $SLOPE \leftarrow 1 \div \div/Q-P$ (see note to problem 5).

7. $SR \leftarrow + \backslash S$
8. $M1 \leftarrow M = A$
      $+ / M1$
9. $\wedge \backslash LV$ makes every element a 0 after the first 0.
      $< \backslash LV$ makes every element a 0 after the first 1.
      $\vee \backslash LV$ makes every element a 1 after the first 1.

Chapter 8   (page 55)

1. $4 * 3 \lceil 3 * 4$
   $5.846006549E48$
         $(4 * 3) \lceil 3 * 4$
   81
         $5 * 3 \times 5$
   $3.051757813E10$
         $1 \div 2 + X \leftarrow {}^- 5 \ 6 \ 0 \ 4 \ 8 \ {}^- 6$
   ${}^- 0.3333333333 \ 0.125 \ 0.5 \ 0.1666666667 \ 0.1 \ {}^- 0.25$
         $76 \div + / 2 + 3 \times 1 \ 2 \ 3 \ 4$
   2
         $6 \div 2 - 4 * 3$
   ${}^- 0.09677419355$
2.   The first, second and fourth expressions are equivalent.
3.   A) $(3 \div 4) + (5 \div 6) - 7 \div 8$ or better, $+ / 3 \ 5 \ {}^- 7 \div 4 \ 6 \ 8$
      B) $(-/9 \ 8 \div 7 \ 10) \div -/1 \ 2 \div 3 \ 5$
4. $(\times / X) * 1 \div \rho X$
   6.386118449
5. B will be compared with $B + A$ for equality, with A added to that result. The expression works only when A is 0. More generally, parentheses are needed around $A + B$.
6.   Brute force solution: $(0 \neq 4000 | Y) \wedge (0 = 4 | Y) \wedge (0 = 400 | Y) = 0 = 100 | Y$
      Better solution: $2 | + / 0 = 4 \ 100 \ 400 \ 4000 | Y$
      Still better solution: $- / 0 = 4 \ 100 \ 400 \ 4000 | Y$
7.   The minus sign in front of the middle term acts on everything to the right of it.
      Correct version: $(X * 2) + ({}^- 2 \times X \times Y) + Y * 2$ or $(X * 2) + (Y * 2) - 2 \times X \times Y$
8. ${}^- 8 + X \times X \times 2 + {}^- 3 \times X * 2$
9. $((+ / X * 2) \div \rho X) * .5$
10.   Jack is to propose if 1) he has the ring, 2) the weather is favorable, 3) Jill is younger than Jack and 4) Jack isn't over the age limit for Jill's beaux.
11.   Annual: $P \times (1 + .01 \times R) * T$
      Quarterly: $P \times (1 + .01 \times R \div 4) * T \times 4$
12. $C \leftarrow 5 \times (A > B) + 4 \times A < B$
      $C \leftarrow 8 + 2 \times (A > B) \wedge D < E$
13.   Shame on you if you said $4 \ \ 4$ is the answer.
         $2 + 2 \ \ 2 + 2$
   $6 \ \ 6$
14.   A) ρV E) $\lceil / V$
      B) $+ / V \div \rho V$ F) $100 \times (+ / \vee > 100) \div \rho V$
      C) $+ / V < 0$ G) $+ / (V \leq 200) \wedge V \geq 100$
      D) $+ / V = 0$ H) $+ / 0 = 100 | V \times V > 0$
15. $A \times A > B$
16. $.25 \times 16.5 \times 16.5 \times 160 \times 144$ or $\times / .25 \ 16.5 \ 16.5 \ 160 \ 144$
   1568160
17. $(7.2 \times 9 \times 5) + 4 \times 235 + 39 \times 3$
   1732

Chapter 9 (page 70)

1.
```
        ⌊‾2.7|‾15
‾2
        *3 4.7 ‾1.5
20.08553692  109.9471725  0.2231301601
        ⌈‾1.8 0 ‾21 5.6
‾1 0 ‾21 6
        ?3 4 5
3 3 4
        ÷3.5 ‾67 ‾.287
0.2857142857 ‾0.01492537313 ‾3.484320557
        ○1÷180
0.01745329252
        |3.1 0 ‾5.6 ‾8
3.1 0 5.6 8
        !3 5 7 4
6 120 5040 24
        ⌊5.5 6.8 ‾9.1 ‾.12
5 6 ‾10 ‾1
        -‾1.2 ‾6.7 .52 19.5
1.2 6.7 ‾0.52 ‾19.5
        14×⌈5.8×‾31.046
‾2520
        4○1 2 3
1.414213562 2.236067977 3.16227766
        ?10 10 10 10
2 8 3 7
```
Your random numbers may be different from those shown.
```
        ⍟14.1 86 .108
2.646174797 4.454347296 ‾2.225624052
        ×‾5.6 0 42
‾1 0 1
        +8.7 ‾19.1 23
8.7 ‾19.1 23
        1○○1 2
1.743934249E‾16 ‾3.487868498E‾16
```
See comparison tolerance, page 299, for why these are not exactly 0.
```
        ‾1 ‾2○1 ○.5
0.5 1.070796327
```

2. Floor: $X-1|X$
   Ceiling: $X+1|-X$ (these expressions work for all real X)

3.
```
        *2+A1←(‾1+A*3)÷2
3269017.372
        ~(2≤A)∧∨/3=B
0
        C≠⌊C←((A*2)+(A+1)*2)*.5
0
```

4. `0=(⌊N÷10)|N`   or   `×(⌊N÷10)|N`

5.
```
A←Y-1969
LY←⌊.25×A
B←1+7|3+A+LY
```
or, on one line: `B←1+7|3+A+⌊.25×A←Y-1969`

6. **A)** `10>|V` or `0=⌊10⍟V`
    B) `10≤|V` or `~0=⌊10⍟V`

7.
```
        (10*‾1)×⌊.5+6.18×10*1
6.2
        (10*‾2)×⌊.5+4.75×10*2
4.75
        (10*-D)×⌊.5+N×10*D
```

8.

$$M \leftarrow 84.6129999993$$
$$M$$
84.613
$$1E5 \times M$$
8461300
$$\lfloor 1E5 \times M$$
8461299

9. $(\lfloor X \times 10* - (\lfloor 1+10 \circledast X) - N) = \lfloor Y \times 10* - (\lfloor 1+10 \circledast Y) - N$

10. A) $\quad D \div B$ B) $\quad \lceil D \div B$

11. The results of these instructions are dependent on your implementation of **APL**. You cannot tell *when* the system evaluates an expression in parentheses. Hence, you should avoid writing commands like those shown in this problem.

12. $(\lfloor X + .5) - 0 = 2 | X - .5 \quad$ or $\quad (\lceil X - .5) + \sim \times 2 | X + .5$

13.

$$(\sim A) \vee \sim B$$
1 1 1 0
$$A \vee C \wedge B$$
1 1 0 1
$$(A \wedge \sim B) \wedge A \vee C$$
0 1 0 0
$$(\sim B) \vee A \vee \sim C$$
0 1 1 1

14.

$$(2 \circ 2 \times \iota 5) = ((2 \circ \iota 5) * 2) - (1 \circ \iota 5) * 2$$
1 1 1 1 1

For X a scalar, try the following: $0 = -/(2 \; 2 \; 1 \circ 2 \; 1 \; 1 \times X) * 1 \; 2 \; 2$

Can you explain why it doesn't work consistently for all X?

15. $1 = +/(1 \; 2 \circ X) * 2$

This version works only for scalar X. For X a vector we can use the outer product as follows:

$\wedge / 1 = +/(1 \; 2 \circ . \circ X) * 2$

16. $?4 \; 4 \rho 100 \quad$ or $\quad 4 \; 4 \rho ? 16 \rho 100$

17. The hard way: $(((|N) \times .5) \times N > 0) + (N * 2) \times N < 0$

Much better: $N * .5 * \times N$

18. A) $S \wedge \sim T \qquad$ B) $T \vee \sim J \qquad$ C) $(T \wedge S) \vee J$

This ambiguous problem points out that it is more difficult to be precise in English than in **APL**.

19.

$$\sim (V1 \wedge V2)$$
1 0 1 0 1 0
$$(\sim V1) \vee (\sim V2)$$
1 0 1 0 1 0
$$\sim (V1 \vee V2)$$
0 0 0 0 1 0
$$(\sim V1) \wedge (\sim V2)$$
0 0 0 0 1 0

These two equivalences are known in logic as De Morgan's rules.

Chapter 10 (page 82)

1.
```
        ∇Z←EQ  X                         ∇Z←EQ1  X
   [1]  Z←0=×/X-2 3∇                [1]  Z←××/X-2 3∇
```
          or

2.
```
        ∇R←H  BB  AB
   [1]  R←H÷AB∇
```
3.
```
        ∇T←HERO  L
   [1]  S←.5×+/L
   [2]  T←(S××/S-L)*.5∇
```
4.
```
        ∇REFUND  E
   [1]  +/.5×E⌊500 200∇
```
5.
```
        ∇RT←PR  M
   [1]  RT←÷+/÷M∇
```

6.   ∇R←SD X   ∇R←SD1 X
   [1]   R←AVG X   or   [1]   R←(AVG(X-AVG X)*2)*.5∇
   [2]   R←R-X
   [3]   R←R*2
   [4]   R←(AVG R)*.5∇

7.   ∇M←MR REL V
   [1]   M←MR÷(1-(V*2)÷9E16)*.5∇

8.   ∇Z←X PLUS Y   ∇Z←X MINUS Y
   [1]   Z←X+Y∇   [1]   Z←X-Y∇
        ∇Z←X TIMES Y   ∇Z←X DIVIDEDBY Y
   [1]   Z←X×Y∇   [1]   Z←X÷Y∇

9.   ∇WHAT X   ∇Z←IS X
   [1]   X∇   [1]   Z←X∇

PLUS is the same as in problem 8 above. Why do *WHAT* and *IS* have the syntax shown?

10.   ∇ R←A HYPOT B
   [1]   R←A×4○B÷A∇

Chapter 11   (page 90)

1.   ∇FICA←P TAX IN
   [1]   FICA←.01×P×15300⌊IN∇

2.   ∇A SQDIF B
   [1]   T←(A-B)*2∇

3.   ∇R←FERMAT N
   [1]   R←1+2*2*N∇

4.   ∇CEILING X
   [1]   X+1|-X∇

5.   ∇R←RANDOM
   [1]   R←?4ρ100∇

6.   ∇COMP   ∇COMP1
   [1]   (0=X|Y)∨0=Y|X∇   or   [1]   0=(X|Y)×Y|X∇

7.   A SQA B   lacks the opening ∇.
     ∇ Z←B HYP   monadic arguments should be on right.
     ∇ A 1FIB B   illegal function name.
     ∇ A HYP B C   **APL** can't handle more than two arguments.

8.   (3 HYP 4) HYP 3 HYP 1
   5.916079783
        4+3 HYP 4-3
   7.16227766
        (4+3)HYP 4-3
   7.071067812

9.   )LOAD 1 CLASS
   SAVED   15.02.39 04/15/74
        ∇ R←ARG1 D ARG2
   DEFN ERROR
        ∇ R←ARG1 D ARG2
                     ∧

   D is a variable in 1 *CLASS*. (Execute) *VARS D* to check.) The system will not let you have two objects in the same block of storage under the same name at the same time.

10.   F←10⊛A←AVG X

Chapter 12 (page 101)

```
 1.            )LOAD 1 CLASS
       SAVED  15.02.39 04/15/74
              ∇STD[□]
          ∇ STD N
      [1]    R←AVG N
      [2]    R←R-N
      [3]    R←AVG R*2
      [4]    ANS←R*0.5
          ∇
 2.   [5]    [4□7]
      [4]    ANS←R*0.5
              ///1
      [4]    R←R*0.5
 3.   [5]    [0□5]
      [0]    STD N
              5
      [0]    R←    STD N
 4.   [1]    [2]
      [2]
              ∨
 5.   [3]    [□]
          ∇ R←STD N
      [1]    R←AVG N
      [3]    R←AVG R*2
      [4]    R←R*0.5
          ∇
 6.   [5]    [3]
      [3]    R←AVG (R-N)*2
 7.   [4]    [□3]
      [3]    R←AVG(R-N)*2
      [4]    R←R*0.5
 8.   [4]    ∇
 9.           ∇STD[1.5]R←R-N
10.  [1.6]  [3□10]
      [3]    R←R*0.5
              /5
      [3]    ANS ←R*0.5
      [4]    [.6]
11.  [0.6]  ρN
     [0.7]  ∇
12.           )ERASE STD
```

Chapter 13 (page 112)

1. A)   )*LOAD 1 CLASS*
    SAVED 15.02.39 04/15/74
            C←5 2 78 90
    SYNTAX ERROR
            C←5 2 78 90
            ∧

There is already a defined function by the name *C* in this workspace, as can be seen by executing
)*FNS C.*

    B)   *A←1+B←3*
            T←F+7
    VALUE ERROR
            T←F+7
              ∧
            T←Z+7
            T
    1 2

F is a function name and has no value. When executed, *Z* receives a value as a global variable.

2.

PERIM1		*S←M PERIM2 R*		*S←PERIM3 R*
R		*R*		*R*
1 4		*3*	*3*	
B		*B*		*B*
2		*2*	*2*	
C		*C*		*C*
5		*5*	*5*	
M		*M*		*M*
7		*7*	*7*	
S		*S*		*S*
1		*20*	*10*	

This exercise is designed to give you practice in distinguishing between local, dummy and global
variables. To reset the values after each execution, define a function like the following:

             ∇*SETUP*
    [1]   *S←1 ◊ B←2 ◊ R←3 ◊ C←5 ◊ M←7*∇

3.   ∇*R←B PERIM2 C;P*
    [1]   *P←B+C*
    [2]   *R←2×P*∇

4.   ∇*M←MARGIN P;S;C*
    [1]   *S←40000-5000×P*
    [2]   *C←35000+2×S*
    [3]   *M←(P×S)-C*∇

Chapter 14 (page 120)

             ∇*FN1 S*
    [1]   *S*10*∇
             ∇*FN2 V*
    [1]   *2⊛V≤X*∇
             VAR1←÷1 2 3 4 5 6
             VAR2←⌈/VAR1
)*SAVE WORKONE*
       10.00.31 05/22/74
)*CLEAR*
    CLEAR WS
             ∇*FN3 T*
    [1]   *×T*∇
             *VAR3←*1 2 3 4 5*
)*SAVE WORKTWO*
       10.01.26 05/22/74

```
        )CLEAR
CLEAR WS
        ∇A FN4 B
[1]     A-B*2∇
        VAR4←4  6  8  9
        )SAVE WORKTHREE
  10.02.22 05/22/74
        VAR5←-3  7  10  78
        )SAVE WORKFOUR
NOT SAVED, WS QUOTA USED UP
        )LIB
WORKONE
WORKTHREE
WORKTWO
        )DROP WORKONE
  10.07.04 05/22/74
        )LIB
WORKTHREE
WORKTWO
        )LOAD WORKTHREE
SAVED  10.02.22 05/22/74
        )FNS
FN4
        )VARS
VAR4
        ∇C FN5 D
[1]     (÷C≤?D)×4∇
        VAR6←1  0  7  ̄6  ̄8
        )SAVE WORKTWO
NOT SAVED, THIS WS IS WORKTHREE
        )SAVE WORKTHREE
  10.11.07 05/22/74
        )CLEAR
CLEAR WS
        )LOAD WORKTHREE
SAVED  10.11.07 05/22/74
        )FNS
FN4     FN5
        )VARS
VAR4    VAR6
        )ERASE FN4 VAR4
        )SAVE
  10.12.14 05/22/74 WORKTHREE
        )LIB
WORKTHREE
WORKTWO
        )FNS
FN5
        )VARS
VAR6
```

Note that when you load one of your own workspaces and then try to save it under a different name, the system prevents you from so doing. Also, when)SAVE is executed, the material will be saved under whatever name the active workspace had prior to saving. The save doesn't take place, however, if the active workspace was not given a name previously.

Chapter 15 (page 132)

```
1.           )LIB 1
    ADVANCEDEX
    APLCOURSE
    CATALOG
    CLASS
    MINIMA
    NEWS
    PLOTFORMAT
    TYPEDRILL
    WSFNS
         )LOAD 1 ADVANCEDEX
    SAVED  9.40.34 02/10/71
         )FNS
    AH      ASSOC    BIN     COMB    DESCRIBE          DTH     ENTER
    F       FC       GC      GCD     GCV     HILB      HTD     IN
    INV     INVP     IN1     LFC     LOOKUP  PALL      PER     PERM
    PO      POL      POLY    POLYB   RESET   TIME      TRUTH   ZERO
         )VARS
    DAH     DASSOC   DBIN    DCOMB   DDTH    DENTER    DESC    DF
    DFC     DGC      DGCD    DGCV    DHILB   DHTD      DIN     DINV
    DINVP   DIN1     DLFC    DLOOKUP DPALL   DPER      DPERM   DPO
    DPOL    DPOLY    DPOLYB  DTIME   DTRUTH  DZERO     J       M
    N       NEW      R       TIMER   X       Z
         DESCRIBE
    EACH OF THE VARIABLES OF THIS WORKSPACE WHICH BEGINS WITH THE
    LETTER D IS THE DESCRIPTION OF THE FUNCTION WHOSE NAME IS
    OBTAINED BY REMOVING THE D. FOR FURTHER
```
(execution interrupted by pressing **ATTN**)
```
         )WSID
    1 ADVANCEDEX
         ∇L RECT W
    [1]   L×W∇
         )COPY 1 CLASS RECT
    SAVED    15.02.39 04/15/74
         ∇RECT[□]∇
       ∇ L RECT H
    [1]   2×L+H
    [2]   L HYP H
    [3]   L×H
       ∇
```
The original *RECT* is replaced by the version in 1 *CLASS*.
```
         )ERASE RECT
         ∇L RECT W
    [1]   L×W∇
         )PCOPY 1 CLASS RECT
    SAVED    15.02.39 04/15/74
```
This command will copy a global object in the same way as *COPY* only if one doesn't exist with the same name in the active workspace.
```
         ∇RECT[□]∇
       ∇ L RECT W
    [1]   L×W
       ∇
         )SAVE JONES
    11.35.53 05/10/74
```

```
        )WSID SMITH
WAS JONES
        )SAVE
   11.36.56 05/10/74 SMITH
        )CLEAR
CLEAR WS
        )LOAD 1 NEWS
SAVED   9.40.34 02/10/71
        )SAVE 1 NEWS
IMPROPER LIBRARY REFERENCE
```
The ordinary user can't save into a common library unless he put it in there originally.
```
        )CONTINUE HOLD
   11.38.19 05/10/74 CONTINUE
058   11.38.20 05/10/74 KGR
CONNECTED      0.08.25  TO DATE   51.27.40
CPU TIME       0.00.00  TO DATE    0.03.03
        )5000:SJ
058) 11.38.45 05/10/74 LGILMAN

        APL*PLUS SERVICE

SAVED  11.38.19 05/10/74
        )LIB
CONTINUE
JONES
SMITH

        )FNS
APLNOW  CLEAR  CLEARSKED       CREATE EDIT      FILE    FLE
FMTDT   INDEX  NJ      POS      POSITION         POSTSKED
PRINT   REWORK RWK     SCHEDULE         SETDATE  SKEDNOTE
START   TDATE  TRYTEXT TXF
        )VARS
DESCRIBE        I       LIBRARY MDX     MSGS     NEWSMAKING
PTX     RLIBRARY        SKD     NS      SD
```
The command *CONTINUE HOLD* saves the active workspace in *CONTINUE* and holds open the phone line for 60 seconds. The workspace is available to the user when he signs on again.

2.
```
        )SAVE CONTINUE
        )LOAD GOOD
        )COPY CONTINUE OK
        )SAVE
```
3.
```
        )LOAD 1 CLASS
SAVED 15.02.39 04/15/74
        )GROUP A TAB0 TAB1 TAB2 TAB3
        )GROUP B AVG1 AVG2 AVG3 AVG4 AVG5
        )GROUP A A PI
        )GRPS
A       B
        )GRP A
TAB0    TAB1    TAB2    TAB3    PI
        )GROUP A
        )GRPS
B
```

Chapter 16 (page 144)

1.
```
        ρA
6
        ρρA
1
        ρρρA
1
        A⌈0.8×⍳6
0.8 8 2.4 4 6 10
        ⍳10
1 2 3 4 5 6 7 8 9 10
        (⍳5)+3
4 5 6 7 8
        ¯7×⍳1
¯7
        ⍳⌈/A
1 2 3 4 5 6 7 8 9 10
        +/⍳15
120
        ÷⍳5
1 0.5 0.3333333333 0.25 0.2
        ⍳28÷3+1
1 2 3 4 5 6 7
        ⍳10000
WS FULL
        ⍳10000
        ∧
```
The active workspace can hold just so much information at one time. See Chapter 32 for a more complete discussion.
```
        ρM
2 4
        (¯2) 1 2
SYNTAX ERROR
        (¯2) 1 2
             ∧
        ¯2,1 2
¯2 1 2
```
Compare these results with problem 6, Chapter 3.
```
        ρρV
2
        5 4ρV
1 2 3 4
5 6 7 8
9 1 2 3
4 5 6 7
8 9 1 2
        V,M
LENGTH ERROR
        V,M
          ∧
```
Why the error message?
```
        6ρ12
12 12 12 12 12 12
        10ρ100
100 100 100 100 100 100 100 100 100 100
        3 3ρ1,3ρ0
1 0 0
0 1 0
0 0 1
```

```
            5  4ρ0
     0  0  0  0
     0  0  0  0
     0  0  0  0
     0  0  0  0
     0  0  0  0
            5,4ρ0
  5  0  0  0  0
            ρρ0ρ9 10 11 12
  1
```

2.   `A←0 8 ¯3 4 6 10`
           `ρA=6`
     6
           `6=ρA`
     1

The first expression tells us how many elements A has, and the second tells us whether A has 6 components.

3.   `)LOAD 1 CLASS`
     `SAVED  15.02.39 04/15/74`
           `×/ρTAB0`
     1
           `×/ρTAB1`
     4
           `×/ρTAB2`
     12
           `×/ρTAB3`
     24

The instructions tell us how many elements are in each of the arrays.

4.   `A←0 8 ¯3 4 6 10`
           `ιρA`
     `1 2 3 4 5 6`
           `ριρA`
     6

The first expression gives us a vector of indices for the elements in A, while the second is equivalent to $ρA$. Compare $ριρA$ with $\lceil/ιρA$. How do they differ? (Don't be too hasty in your answer.)

5. A)   `∇R←A1 N`   B)   `∇R←B2 N`   C)   `∇R←C3 N`
    [1]   `R←+/(ιN)*.5∇`   [1]   `R←(+/ιN)*.5∇`   [1]   `R←(×/ιN)*÷N∇`

6.   `¯1+2×ι8`
   `1 3 5 7 9 11 13 15`
           `¯12+5×ι5`
   `¯7 ¯2 3 8 13`
           `¯.3+.3×ι6`
   `0 0.3 0.6 0.9 1.2 1.5`
           `¯350+100×ι6`
   `¯250 ¯150 ¯50 50 150 250`
           `6-ι5`
   `5 4 3 2 1`
           `2|ι6`
   `1 0 1 0 1 0`

7.   `ι3*ι3`
     `RANK ERROR`
           `ι3*ι3`
            `∧`

The order of execution is such that $ι3$ will be generated first and used as powers for 3, resulting in a vector for the right argument of $ι$ on the left. Since the index generator requires a single element as its argument, the error message appears.

8. `51≠ι50, (ι50)=ι50, (ι50)*0, 50ρ1`, etc.

9. `¯1+2×-/ι5`
    `+/¯1+ι5`
    `+/5=1+ι5`
    `+/0=6=ι5`   or   `+/~6=ι5`

10.   A) $\nabla R \leftarrow SERIES1\ N$ B) $\nabla R \leftarrow X\ \ SERIES2\ \ N;T$
      [1] $R \leftarrow -/ \div \iota N \nabla$ [1] $R \leftarrow +/(X \star T) \div !T \leftarrow {}^{-}1 + \iota N \nabla$

11. $0 = \rho \rho A$

12. $A \leftarrow 3\ 4\ 5$
               $B \leftarrow \iota 8$
               $\rho A , \rho B$
      4
               $(\rho A) , \rho B$
      3   8
The first expression is equivalent to $1 + \rho A$, while the second is the vector consisting of the lengths of A and B.

13. $3\ 1 \rho 2$
      2
      2
      2

14. $?100 \rho 10$

15.   A) $?(?8\ 8) \rho 150$ B) $?(?8\ 8) \rho ?299$

16. $R \leftarrow 12\ 4 \rho (,A) , , B$ This can be done more concisely by $R \leftarrow A , [1]B$. See Chapter 24 for further discussion of catenation.

17.   If E were a dyadic function, we would have to write 6 E 8 to execute it. Spaces or other delimiters (e.g., parentheses) are required around a function name.

18. $S \leftarrow S , \iota 0$ or $S \leftarrow (\iota 0) , S$ or $S \leftarrow | \rho S$

19. $11\ 1 \rho 1000 , .05 \times \iota 10$
      0
      0.156434465
      0.3090169944
      0.4539904997
      0.5877852523
      0.7071067812
      0.8090169944
      0.8910065242
      0.9510565163
      0.9876883406
      1
This expression generates the values required by the problem, but without identification as to the magnitude (in radians) of the associated angles. With the transpose (Chapter 24) such information can be included: $\lozenge 2\ 1\ 1 \rho (\circ A) , 100A \leftarrow ({}^{-}1 + \iota 11) \div 20$. The table can also be generated with the outer product. Do you see how?

20. $+/(\iota N) \times 0 = 2 | \iota N$ or $+/2 \times \iota \lfloor N \div 2$ Looking ahead a bit, once compression is introduced in Chapter 18, a more elegant solution will be $+/(N \rho 0\ 1)/ \iota N$.

21. $0\ 5 \rho \iota 0$

22. $A \leftarrow (321400 \div 27.8 \star .5) - 17 \div 6.5E^{-}4$
      $B \leftarrow 5 \circledast \div (6.8E^{-}6) \star .25$
      $C \leftarrow 32200 \star 2 \div 9$
      $\lfloor /A , B , C$

23. $-/ \div 1 , 2 \times \iota 29$

24. $((\iota N) \circ . = \iota N) \times (N , N) \rho V$

25. $(\iota 4) \circ . + 4 \rho 0$

26.   The sumscan shows that the following series converges fairly rapidly. Try it with some large value of N, say 20:
               $N \leftarrow 20$
               $10000 \times + \backslash \div 2 \star 0 , \iota N$
      10000 15000 17500 18750 19375 19687.5 19843.75 19921.875
             19960.9375 19980.46875 19990.23438 19995.11719
             19997.55859 19998.7793 19999.38965 19999.69482
             19999.84741 19999.92371 19999.96185 19999.98093
             19999.99046

Chapter 17 (page 155)

```
1.              'ABCDE'='BBXDO'
        0  1  0  1  0
                ρV←'3172'
        4
                (ρV)ρV
        3172
                3172=V
        0  0  0  0
                X,Y
        MISSISSIPPIRIVER
                1 2<'MP'
        DOMAIN ERROR
                1 2 <'MP'
                    ∧
                ρX,Y
        16
                +/X='S'
        4
                +/X≠'S'
        7
                X,' ',Y
        MISSISSIPPI RIVER
                ρρAL←3 3ρ'ABCDEFGHI'
        2
                X='S'
        0  0  1  1  0  1  1  0  0  0  0
                +/'P'=X
        2
                +/(X,' ',Y)≠'S'
        13
                ∨/X='R'
        0
```

2. *D* is a character vector consisting of fifteen blanks.

```
3.              ∇F A
        [1]     'THE SHAPE OF A IS ';ρA
        [2]     'THE RANK IS ';ρρA
        [3]     'THE NUMBER OF ELEMENTS IS ';×/ρA∇
```

4. `(10>I)ρ' ';I`
    This is a formatting problem. Further details in Chapter 21.

```
5.              )COPY 1 CLASS GEO3 HYP
        SAVED    15.02.39 04/15/74
                ∇GEO3[0.5]
        [0.5] ⍝THE LITERAL MESSAGES IN THIS FUNCTION
        [0.6] ⍝ARE KEYED TO THE ARGUMENTS USED
        [0.7] ∇
                ∇GEO3[☐]∇
            ∇ L GEO3 H;X;FLAG
        [1]   ⍝THE LITERAL MESSAGES IN THIS FUNCTION
        [2]   ⍝ARE KEYED TO THE ARGUMENTS USED
        [3]     FLAG←((ρ,L)>1)∨(ρ,H)>1
        [4]     X←((4×~FLAG)ρ' IS:'),(6×FLAG)ρ'S ARE:'
        [5]     'PERIMETER',X
        [6]     2×L+H
        [7]     'AREA',X
        [8]     L×H
        [9]     'DIAGONAL',X
        [10]    L HYP H
            ∇
```

```
        3 4 GEO3 5 6
PERIMETERS ARE:
16   20
AREAS ARE:
15   24
DIAGONALS ARE:
5.830951895  7.211102551
```

Comments introduced in this manner don't affect execution of the function, although they do take up space in storage. Note also that in entering the comment the closing del was placed on the next line rather than at the end of the comment. Do you see why?

6.

```
        ∇GPA;GR;CR;M
[1]     M←5 25ρ(25ρ4),(25ρ3),(25ρ2),(25ρ1),(25ρ0)
[2]     GR←M×CR←(3×GR3)+(2×GR2)+GR1
[3]     'STUDENT GRADE POINT AVERAGES ARE ';(+/GR)÷+/CR
[4]     'THE CLASS AVERAGE IS ';(+/+/GR)÷+/+/CR∇
```

Chapter 18 (page 165)

1.
```
        (2<ι5)/ι5
3 4 5
        B/A
0 6.2 ¯2 25
        A[ρA],B[¯2+ρB]
25 0
        (3 2 7)[2 1 3]
2 3 7
        A[3 6]←2E5 4E¯4
        A
0 ¯5 200000 6.2 15 0.0004 25
        C[1 16 12 27 9 19 27 1 12 7 15 18 9 20 8 13 9 3]
APL IS ALGORITHMIC
        M[2;3 1]
7 5
        ρA[2 4 7]
3
        1 1 0 1\'TWO'
TW O
        A[8]
INDEX ERROR
        A[8]
        ∧
        AιΓ/A
3
        1 0 1/M
  1  2  3  4
  9 10 11 12
        A[1]+A[2 3 4]×A[7]
¯125 5000000 155
        1 0 0 1 1 1\M
  1  0  0  2  3  4
  5  0  0  6  7  8
  9  0  0 10 11 12
        A[0ρ3]
        @
        B\2 3 4 5
2 0 0 3 0 4 5
```

Note that A is respecified after fifth drill problem. This will affect the remaining problems.

2. **A)** $(D<.5)/D$ **D)** $((D<0)\wedge D>^-1)/D$
   B) $(D>0)/D$ **E)** $(D=2)/D$
   C) $(4=|D)/D$ **F)** $((D<1)\wedge D\geq^-2)/D$

3. $\nabla Z\leftarrow INSERT1\ V$
   [1] $Z\leftarrow((2\times\rho V)\rho 1\ 0)\backslash V$
   [2] $Z[2\times\iota^-1+\rho V]\leftarrow '\circ' \nabla$ or
                 $\nabla Z\leftarrow INSERT2\ V$
   [1] $Z\leftarrow('\circ',V)[1+((^-1+\rho V,V)\rho 1\ 0)\backslash\iota\rho V]\nabla$
   These functions as written work only for character vectors.

4. $\nabla Z\leftarrow INCR\ V;T$
   [1] $Z\leftarrow V[1+T]-V[T\leftarrow\iota^-1+\rho V]\nabla$
   When the drop function $\downarrow$ is introduced in Chapter 19, line 1 can also be written as $Z\leftarrow V-0,^-1\downarrow V$.

5. $\nabla Z\leftarrow F\ X$
   [1] $Z\leftarrow 3\times X*2\nabla$
                 $\nabla Z\leftarrow I\ AREA\ X$
   [1] $Z\leftarrow+/I\times F\ X[1]+I\times\iota\lfloor|(-/X)\div I\nabla$

6. $\nabla Z\leftarrow W\ WITHIN\ R$
   [1] $Z\leftarrow(R\geq|W-+/W\div\rho W)/W\nabla$

7. $(R=\lfloor R)/R$

8. $\nabla R\leftarrow A\ IN\ INT$
   [1] $R\leftarrow(+/INT[2]>|A-INT[1])\times 100\div\rho A\nabla$
   INT is defined here as the vector B,C.

9. $(\lceil/V)>(+/V)-\lceil/V$ or $(\lceil/V)>+/(V\neq\lceil/V)/V$

10. $Y[2\times\iota\lfloor(\rho Y)\div 2]$ or $(2|1+\iota\rho Y)/Y$ or $(\sim 2|\iota\rho Y)/Y$

11. $\nabla R\leftarrow S\ INS\ X$
   [1] $R\leftarrow((S\geq X)/X),S,(S<X)/X\nabla$ or
                 $\nabla R\leftarrow S\ INS1\ X$
   [1] $R\leftarrow X<S$
   [2] $R\leftarrow((R,0)\vee 0,\sim R)\backslash X$
   [3] $R[R\iota 0]\leftarrow S\nabla$

12. **A)** $A\leftarrow 3$
                 $\iota A[2]$
   $RANK\ ERROR$
                 $\iota A[2]$
                 $\wedge$
                 $(\iota A)[2]$
   2
   The first expression is nonsense if A is a scalar or vector of length 1, while the second one is invalid if A isn't a positive integer ≥ 2.
   B) $M\leftarrow 1\ 2$
                 $N\leftarrow 3\ 4$
                 $\rho M,\rho N$
   3
   (This is equivalent to $\rho 1\ 2,2$.)
                 $(\rho M),\rho N$
   2 2

13. $V[\rho V]$

14. The indices as given start with 0, which will result in an index error. See page 301.

15. $(W=\lceil/W)/\iota\rho W$ or $W\iota\lceil/W$

16. $\nabla Z\leftarrow DELE\ V$
   [1] $Z\leftarrow((\iota\rho V)=V\iota V)/V\nabla$

17. $+/Q[\iota 8\lfloor\rho Q]$ or $+/Q\times 8\geq\iota\rho Q$

18. $\nabla R\leftarrow X\ SELECT\ Y$
   [1] $R\leftarrow X[Y\iota\lceil/Y]\nabla$

19. **A)** $((^-1+\rho V,V)\rho 1\ 0)\backslash V$
    B) $(((2|\rho V)+3\times\lfloor.5\times\rho V)\rho 1\ 0\ 1)\backslash V$
    C)   Same as **B)** provided we don't want a zero on the right end when ρV is odd.

20. $\nabla R\leftarrow FACTORS\ N$ or $\nabla R\leftarrow FACTORS1\ N$
   [1] $R\leftarrow(0=(\iota N)|N)/\iota N\nabla$ [1] $R\leftarrow(\sim 1|N\div\iota N)/\iota N\nabla$

21. $\nabla Z\leftarrow LIT\ N$
   [1] $Z\leftarrow+/(10*(\rho N)-\iota\rho N)\times^-1+'0123456789'\iota N\nabla$

This conversion of literal numbers to numerics can be done somewhat more compactly with the decode function $\perp$ to be introduced in Chapter 20, as well as by the inner product (Chapter 26) and the execute function (Chapter 33).

22.　　　　　$\nabla R \leftarrow A\ \ COMFACT\ \ B$
　　[1]　　$R \leftarrow (0=R|B)/R \leftarrow (0=(\iota A)|A)/\iota A \nabla$

23.　　　　　$\nabla R \leftarrow LONGEST\ \ X;J;M;N;P$
　　[1]　　$J \leftarrow (X=' ')/\iota \rho X$
　　[2]　　$M \leftarrow \lceil /N \leftarrow ^-1+(P \leftarrow J,1+\rho X)-0,J$
　　[3]　　$R \leftarrow X[((P[N \iota M]+\iota M)-(1+\rho \iota M)]\nabla$

In this solution, J (line 1) locates the blanks in X. N (line 2) is a vector of word lengths, the largest word length being represented by M. Line 3 brackets this longest word and generates the indices needed to pick it out of X.

24.　The second is a 1 1 matrix, while the first is a scalar. Try ρ of each to check.

25.　$W \leftarrow (W \neq 'A')/W$

26.　A)　　$((0=2|X)\lceil(0=3|X))/X$　　　　　($\vee$ may be substituted for $\lceil$).
　　B)　　$((0=2|X) \not\vee (0=3|X))/X$

27.　　　　　$\nabla Z \leftarrow CLOSEST\ \ A;M$
　　[1]　　$M \leftarrow (1000 \times (\iota \rho A)\circ.=\iota \rho A)+|A \circ.-A$
　　[2]　　$M \leftarrow ,M=\lfloor M$
　　[3]　　$Z \leftarrow A[\lceil(M/\iota \rho M) \div \rho A]\nabla$

After looking at the matrix $A \circ.-A$, you should be able to figure out for yourself why the rest of line 1 was necessary. Also compare with the solution given in problem 4.

28.　A)　$M[\iota 3;]$　B)　　$M[1\ 2;1\ 2]$　C)　　$M[;4\ 5]$　D)　　$M[1\ 5;1\ 5]$

29.　$P \leftarrow 6.99+.01 \times \iota 51$
　　$Q \leftarrow 600-3.7 \times P \star 2$
　　$TR \leftarrow P \times Q$
　　Price: $P[TR \iota \lceil /TR]$
　　Production: $Q[TR \iota \lceil /TR]$

30.　$N \leftarrow \iota 50$
　　$COST \leftarrow (.08 \times N)+10.24 \div M \star .5$　　(cost)
　　$(COST=\lfloor /COST)/N$　　(number of items sampled)

Chapter 19　(page 176)

1.　　　　　$3 \phi A$
　$^-1\ 5\ ^-8\ 3\ 2\ 0$
　　　　　$2 \phi A[\iota 4]$
　$0\ ^-1\ 3\ 2$
　　　　　$4 \uparrow A$
　$3\ 2\ 0\ ^-1$
　　　　　$2 \uparrow ^-3 \phi A$
　$^-1\ 5$
　　　　　　$^-2\ 1\ 3 \phi M$
　　$3\ \ 4\ \ 1\ \ 2$
　　$6\ \ 7\ \ 8\ \ 5$
　$12\ \ 9\ 10\ 11$
　　　　　$\phi 0,\iota 3$
　$3\ 2\ 1\ 0$
　　　　　$2 \phi \phi \iota 7$
　$5\ 4\ 3\ 2\ 1\ 7\ 6$
　　　　　$^-3 \uparrow A$
　$3\ 2\ 0$
　　　　　$A[\blacktriangle \blacktriangle A]$
　$5\ ^-1\ 0\ 2\ ^-8\ 3$
　　　　　$1\ 2 \downarrow M$
　　$7\ \ 8$
　$11\ 12$

```
        A[⍒0 1 0 1 0 1]
  2 ¯1 ¯8 3 0 5
        (⍳4)∊A
 0 1 1 0
        (3↑A)∊⍳4
 1 1 0
        (⍳6)=⍋A[⍋A]
 1 1 1 1 1 1
        A∊M
 1 1 0 0 1 0
```

2. `(((|V)∊0,⍳9)/V`

3. `∧/(S1∊S2),S2∊S1` or `~0∊(S1∊S2),S2∊S1`

4. `+/S∊'ABCDEFGHIJKL'`

5. `ALF←'ABCDEFGHIJKLMNOPQRSTUVWXYZ '`
   `S[⍋ALF⍳S]`

6.   `∇Z←BL S`
   `[1]`   `Z←(C∨1⌽C←S≠' ')/S∇`

7. `(V,V1)[⍋V,V1]`

8. `∧/V[⍋V]=⍳N` or `∧/(V∊⍳N),(⍳N)∊V`

9. `C[('X'=C)/⍳⍴C]←'Y'`

10. `(5<⍳8)/X` and `¯3↑X`

11.   `∇R←MED X`
    `[1]`   `R←.5×+/X[(⍋X)[⌈|⌈¯.5 .5×1+⍴X]]∇`

12. A)   This is a difficult problem. The expression corresponds to a perfect shuffle, in which a deck of cards is cut exactly in half and cards fed alternately first from the top half, then from the bottom half to form a new deck.

    B)   This expression is the algorithm used in **APL** for the deal function, $A?B$. For an explanation of $⌊/⍳0$ see the answer to problem 4, Chapter 26.

13.   `∇R←DECODE C`
    `[1]`   `R←ALF[P⍳ALF⍳C]∇`

14.   `∇COVIG M;C;D`
    `[1]`   `N←ALF⍳M`
    `[2]`   `M`
    `[3]`   `C←1+26|N+D←((⍴N)⍴KB)+(⍴N)⍴KA`
    `[4]`   `ALF[D]`
    `[5]`   `(⍴M)⍴'¯'`
    `[6]`   `ALF[C]∇`

    VIG, incidentally, is an example of a well-known cryptographic scheme, the Vigenère code, with *COVIG* being a more complicated variation.

15.   `∇VERNAM M;V;N;C`
    `[1]`   `M`
    `[2]`   `V←?(⍴M)⍴26`
    `[3]`   `C←1+26|V+ALF⍳M`
    `[4]`   `ALF[V]`
    `[5]`   `(⍴M)⍴'¯'`
    `[6]`   `ALF[C]∇`

16. `(,M)[N?⍴,M]`

17. `M←M+(⍴M)⍴(1↓⍴M)⍴0,N`

18.   `∇AR`
    `[1]`   `M←5 15⍴V1,V2,V3,V4,V5`
    `[2]`   `'TOTALS BY CATEGORY ARE ';+/M`
    `[3]`   `'TOTALS BY CUSTOMER ARE ';+⌿M`
    `[4]`   `'THE TOTAL OF ALL ACCOUNTS RECEIVABLE IS ';+/+⌿M`
    `[5]`   `'CUSTOMERS WITH OVERDUE INVOICES: ';(∨⌿0≠¯3 15↑M)/⍳15∇`

19.   `∇Z←MS N;Q`
    `[1]`   `Z←(N,N)⍴⍳N*2`
    `[2]`   `Q←(-⌈.5×N)+⍳N`
    `[3]`   `Z←Q⊖Q⌽Z∇`

20. `¯3↑5↑V` and `2↓¯6↓V`

21.   `∇C←ISITLIT D;B`   or   `∇C←ISITLIT2 D;B`
    `[1]`   `B←0∈(0 1)\1↑D`   `[1]`   `B←0∈0\0/D`
    `[2]`   `C←((~B)/'YES'),B/'NO'∇`   `[2]`   `C←((~B)/'YES'),B/'NO'∇`
Besides the algorithms on lines 1 above, try `0=1↑0ρD`.

22.   `(B∈A←50?100)/B←50?100`

23.   `∇R←V LOC W`
    `[1]`   `R←(∧/(¯1+ιρW)⌽W∘.=V)/ιρV∇`

24.   `¯2↑G[⍋G]`

25.   A)   `(V1∈V2)/V1`
If there are duplicate elements in either $V1$ or $V2$, this expression is *not* symmetric with respect to $V1$ and $V2$, i.e., the above would not then be the same as `(V2∈V1)/V2`.
    B)   `V1,(~V2∈V1)/V2`
    C)   `(~V1∈V2)/V1`
You may recognize these expressions as corresponding to the intersection, union and difference of the two vectors.

26.   `B←4 13ρ52?52`
Each row of B represents one bridge hand, with numbers 1 to 13 corresponding, say, to hearts, 14 to 26 to diamonds, etc.

27.   `1++/(.5×+/S)>+\S[⍒S]`

28.   `(+/V[4↓⍋V])÷¯4+ρV`

29.   `1/⍋V` This function is dependent on the index origin (page 301).
The authors concede that this is a dirty problem.

30.   `+/∨\⌽0≠V`

31.   `M1←(((R-1),1↓ρM)↑M),[1](R,0)↓M`   or   `M1←(R≠ι1↑ρM)⌿M`

Chapter 20   (page 187)

1.   `(3ρ40)⊥8 7 2`
  `13802`
        `1 ¯4.1 .8⊥1 2 3`
  `1.32`
        `3 3⊤5217`
  `2 0`
        `(4ρ8)⊥¯14`
  `¯8190`
        `2⊥5 1 9 6`
  `68`
        `7 8 9⊥7 8 9`
  `585`
        `3 3 3⊤5217`
  `0 2 0`
        `1 4 6⊤345`
  `0 1 3`
        `1 4 7⊥3 5 ρι15`
 `81 117 153 189 225`
        `3⊤5217`
  `0`
        `(5ρ3)⊤5217`
  `1 1 0 2 0`
        `2 4 5⊤78`
  `1 3 3`

2.   A)   `0 4 2⊥2 8 1`
    B)   `0 2000 16⊥3 568 13`

3.   A)   `8⊥2 1 7 7`
    B)   `2⊥1 0 1 1 0 1`
    C)   `(10ρ3)⊤8933`
    D)   `(10ρ5)⊤4791`

4. $X \top X \bot Y$ and $X \bot X \top Y$
5. $\nabla P \leftarrow CONV\ D$
    [1] $P \leftarrow 10 \bot {}^-1 + '0123456789' \iota (D \neq '\ ,\ ') / D \nabla$
6. $N = +/(10\ 10\ 10 \top N) * 3$
7. A)   converts M into a vector of digits.
    B)   converts M into the corresponding scalar.
    C)   same as B.
8. $0 = 11 | -/((1 + 10 \circledast N) \rho 10) \top N$
9. $\nabla TRICK\ N; D1$
    [1] $D1 + 10 \bot \phi (3 \rho 10) \top D1 \leftarrow |N - 10 \bot \phi (3 \rho 10) \top N \nabla$
10. $0\ 1 \top N$
11. $\nabla Z \leftarrow C\ EVAL\ X$
    [1] $Z \leftarrow X \bot C \nabla$ (put 0's in for missing powers of X.)
12. $0 \bot V$
13. $1 \bot V$ and ${}^-1 \bot \phi V$
14. $.1 \bot \phi V$
15. $0\ 20\ 12 \top 0\ 20\ 12 \bot + / C$ Jefferson was correct.

Chapter 21 (page 205)

1. A) $10\ 4 \overline{\!\phi} TABLE$
    B) $10\ {}^-3 \overline{\!\phi} TABLE$
    C) $0\ 3 \overline{\!\phi} TABLE$
    D) $(8\ 3\ 10\ 5\ 8\ 3,(2 \rho 10\ 5)) \overline{\!\phi} TABLE$
2. $(\overline{\!\phi} Q)[;2 \times \iota (\rho Q)[2]]$ or $1\ 0 \overline{\!\phi} Q$
3. $L, \overline{\!\phi} N$

Chapter 22 (page 210)

1. A)   If $5 < W$, go to step 3; if $5 > W$, go to 2; if $5 = W$, go to the next step. W is assumed to be a scalar
           or vector of length 1.
    B)   Go to step 3 if $A = 8$, otherwise drop through to the next step.
    C)   Go to END if $Y > 1$, otherwise branch out of the program. At the same time R is reshaped as
           $1\ 1$ matrix containing a 1.
    D)   Go to step 7 if any element of B is a member of C, otherwise drop through to the next step.
    E)   If $A \leq C$ go to 5, otherwise branch out of the program.
    F)   Go to step 3.
    G)   Go to step 8 if $0 \neq J$, otherwise go to the next step. At the same time J is decreased by 1.
    H)   If the absolute value of X is greater than or equal to I, go to step 4, otherwise leave the
           program. I is also incremented by 1.
    I)   Go to $AGAIN$ if $N = 10$, otherwise execute the next line. R is reshaped as a 2 4 matrix.
2. $\nabla REM\ T$
    [1] $I \leftarrow 1$
    [2] $L2: V \leftarrow (T[I] \neq V)/V$
    [3] $\rightarrow (I \geq \rho T)/0$
    [4] $\rightarrow L2, I \leftarrow I + 1 \nabla$
    This function, which involves branching, solves the problem by brute force. You'll appreciate the
    power of **APL** from the following:
          $\nabla REM1\ T$
    [1] $V \leftarrow (\sim V \in T)/V \nabla$
3. $\nabla Z \leftarrow P\ DIGIT\ Q; M$
    [1] $Z \leftarrow \iota 0$
    [2] $M \leftarrow \lfloor P \div 10$
    [3] $\rightarrow (0 \neq M | P)/5$
    [4] $Z \leftarrow Z, P$
    [5] $\rightarrow (Q \geq P \leftarrow P + 1)/2 \nabla$

4.
```
          ∇R←MED N
[1]       →(R=⌊R←.5×ρN←N[♠N])/ST   or
[2]       →0,R←N[⌈R]
[3]       ST:R←.5×N[R]+N[R+1]∇
```

```
          ∇R←MED1 N
[1]       N←N[♠N]
[2]       R←N[⌈.5×ρN]
[3]       →4×~2|ρN
[4]       R←.5×R+N[1+.5×ρN]∇
```

5.
```
          ∇R←N DUPL V
[1]       →0×ιρR←(N=V)/ιρV
[2]       'SCALAR NOT PRESENT'∇
```

6.
```
          ∇Z←ROOT S
[1]       →(0≠ρρS)/0
[2]       Z←S*.5∇
```

7.
```
          ∇R←SORT TEXT
[1]       ALF←'ABCDEFGHIJKLMNOPQRSTUVWXYZ'
[2]       R←''
[3]       →0×ι0=ρTEXT
[4]       R←R,(TEXT=1↑ALF)/TEXT
[5]       TEXT←(TEXT≠1↑ALF)/TEXT
[6]       ALF←1↓ALF
[7]       →3∇
```

or, without branching
```
          ∇R←SORT1 TEXT
[1]       TEXT←((ALFιTEXT)≤ρALF)/TEXT
[2]       R←ALF[R[♠R←ALFιTEXT]]∇
```

Incidentally, a long vector of arbitrary characters can be entered in the following way: define one line of *TEXT* as *TEXT←'...'* and each succeeding line *TEXT←TEXT,'...'*. It is also possible to enter large amounts of information into the system through a card reader attached to an appropriate terminal or from a tape generated in some other system.

8.
```
          ∇R←MODE N;V
[1]       V←R←ι0
[2]       AT:V←V,+/N[1]=N
[3]       R←R,N[1]
[4]       →(0≠ρN←(N[1]≠N)/N)/AT
[5]       R←R[(V=⌈/V)/ιρV]∇
```

9.
```
          ∇R←FIB N
[1]       R←1 1
[2]       END:→(N>ρR←R,+/¯2↑R)/END∇
```

10.
```
          ∇HISTOG A;I
[1]       I←⌈/A
[2]       I≤A
[3]       →2××I←I-1∇
```

To "clean up" the histogram, change line 2 to ' *'[1+I≤A]. This function produces a vertical histogram. For a horizontal histogram try the following:
```
          ∇HISTOG1 A
[1]       A[1]ρ'*'
[2]       →×ρA←1↓A∇
```

The outer product further simplifies the construction of histograms:
```
          ∇HISTOG2 A
[1]       '.□'[1+A∘.≥ι⌈/A]∇
```

11.
```
          ∇R INT P
[1]       'YR PRIN INT
          '
[2]       I←1
[3]       IN←.01×⌊.5+100×P×R[1]
[4]       I,P,IN
[5]       P←P+IN
[6]       →((I←I+1)>R[2])/0
[7]       →3∇
```

Here $R[1]$ is the yearly interest rate in decimal form and $R[2]$ the number of years to be evaluated. As in problem 10, the outer product will greatly simplify the job of generating the table. Your table probably will not be formatted properly. If this bothers you, use the formatting operator introduced in Chapter 21.

```
12.            ∇R←ODDS N;A;I
     [1]       I←1+R←0
     [2]       A←5?52
     [3]       R←R+3≤+/A≤13
     [4]       →2×ιN≥I←I+1
     [5]       R←4×R÷N∇
```

Note that the odds are figured for only one suit (random numbers 1 to 13) on line 3, and the result is multiplied by 4 on line 5, assuming each suit to be equally probable.

```
13.            ∇A PICT M;I
     [1]       I←0
     [2]       M←1+M
     [3]       A[M[I←I+1;]]
     [4]       →(I≠(ρM)[1])/3∇
```

Chapter 23   (page 223)

```
1.             V←'HELLO εωTHERE?'
               T←'?~ρεω'
               TΔREM←2 3 4
               REM T
     REM[2]    HELLO εωTHERE
     REM[3]    →4
     REM[4]    →2
     REM[2]    HELLO εωTHERE
     REM[3]    →4
     REM[4]    →2
     REM[2]    HELLO εωTHERE
     REM[3]    →4
     REM[4]    →2
     REM[2]    HELLO ωTHERE
     REM[3]    →4
     REM[4]    →2
     REM[2]    HELLO THERE
     REM[3]    →0
               TEXT←'DAB'
               TΔSORT←3 4 5 6
               SORT TEXT
     SORT[3]   →4
     SORT[4]   A
     SORT[5]   DB
     SORT[6]   BCDEFGHIJKLMNOPQRSTUVWXYZ
     SORT[3]   →4
     SORT[4]   AB
     SORT[5]   D
     SORT[6]   CDEFGHIJKLMNOPQRSTUVWXYZ
     SORT[3]   →4
     SORT[4]   AB
     SORT[5]   D
     SORT[6]   DEFGHIJKLMNOPQRSTUVWXYZ
     SORT[3]   →4
     SORT[4]   ABD
     SORT[5]
     SORT[6]   EFGHIJKLMNOPQRSTUVWXYZ
     SORT[3]   →0
     ABD
```

```
              N←2  5  7  3  2  8  2  5  2
              T∆MODE←2  3  4  5
              MODE  N
MODE[2]  4
MODE[3]  2
MODE[4]  →2
MODE[2]  4  2
MODE[3]  2  5
MODE[4]  →2
MODE[2]  4  2  1
MODE[3]  2  5  7
MODE[4]  →2
MODE[2]  4  2  1  1
MODE[3]  2  5  7  3
MODE[4]  →2
MODE[2]  4  2  1  1  1
MODE[3]  2  5  7  3  8
MODE[4]  →5
MODE[5]  2
2
```

2.
```
              T∆GCD←ι4
              75  GCD  105
GCD[1]  75
GCD[2]  30
GCD[3]  75
GCD[4]  →1
GCD[1]  30
GCD[2]  15
GCD[3]  30
GCD[4]  →1
GCD[1]  15
GCD[2]  0
GCD[3]  15
GCD[4]  →0
15
```

3.
```
              T∆ACK←ι4
              2  ACK  1
ACK[1]  →2
ACK[1]  →3
ACK[1]  →2
ACK[1]  →3
ACK[1]  →4
ACK[4]  2
ACK[3]  →0
ACK[1]  →4
ACK[4]  3
ACK[2]  →0
ACK[3]  →0
ACK[1]  →2
ACK[1]  →2
ACK[1]  →2
ACK[1]  →3
ACK[1]  →4
ACK[4]  2
ACK[3]  →0
ACK[1]  →4
ACK[4]  3
```

```
         ACK[2]  →0
         ACK[1]  →4
         ACK[4]  4
         ACK[2]  →0
         ACK[1]  →4
         ACK[4]  5
         ACK[2]  →0
         ACK[2]  →0
         5
4.           ∇R←N FIB1 A
     [1]     R←A
     [2]     →(N=2)/0
     [3]     R←(N-1) FIB1 R
     [4]     R←R,¯1↑R+(¯1ϕR)∇
```

Chapter 24 (page 231)

```
1.           S+T
         21 21 21 21 21
         21 21 21 21 21
         21 21 21 21 21
         21 21 21 21 21
             2×S+T÷2
         41 40 39 38 37
         36 35 34 33 32
         31 30 29 28 27
         26 25 24 23 22
             S⌊T
          1  2  3  4  5
          6  7  8  9 10
         10  9  8  7  6
          5  4  3  2  1
             3|T
         1 2 0 1 2
         0 1 2 0 1
         2 0 1 2 0
         1 2 0 1 2
             S≤T
         0 0 0 0 0
         0 0 0 0 0
         1 1 1 1 1
         1 1 1 1 1
             +/[2]T
         15 40 65 90
             +⌿T
         34 38 42 46 50
             4+T
          5  6  7  8  9
         10 11 12 13 14
         15 16 17 18 19
         20 21 22 23 24
             ⌈/⌈/⌈/U
         24
             ⌈/,U
         24
```

```
        ×/U
  13    28    45    64
  85   108   133   160
 189   220   253   288
        +/+/[1]T
210
        A[;2 5]
   2   5
   7  10
  12  15
        C[1;2 3;]
   5   6   7   8
   9  10  11  12
        ¯1 1 2↓⊖C
  4  5
  8  9
        1 1 1 1 0 1\A
   1   2   3   4   0   5
   6   7   8   9   0  10
  11  12  13  14   0  15
        ⊖A
  11  12  13  14  15
   6   7   8   9  10
   1   2   3   4   5
        ¯1 ¯1 2 1 1⊖A
  11  12  13   9  10
   1   2   3  14  15
   6   7   8   4   5
        +/C[1 2;2;3]
11
        A[1 3;ι4]
   1   2   3   4
  11  12  13  14
        1 0 1 1\[2]C
   1   2   3   4
   0   0   0   0
   5   6   7   8
   9  10  11  12

  13  14  15   1
   0   0   0   0
   2   3   4   5
   6   7   8   9
        0 1/[1]C
  13  14  15   1
   2   3   4   5
   6   7   8   9
        3 1 2ϕA
   4   5   1   2   3
   7   8   9  10   6
  13  14  15  11  12
        ,ϕB
CBAFEDIHG
        B[1;2 3]
BC
```

```
                2  2  2+⍴C
      4    3
      8    7

      1   15
      5    4
              1  0  1⍴B
  ABC
  GHI
              ⍴A
      5    4   3   2   1
     10    9   8   7   6
     15   14  13  12  11
             ¯1  ¯2  2⍴B
  CAB
  EFD
  IGH
              1  3  3⍴3  1  1  2  4⍴[1]A
      7    8  14  10   1
      4   15   6  12  13
      9    5  11   2   3
              1  1⍴M
  1 6 1
              1  1  2⍴N
      1    2   3   4
     17   18  19  20
             ρ2  1  3⍴N
  3 2 4
              2  1  3⍴N
      1    2   3   4
     13   14  15  16

      5    6   7   8
     17   18  19  20

      9   10  11  12
     21   22  23  24
             ⍴⍴⊖M
      2    8   4
      1    7   3
     10    6   2
      9    5   1
              1  2  1⍴N
      1    5   9
     14   18  22
             ⍴2  1⍴M
      9    5   1
     10    6   2
      1    7   3
      2    8   4
             ⍴M
      1    5   9
      2    6  10
      3    7   1
      4    8   2
```

```
        ⍉⍉M
  1    2    3    4
  5    6    7    8
  9   10    1    2
```

2. `B[1;]←B[;3]`

3. Assume each row is a name with no blanks on the left and filled out on the right with blanks.

```
        ∇DELE NAME;J
[1]     J←0
[2]     →6×⍳(ρA)[1]≤J
[3]     →2×⍳~∧/A[(J←J+1);]=(1↓ρA)↑NAME
[4]     A←(((J-1)ρ1),0,((ρA)[1]-J)ρ1)/A
[5]     →0
[6]     'NAME NOT FOUND'∇
```

When the inner product is introduced in Chapter 26, this function can be rewritten as

```
        ∇DELE1 NAME;T
[1]     →4×⍳∨/T←A∧.=(1↓ρA)↑NAME
[2]     'NAME NOT FOUND'
[3]     →0
[4]     A←(~T)/A∇
```

4. `R←M[;M]`   Reminder: the indices themselves may have rank >1.

5. `1 1⍉⍉B` or `1 1⍉2 0 1⍉B`

6.
```
        ∇R←DIAG M
[1]     R←10⊥1 1⍉M∇
```

7.
```
        ∇Z←LIST N
[1]     Z←⍉(3,N)ρZ,(⍳Z),÷Z←⍳N∇
```

8. `∧/,S=⍉S`

9. The result shows that A×B is a maximum when A=B, a conclusion well known to calculus students who have worked since time immemorial on problems like the following: Show that a square is that rectangle of the greatest area for a given perimeter.

10.
```
        ∇Z←PERM N;B
[1]     Z←1 1ρ1
[2]     →(1=N)ρ0
[3]     Z←B←(PERM N-1),N
[4]     L1:B[;N-0 1]←B[;N-1 0]
[5]     Z←Z,[1]B
[6]     →L1×1≠N←N-1∇
```

11. `⍉4 3ρ0 1 2 3`

12. A)   `+/+/[2]BUDG[;;4 10]`

    B)   `BUDG[;3;6]`   (per month) or `+/BUDG[;3;6]`   (per year)

    C)   `+/+/[2]BUDG`

    D)   `10|Z1←(,Z)⍳⌊/,Z←BUDG[;2;]` (identifies account)

          `⌈/Z1÷12`   (identifies month)

    E)   `BUDG[;4 5;1 3]`

    F)   `∇FORMAT;M`
```
[1]     'ACC', 6 0 ⍕⍳10
[2]     (3ρ'¯'),(54ρ'         ¯'),'      ¯¯'
[3]     M← 12 3 ρ'JANFEBMARAPRMAYJUNJULAUGSEPOCTNOVDEC'
[4]     M, 6 0 ⍕+/[2] BUDG∇
```

    G)   `BUDG←D,[1](+/D←BUDG[⍳6;;]),[1]C,[1]+/C←BUDG[6+⍳6;;]`

13. `ROWHEAD←5 6ρ'STORE1STORE2STORE3STORE4STORE5'`

    `COLHEAD←9+⍳5`

    `M←.15×¯3000+?5 5ρ6000`

    `M←(' ',[1]ROWHEAD),(1⌽10 0 ⍕ COLHEAD),[1] 10 1 ⍕ M`

14.   ∇R←M COMB N
   [1]   →(M=1,N)/L,R
   [2]   R←1+(0,(M-1) COMB N-1),[1] M COMB N-1
   [3]   →0
   [4]   L:R←(ιN)∘.×ι1
   [5]   →0
   [6]   R:R←(ι1)∘.×ιN∇
15.   ,V,[1.5]';'
16.   ∇WINNER;A;B;B1
   [1]   A←⌈/B←+/MAGSALES
   [2]   B1←B=A∘.+25ρ0
   [3]   CAL,MAGNAMES[⌈/B1×(12ρ0)∘.+ι25;]∇
17.   ∇Z←V REPEAT W
   [1]   Z←(,V∘.≥ι⌈/V)/,⍉((⌈/V),ρV)ρW∇

Chapter 25 (page 238)

1.   C∘.=B
      1 0 0
      0 0 0

      0 1 0
      0 0 0

      0 0 0
      1 0 0
              D∘.×A
       1   2   3   4

       2   4   6   8

       3   6   9 12
              1 3 9∘.>D
      0
      0
      0

      1
      1
      0

      1
      1
      1

```
      A∘.+3×D
  4
  7
 10

  5
  8
 11

  6
  9
 12

  7
 10
 13
      D∘.÷A
  1                    0.5           0.3333333333    0.25

  2                    1             0.6666666667    0.5

  3                    1.5           1               0.75
      B∘.≠C
 0 1 1
 1 0 1
 1 1 1

 1 1 0
 1 1 1
 1 1 1
      ~(A∘.=A)∘.∧1 0 0 1
 0 1 1 0
 1 1 1 1
 1 1 1 1
 1 1 1 1

 1 1 1 1
 0 1 1 0
 1 1 1 1
 1 1 1 1

 1 1 1 1
 1 1 1 1
 0 1 1 0
 1 1 1 1

 1 1 1 1
 1 1 1 1
 1 1 1 1
 0 1 1 0
```

```
            ⍉D∘.*A
   1
   1
   1
   1

   2
   4
   8
  16

   3
   9
  27
  81
            A∘.⌈¯1 3 2 4
   1  3  2  4
   2  3  2  4
   3  3  3  4
   4  4  4  4
```

2.   4 2 2   or   2 2 4

3.
```
            ∇R←DIST L
     [1]    R←⌊.5=((((L[;1]∘.-L[;1])*2)+(L[;2]∘.-L[;2])*2)*.5∇
                or
            ∇R←DIST1 L
     [1]    R←⌊.5+(+/1 3 2 3⍉(L∘.-L)*2)*.5∇
```

4.   +/'ABCDEFG'∘.='CABBAGE'

5.
```
     SUM←B|C+D
     CARRY←B≤C+D
            ∇ADDTAB B;T
     [1]    T←INT∘.+INT←¯1+⍳B
     [2]    (B|T)+10×B≤T∇
```

6.
```
            ∇Z←C1 MULT C2
     [1]    Z←+/(1-⍳⍴C1)⍉C1∘.×C2,0×1↓C1∇
```

7. A)   `X←¯5+⍳9 ◊ F←(⌽X)∘.=|X`   B)   `F←(⌽X)∘.=¯5+X*2`

```
          GRAPH                                         GRAPH
   o           +           o                   o           +           o
      o        +        o                                  +
         o     +     o                                     +
            o  +  o                                        +
   +  +  +  +  o  +  +  +  +                  +  +  +  +  +  +  +  +  +
            +                                       o     +     o
            +                                             +
            +                                             +
            +                                             +
                                                    o     +     o
```

  C)   `F←(⌽X)∘.≤X+1`   D)   `F←(⌽X)∘.≤3|X`

```
          GRAPH                                         GRAPH
            +        o  o                                  +
            +        o  o  o                               +
            +     o  o  o  o                      o        o  +  o
            +  o  o  o  o  o                       o  o  o  +  o  o  o
   +  +  +  o  o  o  o  o  o                  o  o  o  o  o  o  o  o  o
            o  o  o  o  o  o                  o  o  o  o  o  o  o  o  o
         o  o  o  o  o  o  o                  o  o  o  o  o  o  o  o  o
      o  o  o  o  o  o  o  o                  o  o  o  o  o  o  o  o  o
   o  o  o  o  o  o  o  o  o                  o  o  o  o  o  o  o  o  o
```

E) $F \leftarrow ((\phi X) \circ . \leq X+1) \wedge ((\phi X) \circ . \geq 3-|X$
       $GRAPH$

```
            +           o   o
            +       o   o   o
            +   o   o   o   o
            +       o   o   o
+   +   +   +   +   +   +   o   o
            +                   o
            +
            +
            +
```

8. $Y \leftarrow \phi X \leftarrow {}^-13+\iota 25$
       $R \leftarrow (0 = ({}^-3 \times Y) \circ .+(2 \times X)-2) \vee 0 = (2 \times Y) \circ .+X-8$

```
0 0 0 0 0 0 0 0 0 0 0 0 0 0 0 0 0 0 0 0 0 0 0 0 0
0 0 0 0 0 0 0 0 0 0 0 0 0 0 0 0 0 0 0 0 0 0 0 0 0
1 0 0 0 0 0 0 0 0 0 0 0 0 0 0 0 0 0 0 0 0 0 0 0 0
0 0 1 0 0 0 0 0 0 0 0 0 0 0 0 0 0 0 0 0 0 0 0 0 0
0 0 0 0 1 0 0 0 0 0 0 0 0 0 0 0 0 0 0 0 0 0 0 0 0
0 0 0 0 0 0 1 0 0 0 0 0 0 0 0 0 0 0 0 0 0 0 0 0 0
0 0 0 0 0 0 0 0 1 0 0 0 0 0 0 0 0 0 0 0 0 1 0 0
0 0 0 0 0 0 0 0 0 0 1 0 0 0 0 0 0 0 0 0 0 0 0 0
0 0 0 0 0 0 0 0 0 0 0 0 1 0 0 0 0 0 1 0 0 0 0 0
0 0 0 0 0 0 0 0 0 0 0 0 0 0 1 0 0 0 0 0 0 0 0 0
0 0 0 0 0 0 0 0 0 0 0 0 0 0 0 0 1 0 0 0 0 0 0 0
0 0 0 0 0 0 0 0 0 0 0 0 0 0 0 0 0 0 1 0 0 0 0 0
0 0 0 0 0 0 0 0 0 0 0 0 1 0 0 0 0 0 0 0 1 0 0 0
0 0 0 0 0 0 0 0 0 0 0 0 0 0 0 0 0 0 0 0 0 0 1 0
0 0 0 0 0 0 0 0 0 0 1 0 0 0 0 0 0 0 0 0 0 0 0 0 1
0 0 0 0 0 0 0 0 1 0 0 0 0 0 0 0 0 0 0 0 0 0 0 0 0
0 0 0 0 0 0 0 0 0 0 0 0 0 0 0 0 0 0 0 0 0 0 0 0 0
0 0 0 0 1 0 0 0 0 0 0 0 0 0 0 0 0 0 0 0 0 0 0 0 0
0 0 0 0 0 0 0 0 0 0 0 0 0 0 0 0 0 0 0 0 0 0 0 0 0
0 1 0 0 0 0 0 0 0 0 0 0 0 0 0 0 0 0 0 0 0 0 0 0 0
0 0 0 0 0 0 0 0 0 0 0 0 0 0 0 0 0 0 0 0 0 0 0 0 0
0 0 0 0 0 0 0 0 0 0 0 0 0 0 0 0 0 0 0 0 0 0 0 0 0
0 0 0 0 0 0 0 0 0 0 0 0 0 0 0 0 0 0 0 0 0 0 0 0 0
0 0 0 0 0 0 0 0 0 0 0 0 0 0 0 0 0 0 0 0 0 0 0 0 0
```

The 1's correspond to integer number pairs satisfying the simultaneous linear equations 3Y=2X-2 and 2Y=8-X (conventional notation). The point of intersection (4,2) is the common solution of both equations.

9.   Change X to $X \leftarrow \lfloor .5 + X \div S$

10. $\nabla W \ FORM \ M;U;R$
    [1] $R \leftarrow \rho M$
    [2] $M \leftarrow (U \leftarrow M \neq 0)/M \leftarrow ,M$
    [3] $M \leftarrow W \Phi ((\rho M),1)\rho M$
    [4] $M \leftarrow (R \times 1, W[1])\rho M \leftarrow U \setminus M \nabla$

11.   A)

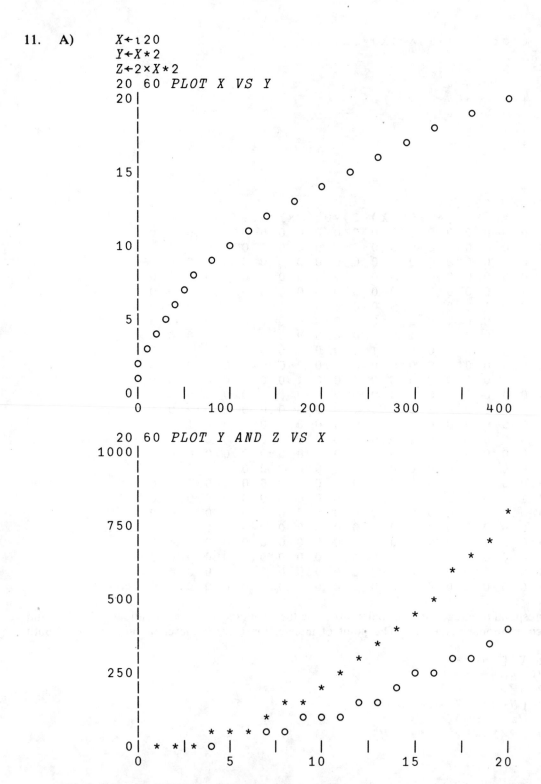

```
        X←ι20
        Y←X*2
        Z←2×X*2
  20  60  PLOT X VS Y
```

```
  20  60  PLOT Y AND Z VS X
```

This last plot looks like something the cat dragged in. If we use only one symbol for each "curve," we are constrained in the fineness of the plot by the "size" of a print position (1/6 inch vertical by 1/10 inch horizontal). Many **APL** systems have an alternate plotting routine which uses a special typeball and produces a much neater plot, like the following. Your *DESCRIBE* or *HOWPLOT* may contain information on how this may be done.

Here is the previous example, using a special typeball:

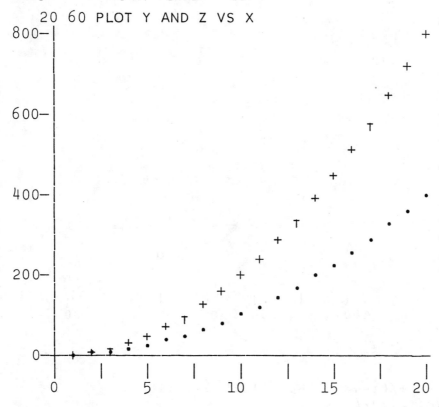

```
                20  60  PLOT  Y  AND  Z  VS  X
```

B) $X \leftarrow 1,50 \times \iota 7$
          $Y \leftarrow \div X$
          $20 \quad 60 \quad PLOT \quad Y \quad VS \quad X$

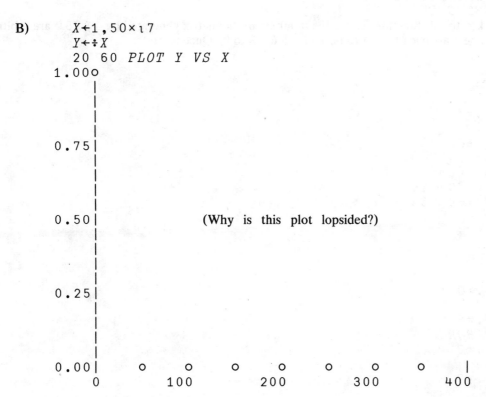

(Why is this plot lopsided?)

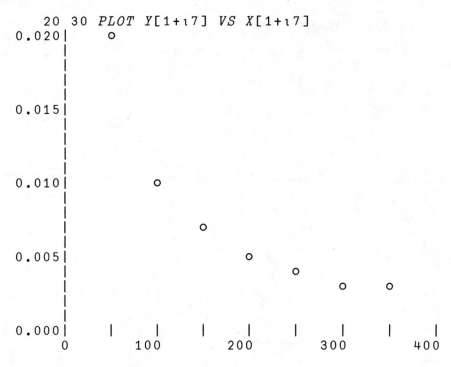

```
        20 30 PLOT Y[1+ι7] VS X[1+ι7]
```

12.   ∇HCP N;I;T
[1]   I←1
[2]   T←ι0
[3]   L1:T←T,+/(ι4)×+/4 4ρ+⌿(13?52)∘.=ι16
[4]   →(N≥I←I+1)/L1
[5]   HISTOG T∇

Line 3 is the key to this function. Since the numbers in the matrix generated by 13?52 are arbitrary and random, line 3 assumes 1 2 3 4 to be Jacks, 5 6 7 8 to be Queens, etc.

Chapter 26 (page 248)

1.   A+.=A
    3
          B×.-C
    ⁻18   0   4   0
      0   ⁻6   ⁻8   0
      0   24   70   18
     24   12   0   36
          B∨.<C
    1 1 1 1
    1 1 1 1
    0 0 0 0
    1 1 1 1
          A∧.>C
    0 0 0 0
          A∨.≠B
    LENGTH ERROR
          A∨.≠B
          ∧
          3+.×B
    66 48 60
          B×.=A
    0 0 0 0
```
```

```
        C|.-B
  0  0  2
  1  0  1
  0  2  0
        (⍉C)⌈.+A
11  10  9  11
```

2.   A) $A \wedge . = B$ results in a 1 if A and B are identical, 0 otherwise.

            $M \wedge . = B$ yields a logical vector with a 1 for each row of M which is identical to B.

            $A + . \neq B$ gives the number of pairs of corresponding dissimilar elements in A and B.

            $(M = 0) \wedge . \geq U$ produces a logical matrix which reproduces the initial 1's in each row of $M = 0$ and fills the rest of the row with 0's, i.e.,

```
        M
  0  0  0  3  2  0  0  0
  0  0  1  7  9  2  8  0
  6  4  0  0  0  1  6  0
        M=0
  1  1  1  0  0  1  1  1
  1  1  0  0  0  0  0  1
  0  0  1  1  1  0  0  1
        (M=0)∧.≥(⍳8)∘.≤⍳8
  1  1  1  0  0  0  0  0
  1  1  0  0  0  0  0  0
  0  0  0  0  0  0  0  0
```

            It may be considered a simulation of the "and-scan" $\wedge \backslash M = 0$.

            $A \times . * B$ is equivalent to the times reduction of A raised to the B power. One possible use could be in getting a number from its prime decomposition. Here is an example of this latter use:

            `2  3  5  7×.*2  1  0  1`

```
84
```

   B) $R[I;J]$ is 1 if and only if the Ith column and the Jth row of N have at least 1 in the same location. It is used to represent two-stage connections, as in pecking orders or circuitry. (See the defined function RUN in this chapter.)

   C)   For $R \leftarrow C + . = D$, $R[I;J]$ is the number of matching pairs of elements of $C[I;]$ and $D[;J]$. For $R \leftarrow C \lceil . \lfloor D$, $R[I;J]$ is the largest of the smaller of $C[I;]$ and $D[;J]$ taken pairwise.

3.   `∇R←X  POLY  C`
   [1]   `R←C+.×X∘.*⁻1+⍳⍴,C∇`

4.   `∇Z←EXP  A`
   [1]   `Z←.14  .10  .06+.×(75⌊A),(50⌊0⌈A-75),0⌈A-125∇`

           or

       `∇Z←EXP1  A`
   [1]   `Z←.01×4  4  6+.×(75  25,⌊/⍳0)∘.⌊A∇`

which will handle both vector and scalar arguments. $\lfloor/\iota0$ is the so-called *identity element* for the dyadic operation $\lfloor$. It yields $7.237005577E75$, the largest number generated by the **APL** system. The reason it is called an identity element is that when paired with any other number N with $\lfloor$, it yields N. (Try $+/\iota0$, $-/\iota0$, $\times/\iota0$, $*/\iota0$, $\lceil/\iota0$, etc.)

5.   A)   `R←0≠.=4  100  400  4000∘.|Y`
   B)   `∇REFUND1  E`
   [1]   `.5×200  500+.⌊1  1∘.×E∇`
   C)   `∇Z←LIT1  N`
   [1]   `Z←(⁻1+'0123456789'⍳N)+.×10*⌽⁻1+⍳⍴N∇`
   D)   `∇R←N  DUPL1  V`
   [1]   `R←'SCALAR  NOT  PRESENT'`
   [2]   `→0×⍳0=N∨.=V`
   [3]   `R←(N=V)/⍳⍴V∇`

6.
```
        ORDERS←300 500 200 1000
        PARTS←4 5ρ1 2 0 5 2 0 3 0 1 5 1 1 4 2 2 1 2 4 5 5
        PRICES←32 9.75 3.2 .78 7.2
        COSTOFALLPARTS←ORDERS+.×PARTS+.×PRICES
        COSTOFALLPARTS
172257
        COSTFOREACHMODEL←PARTS+.×PRICES
        COSTFOREACHMODEL
69.8 66.03 70.51 104.2
```

Chapter 27 (page 257)

1.
```
        ∇R←F X
[1]     R←*X∇
        1E¯6 SLOPE ι10
2.718283187 7.389059793 20.08554696 54.59817733
        148.413233 403.4289952 1096.633707 2980.959477
        8103.087978 22026.47681
        *ι10
2.718281828 7.389056099 20.08553692 54.59815003
        148.4131591 403.4287935 1096.633158 2980.957987
        8103.083928 22026.46579
```
In calculus courses it is shown that $*X$ is its own derivative.

2. In general execute $⊞(N,N)ρ1,Nρ0$. A specific example might be
```
        ⊞3 3ρ1 0 0 0
  1 0 0
  0 1 0
  0 0 1
```
from which it should be evident that the identity matrix is its own inverse.

3.
```
        10 13 3⊞3 3ρ2 13 4 3 ¯1 2 1 ¯4
3.5 2.220446049E¯16 1
```

4.
```
        ∇LIN W;G
[1]     →(0=G←(W[1]×W[5])-W[4]×W[2])/L1
[2]     'X IS ';((W[5]×W[3])-W[2]×W[6])÷G
[3]     'Y IS ';((W[1]×W[6])-W[4]×W[3])÷G
[4]     →0
[5]     L1:'NO UNIQUE SOLUTION'∇
        ∇ABC SOLVE DEF
[1]     ⍝ABC IS A 3-ELEMENT VECTOR A,B,C
[2]     ⍝DEF IS A 3-ELEMENT VECTOR D,E,F
[3]     →OK×ι0≠-/×/(ABC,DEF)[2 2ρ1 5 2 4]
[4]     'NO UNIQUE SOLUTION'
[5]     →0
[6]     OK:(ABC,DEF)[3 6]⊞(ABC,DEF)[2 2ρ1 2 4 5]∇
```

5.
```
        ∇R←F X
[1]     R←X×300+¯2×X∇
        1E¯6 SLOPE 0 100 200
299.999998 ¯100.000002 ¯500.0000001
        1E¯6 SLOPE 0 20 40 60 80
299.999998 219.9999972 139.9999974 59.99999757 ¯20.00000222
        1E¯6 SLOPE 60 65 70 75
59.99999757 39.99999717 19.99999768 ¯2.728484105E¯6
```
The sides of the rectangle are each about 75 feet long.

6.
```
        ∇R←F X
 [1]    R←÷X∇
        .001 AREA 1 2
0.6928972431
        ⊛2
0.6931471806
```
Readers with a background in calculus will recall that ⊛N is equivalent to the area under the curve $Y←÷X$ from $X=1$ to $X=N$.

7.
```
        YR←74+ι7
        SALES←38 52 64 82 98 128 156
        SALES⌹YR∘.*0 1
¯1416 19.28571429
```
The linear equation best fitting the data is $SALES←¯1416+19.28×YR$.

8. To solve for R:

R-UR=I

IR-UR=I

(I-U)R=I

(I-U)⁻¹(I-U)R=(I-U)⁻¹I   where (I-U)⁻¹ is the inverse of I-U

IR=(I-U)⁻¹I

R=(I-U)⁻¹

Therefore the **APL** solution is
```
        ⌹((ι1↑ρU)∘.=ι1↑ρU)-U
  1  0  0  0  0  0  0  0  0
  0  1  0  0  0  0  0  0  0
  0  0  1  0  0  0  0  0  0
  1  2  0  1  0  0  0  0  0
  0  1  1  0  1  0  0  0  0
  1  3  3  1  1  1  0  0  0
  3 10  8  3  4  2  1  0  0
  6 12  8  3  4  2  1  1  0
 10 33 27 10 13  7  3  0  1
```

9.
```
        W←2000 2200 2500 2750 3000 3500 4000 4500 5000 5500
        C←4.14 4.67 5.35 5.61 6.77 7.39 9.29 10.45 10.95 12.16
        C⌹W∘.*0 1
1.929687474 0.001734030928
```
The equation is $C←1.93+.001734×W$. In these days of energy conservation, what can you deduce from these results?

Chapter 28 (page 269)

1.
```
        ∇MULT1 N;X
 [1]    X←?N,N
 [2]    1↑X;'×';1↓X
 [3]    →(□=STOP,×/X)/0,CORRECT
 [4]    'TRY AGAIN'
 [5]    →3
 [6]    CORRECT:'CORRECT'
 [7]    →1∇
```
2.
```
        ∇MULT2 N;X
 [1]    X←?N,N×I←1
 [2]    1↑X;'×';1↓X
 [3]    →(□=STOP,×/X)/0,CORRECT
 [4]    →ANS×ι4=I←I+1
 [5]    'TRY AGAIN'
 [6]    →3
 [7]    ANS:'ANSWER IS ';×/X
 [8]    →1
 [9]    CORRECT:'CORRECT'
 [10]   →1∇
```

```
3.              ∇MULT3 N;X
      [1]       X←?N,N×I←1
      [2]       1↑X;'×';1↓X
      [3]       →(□=HELP,STOP,×/X)/AID,0,CORRECT
      [4]       →ANS×ι4=I←I+1
      [5]       'TRY AGAIN'
      [6]       →3
      [7]       ANS:'ANSWER IS ';×/X
      [8]       →1
      [9]       CORRECT:'CORRECT'
      [10]      →1
      [11]      AID:'COUNT THE STARS FOR THE ANSWER:'
      [12]      Xρ'*'
      [13]      →5∇
4.    ∇SPELL[6]'THE CORRECT SPELLING IS ',SPL[N+1;]∇
5.              ∇ENTER;A
      [1]       R←''
      [2]       →DONE×ι0=ρA←,□
      [3]       R←R,20↑A
      [4]       →2
      [5]       DONE:R←(1+,0 20⊤¯1+ρR)ρR∇
6.              ∇N LIST L;I
      [1]       M←ρI←1
      [2]       M←M,L←□
      [3]       →2×ιN≥I←I+1
      [4]       □←M←(N,L)ρM∇
7.              ∇LOOK UP L;M
      [1]       'ENTER NAME'
      [2]       NAME←□
      [3]       NAME←(¯1↑ρL)↑NAME
      [4]       M←(L∧.=NAME)/ι1↑ρL
      [5]       →(0=ρM)/NOGO
      [6]       'NAME IS ON ROW(S) ';M;' IN THE LIST'
      [7]       →0
      [8]       NOGO: 'NAME NOT FOUND'∇
```

Chapter 32 (page 305)

```
1.              ∇R←TIME;T;W
      [1]       W←3↑3↓□TS
      [2]       T←(12|1↑W),1↓W
      [3]       T←((0=1↑T)/12),((0≠1↑T)/1↑T),1↓T
      [4]       R←⍕T
      [5]       R[(R=' ')/ιρR]←':'
      [6]       R←R,' ',('AP')[1+12≤1↑W],'M EASTERN'∇
2.              ∇DATE;S
      [1]       S←3↑□TS
      [2]       S[ι3]←S[2 3 1]
      [3]       S←⍕S
      [4]       S[(S=' ')/ιρS]←'/'
      [5]       S∇
3.              ∇CPUTIME
      [1]       0 60 60 1000⊤□AI[2]-PREVIOUSTIME
      [2]       PREVIOUSTIME←□AI[2]∇
                PREVIOUSTIME←0
```

```
           ∇CHECK
[1]        CPUTIME
[2]        I←1
[3]        S←2!10
[4]        →3×ι1001≠I←I+1
[5]        CPUTIME
[6]        I←1
[7]        S←(!10)÷(!2)×!8
[8]        →7×ι1001≠I←I+1
[9]        CPUTIME∇
           CHECK
 0  0  2 917
 0  0  3 650
 0  0  5 516
```

4.
```
           ∇FORYOUONLY
[1]        →(1421≠□AI[1])/0
[2]        'THIS IS THE MESSAGE'∇
```
How would you modify line 1 for a vector of numbers?

5.
```
           ∇MULT4 N;X
[1]        X←?N,N×I←1+0×AKT←□AI[4]
[2]        1↑X;'X';1↓X
[3]        →(□=HELP,STOP,×/X)/AID,0,CORRECT
[4]        →ANS×ι4=I←I+1
[5]        'TRY AGAIN'
[6]        →3
[7]        ANS:'ANSWER IS ',⍕×/X
[8]        →1
[9]        CORRECT:⌊((□AI[4])-AKT)÷1000;' SECONDS'
[10]       →1
[11]       AID:'COUNT THE STARS FOR THE ANSWER'
[12]       Xρ'*'
[13]       →5∇
```

6.   Problem self-explanatory

7.
```
           )LOAD 1 CLASS
SAVED   15.02.39 04/15/74
           Y←ι10
           □IO←0
           TAB3[0;2;1]
 132
           Yι4 5 6
 3  4  5
           □PP←5
           ÷TAB3
     0.009009      0.0089286     0.0088496
     0.0082645     0.0081967     0.0081301
     0.0076336     0.0075758     0.0075188
     0.0070922     0.0070423     0.006993

     0.0047393     0.004717      0.0046948
     0.0045249     0.0045045     0.0044843
     0.004329      0.0043103     0.0042918
     0.0041494     0.0041322     0.0041152
           □PW←50
           )FNS J
 MEAN        NAMESONLY         NUMCODE  PEREL     PI
 RECT        ROWNAMES          RUN      S         SD
 SIGN        SLOPE      SORT   SPELL    SPLINECALC
 SPLINEEVAL         SPRED   SQRT    STAT     STATEMENT
```

```
      STATISTICS        SUB      SUBST    SUSPENDED
      TRANSP  VIG
            □WA
60208
            B←ı1000
            □WA
56232
```

8.
```
            A←9.222222222222222
            B←9.222222222222227
            A=B
1
            A∈B
1
            A-B
¯4.884981308E¯15
            □CT←0
            A=B
0
            A∈B
0
```

9.   Because both indexing and the index generator are affected in the same way by the change of origin.

10.
```
            □IO←0
            ı0
            @
            ı1
0
            ρı0
0
            ρı1
1
```

11.
```
            ∇SUB[1.1]
[1.1]  T←□IO←0
[1.2]  P←P,?P
[1.3]  T←□IO←1∇
[1.4]  [2]
[2]    ∇

[10]   →5
[11]   [15]
[15]   →5∇
```
The last two editing changes would not have been necessary if we had used labels.

12.
```
            ALF←' ABCDEFGHIJKLMNOPQRSTUVWXYZ'
            ∇A←N ALFSORT M
[1]    M←ALFıM
[2]    M←M[⍋,M[;N];]
[3]    →2×ı0≠N←N-1
[4]    A←ALF[M]∇
```
        or, more concisely
```
            ∇A←N ALFSORT1 M
[1]    →(0<N←N-1)/1,ρM←M[⍋,ALFıM[;N];]
[2]    A←M∇
```
Both *ALFSORT* and *ALFSORT*1 are straightforward sorts by columns. *ALFSORT*2 and *ALFSORT*3 are somewhat more devious:
```
            ∇A←ALFSORT2 M
[1]    A←M[⍋,27⊥⍉ALFıM;]∇
            ∇A←N ALFSORT3 M
[1]    A←M[⍋,ALFı((1↑ρM),N)↑M+.×(30*(¯1+φıN));]∇
```
Are there any limitations on the latter two versions?

```
13.     →(□AI[2]≥120000)/0
14.           ∇TIMEOFDAY;T
  [1]     T←4 9ρ(18ρ'MORNING   '),'AFTERNOONEVENING  '
  [2]     'GOOD ',T[1+⌊□TS[4]÷6;]∇
15.           ∇N CRAPS D;I
  [1]     I←0
  [2]     L1:DICE
  [3]     □DL D
  [4]     →(N>I←I+1)/L1∇
16.     'S',□AV[159],'/'
```

Chapter 33 (page 317)

```
1.            )LOAD 1 CLASS
       SAVED 15.02.39  04/15/74
              AVG4 5 6 7
       VALUE ERROR
       AVG4[2] COUNT←COUNT+1
                       ^
              AVG5 4 2 1
       VALUE ERROR
       AVG5[2] COUNT←COUNT+1
                       ^
              AVG4 8 9 6
       VALUE ERROR
       AVG4[2] COUNT←COUNT+1
                       ^
              )SI
       AVG4[2] *
       AVG5[2] *
       AVG4[2] *
              □LC
       2 2 2
              S∆RECT←3
              3 RECT 4
       14
       5
       RECT[3]
              □LC
       3 2 2 2
              →□LC
       12
              □LX←'→□LC'
              S∆SPELL←4
              SPELL
       1
       ONE
       SPELL[4]
              )SAVE CONTINUE
       10.13.14 04/17/74
              )LOAD CONTINUE
       SAVED  10.13.14 04/17/74
       THATS RIGHT
       7
```

2.   Problem self-explanatory.

3.   ∇ADD[4]
     [4]   A←⍕A∇

The combination of ⍕ and ⎕, though the net effect is practically the same as ⎕, does allow you to check, as in this function, to exclude certain kinds of input.

4.   )LOAD 1 CLASS
     SAVED 15.02.39 04/15/74
             ∇DRILL
     [1]   'ENTER YOUR CHOICE OF DRILL EXERCISES'
     [2]   'SUB, ADD OR SPELL'
     [3]   ⍕⎕∇

5.   FALSE←'FALSE'
            TRUE←'TRUE'
            ∇A CHECK B
     [1]   ⍕5 ¯4[1+A>B]↑'FALSE   TRUE'∇
            3 CHECK 4
     FALSE
            6 CHECK 3
     TRUE

This illustrates using ⍕ to execute only that expression determined by the stated condition. Although in this example the expressions selected are literal, had they instead been instructions requiring considerable computation, some savings could result from avoiding unnecessary calculations. Note that ⍕ isn't really necessary in this function; it is used only to make a point.

6.   ∇CMP[⎕]∇
                ∇A CMP B
     [1]   ((A>B)/'GREATER'),((A=B)/'EQUAL'),(A<B)/'LESS'
            ∇
            R←⎕CR 'CMP'
            R
     A CMP B
     ((A>B)/'GREATER'),((A=B)/'EQUAL'),(A<B)/'LESS'
            R[2;8+⍳7]←'MORE
            ⎕FX R
     CMP
            ∇CMP[⎕]∇
        ∇ A CMP B
     [1]   ((A>B)/'MORE   '),((A=B)/'EQUAL'),(A<B)/'LESS'
        ∇

7.   )CLEAR
     CLEAR WS
)COPY 1 CLASS HYP RECT
     SAVED 15.02.39 04/15/74
            D←⎕CR 'HYP'
            ⎕EX 'HYP'
            ∇RECT[0⎕0]
     [0]   L RECT H;HYP
     [1]   [2]
     [2]   ⍕'L ',(⎕FX D),' H'∇
            ∇RECT[⎕]∇
        ∇ L RECT H;HYP
     [1]   2×L+H
     [2]   ⍕'L ',(⎕FX D),' H'
     [3]   L×H
        ∇
)FNS
     RECT

```
                3 RECT 4
        14
         5
        12
  8.             ∇DISP;R;L;M
        [1]     'WHAT LETTER(S)?'
        [2]     L←⎕
        [3]     'LABELS (1), VARIABLES (2) OR FUNCTIONS (3)?'
        [4]     R←⎕
        [5]     ⎕←M←L ⎕NL R
        [6]     I←1
        [7]     ⎕CR M[I;]
        [8]     →((I←I+1)≤1↑ρM)/7∇
  9.    ⎕LX←'M[1+(1↑⎕AI)∈1500 1600;]'
 10.    [1]     →(6<ρ⎕LC)/EXIT
        [2]     ⍝ NORMAL ROUTE HERE
        [3]     EXIT:→
 11.             ∇ADD1;A;P
        [1]     NEW:⎕←P←?10 10
        [2]     LOOP:→(0=ρA←,⎕)/0
        [3]     →(~∧/A←⎕AV[140+ι10])/WRONG
        [4]     →((⍎A)=+/P)/NEW
        [5]     WRONG:'???????'
        [6]     'TRY AGAIN'
        [7]     →LOOP∇
 12.             ∇LIST;A;B;I;⎕IO
        [1]     ⎕IO←1
        [2]     I←1↑ρA←⎕NL 3
        [3]     →(0∧.=ρA)/0
        [4]     ⎕←B←10ρ'_'
        [5]     L1:⎕CR,A[I;]
        [6]     B
        [7]     →(0≠I←I-1)/L1∇
```

Index